OUTDOORS

PA
917.48
MIL

D0932673

"are we there yet?"
  -heidi ruby miller

PENNSYLVANIA CAMPING

SOMERSET COUNTY LIBRARY
6022 GLADES PIKE, SUITE 120
SOMERSET, PA 15501
814-445-5907

JASON & HEIDI RUBY MILLER

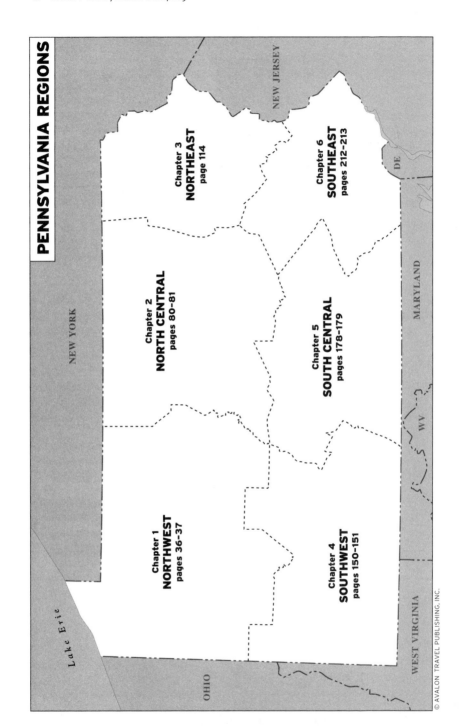

PENNSYLVANIA REGIONS

Chapter 1
NORTHWEST
pages 36–37

Chapter 2
NORTH CENTRAL
pages 80–81

Chapter 3
NORTHEAST
page 114

Chapter 4
SOUTHWEST
pages 150–151

Chapter 5
SOUTH CENTRAL
pages 178–179

Chapter 6
SOUTHEAST
pages 212–213

Lake Erie

NEW YORK

NEW JERSEY

OHIO

WEST VIRGINIA

WV

MARYLAND

DE

© AVALON TRAVEL PUBLISHING, INC.

Contents

How to Use This Book

ABOUT THE CAMPGROUND PROFILES

The campgrounds are listed in a consistent, easy-to-read format to help you choose the ideal camping spot. If you already know the name of the specific campground you want to visit, or the name of the surrounding geological area or nearby feature (town, national or state park, forest, mountain, lake, river, etc.), look it up in the index and turn to the corresponding page. Here is a sample profile:

Campground name and number →

General location of the campground in relation to the nearest major town or landmark →

1 SOMEWHERE USA CAMPGROUND

← Icons noting activities and facilities at or nearby the campground

Rating: 10 ← Rating on a scale of 1-10

south of Somewhere USA Lake

BEST (← Symbol indicating that the campground is listed among the authors' top picks

Each campground in this book begins with a brief overview of its setting. The description typically covers ambience, information about the attractions, and activities popular at the campground.

Campsites, facilities: This section notes the number of campsites for tents and RVs and indicates whether hookups are available. Facilities such as restrooms, picnic areas, recreation areas, laundry, and dump stations will be addressed, as well as the availability of piped water, showers, playgrounds, stores, and other amenities. The campground's pet policy and wheelchair accessibility is also mentioned here.

Reservations, fees: This section notes whether reservations are accepted, and provides rates for tent sites and RV sites. If there are additional fees for parking or pets, or discounted weekly or seasonal rates, they will also be noted here.

Directions: This section provides mile-by-mile driving directions to the campground from the nearest major town or highway.

Contact: This section provides an address, phone number, and website, if available, for the campground.

ABOUT THE ICONS

The icons in this book are designed to provide at-a-glance information on activities, facilities, and services available on-site or within close proximity of each campground.

- Hiking trails
- Biking trails
- Swimming
- Fishing
- Boating opportunities available (includes motorboats and personal watercrafts)
- Winter sports (such as downhill skiing, cross-country skiing, snowshoeing, snowmobiling, snowboarding, and ice-skating)
- Pets permitted (restrictions or additional fees may apply)
- Playground
- Wheelchair access (concerned persons should always call the campground to verify that their specific needs will be met)
- RV sites
- Tent sites

MAP SYMBOLS

═══ Expressway	(80) Interstate Freeway	✗ Airfield
═══ Primary Road	(101) US Highway	✗ Airport
─── Secondary Road	(29) State Highway	○ City/Town
---------- Unpaved Road	66 County Highway	▲ Mountain
·············· Ferry	Lake	▲ Park
—·—·—· National Border	Dry Lake	↘ Pass
—··—·· State Border	Seasonal Lake	◉ State Capital

ABOUT THE RATINGS

1 to 3: These camping sites are farther away from natural settings and may have limited views, but are often convenience stops for activities like shopping, taking in a show, or visiting friends.

4 to 6: With a bit more seclusion, these campgrounds make good base camps for further outdoor adventures.

7 to 9: Campgrounds rated in this category allow campers to split their time evenly between staying and going. They may adjoin state parks and forests or border a body of water, but also provide aesthetic settings and lots of amenities on-site.

10: These are the ultimate camping spots. Whether the magic comes from a spectacular view, a secluded grove, or a unique natural formation, you know it when you're there. Often these camping sites are destinations in and of themselves (for example, in state parks and forests).

INTRODUCTION

© JASON MILLER

Authors' Note

Green plateaus protruding through a dense fog. Pink and white laurel petals falling into a clear cool stream. Rushing rivers spilling through a mountain gorge. These are the images that welcome us back to Pennsylvania after we've been away for too long. And when we hit the trail again, inhaling the scent of fallen pine needles and air charged with the mist of cascades, we know that we are home.

A thousand times we've felt the pull of wanderlust, and a thousand times we've driven into the ancient Appalachians and been reminded why we couldn't leave: Our forests and wilderness areas are the fuel that keep us running.

It's easy to take out-of-state visitors into parks that leave them gushing in a matter of minutes. Our steep ridges and broad valleys look fine no matter what color they're wearing. It doesn't matter if it's autumn and the leaves of our mixed mesophytic forests are releasing reds and oranges back to the star from which they came, or spring when green fiddleheads push through the snowmelt—visitors leave with a sense of surprise. Waterfalls suspended by winter's grip provide a rare counterpoint to their plunging summer versions. Bluets and wild bleeding hearts announce in subtle verse that long days have returned.

Pennsylvania lacks a Yellowstone or a Yosemite, a Grand Canyon or an Everglades, yet millions of people visit every year. So why do tourists still come?

We like to think it's because Pennsylvania has nature on an accessible, human scale that encourages exploration and play. We have waterfalls and slides to play in, boulders to climb, swimming holes deeper than they are wide, and trails winding through virgin hemlock stands to secluded overlooks. Most people who go to the Grand Canyon or Yosemite just look and take pictures; some might hike a few miles. But here visitors can touch the rock, dip a toe in the river, or bend down and smell a wildflower without having to wait in line. Rivers like the Youghiogheny and Lehigh are where many paddlers get their first taste of whitewater. This is nature to be experienced rather than viewed.

Our wonderful state park system, one of the largest in the country, brings nature to overnight scout troops and urban children on field trips. We have cool air, fine trails, clean waterways, old growth forest, abundant wildlife, scenic byways, a rich history, and a culture that goes back almost 15,000 years. The scenic rivers permit families to introduce their children to the wonders of frictionless travel, propelled only by a wooden paddle. Wilderness areas invite travelers to forget time, forget culture, and see stars brighter than they could ever imagine. Historical parks and national battlefields remind all Pennsylvanians and all visitors that this was where liberty was born and defended.

Some of our favorite Pennsylvania adventures involved little more than a backpack and feet bared to the warm Pottsville sandstone that lines the shaded banks of Meadow Run just outside of Ohiopyle. Hiking upstream through rapids, waterfalls, and swimming holes, stopping to take pictures of mink and painted trillium, and having a lunch of crusty bread, baby Swiss, and dark chocolate at the edge of a waterfall.

But we plan on topping that next week somewhere up in those old mountains—and of course we'll take pictures and let you know how it goes.

Best Campgrounds

◖ Best for Families

Family Affair Campground, Northwest chapter, page 39
Red Oak Campground, Northwest chapter, page 44
Shenango Valley RV Park, Northwest chapter, page 54
Farma Travel Trailer Park, Northwest chapter, page 55
Two Mile Run County Park, Northwest chapter, page 57
Shangri-La on the Creek, North Central chapter, page 103
Knoebels Amusement Resort and Campground, North Central chapter, page 109
Yogi Bear's Jellystone Park Camp-Resort, Southwest chapter, page 169
Pine Grove KOA at Twin Grove Park, South Central chapter, page 183
Lake Raystown Resort and Lodge, South Central chapter, page 187

◖ Best for Leisure Hiking

Sizerville State Park, Northwest chapter, page 53
Parker Dam State Park, Northwest chapter, page 68
Black Moshannon State Park, North Central chapter, page 97
Lackawanna State Park, Northeast chapter, page 118
Keen Lake Camping & Cottage Resort, Northeast chapter, page 119
Lower Lake Campground, Northeast chapter, page 128
Foxwood Family Campground, Northeast chapter, page 138
Blue Ridge Campground, Northeast chapter, page 140
Codorus State Park, South Central chapter, page 207
French Creek State Park, Southeast chapter, page 231

◖ Best for Mountain Hiking

Tracy Ridge Campground, Northwest chapter, page 44
Chapman State Park, Northwest chapter, page 45
Red Bridge Campground, Northwest chapter, page 47
Worlds End State Park, North Central chapter, page 92
Frances Slocum State Park, Northeast chapter, page 125
Tobyhanna State Park, Northeast chapter, page 130
Hickory Run State Park, Northeast chapter, page 134
Kentuck Campground, Southwest chapter, page 171
Pine Grove Furnace State Park, South Central chapter, page 197
Deer Run Appalachian Campground, South Central chapter, page 198

◖ Best for Trout Fishing

Loleta Campground, Northwest chapter, page 59
Sinnemahoning State Park, Northwest chapter, page 60
S. B. Elliott State Park, Northwest chapter, page 69
Kettle Creek State Park, North Central chapter, page 91
Hyner Run State Park, North Central chapter, page 91
Riverside Campground, North Central chapter, page 94
Poe Paddy State Park, North Central chapter, page 104

◖ Best Historic-Area Campgrounds

◖ Best Swimming Beaches

◖ Most Pet-Friendly

◖ Most Scenic

Camping Tips

CAMPING GEAR
Tents
The type of activities you pursue will decide the type of tent you need. If you're a hiker, the lighter, the better. If you've got the whole family along, you may want to opt for a large domed tent with a vestibule and maybe separate rooms. No matter the size, however, the purpose of any tent is to keep you dry and bug-free.

The North Face and REI both make several lightweight expedition and trekking tents that sleep two people. The North Face-Rock 22 weighs in at five pounds, 14 ounces. The REI Clipper is slightly lighter at five pounds, 2 ounces. Both tents are rated for optimal use during spring, summer, and fall.

Larger tents that also have the three-season rating and sleep four are the Venture 4 from EMS and the Silver Moon 4 from Kelty, Inc. These tents have more head room and floor space and are much heavier because of it. The Venture 4 is 13 pounds, three ounces, while the Silver Moon 4 is 10 pounds, one ounce. Those few pounds don't seem like much unless you're carrying them several miles on your back.

Sleeping Bags
When selecting a sleeping bag, you should check out its temperature range, filling, and size. Don't be afraid to test out several bags to decide on comfort and fit.

You'll need to decide between natural and

food cache
(hang downwind)

escape tree

minimum 100 feet

minimum 100 feet

minimum 200 feet

6-8 inch "cat hole" for
depositing human waste

minimum 200 feet

In setting up camp, always be mindful of potential ecological disturbances. Pitch tents and dispose of human waste at least 200 feet from the water's edge. In black bear territory, increase the distance between your tent and your cooking area, food-hang, and the water's edge threefold. In other words, if you're in black bear country, do all your cooking 100 yards (not feet) downwind of your sleeping area. If you can establish an escape tree nearby, all the better.

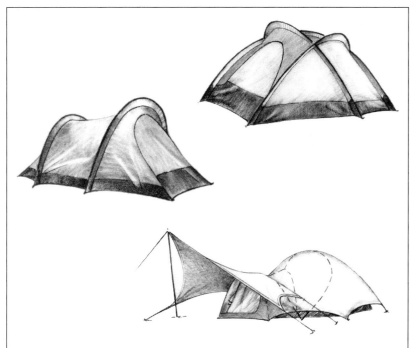

With the world going high-tech, **tents** of today vary greatly in complexity, size, price, and put-up time. And they wouldn't be fit for this new millennium without offering options such as moon roofs, rain flies, and tent wings. Be sure to buy the one that's right for your needs.

synthetic fillings. Down is light and warm unless it gets wet—then the bag becomes a heavy, lumpy mess that doesn't insulate well. When poly-fill is wet, on the other hand, it will still hold in up to 90 percent of your body heat. Backpackers need to consider weight more than car campers, so take your time to find a bag that will serve you well. A trip will go from bad to worse if you're unable to get a good night's rest.

To make tent camping just a bit more comfortable, you can put down a sleeping pad such as a Therm-a-Rest pad. These pads roll up for easy transport and provide a surprisingly good cushion for their relative thinness. They can be expensive, but are self-inflating and light to carry.

Other options for use inside RVs or tents are fold-up cots, bulky foam mattresses, and air mattresses. The first two are pretty self-contained and can be unfolded or unrolled and used immediately. Air mattresses will need to be inflated. You can use a foot pump or a motorized pump that plugs into a cigarette lighter or can be hooked up to a generator.

Camp Stoves

Camp stoves vary in price and in style. What you choose will be determined by whether you are backpacking or driving to the campsite.

The range of options for RVers and car campers are greater due to the lack of weight restrictions. Fifteen pounds is too heavy for a backpacker counting ounces, but to a car camper, the convenience of three burners may be well worth the price. Coleman makes a variety of stoves that burn any number of fuels. Some use propane or butane, which

Stoves are available in many styles and burn a variety of fuels. These are three typical examples. Top left: **White gas stoves** are the most popular because they are inexpensive and easy to find; they do require priming and can be explosive. Top right: **Gas canister stoves** burn propane, butane, isobutane, and mixtures of the three. These are the easiest to use but have two disadvantages: 1) Because the fuel is bottled, determining how much fuel is left can be difficult. 2) The fuel is limited to above-freezing conditions. Bottom: **Liquid fuel stoves** burn Coleman fuel, denatured alcohol, kerosene, and even gasoline; these fuels are economical and have a high heat output, but most must be primed.

can usually be found at gas stations, hardware stores, and outdoors supply stores. Some Coleman stoves use a proprietary fuel similar to white gas. Gasoline should never be used unless recommended by the manufacturer. It contains additives that may damage a stove or cause fire or explode if not used properly.

Backpackers will prefer something lighter, and there are a variety of options for the weight-conscious trekker. Mountain Safety Research (MSR) makes a series of stoves perfect for backpackers. The WhisperLite weighs in at a mere 11 ounces, making it a great choice for multi-night trips. With a recom-

mended four ounces of fuel per person per day, it's a light, reliable option. We've used our WhisperLite on all of our trips and it's cooked without fail in even the wettest and windiest conditions. An international version, the WhisperLite International, burns a variety of fuels more easily found by international travelers, including white gas, kerosene, and unleaded auto fuel. Brunton, Suunto, Optimus, Primus, and Snow Peak USA all make backpacking stoves with similar features in a similar price range.

Cooking on camp stoves is more a matter of boiling water and adding contents to premade meals than mastering the culinary skills of the world's finest chefs. Fresh veggies or herbs can definitely spice up an otherwise bland meal, but sautéing, simmering, and spatchcocking are best left to the kitchen. With practice and experience campers will learn that some foods travel better than others. Nothing beats the joy of fresh parmesan cheese on ready-to-eat ravioli. Hummus, pepperoni, olives, soy sauce, chocolate chips, olive oil, chili peppers, and garlic are just a few of the crush-proof, transportable items that can make camp cooking a little more exciting.

Car campers will have a wider variety of options, limited only by the amount of cooler space or proximity to a grocery store. Some campgrounds even have weekly potluck dinners where campers can show off their best butane stove recipes. The good news for car campers is that a burnt meal isn't a tragedy as long as there's takeout nearby.

The main safety concern with camp stoves is a clogged fuel line. If it's clogged, you'll most likely notice a black residue rising from a sputtering flame. This sputtering can lead to flare-ups or cause the stove to catch fire. Most stoves are field repairable. Scrub them often and clean the fuel line with a pipe cleaner. The best way to avoid a clog is by using only the fuel recommended specifically for your camp stove. White gas stoves are safer and more efficient because the gas's flashpoint is much higher than that of gasoline, plus white gas vaporizes easier and burns much cleaner.

A hot stove should never be left unattended, even for a second, and under no circumstances should a stove ever be used inside a tent. The potential for accidents is too great when a hiker is fatigued or cold.

Water Treatment

Outdoor water treatment can be divided into two categories—chemical and mechanical. Iodine and chlorine are two suitable methods for killing bacteria and viruses when administered properly. AquaMira, Katadyn, Polar Pure, Potable Aqua and Pristine Water Purification make tablets that can be administered without measuring or counting drops. Unfortunately, chemical purification doesn't

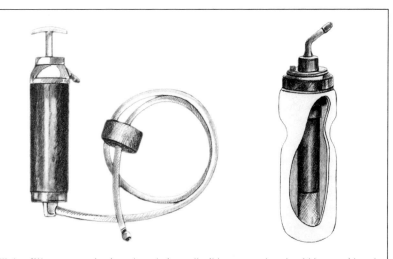

Water filters are a wise investment since all wilderness water should be considered contaminated. Make sure the filter can be easily cleaned or has a replaceable cartridge. The filter pores must be 0.4 microns or less to remove bacteria.

remove suspended solids from drinking water, a problem when the water source is muddy or cloudy. Additionally, some forms of chemical treatment leave an aftertaste that some people find disagreeable.

Mechanical treatment is an alternative. Plastic pumps housing ceramic, carbon, or other proprietary filters are both lightweight and convenient for use by backpackers and car campers. Filtering occurs as water is squeezed through the filter material, which contains pores that allow water to pass, but not bacteria, protozoa (including crypto and giardia), and particulate matter. The carbon filter improves taste in water that may contain iron or other less-than-pleasant odors.

We've used the MSR MiniWorks on all of our trips and have found it to be a dependable, easy-to-use system. It pumps about one liter per minute and involves occasional cleaning that can be easily done in the field. It must be noted that extra care must be taken with the ceramic filter in very cold temperatures. If dropped or jarred in the pack, it could crack and would need to be replaced.

Katadyn, PUR, and Sweetwater also make mechanical systems similar to the MSR pump. All operate in a similar fashion, by forcing water through a porous filter. Katadyn makes a gravity filter that eliminates the need to pump. Just hang it from a tree and let gravity do the rest.

It should be noted that mechanical filters are ineffective for treating viruses. Some debate exists among outdoor enthusiasts about the necessity to treat viruses, since common waterborne viruses such as hepatitis A, polio, and typhoid aren't commonly associated with areas frequented by hikers and campers. Chlorine or iodine can be added to treat viruses if desired.

Water, of course, can still be boiled. A tried and true method, boiling kills bacteria, protozoa, and viruses. The main arguments against boiling are that it can be time consuming and inconvenient. Some say they don't prefer the taste of boiled water, but aeration by passing it from one container to another can improve taste somewhat.

CLIMATE AND WEATHER

Pennsylvania's climate and weather can be summed up in one word…. Well, actually it can't, and therein lies the problem. Tornadoes, tropical storms, drought, microbursts, blizzards, and flooding can all occur in a 12-month period. Ice storms haunt the nether regions between fall and winter and between winter and spring. Flooding can occur after heavy summer rains or in January when warm temperatures follow a blizzard. A 90-degree summer day can be followed by a 40-degree night under a clear sky in the mountains.

But that's weather, and when observed over a long period of time, it's not so bad. Freakish events can occur, but generally summer will be warm, winter cold, and the periods in between something altogether different. Overall, the state has an average July temperature of 83°F and typically receives four inches of rainfall during that time period. January, on the other hand, sees an average temperature of 24°F and usually about three inches of precipitation.

Philadelphia experiences about 40 inches of rain a year, a little over four inches of it coming in July, the wettest month. Snowfall totals of six or seven inches are not uncommon in January or February.

Just a little further north in Allentown, annual precipitation averages between 44 and 45 inches a year. Mid- to late summer are usually the wettest times. Snowfall totals are only slightly higher here as well. January and February are the worst months—unless you ski, in which case they are the best months. Allentown receives a little over 30 inches of the white stuff every year.

Scranton, in northeastern Pennsylvania, sees an average of 12 to 13 inches of snow during January alone, due to its higher elevation. The area can receive a little over 50 inches of snow in an average year. Total precipitation for the year averages about 36 inches, most of it coming during the summer months.

The central part of the state doesn't deviate much. Williamsport averages 40 inches of precipitation a year, most of it in mid- to late summer. Mid-June to mid-August are the wettest periods, and Williamsport can receive an average of 40 inches of snowfall per year.

Downstream from Williamsport lies Harrisburg, a city with slightly milder winters due to its location a little further south. Snowfall total for the year is about 35 inches.

The Appalachians and Lake Erie are two of the largest geographic factors affecting weather and climate in Pennsylvania. Pittsburgh and Erie can see lake-effect snows factored into totals, but those local totals can vary greatly. Overall, the Pittsburgh area experiences an average of 45 inches per year. But just to the east in the Laurel Highlands, numbers can be greater by as much as 20 percent. June and July are also the wettest months, getting an average of almost four inches each month. Pittsburgh usually gets about 38 inches of rain per year.

Erie lies in Pennsylvania's northwestern corner, adjacent to its namesake lake. Winter here means something completely different due to the lake's effect on weather. Erie averages an astounding 85 inches of snow per year. That's double Green Bay's measly 40 inches. Denver, with its 60 inches, doesn't even come close. Erie's 85 inches put it in the same league as Casper, Wyoming, and Burlington, Vermont. Summer is the wettest time, as most of the city's 42 inches of precipitation fall during this three-month period.

An understanding of how the geography affects the climate can greatly enhance your experience. If your plans take you to the Poconos or Laurel Highlands in May, a jacket may be necessary around the campfire at night. Frost can occur in some parts of the state as late as early June. Rain can fall anytime of the year, and it's not uncommon to see a late January storm cover the streets with a layer of water that will become ice as soon as the sun sets. Summer thunderstorms can be common in July and August when convection currents, aided by mountains, push air high into the atmosphere. The resulting cumulonimbus clouds can bring lightning, and campers should make every effort to get to a lower area away from trees. Stream crossings can become treacherous, and alternate routes should be sought. Use common sense, seek shelter if things get too bad, and above all, don't panic.

So pack a raincoat and a jacket, armed with the knowledge that summer travel in Pennsylvania can throw surprises your way. Who among us doesn't recount being caught in a summer downpour with a smile on our face? What backpacker holds back when telling his coworkers how snow kept him in his tent all weekend? After all, isn't that why we went outside to begin with?

Clothing and Weather Protection

Layering is the best method to maintain comfort in the outdoors, no matter the time of year. Avoid cotton and opt for synthetic materials whenever possible. Wet cotton, especially blue jeans, can zap body heat and cause hypothermia, an especially dangerous situation when relief isn't nearby. Many clothing companies, like Patagonia, EMS, REI, and Mountain Hardware offer a variety of proprietary synthetics that wick moisture, have flat seams to prevent chafing, and are tapered and tailored to permit layering.

Rain gear can be a hiker's best friend. When showers hit the mountains, even in summer, temperatures can fall to a point where shivering can occur. Prevent this by being prepared—most modern raingear weighs ounces and is breathable, not like the heavy ponchos of old. But even in a pinch that old poncho is better than nothing. Wear a hat to prevent sunburn in the summer and hypothermia in the winter. And when hiking don't neglect your feet. Blisters and sore spots should be tended to immediately.

Winter Camping

Campgrounds that are open year-round are usually close to ski resorts or state parks and forests that offer winter activities. Pennsylvania has many cross-country ski trails that are also open to snowshoers. Separate trails for snowmobiles are always marked. Many lakes throughout the state allow ice fishing, ice boating, and ice skating in designated areas. Always pay attention to posted signs warning about thin ice.

Other safety considerations for winter camping include exposure, hypothermia, and frostbite. Consider the type of activity you'll be pursuing, the day's weather forecast, including temperature ranges and wind chill, and how long you'll be out. Then you can select the appropriate layers of clothing.

The entire state should be driven with caution from late November to mid-March. When heavy snowfall threatens, special consideration should be taken to avoid traveling on roads that could easily become icy or impassable. Even though it may seem safe, conditions can often deteriorate, especially in the higher elevations or near Erie.

SAFETY
Preparation and Planning

Preparation and planning are important to any traveling experience. You should always know your destination and its surrounding area by checking out guidebooks and maps ahead of time. Take the proper equipment depending on which activities you have planned to do and find out if specialty equipment can be rented on site (e.g., paddles and life jackets or skis).

Always know your party's limitations. For instance, do you need to find areas with wheelchair accessibility? Are you traveling with small children or the elderly? Do you or any of your party have prior experience with the intended activities?

And, finally, be sure to notify someone back home when you intend to return should complications arise.

Health
Giardia

Even water that appears clean may contain animal-borne parasites such as *Giardia intestinalis* (also known as *Giardia lamblia*). Mountain streams, no matter how far from civilization, may contain nasties that cause diarrheal illness or some other malady that can ruin a trip or become potentially dangerous if medical help is more than a day away. Water treatment is an area that campers should not take lightly.

Poison Ivy

You probably know poison ivy when you see it—that three-leafed vine that serves as ground cover or attaches itself to an unsuspecting tree. The leaves are green, arrow-shaped, and sometimes have small black bumps erupting from them. It is the oil from the plant that causes the irritation.

Wash exposed body parts, clothing, and your dog immediately after being in an area where you've seen poison ivy. If you do get red and blistered skin from exposure to the plant, Caladryl or another antihistamine product will soothe the itch and dry out the blisters.

Ticks and Mosquitoes

After spending time in the woods, always check exposed skin and areas where clothing tightens around the skin such as waistbands and the tops of socks. Should you find a tick attached to your skin, be careful when removing it, as mouth parts left in the wound can cause infections, even Lyme disease. Many outdoor stores sell tick removal kits. If in doubt, see a doctor to have the tick removed.

To protect against mosquitoes, you have your choice of DEET-based repellents or citronella-based repellents. If something natural like the EPA-approved citronella product Avon's Skin-So-Soft doesn't seem to work for you, you could try one of those riskier products that contain DEET (the common name for N, N-diethyl-m-toluamide). You should check with a doctor before applying any DEET-based substance, as medical problems and even deaths have resulted from its use.

Snakes

The two venomous snakes in Pennsylvania are the copperhead and the Eastern diamondback rattlesnake. They can most often be found sunning themselves on rocks or hiding under them. In more wooded areas, you may encounter them in leaf detritus at the base of trees, wedged under fallen logs, or curled among exposed tree roots.

To cut down on your risk of injury from snakebites, wear boots that cover the ankle while hiking and stay on existing paths. Some outdoor stores sell snakebite kits. Should you sustain a bite, seek medical help immediately.

BEARS

If you see a bear in the wild, it's best to avoid any encounters, especially if there are cubs involved. Sometimes a whistle can scare away a black bear. If you can, safely vacate the immediate area and find an alternate route.

For more wild and remote campsites, bear-bagging food is a good idea. Place food in a plastic bag and use a long rope to hang it from a limb that is approximately 10 feet from the tree's trunk and around 20 feet from the ground.

Recreation
TRAIL TIPS

Pennsylvania is popular among hikers from all over because of the many trail systems contained within and passing through the state. You can hike the Mid-State Trail System and the Laurel Highlands Hiking Trail and never leave the Keystone State.

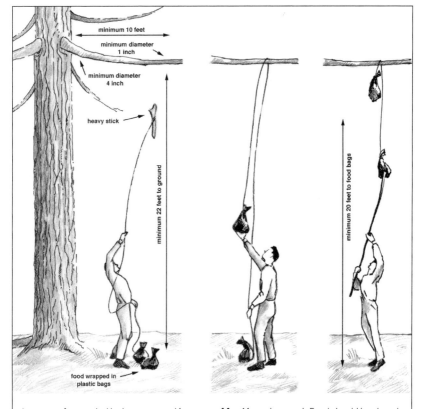

In an area frequented by bears, a good **bear-proof food hang** is a must. Food should be stored in a plastic bag 10 feet from the trunk of the tree and at least 20 feet from the ground.

Or pick up parts of the Appalachian Trail system on its way from Georgia to Maine or the North Country National Scenic Trail as it travels from North Dakota to upstate New York.

•When hiking, wear sturdy hiking boots and two pairs of socks to avoid blisters.

•Trekking poles can help on steep or uneven trails.

•Watch for sudden changes in weather and keep track of how much daylight is left.

•Stay on existing trails and be mindful of blazes and other trail markers. This is not only for your own safety, but also to preserve the ecosystems surrounding the trails.

Leave No Trace

PLAN AHEAD AND PREPARE
•Know the regulations and special concerns for the area you'll visit.
•Prepare for extreme weather, hazards, and emergencies.
•Schedule your trip to avoid times of high use.
•Visit in small groups. Split larger parties into groups of 4-6.
•Repackage food to minimize waste.
•Use a map and compass to eliminate the use of marking paint, rock cairns or flagging.

TRAVEL AND CAMP ON DURABLE SURFACES
•Durable surfaces include established trails and campsites, rock, gravel, dry grasses or snow.
•Protect riparian areas by camping at least 200 feet from lakes and streams.
•Good campsites are found, not made. Altering a site is not necessary.
   In popular areas:
•Concentrate use on existing trails and campsites.
•Walk single file in the middle of the trail, even when wet or muddy.
•Keep campsites small. Focus activity in areas where vegetation is absent.

DISPOSE OF WASTE PROPERLY
•Pack it in, pack it out. Inspect your campsite and rest areas for trash or spilled foods. Pack out all trash, leftover food, and litter.
•Deposit solid human waste in catholes dug 6-8 inches deep at least 200 feet from water, camp, and trails. Cover and disguise the cathole when finished.
•Pack out toilet paper and hygiene products.
•To wash yourself or your dishes, carry water 200 feet away from streams or lakes and use small amounts of biodegradable soap. Scatter strained dishwater.

•Avoid strenuous hikes during the hottest part of the day (noon–4 P.M.) and eat lightly when the temperature is high.

•Dress in lightweight, light-colored clothing made of natural fibers.

•Drink plenty of water and electrolyte-replacing fluids, such as Gatorade, and gauge your levels of consumption.

•Wear sunscreen and keep skin moisturized and covered.

LEAVE WHAT YOU FIND
•Preserve the past: examine, but do not touch, cultural or historic structures and artifacts.
•Leave rocks, plants and other natural objects as you find them.
•Avoid introducing or transporting non-native species.
•Do not build structures, furniture, or dig trenches.

MINIMIZE CAMPFIRE IMPACTS
•Campfires can cause lasting impacts to the backcountry. Use a lightweight stove for cooking and enjoy a candle lantern for light.
•Where fires are permitted, use established fire rings, fire pans, or mound fires.
•Keep fires small. Only use sticks from the ground that can be broken by hand.
•Burn all wood and coals to ash, put out campfires completely, then scatter cool ashes.

RESPECT WILDLIFE
•Observe wildlife from a distance. Do not follow or approach them.
•Never feed animals. Feeding wildlife damages their health, alters natural behaviors, and exposes them to predators and other dangers.
•Protect wildlife and your food by storing rations and trash securely.
•Control pets at all times, or leave them at home.
•Avoid wildlife during sensitive times: mating, nesting, raising young, or winter.

BE CONSIDERATE OF OTHER VISITORS
•Respect other visitors and protect the quality of their experience.
•Be courteous. Yield to other users on the trail.
•Step to the downhill side of the trail when encountering pack stock.
•Take breaks and camp away from trails and other visitors.
•Let nature's sounds prevail. Avoid loud voices and noises.

This copyrighted information has been reprinted with permission from the Leave No Trace Center for Outdoor Ethics. For more information or materials, please visit www.LNT.org or call 303/442-8222 or 800/332-4100.

River Tips

Paddling opportunities abound in Pennsylvania's scenic mountains and pastoral hills. Whether you paddle a canoe, a kayak, or a raft there's something here that will challenge you or make you wish the pull of the river were just a little slower. Flatwater enthusiasts will seek the tranquil beauty of the Allegheny, the Clarion, or the Delaware to marvel at the wilderness setting and abundant wildlife along their rocky banks. Paddlers seeking wildness of a different sort will head to Ohiopyle, where commercial whitewater rafting first reared its head east of the Mississippi. Dam-controlled flows ensure good levels all summer long and the scene can't be beat. During spring snowmelts or after a good summer rain, Pennsylvania paddlers head to Slippery Rock Creek, the Lehigh, or the Loyalsock for their abundant rapids and waves.

Before you set out on a river trip, whether by canoe, kayak, raft, or motorboat, always follow these tips:

•Know the hazards and obstacles on your route and always scout unknown rapids before attempting them.

•Wear a Coast Guard approved type III-V personal flotation device (PFD) and keep it properly adjusted and buckled while on the water.

•Know the capacity of your watercraft and do not exceed it.

•Never boat alone; always have at least one other boat with you on any trip.

•Stay away from rivers during high water.

•When a river is frozen, never walk onto the ice.

•Keep all ropes coiled when not in use (never tie a rope to yourself or another person, especially a child) and know how to use a throw rope should someone fall in. Be aware that hypothermia can set in even in summer after someone has been in the water.

FLORA AND FAUNA

Travelers to Pennsylvania see a state that has been largely manipulated by the hand of man. One doesn't have to travel far to see old strip mines picked over by earth moving machines, farmland molded by the plow, third-growth forests seemingly more familiar with the ax than birdsong. Urbanization caps the eastern and western borders of the state like bookends, but what's in between often surprises visitors, and can even inspire a sense of awe that seems out of place in this well-populated chunk of land. Despite industrial and agricultural threats, Pennsylvania still has large tracts of land worth exploring. Pristine streams fall through isolated canyons. Groves of old growth hemlocks slumber on remote mountainsides. Sphagnum bogs, left over from the ice age, wait in rocky gullies for the next one. In some instances these natural treasures are just a short walk from a parking area or visitors center. But it's usually the traveler who hikes that extra mile who finds the rewards of nature in relative solitude.

Forest Types

Pennsylvania's location astride the Appalachians makes it an important keystone in the region's ecology. Migratory birds make use of Presque Isle's wetlands and the muddy banks of Susquehannock State Park. Pennsylvania's wooded ridges and valleys shelter a plethora of threatened or endangered species, a group that ranges from bald eagles to Indiana bats. Freshwater streams, some of the richest in the world, hold an abundance of species that diversified in the periods between glaciations. No other place on earth has the variety of salamanders that some of Pennsylvania's forests have.

What follows are brief descriptions of the main forest types found in the state.

Allegheny Highlands

In the Allegheny Highlands forests, hemlock and beech represented 60 percent of observed species in what is now the Allegheny National

Fossil Finds

NORTHWEST
In Erie Bluffs State Park, you can see a rare fossil sand dune ridge that formed more than 12,000 years ago.
   Nearby campgrounds: Camp Eriez Campground; Sparrow Pond Family Campground.

NORTH CENTRAL
Worlds End State Park boasts fossil lungfish burrows in its weathered red siltstones.
   Nearby campground: Pioneer Campground.

NORTHEAST
Located in Delaware Water Gap National Recreation Area, the Pocono Environmental Education Center has a 1.5-mile trail that leads to a rock outcrop with marine fossils.
   Nearby campgrounds: Four Seasons Campgrounds; Mount Pocono Campground; Silver Valley Campsites.

SOUTHWEST
At Ohiopyle State Park's Ferncliff Peninsula you can see lepidodendron and calamite tree fossils in the rock underfoot as you hike.
   Nearby campgrounds: Pioneer Park Campground; Yogi Bear's Jellystone Park Camp-Resort (Mill Run); Scarlett Knob Campground; Kentuck Campground; Tall Oaks Campground, Inc.; Benner's Meadow Run Camping & Cabins.

SOUTH CENTRAL
The collectible trilobites, insect ancestors, and starfish fossils in Swatara State Park's Fossil Pit were unearthed and dumped here during I-81 road construction.
   Nearby campgrounds: Pine Grove KOA at Twin Grove Park; Lickdale Campground & General Store; KOA Jonestown; Shady Oaks Campground.

SOUTHEAST
In Joliette you can collect Pennsylvanian-aged petrified wood and fern fossils from the shale and sandstone in the anthracite coal mine dumps.
   Nearby campgrounds: Camp-A-While, Inc.; Echo Valley Campground.

Forest when the first Europeans arrived. When periodic fires burned through drier portions of the region, sugar maple often replaced hemlock as a major component of the forest. Other species found in the Allegheny Highlands forest include red maple, yellow and black birch, black cherry, and white ash. White pine is found in homogeneous stands that may have originated after fire or wind flattened the original hemlock.

Logging took its toll between 1890 and 1920. Except for a few stands of old growth on steep mountain slopes or in isolated ravines, most of the hardwoods fell and were dragged to mills for processing. The resulting slash was easily burned, and fierce forest fires were common after logging companies had moved on. The fires resulted in the loss of most of the hemlock and white pine and greatly reduced populations of beech, sugar maples, and other related hardwoods. Species such as aspen, pin cherry, grasses, sedges, and honeysuckles grasped a firmer foothold at this point.

Even the surviving Allegheny Highland old growth remains threatened. Exploding deer populations have resulted in the loss of size diversity, resulting in a forest that trends toward larger species that produce a heavy canopy and sparse undergrowth.

A few important pockets of Allegheny Highland forest remain. The Pennsylvania State Forest in Potter and Clinton Counties has over 247,000 acres of habitat. The Allegheny National Forest in McKean and Warren Counties in northwestern Pennsylvania has over 4,000 acres.

APPALACHIAN MIXED MESOPHYTIC

The Appalachian mixed mesophytic forest reaches its northern extent in southwestern Pennsylvania. This region acted as a refuge for many plants and animals during the periods between glaciations, and as a result this region experiences rich species diversity and a plethora of endemic species. Dense understories of ferns, mosses, fungi, perennial and annual herbaceous plants, small trees, and shrubs reside below a canopy that may contain over 30 species of trees at any given site. In an interesting twist of evolution, this forest mirrors the temperate forests of central and eastern China almost on a species-to-species basis. For almost any given genera, the Asian forest can produce a match.

The diversity of the mixed mesophytic forest can be seen in the variety of songbirds, snails, and amphibians that live there. Pennsylvania alone has 22 species of salamanders representing five families and 11 genera. Nowhere else in the United States or Canada is the diversity of endemic land snail communities or herbaceous plant biotas as rich. Appalachia's mixed mesophytic forests, along with the Appalachian–Blue Ridge forests, are unrivaled in the world for diversity and endemism of the region's freshwater communities. No other region can boast the variety of fish, mussels, crayfish, and other invertebrates that this one can.

In the lower elevations, magnolias, elms, hickories, oaks, ashes, basswoods, walnuts, maples, and pines dominate. Prior to 1904, American chestnuts were so abundant that it was said that a squirrel could go from Pittsburgh to Atlanta, hopping from chestnut to chestnut without ever touching the ground. But a fungus introduced to the United States via New York made short work of the species.

As one ascends mountain roads to some of the region's higher elevations the canopy begins transitioning to sugar and mountain maple, yellow birch, beech, and eastern hemlock. The understory here is dense with mountain laurel and rhododendron, which are particularly beautiful when in bloom. The best time to see blooms is from late May to early July. Actual times vary with elevations.

It's at these higher elevations where pockets of ice age environs resist global warming and deforestation. Cranberry glades, heath barrens, shale barrens, and sphagnum bogs reside in isolated valleys where cooler temperatures allowed them to resist succession to forest types typical of warmer areas. The uniqueness of cranberry bogs is especially apparent when compared to surrounding woodland. The representative species are more commonly associated with ecoregions found much further to the north. Cranberries, blueberries, buckbean, and bog rosemary coexist in relic forests of balsam fir, red pine, eastern larch, and the Canada yew. Atypical wildlife species found in these relic bogs include martins, northern goshawks, and black-billed magpies.

Unfortunately, Pennsylvania has lost many of its larger tracts of these unique forest types, but some vestiges remain. (To see large, unbroken tracts of mixed mesophytic forests, one has to travel south to West Virginia's Monongahela National Forest.) In Monroe County, Bender and Black Bear Swamps embrace 1600 acres of sphagnum bogs and acidic shrub swamps, which are home to rare animals and plants. In Ohiopyle State Park in southwestern Pennsylvania, Ferncliff Peninsula is a National Natural Landmark with abundant wildflowers, old-growth hemlocks, and a mixed oak forest that shelters species of concern like white monkshood. In eastern Pennsylvania are the Pine Swamps of French Creek State Park. These acidic broadleaf swamps contain rare plant species and feature mucky, water-filled channels separating vegetated sphagnum hummocks.

APPALACHIAN–BLUE RIDGE

The last major forest type to be found in Pennsylvania is the Appalachian–Blue Ridge forests found in the central portion of the state. A variety of climate, soil, and landform types in association with a long stretch of evolutionary history have resulted in a diversity of plants and animals nearly unmatched in the world's temperate deciduous forests. Over 158 species of trees can be found here, making it one of the most diverse ecoregions in North America for floral diversity. These forests acted as a seed bank in times of glaciation,

much in the same way that the mesophytic forests described above did.

With a geology that has been relatively stable since pre-Mesozoic times, and a climate that varies regionally with changes in elevation, latitude, and physiography, a large number of species have been able to survive despite glacial retreat. In addition to these factors, a type of limestone landscape known as karst has resulted in a network of caves that provide additional habitat for a large number of unusual species, including nine varieties of bats. Variations include the hoary bat, which can have a wingspan of up to 16 inches, and the rare small-footed bat, one of the tiniest in North America.

Forest types in this region vary with elevation much in the way the mixed mesophytic forests do. At higher elevations, spruce-fir forests dominate. Typical species include red spruce, Fraser fir, and balsam fir, usually situated along the tops of narrow ridges.

The transition from spruce-fir to mixed oak is usually a very noticeable one. Even a short descent will reveal a transition to tulip poplars and oaks. At the beginning of the 20th century, chestnuts would have dominated here, but the aforementioned blight took care of that species. Other species include birch, pines, red maples, and hickory, red, chestnut, and black oaks.

Another component that adds a layer of complexity to this forest type is the tremendous expanse of microhabitats found here. The prolonged geologic stability permitted speciation among certain groups. As temperatures fluctuated, groups from the same species became separated and isolated on adjacent ridge tops. Many species of plants, invertebrates, fish, and salamanders diverged after millions of years of isolation. In some cases it seems that each ridge or watershed has its own unique species.

Mountain ridges in central Pennsylvania, including South Mountain and Allegheny Mountain, are the best places to see the remaining Appalachian–Blue Ridge forests. Their range has been restricted primarily to ridge tops; the limestone valley floors were too fertile for early American farmers to resist. Subsequent logging and additional agriculture has made this forest all but nonexistent at lower elevations.

Fauna

MAMMALS

Whitetail deer and black bear are plentiful. Sightings of coyotes and bobcats are rarer, but occur throughout the state. Smaller animals such as cottontail rabbits, raccoons, woodchucks, chipmunks, skunks, opossums, bats, and red, gray, and fox squirrels are found just as often in urban areas as in the forests and state parks. In the northwest, don't be surprised to spot porcupines in the woods or along the rural roads. Near the water, you're likely to see muskrats, minks, beavers, and otters.

BIRDS

Birdlife includes year-round residents as well as their migrating cousins. Raptors such as eagles, red-tail hawks, and osprey share the skies with crows, ravens, and turkey vultures. Within the woods, you'll encounter ruffed grouse (the state bird), wild turkeys, and woodpeckers. And just about anywhere you can see cardinals, bluebirds, tree swallows, wrens, and chickadees. Waterside brings mallard and wood ducks, green-wing teal, gadwall, herons, and egrets. Near Lake Erie's shore, you'll find gulls. During spring migration and into the summer, you can watch for flycatchers, thrushes, vireos, warblers, orioles, tanagers, cormorants, and Canadian geese.

REPTILES AND AMPHIBIANS

Among the reptiles and amphibians found in Pennsylvania are 15 types of toads and frogs, two varieties of skinks, the Northern fence lizard, 18 species of salamanders and newts (including hellbenders, which can reach a length of 12–18 inches), 11 types of turtles,

and 22 different snake species. Most commonly encountered are black snakes, garter snakes, and water snakes. Rare is a sighting of Eastern diamondback rattlesnakes or copperheads. Often the Northern brown water snake is confused with the copperhead because they have similar markings; note the water snake's nose is blunt, however.

FISH

Within the numerous streams, rivers, and lakes of Pennsylvania are native species and those of the stocked variety. Anglers can cast for brook, brown, and rainbow trout as well as striped, largemouth, and smallmouth bass. Other fish include northern and yellow perch, bullhead, carp, sunfish, bluegill, catfish, crappie, salmon, walleye, muskellunge, sucker, pumpkinseed, steelhead, northern pike, and pickerel.

© JASON MILLER

litter frog, one of the many types of frogs found in Pennsylvania

Camping Gear Checklist

GENERAL GEAR
Cooking Utensils

aluminum foil
ax or hatchet
barbecue tongs
camp stove
can opener
candles
Clif and granola bars
coffee packets
cream packets
cups
dish soap and scrubber
fire-starter cubes
forks, knives, and spoons
fuel
grill

ice chest
knife sharpener
matches
paper plates
paper towels
plastic wrap
potholder
pots and pans
spatula
spices
sugar packets
tablecloth
tea bags
water jug
wood or charcoal for barbecue

Clothing

ballcap or wide-brimmed hat
breathable shirt
canvas/cotton pants
fleece vest
gloves (seasonal)
lightweight fleece jacket

rain jacket, pants, and poncho
scarf (seasonal)
shorts (seasonal)
swimsuit or trunks (seasonal)
underwear

First-Aid Kit

Ace bandage
aspirin or ibuprofen
Band-Aids
biodegradable soap
Caladryl for poison and bites
gauze bandages
insect repellent
lip balm

list of local emergency numbers
medical insurance card
medical tape
Neosporin for cuts
snakebite kit
sunscreen
thermometer
tweezers

Packing Supplies

bungee cords
duct tape

garbage bags
nylon rope

Personal Items

biodegradable shampoo
brush or comb
cash

cell phone
credit cards
earplugs

(continued on next page)

Personal Items *(continued)*

feminine hygiene products
hand sanitizer
handkerchief
mirror
moisturizer
prescription medications
sewing kit
spare glasses or contacts

sunglasses
toilet paper
tooth brush and toothpaste
towel
towelettes
traveler checks
watch

Pet Supplies

brush
carrier
collar and tags
food
food dish
health and rabies certificate
leash

litter box
litter Scoop Bags
medication
picture in case pet gets lost
toys
water dish

RVing

30 and 50 amp adapters
airbed
board games
camping guide
catalytic heater
coins
coolant hoses
cot
cotter pins
driver's license
emergency flares
extension cords
fan belts
first-aid kit with ibuprofen and
    prescriptions
flashlight
folding chairs
fuses

insurance card
jumper cables
keys
light bulbs
motor oil and transmission fluid
Mr. Heater
pillow
plastic tarp
power adapters
propane gas for Mr. Heater
registration card
road map
RV Windshield light screen
slide-out pins or bolts
tire pressure gauge
tool kit
water filtration
water hose

Tenting

deck of cards
flashlight and batteries
ground tarp
lantern and fuel
mosquito net
radio
rain fly
reading material
Seam Lock for tent repair

sleeping bag
stuff sack
tent
tent poles
Therm-a-Rest pad
waste spade
water filter or iodine for purification
waterproof tent bag
toilet paper

RECREATIONAL GEAR
Biking

altimeter	helmet
backpack with snacks	mountable compass
bike	pump
cycling gloves	security lock
cycling jersey	spare tube for long rides
cycling shorts	tool kit
fleece	water bottle and carrier
heart rate monitor	

Birding

binoculars	camera
bird guide	notebook and pen

Fishing

chest pack	permits and licenses
fishing vest	pliers
float tube	reel
fly reels	rod
fly rods	spare spools
fresh line	tacklebox with lures, hooks, flies
knife	waders
net	wading boots

Hiking

altimeter	lightweight hiking shoes
backpack	rain gear
boot inserts	sock liners
compass	topographic map
daypack	trekking poles
extra boot laces	trail map
gaiters	water purifier
GPS unit	whistle
headlamp with extra batteries	wool socks
hiking boots	

Paddling

bailer	spray jacket
canoe	waste bucket
dry bag	water shoes or sandals
inflatable boat	wetsuit
kayak	wool sweater or fleece
personal flotation device (PFD)	

NORTHWEST

© HEIDI MILLER

BEST CAMPGROUNDS

Lake Erie's cold waters lap against the shores of northwest Pennsylvania, a region that contains some of the state's largest unspoiled wooded areas. The campgrounds here reflect this mixing of shore and forest and offer wonderful views and many recreational opportunities – yet they are refreshingly not as crowded as their eastern counterparts.

Glaciation during the Pleistocene epoch was the primary force to shape this area. Massive glaciers left behind a legacy of lakes, rerouted streams, moraines, eskers, swamps, and bogs. The glaciers acted like a dam, preventing north-flowing rivers and streams from reaching an outlet to the ocean. The water backed up and formed Lake Monongahela, a tremendous body of water that once covered most of Western Pennsylvania and parts of Ohio and West Virginia.

The water rose until it crested the low hills that defined its drainage basin. The flood rushed southwest toward the present location of Three Rivers in a dramatic fashion, sculpting and reshaping to fit its needs. The best place to see the result, not coincidentally, is the best place to start your exploration of northwest Pennsylvania.

Slippery Rock Creek Gorge, the scenic highlight of McConnells Mill State Park, was created when a series of ancient lakes spilled over their damming ridges. The torrent carved a steep-walled gorge more than 400 feet deep. Today this National Natural Landmark is a geological wonderland, containing scenic hiking trails to overlooks, waterfalls, potholes, and flumes, areas for bouldering and rappelling, and arguably the best whitewater in this corner of the state. With enough rainfall, Slippery Rock Creek can become a pushy Class V. Even at normal levels, the eight most frequently run miles have more than 16 Class II and III rapids.

For a different experience, visitors can try Moraine State Park, home to 3,225-acre Lake Arthur. A seven-mile bike trail follows this warm-water fishery's north shore. Some visitors will even be lucky enough to spy one of the osprey reintroduced into the park.

Erie Bluffs, located 12 miles west of the city of Erie, is one of Pennsylvania's newest state parks. Its 540 acres contain the largest undeveloped parcel of Great Lake shoreline in the state, 90-foot bluffs overlooking this important waterway, and a world-class steelhead fishery.

Further east is Presque Isle State Park, a massive sand spit that hooks into Lake Erie. Its location makes it a valuable migratory stopover, providing excellent bird-watching opportunities and fine fishing. The park has six distinct ecological zones. Visitors can follow trails from climax forest to thicket and sub-climax forest, past old ponds and marshes to sand plains and new ponds, and down to the bay and shoreline zones to Lake Erie. Among the park's 11 beaches is the only surf beach in the Commonwealth.

No visit to the northwest region would be complete without a visit to Allegheny National Forest. Visitors here can view grouse, turkey, hawks, raccoons, porcupines, and deer from forest roads. Black bear and bobcat sightings are rarer, despite a recent increase in the bobcat population.

Hickory Creek Wilderness and Allegheny Islands Wilderness, both located in the national forest, are Pennsylvania's only Congressionally designated wilderness areas. Hickory Creek Wilderness sits on gentle terrain drained by East Hickory Creek and Middle Hickory Creek. Small native brook trout reside in both streams, and wildlife typical of Pennsylvania can be found in the northern hardwood forest. Twelve-mile Hickory Creek Trail is the major attraction for backpackers and day hikers. Allegheny Islands Wilderness is comprised of seven islands on the Allegheny River between Buckaloons Recreation Area and Tionesta; access is by canoe. Crull's Island is the largest, with 93 acres, and has many fine specimens of willow, sycamore, and silver maple. Eighty-five miles of the placid Allegheny have designated recreational status under the National Wild and Scenic River Act.

The Clarion River, a tributary of the Allegheny, has almost 52 miles designated as scenic or recreational. Narrow valleys lined with hardwoods characterize this undeveloped stretch and small rapids, rock outcrops, virgin hemlock and white pine, and abundant wildlife keep the paddler interested, always wanting more, yet content to let the current do most of the work.

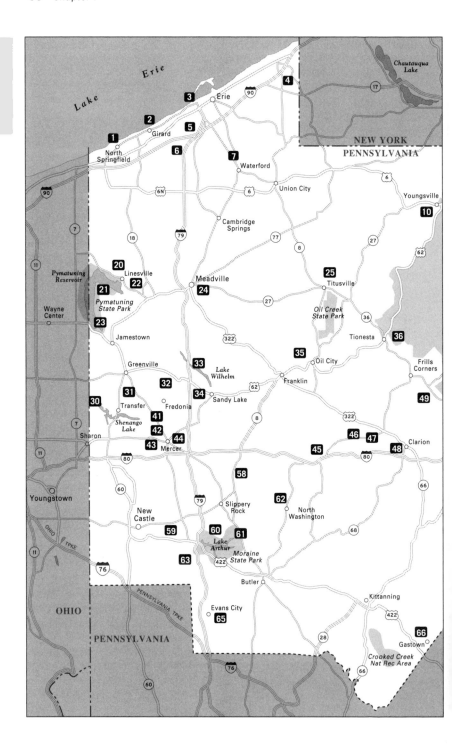

NORTHWEST

Jamestown

Olean

17

219

417

NEW YORK
PENNSYLVANIA

449

Allegheny Reservoir **8**

9 Bradford

49

12 Scandia

11

13

59 Marshburg

Warren

16

18

19

59

Smethport

6

Coudersport 6

Clarendon

15

17

6

14

Sheffield

Kane

Lafayette

6

Allegheny

27

46

see
North Central
pages 80-81

26

National

219

28

East Branch
Clarion River
Reservoir

29 Sizerville

Forest

Emporium

144

66

38

37

120

40

Cook Forest
State Park

39

Ridgway

255

Renovo

50

120

Cooksburg

Sinnamahoning

51

52

Sigel

144

53

28

54 Penfield

Brookville

219

55

80

153

56

28

DuBois

57

Susquehanna River

Clearfield

Woodland

80

64

322

Punxsutawney

219

Phillipsburg

220

119

26

see
Southwest
pages 150-151

State
College

322

0   10 mi

0   10 km

Indiana

219

99

422

Altoona

© AVALON TRAVEL PUBLISHING, INC.

1 VIRGINIA'S BEACH CAMPGROUND

🧍🚵🏊🛶🛥🏕🏇🚐🏔

Rating: 10

at Lake Erie

BEST (

This campground is a steelhead angler's dream. Not only do you have access to several streams and creeks like Elk, Raccoon, and Crooked Creek, but also to Lake Erie, the eleventh largest lake in the world. Virginia's Beach Campground has a private boat ramp for vessels up to 20 feet in length. Jet skis are welcome. The beach in front of the campground is a mixture of sandy and rocky spots. You can swim, bike, or hike here. There is also a 0.75-mile wooded hiking trail on the property. Birders will enjoy spying warblers, sparrows, and occasional sea birds. You can also cast for walleye, carp, perch, smallmouth and largemouth bass, catfish, salmon, brown trout, and bluegill. Open, wooded, and lakefront sites are available.

Campsites, facilities: There are 141 sites for tents or RVs up to 90 feet: 90 have full hookups; 35 have water and electricity; 16 have no hookups. There are 15 pull-throughs. Picnic tables and fire rings are provided. Drinking water, restrooms with flush toilets, a dump station, a portable dump, showers, a public phone, groceries, ice, wood, a camp store, a pavilion, a playground, basketball, horseshoes, a sports field, and RV supplies are available. Leashed pets are permitted.

Reservations, fees: Reservations are accepted. The rate is $24–34 per night for up to two people. Each additional person is $7. Weekly, monthly, and seasonal rates are available. Major credit cards are accepted. Open mid-May through mid-October.

Directions: From the junction of Highway 5 and Highway 215 and Holliday Road, travel one mile north on Holliday Road, then 0.25 mile west on an unnamed gravel road to the campground entrance on the right.

Contact: Virginia's Beach Campground, 352

Holliday Road, North Springfield, PA 16430, 814/922-3261, www.virginiasbeach.com.

2 CAMP ERIEZ CAMPGROUND

🏊🛶🏕🏇♿🚐

Rating: 5

near Erie Bluffs State Park

You have your choice of shaded and open sites at this quaint private campground near one of Pennsylvania's newest state parks, Erie Bluffs. Established on June 4, 2004, the 540-acre park covers one mile of shoreline along Lake Erie, making it a great destination for swimming or fishing. The 90-foot bluffs that look over Lake Erie give the park its name. Among the species of fish found within the great lake are crappie, catfish, smallmouth, largemouth, and striped bass, northern pike, perch, walleye, muskie, bluegill, and sunfish. There are also wetlands that attract waterfowl such as great blue heron, osprey, Canada geese, wood ducks, and mallard ducks. If you'd prefer the campground's entertainment, Camp Eriez has planned activities like bingo and ceramics on weekends.

Campsites, facilities: There are 190 sites for RVs up to 26 feet; all have water and electricity. There are 15 pull-throughs. No tents are permitted. Picnic tables and fire rings are provided. Drinking water, restrooms with flush toilets, a dump station, showers, a public phone, modem access, a phone hookup, wood, a swimming pool, a rec hall, an arcade, a playground, badminton, a basketball court, a volleyball court, and a sports field are available. Some sites are wheelchair accessible. Leashed pets are permitted. The campground has a traffic control gate for security.

Reservations, fees: Reservations are accepted. The rate is $20 per night for up to four people. Each additional person is $4. Open mid-April through mid-October.

Directions: From the junction of I-90 Exit

16/4 and Highway 98, travel 3.5 miles north on Highway 98, then three miles west on Highway 5 to the campground entrance on the right.

Contact: Camp Eriez Campground, 9356 West Lake Road, Lake City, PA 16423, 814/774-8381, bart2@velocity.net.

3 SARA'S BEACHCOMBER CAMPGROUND

🚶 🚴 🏊 ⛵ 🚤 🐴 👨‍👩‍👧 🚐 ⛺

Rating: 10

near Presque Isle State Park

BEST (

Located on the shores of Lake Erie, between Presque Isle State Park and Waldameer Amusement Park, Sara's is one of the most scenic campgrounds in Pennsylvania. With a choice between bayside and lakeside campsites, Sara's is sure to make even the most jaded camper sigh. Beachcombing, as the name implies, is a favorite activity, and it's easy to take long strolls while gazing into Erie's placid waters. Lake fishing and swimming are available just beyond your campsite, and long walks in the early morning or late evenings is an activity that no guide can place a value to. Weekly activities and theme weekends provide extra incentive for the camper to stay close to this campground, but with Presque Isle so close, the temptation to visit is hard to resist. Home to many swimming beaches, Presque Isle provides a balance of developed and primitive beach areas. There are hiking trails and bicycle routes, volleyball courts, and picnic pavilions on Presque Isle as well.

Campsites, facilities: There are 75 sites for tents and RVs up to 30 feet: 25 have full hookups; 50 have water and electricity. Picnic tables and fire rings are available. Drinking water, restrooms with flush toilets, a dump station, showers, groceries, a camp store, a playground, and a rec room are available. Leashed pets are permitted.

Reservations, fees: No reservations are accepted. The rate is $20–28 per night for up to two people. Each additional person is $7. Weekly and seasonal rates are available. Open end of May through beginning of September.

Directions: From I-79 Exit 183B, travel west four lights to Highway 832, then north one mile on Highway 832 to the campground entrance on the right.

Contact: Sara's Beachcomber Campground, 50 Peninsula Drive, Erie, PA 16505, 814/833-4560, www.sarascampground.com.

4 FAMILY AFFAIR CAMPGROUND

🚶 🚴 🏊 ⛵ 🚤 🐴 👨‍👩‍👧 ♿ 🚐 ⛺

Rating: 7

near Presque Isle State Park

BEST (

Located in Pennsylvania's northern tip, Family Affair Campground offers proximity to Lake Erie and Orchard Beach. This is the heart of the Keystone State's wine country so many trips to vineyards are possible from the campground. Just to the east is the famous Chautauqua Region of New York. Lake Chautauqua is one of the highest navigable lakes in North America, and is world renowned for its beauty and arts community. Presque Isle State Park is located just to the west on Lake Erie's sandy shore. Swimming is permissible at one of the park's many beaches, and boating, fishing, biking, and hiking can be enjoyed there as well. Back at the campground, you can take advantage of paddleboats, fishing, or canoeing on the property's lake, hiking on one of the many trails, or planned activities on weekends.

Campsites, facilities: There are 280 sites for tents or RVs up to 31 feet: 33 have full hookups; 197 have water and electricity; 50 have no hookups. There are 12 pull-throughs. Picnic tables and fire rings are provided. Drinking water, restrooms with flush toilets, a dump

SOMERSET COUNTY LIBRARY
6022 GLADES PIKE SUITE 120
SOMERSET, PA 15501
814-445-5907

station, a portable dump, showers, a public phone, groceries, ice, LP gas, wood, a camp store, a pavilion, a rec hall, a playground, two swimming pools, miniature golf, horseshoes, volleyball, and a sports field are available. Some sites are wheelchair accessible. Leashed pets are permitted.

Reservations, fees: Reservations are accepted at 800/729-8112. The rate is $22–24 per night for up to two people. Each additional person is $5. Open April through mid-October.

Directions: From the junction of I-90 Exit 41/11 and Highway 89, travel 0.75 mile south on Highway 89, then turn left onto Cole Road and travel two miles to Highway 426 south, and continue one mile on Highway 426 to the campground entrance on the right.

Contact: Family Affair Campground, 9640 Findley Lake Road, North East, PA 16428, 814/725-8112, www.facinfo.com.

5 HILL'S FAMILY CAMPGROUND

Rating: 6

near Presque Isle State Park

At Hill's Family you can choose from shaded or sunny sites. The relaxing setting makes you want to take it easy—you know the fishing, swimming, and boating will be good this close to Lake Erie. Nearby Presque Isle State Park is a 3,200-acre sandy peninsula that can be reached by highway or by boat. There are four boat launches within the park. Vista Launch is for small craft and Jet skis. Niagara and Lagoon have space for small and medium-sized craft. For larger watercraft use West Pier. A 500-slip marina is also available in the park. Presque Isle has 11 sand beaches along the lake. Other water activities include scuba diving and waterskiing. There are 11 miles of hiking trails and 13.5-mile Karl Boyes Multi-Purpose National

Recreation Trail, which accommodates both hikers and bikers.

Campsites, facilities: There are 139 sites for tents or RVs up to 30 feet: 82 have full hookups; 20 have water and electricity; 37 have no hookups. There are 60 pull-throughs. Picnic tables and fire rings are provided. Drinking water, restrooms with flush toilets, a dump station, a portable dump, showers, a laundry, modem access, a phone hookup, a public phone, cable TV hookup, groceries, ice, wood, a camp store, a pavilion, a playground, a rec hall, an arcade, horseshoes, and RV rentals and supplies are available. Some sites are wheelchair accessible. Leashed pets are permitted.

Reservations, fees: Reservations are accepted. The rate is $24–28 per night for up to two people. Each additional person is $6. Group discounts are available. Major credit cards are accepted. Open April through October.

Directions: From the junction of I-90 Exit 18 and Highway 832, travel 500 feet north on Highway 832 to the campground entrance on the left.

Contact: Hill's Family Campground, 6300 Sterrettania Road, Fairview, PA 16415, 814/833-3272, hillscampground@aol.com.

6 KOA ERIE

Rating: 8

near Presque Isle State Park

Located close to Presque Isle State Park, a 3,200-acre peninsula that thumbs its way into Lake Erie, KOA Erie has plenty of on-site and nearby activities to keep visitors interested. Paddleboats are available for rent on the site's three-acre lake, which is stocked with catfish and sunfish. Local streams are also popular for trout fishing. Check schedules on the premises for a list of planned weekly activities. If the nature bug bites you, apply ointment, then head to Presque Isle for its fine swimming beaches, boating, fishing, or bird watching. Because of its location along migratory flyways, Presque Isle is a nature lover's dream. Species will vary seasonally, but waterfowl dominate. Presque Isle's various habitats shelter threatened and endangered species. Hiking trails and a bicycle path can also be found on Presque Isle, which has both rustic and developed beaches.

Campsites, facilities: There are 135 sites for tents or RVs up to 28 feet: 95 have water and electricity; 40 have no hookups. There are 23 pull-throughs. Picnic tables and fire rings are provided. Drinking water, restrooms with flush toilets, a dump station, a portable dump, showers, a laundry, modem access, a phone hookup, a public phone, groceries, ice, LP gas, wood, a general store, grills, a pavilion, a rec hall, a playground, a swimming pool, badminton, horseshoes, and a volleyball court are available. Some sites are wheelchair accessible. Leashed pets are permitted.

Reservations, fees: Reservations are accepted. The rate is $38–45 per night for up to two people. Each additional person is $6. Open April through October.

Directions: From the junction of I-90 Exit 18/5 and Highway 832, travel south one mile on Highway 832, then turn left onto West Road and travel 0.5 mile to the campground entrance on the right.

Contact: KOA Erie, 814/476-7706, 6645 West Road, McKean, PA 16426, www.koakampgrounds.com/where/pa/38112/index.htm.

▊ SPARROW POND FAMILY CAMPGROUND
👫 🏊 🛶 🐕 🚴 ♿ 🚐 ⛺

Rating: 6

near Erie Bluffs State Park

Located just south of Erie, Sparrow Pond Family Campground provides convenient access to a variety of recreational activities. Presque Isle State Park is just to the north, in Erie, and one of Pennsylvania's newest state parks, Erie Bluffs, is just to the northwest. Erie Bluffs boasts a world-class steelhead fishery and the largest stretch of unspoiled Erie shoreline in Pennsyl-

vania. There are significant archaeological sites on the park property, as well as endangered and threatened plants. The 90-foot bluffs are the scenic highlight, though, and are not to be missed. At press time, there were no facilities, so pack a picnic lunch and visit before development brings crowds. Back at the campground you can enjoy fishing in the pond, swimming, hiking, or organized outdoor games and activities.

Campsites, facilities: There are 135 sites for tents or RVs up to 45 feet: 100 have full hookups; 35 have water and electricity. There are three pull-throughs. Picnic tables and fire rings are provided. Drinking water, restrooms with flush toilets, a dump station, a portable dump, showers, a laundry, modem access, a phone hookup, groceries, ice, LP gas, wood, a camp store, grills, a rec hall, an arcade, a playground, a swimming pool, a wading pool, basketball, horseshoes, volleyball, a sports field, and RV storage and supplies are available. Some sites are wheelchair accessible. Leashed pets are permitted.

Reservations, fees: Reservations are accepted. The rate is $30–35 per night for up to four people. Each additional person is $5. Major credit cards are accepted. Open mid-April through mid-October.

Directions: From the junction of I-90 and Highway 19 Exit 24, travel four miles south on Highway 19 to the campground entrance on the left.

Contact: Sparrow Pond Family Campground, 11103 Route 19 North, Waterford, PA 16441, 814/796-6777, www.campingfriend.com/sparrowpondcampground.

▊ WILLOW BAY CAMPGROUND
👫 🏊 🛶 🚤 🎣 🐕 🚴 ♿ 🚐 ⛺

Rating: 7

in Allegheny National Forest

You can choose from shaded or open sites at this campground, looking out over the southern shore of Willow Bay. The bay is an eastern branch of Allegheny Reservoir and part of Allegheny National Forest. You can go fishing or boating on the bay or on the reservoir itself. Among the species of fish you might hook are sunfish, smallmouth and largemouth bass, bluegill, trout, crappie, northern perch, and catfish. For hiking there is the North Country National Scenic Trail just south of Willow Bay Recreation Area. This 86.4-mile trail offers views of the many bays and waterfalls in the area. You may observe black bear, white-tailed deer, raccoons, opossums, red and gray squirrels, chipmunks, cotton tail rabbits, minks, or skunks. The trail takes you through many types of forest from black cherry, oak, and beech to white pine and mountain laurel. The trail is challenging at times due to steep grades, stream crossing, and rock ledges. It is accessible in the winter.

Campsites, facilities: There are 102 sites for tents or RVs up to 60 feet: 33 have electricity; 69 have no hookups. Picnic tables and fire rings are provided. Drinking water, vault toilets, restrooms with flush toilets, showers, a dump station, public phones, a pavilion, a concrete boat launch, and a playground are available. Some sites are wheelchair accessible. Leashed pets are permitted.

Reservations, fees: Reservations are accepted at 877/444-6777. The rate is $18–23 per night for up to eight people; a fee may apply for additional guests. Major credit cards are accepted. Open beginning of May through mid-October.

Directions: From Bradford, travel west 15 miles on Highway 346 to the campground entrance.

Contact: Allegheny National Forest, P.O. Box 847, Warren, PA 16365, 814/362-4613, www.fs.fed.us/r9/forests/allegheny.

9 KOA KINZUA EAST

Rating: 7

near Allegheny National Forest

Most of this property is wooded, but you can still find open sites if you want. Nearby Allegheny National Forest will amaze you with its offerings for outdoor recreation. There are trails for hiking, biking, horseback riding, ATV riding, cross-country skiing, and snowmobiling. Wildlife- and bird-viewing opportunities are abundant. Among the animals found in the forest are black bear, white-tailed deer, red and gray squirrels, raccoons, porcupines, opossums, skunks, cottontail rabbits, chipmunks, beaver, and mink. Birders can glimpse turkey buzzards, red-tailed hawks, eagles, osprey, warblers, and heron. On and around the water are areas for swimming, boating, canoeing, and fishing. You can choose from Allegheny and Tionesta Reservoirs, the Clarion and Allegheny Rivers, Beaver Meadows Lake, and Tionesta, Brokenstraw, and Conewango Creeks. There are also two wilderness areas within the national forest: Hickory Creek and Allegheny Islands. On weekends the campground has planned activities like bingo and hayrides.

Campsites, facilities: There are 120 sites for tents or RVs up to 27 feet: 62 have full hookups; 30 have water and electricity; 28 have no hookups. There are 42 pull-throughs. Picnic tables and fire rings are provided. Drinking water, restrooms with flush toilets, a dump station, a portable dump, a laundry, groceries, ice, wood, LP gas, a camp store, a swimming pool, a rec hall, a rec room, a playground, badminton, horseshoes, volleyball, a shuffleboard court, and hiking trails are available. Some sites are wheelchair accessible. Leashed pets are permitted.

Reservations, fees: Reservations are accepted. The rate is $32–37 per night for up to two people. Each additional person is $6. Open April through December.

Directions: From the junction of U.S. 219 and Highway 770, travel seven miles west on Highway 770, then 1.5 miles west on Highway 59, then turn right onto Klondike Road and travel 0.2 mile to the campground entrance on the right.

Contact: KOA Kinzua East, Kinzua Heights,

Bradford, PA 16701, 814/368-3662, koa@
penn.com.

10 BUCKALOONS CAMPGROUND

🥾 🚴 ❄️ 🛖 🏕️ ♿ 🚐 ⛰️

Rating: 8

in Allegheny National Forest

Circling Buckaloons Campground is Seneca
Interpretive Trail, which can be used by hikers, bikers, and cross-country skiers. Horseback riding and ATVs are not permitted.
There are 20 stops along this one-mile loop
trail following the Allegheny River and Irvine
Run. Number 8 gives you a nice view of the
Allegheny River. At stop 12 you cross over
the junction of Irvin Run and Brokenstraw
Creek; from a bridge here you can observe
aquatic life in a pool of water. The last is
a nesting area for purple martins, which
migrate all the way from South America
each April.

Campsites, facilities: There are 51 sites for
tents or RVs up to 45 feet: 43 have electricity; eight have no hookups. Picnic tables,
fire rings, and charcoal grates are provided.
Drinking water, restrooms with flush toilets,
a dump station, showers, a boat launch, a pavilion, and a playground are available. Some
sites are wheelchair accessible. Leashed pets
are permitted.

Reservations, fees: Reservations are accepted at 877/444-6777. The rate is $14–16
per night for up to eight people; a fee
may apply for additional guests. Major
credit cards are accepted. Open end of May
through beginning of October.

Directions: From Warren, travel six miles west
on U.S. 6 to the campground entrance.

Contact: Allegheny National Forest, P.O.
Box 847, Warren, PA 16365, 814/723-5150,
www.fs.fed.us/r9/forests/allegheny.

11 DEWDROP CAMPGROUND

🥾 🚴 🏊 🛶 🛥️ 🏕️ 🎣 ♿ 🚐 ⛰️

Rating: 8

in Allegheny National Forest

The natural setting of this campground provides
mostly shaded sites. Dewdrop Recreation Area is
part of Allegheny National Forest and is located
along the Longhouse National Scenic Byway. It
also borders Kinzua Bay off Allegheny Reservoir.
You can fish here for bluegill, catfish, trout,
smallmouth and largemouth bass, crappie, sunfish, northern pike, and perch. Travel three miles
south to Elijah Run Boat Launch for swimming,
boating, and more fishing, or take one of the scenic trails. There is also a small interpretive trail
back at Dewdrop Recreation Area. Kinzua Bay
is only four miles away. It shares a marina with
Wolf Run and offers swimming, sand beaches,
canoe, rowboat, and paddleboat rentals, boat
docking, boat launches, changing rooms, showers, a concession stand, and a restaurant. Bikes
are permitted on most national forest roadways
and certain multi-use trails.

Campsites, facilities: There are 74 sites for
tents or RVs up to 50 feet: 67 have electricity;
seven have no hookups. Picnic tables and fire
rings are provided. Drinking water, restrooms
with flush toilets, a dump station, showers, a
playground, and a concrete boat launch are
available. Some sites are wheelchair accessible.
Leashed pets are permitted.

Reservations, fees: Reservations are accepted
at 877/444-6777. The rate is $17–19 per night
for up to eight people; a fee may apply for
additional guests. Major credit cards are accepted. Open end of May through beginning
of September.

Directions: From Warren, travel 11 miles east
on Highway 59, then four miles south on
Longhouse Scenic Drive to the campground
entrance.

Contact: Allegheny National Forest, P.O.
Box 847, Warren, PA 16365, 814/723-5150,
www.fs.fed.us/r9/forests/allegheny.

12 RED OAK CAMPGROUND

👫 🚴 🛶 🎣 🏕 🎿 🐴 🛷 ♿ 🚐 ⛺

Rating: 10

near Allegheny Reservoir

BEST (

You can choose from open or shady sites at this campground, which offers trails for hiking, biking, horseback riding, and ATVs. On weekends there are planned activities like bingo and ceramics. At nearby Kinzua Dam and Allegheny Reservoir, anglers can cast for trout, smallmouth and striped bass, northern perch, bluegill, catfish, crappie, sunfish, and muskie. For boating on the lake, you can bring your own motorboat so long as it has an electric motor or rent one from Kinzua-Wolf Run Marina. You can launch from the marina or Elijah Run, Roper Hollow, Webbs Ferry, Willow Bay, or Kiasutha. The lake is also great for swimming, waterskiing, and canoeing. There are several hiking trails within Allegheny National Forest such as Deer Lick, Tanbank, and Little Drummer. During the winter, ice fishing, snowmobiling, and cross-country skiing are favorite activities.

Campsites, facilities: There are 225 sites for tents or RVs up to 35 feet: 145 have full hookups; 60 have water and electricity; 20 have no hookups. Picnic tables and fire rings are provided. Drinking water, restrooms with flush toilets, a dump station, showers, a laundry, a public phone, groceries, ice, LP gas, wood, a camp store, a bakery, a soda fountain, a pavilion, a swimming pool, a playground, a rec area, a game room, miniature golf, horseshoes, volleyball, basketball, kick ball, whiffle ball, and a sports field are available. Some sites are wheelchair accessible. Leashed pets are permitted.

Reservations, fees: Reservations are accepted. The rate is $18–25 per night for up to two people. Each additional person is $2. Weekly, monthly, and seasonal rates are available. Open year-round.

Directions: From Scandia, travel six miles north on Reservoir Road to the campground entrance on the right.

Contact: Red Oak Campground, R.D. #1, Russell, PA 16345, 814/757-8507, bsda@westpa.net.

13 TRACY RIDGE CAMPGROUND

👫 🎿 🐴 🚐 ⛺

Rating: 9

in Allegheny National Forest

BEST (

These wooded sites are part of the Tracy Ridge Recreation Area within Allegheny National Forest. The ridge itself is 2,245 feet in elevation and can be reached via the Tracy Ridge Hiking Trails System. The 8.7-mile triangular loop is located within Allegheny National Recreation Area, a roadless part of Allegheny National Forest. Established in 1984 as part of the Pennsylvania Wilderness Act, Allegheny National Recreation Area preserves the natural and cultural aspects of the forest while providing recreational opportunities with limited impact. Many parts of the trail system are difficult due to steep grades, stream crossings, and rock ledges. Among the many tree species you will encounter are oak, beech, black cherry, hickory, hemlock, and white pine. The chances for wildlife sightings are wonderful, since raccoons, red and gray squirrels, black bears, opossums, chipmunks, and white-tailed deer frequent these second-growth woods. The bird species are numerous and include woodpeckers, eagles, red-tailed hawks, and turkey buzzards. Trails are open to foot traffic even in winter, but no horseback riding is permitted. Be advised that hunting is allowed seasonally in the area.

Campsites, facilities: There are 119 sites for tents or RVs up to 60 feet. No sites have hookups. Picnic tables and fire rings are provided. Vault toilets, a dump station, and hand pumps for drinking water are available. The Forest Service recommends boiling water before consumption. Leashed pets are permitted.

Reservations, fees: Reservations are

accepted at 877/444-6777. The rate is $10 per night for up to 8 people. Major credit cards are accepted. Open mid-April through mid-December.

Directions: From Bradford, travel west 16 miles on Highway 346, then southeast three miles on Highway 321 to the campground entrance.

Contact: Allegheny National Forest, P.O. Box 847, Warren, PA 16365, 814/368-4158, www.fs.fed.us/r9/forests/allegheny.

14 HEARTS CONTENT CAMPGROUND

🚶 🚲 ❄️ 🐴 🏕️ 🚐 ⛺

Rating: 10

in Allegheny National Forest

These wooded sites are located next to the Hearts Content National Scenic Area in the Allegheny National Forest and the Hickory Creek Wilderness. The 8663-acre wilderness area has a challenging 11-mile hiking trail that loops in and out of the surrounding valleys. The one-mile Hearts Content Scenic Interpretive Trail also loops; it begins and ends at the picnic area and travels through the surrounding woods. Here you will see examples of native tree species such as white pine, beech, and hemlock. In this same area are Tom's Run Loop and Ironwood Loop. Tom's Run Loop moderately ascends to a plateau at the headwaters of Tom's Run where it connects to the lesser used Ironwood Loop. In the winter cross-country skiing is a favorite activity on both trails. Foot and bike traffic are welcome on all trails, but horseback riding and motor vehicles are not permitted. Among the wildlife you can spot are red and gray squirrels, white-tailed deer, opossums, raccoons, skunks, chipmunks, and woodchucks. Birders can look for turkeys, red-tailed hawks, and ravens.

Campsites, facilities: There are 26 sites for tents or RVs up to 30 feet. No sites have hookups. Picnic tables and fire rings are available. Vault toilets and hand pumps are available, but the Forest Service recommends boiling water before consumption. A playground and a sandbox are available. Leashed pets are permitted.

Reservations, fees: Reservations are not accepted. The rate is $10–12 per night for up to eight people; a fee may apply for additional guests. Major credit cards are accepted. Open end of May through beginning of October.

Directions: From Warren, travel 12 miles southwest on Highway 337, then four miles south on FR 18 to the campground entrance.

Contact: Allegheny National Forest, P.O. Box 847, Warren, PA 16365, 814/723-5150, www.fs.fed.us/r9/forests/allegheny.

15 CHAPMAN STATE PARK

🚶 🚲 🏊 🛶 🚐 ❄️ 🏕️ ♿ 🚐 ⛺

Rating: 9

near Clarendon

BEST (

Adjacent to Allegheny National Forest, 805-acre Chapman State Park provides wooded campsites and offers picnicking, biking, swimming, hiking, backpacking, fishing, and boating. Chapman Lake covers 68 acres and has both warm-water and cold-water fish. Among the species found here are bluegill, brook trout, sucker, largemouth bass, sunfish, crappie, catfish, and brown trout. Motorboats must have electric motors. There is a sand beach where swimming is permitted. Chapman State Park has 12 miles of hiking trails and has trailheads for backpacking trails in the adjacent state game lands and Allegheny National Forest. The hiking trails are for foot and ski traffic only. Bikes are welcome on park and national forest roads. Summer offers environmental and interpretive programs with guided walks, slide presentations, and stream studies. Check the park office for a program of these changing events. During the winter, snowmobiling, sledding, toboganing, cross-country skiing, and ice fishing are favorite activities. Be advised that hunting is allowed seasonally in Chapman State Park.

Campsites, facilities: There are 83 sites for tents or RVs up to 30 feet: 39 have electricity; 44 have no hookups. Picnic tables and fire rings are provided. Rustic restrooms with non-flush toilets, a dump station, a public phone, groceries, a camp store, a pavilion, a playground, and a sports field are available. Some sites are wheelchair accessible. No pets are permitted.

Reservations, fees: Reservations are accepted at 888/PA-PARKS (888/727-2757). The rate is $14–19 per night for up to five people; a fee may apply for additional guests. Senior and Pennsylvania resident discounts are available. Open April through December.

Directions: From U.S. 6 in Clarendon, travel five miles southwest on Chapman Dam Road/Railroad Street to the campground entrance.

Contact: Chapman State Park, RR 2 Box 1610, Clarendon, PA 16313, 814/723-0250, chapmansp@state.pa.us.

16 KIASUTHA CAMPGROUND
🏊 🚤 �RV 🏕️ 🚶 ♿ �RV ⛺

Rating: 7

on Kinzua Bay in Allegheny National Forest

Kiasutha Campground is located in Kiasutha Recreation Area, part of Allegheny National Forest. It lies along Kinzua Bay, a southern branch of Allegheny Reservoir. The reservoir is 27 miles long, covers 12,080 acres, and has 90 miles of shoreline. The water level is controlled by Kinzua Dam, which is administered by the U.S. Army Corps of Engineers. Swimming and fishing can be enjoyed at the bay. Among the species living in the bay are perch, walleye, northern pike, crappie, smallmouth and largemouth bass, catfish, bluegill, muskie, and sunfish. A grass beach with concession is easily accessible. Across from the beach is Kinzua Wolf Run Marina.

Here you can rent, dock, and launch boats. There is also a full-service restaurant and carp feeding at the marina. Nearby are the Red Bridge Recreation Area, Jakes Rocks Overlook, Dewdrop Recreation Area, and Elijah Boat Launch.

Campsites, facilities: There are 90 sites for tents or RVs up to 45 feet. Picnic tables and fire rings are provided. Drinking water, restrooms with flush toilets, a dump station, showers, a concrete boat launch, a picnic area, a playground, and a bathhouse are available. Some sites are wheelchair accessible. Leashed pets are permitted.

Reservations, fees: Reservations are accepted at 877/444-6777. The rate is $19–21 per night for up to eight people; a fee may apply for additional guests. Major credit cards are accepted. Open end of May through beginning of September.

Directions: From Kane, travel northwest eight miles on Highway 321, then northwest two miles on FR 262 to the campground entrance.

Contact: Allegheny National Forest, P.O. Box 847, Warren, PA 16365, 814/723-5150, www.fs.fed.us/r9/forests/allegheny.

17 WHISPERING WINDS CAMPGROUND
🚶 🚴 🏊 🚤 🚣 ❄️ 🐕 🚶 �RV ⛺

Rating: 3

near Allegheny Reservoir

You have your choice of shaded and open sites here. If this property's stream fishing and hiking trails aren't enough, nearby Kinzua Dam and Allegheny Reservoir offer many additional activities, including swimming, boating, waterskiing, and fishing. Among the species found in the lake are smallmouth and largemouth bass, striped bass, crappie, bluegill, northern perch, sunfish, catfish, muskie, and walleye. There are several boat launches and marinas in Allegheny National Forest, some of which also rent boats. They are Big Bend Access Area, Elijah Run, Friends Quaker Area, Highbanks, Kiasutha, Kinzua-Wolf Run Marina, Onoville Marina, and Webbs Ferry. Due to the lack of maneuverability and poor wind conditions caused by the narrow valleys and steep hills, sailboats may find the lake unsuitable. If you prefer to stay on land, the forest offers many hiking, biking, interpretive, and ATV trails. Biking is also allowed on most forest roadways. During the winter the Kinzua Dam and Allegheny Reservoir offer opportunities for ice fishing, cross-country skiing, and snowmobile riding.

Campsites, facilities: There are 72 sites for tents or RVs up to 30 feet: 30 have full hookups; 22 have water and electricity; 20 have no hookups. There are 10 pull-throughs. Picnic tables and fire rings are provided. Drinking water, restrooms with flush toilets, a dump station, a portable dump, showers, modem access, ice, groceries, LP gas, wood, a pavilion, a swimming pool, a rec room, a playground, volleyball, and a sports field are available. Leashed pets are permitted.

Reservations, fees: Reservations are accepted at 888/554-4377. The rate is $20 per night for up to two people. Open year-round.

Directions: From the junction of Highway 666 and U.S. 6, travel 0.75 mile east on U.S. 6, then 0.25 mile north on Tollgate Road to the campground entrance on the right.

Contact: Whispering Winds Campground, Tollgate Road, Sheffield, PA 16347, 814/968-4377, bowwow@penn.com.

18 RED BRIDGE CAMPGROUND

Rating: 10

in Allegheny National Forest

BEST (

This wooded campground, nestled within Allegheny National Forest, offers mostly shaded sites. Red Bridge Recreation Area is located on the eastern shore of Kinzua Bay on the southern branch of Allegheny Reservoir within the national forest. It abuts the Red Bridge Bank Fishing Area and is near the end of the Longhouse National Scenic Byway. Red Bridge Recreation Area was built in the 1960s as part of the Kinzua Dam development. The North Country National Scenic Trail is 0.75 mile south of the campground. This 86.4-mile trail is difficult due to steep inclines, stream crossings, and rock ledges. It is open to hikers, bikers, and cross-country skiers, but horseback riding and motorized vehicles like ATVs and snowmobiles are not permitted. If you'd prefer to play at the reservoir, boat launches are available at Elijah, Webbs Ferry, and Roper Hollow. Anglers can fish for perch, trout, smallmouth and bigmouth bass, bluegill, sunfish, crappie, and catfish at the Red Bridge Bank Fishing Area. Among the wildlife you may see in the area are white-tailed deer, raccoons, chipmunks, black bear, red and gray squirrels, woodchucks, cottontail rabbits, and opossums.

Campsites, facilities: There are 55 sites for tents or RVs up to 50 feet. Picnic tables and fire rings are provided. Drinking water, vault toilets, restrooms with flush toilets, a dump station, showers, a playground, and a sandbox are available. Leashed pets are permitted.

Reservations, fees: Reservations are accepted at 877/444-6777. The rate is $12–15 per night for up to eight people; a fee may apply for additional guests. Major credit cards are accepted. Open end of May through beginning of October.

Directions: From Kane, travel nine miles northwest on Highway 321 to the campground entrance.

Contact: Allegheny National Forest, P.O. Box 847, Warren, PA 16365, 814/723-5150, www.fs.fed.us/r9/forests/allegheny.

19 BETTUM'S IDLEWOOD FAMILY CAMPGROUND

🚶 ⛵ 🎿 🛖 ⛺ 🚐 ⛺

Rating: 5

near Kinzua Bridge State Park

You have your choice of open or shaded sites on this 46-acre campground. Nearby 329-acre Kinzua Bridge State Park offers a wonderful view of the Kinzua Creek Valley and the viaduct from the high railroad bridge. There are also trails for hiking and picnicking areas. Among the wildlife you may see in the area are raccoons, black bear, woodchucks, red and gray squirrels, opossums, white-tailed deer, cottontail rabbits, and chipmunks. Birders can expect to view red-tailed hawks, woodpeckers, bluebirds, and warblers. To catch an excursion train through Allegheny National Forest to Kinzua Bridge State Park, go to nearby Kane or Marienville. For on-site entertainment back at the campground, you can participate in fire truck rides, hayrides, and planned activities on the weekends.

Campsites, facilities: There are 66 sites for tents or RVs up to 30 feet; 10 have full hookups; 56 have water and electricity. Picnic tables and fire rings are provided. Drinking water, a dump station, a portable dump, restrooms with flush toilets, a laundry, a general store, ice, wood, LP gas, a rec hall, a swimming pool, a pavilion, an arcade, a playground, horseshoes, volleyball, a sports field, hiking, ATV, and snowmobile trails, snowshoeing, and cross-country skiing are available. Leashed pets are permitted.

Reservations, fees: Reservations are accepted. The rate is $14–21.50 per night for up to two people. Each additional person is $4. Weekly, monthly, and seasonal rates are available. Open year-round.

Directions: From the junction of U.S. 219 and Highway 59, travel 0.75 mile east on Highway 59, then turn left onto Big Shanty Road and travel 0.5 mile to the campground entrance on the left.

Contact: Bettum's Idlewood Family Campground, 299 Big Shanty Road, Lewis Run, PA 16738, 814/362-1719, bettumcamping.tripod.com.

20 LINESVILLE CAMP

🚶 ⛵ 🚣 🚐 🎿 🛖 🚵 ♿ 🚐 ⛺

Rating: 10

in Pymatuning State Park

BEST (

This campground located within Pymatuning State Park offers mostly wooded sites. Pymatuning Lake provides wonderful opportunities for recreation on the water. You can fish for crappie, walleye, largemouth and smallmouth bass, perch, muskie, bluegill, carp, and sun fish. If you have an electric-powered motorboat you can launch or moor your boat at the lake. There are three marinas in the area that will rent motorboats, canoes, and floatboats, and four beaches provide swimming access. Other sights in and around the water are the Linesville spillway, the Parker Dam, a fish hatchery, the PA Game Commission Visitor Center and Waterfowl Museum, and two causeways. You can also explore the two natural areas for hiking within the park: Blackjack Swamp is a 725-acre wetlands with palustrine scrub; Clark Island has an inland, lake-fed pond, as well as a 161-acre forest of mature hardwoods and white pine. During the winter ice skating, ice fishing, iceboating, sledding, snowmobiling, and cross-country skiing are favorite activities. Be advised that hunting is allowed seasonally in Pymatuning State Park.

Campsites, facilities: There are 115 sites for tents or RVs up to 30 feet; 68 have electricity; 47 have no hookups. No sites have full hookups. Picnic tables and fire rings are provided. Drinking water, restrooms with flush toilets, a dump station, showers, a laundry, a public phone, a playground, and volleyball are available. Some sites are wheelchair accessible. Leashed pets are permitted.

Reservations, fees: Reservations are accepted

at 888/PA-PARKS (888/727-2757). The rate is $14–19 for up to five people per night. Pets are $2 for up to two pets per night. Senior and Pennsylvania resident discounts are available. Open April through December.

Directions: From Linesville, travel west two miles on West Erie Street to the campground entrance at the end.

Contact: Pymatuning State Park, 2660 Williams Field Road, Jamestown, PA 16134, 724/932-3141, pymatuningsp@state.pa.us.

21 TUTTLE CAMP

🏃 🚣 🛶 🌊 🚤 🎣 🏕 🐕 ♿ 🚐 ⛺

Rating: 9

in Pymatuning State Park

Tuttle Camp sits on a peninsula in the northern half of Pymatuning State Park. A boat launch area for Pymatuning Reservoir is located within the campground, and Tuttle Beach is just to the south along North Lake Road. Non-powered boats and boats with engines less than 10 horsepower are permitted on the lake, and there are three marinas in the park where boats can be rented. Clark Island is a 161-acre natural area containing a forest of mature white pines and hardwoods, and a lake-fed pond. Because of its relative isolation, many species of concern flourish on the island. Please note that the lake straddles the border between Pennsylvania and Ohio, where the Ohio Department of Natural Resources maintains a state park as well. The Ohio side also has beaches and over two miles of hiking trails. No visit to Pymatuning State Park would be complete without a visit to the spillway, famous for its proliferation of carp. The fish are so abundant here that the ducks actually walk on their backs to get breadcrumbs. During the winter, cross-country skiing, sledding, ice fishing, ice-skating, iceboating, and snowmobiling are favorite activities. Be advised that hunting is allowed seasonally in Pymatuning State Park.

Campsites, facilities: There are 200 sites for tents or RVs up to 60 feet; 99 have electricity; 101 have no hookups. Picnic tables and fire rings are provided. Drinking water, restrooms with flush toilets, a dump station, showers, a laundry, a pavilion, a playground, a public phone, groceries, and a sports field are available. Some sites are wheelchair accessible. Leashed pets are permitted.

Reservations, fees: Reservations are accepted at 888/PA-PARKS (888/727-2757). The rate is $14–19 per night for up to five people; a fee may apply for additional guests. Pets are $2 for up to two pets per night. Senior and Pennsylvania resident discounts are available. Open year-round.

Directions: From the junction of Highway 285 and North Lake Road, travel north two miles on North Lake Road to the campground entrance at the end.

Contact: Pymatuning State Park, 2660 Williams Field Road, Jamestown, PA 16134, 724/932-3141, pymatuningsp@state.pa.us.

22 MALLARDS LANDING FAMILY CAMPGROUND

🏃 🚣 🛶 🌊 🚤 🏕 🐕 🚐 ⛺

Rating: 4

near Pymatuning State Park

Mallards Landing has a fishing pond filled with bluegill, sunfish, and bass. There are also hiking trails on the property and planned activities on the weekends. At nearby Pymatuning State Park, you can enjoy water activities on Pymatuning Lake. Cast your line for smallmouth and largemouth bass, muskie, carp, crappie, perch, bluegill, sunfish, and walleye. If you don't have your own boat, rentals of motorboats, canoes, rowboats, and paddleboats are available at three marinas. The state park has four swimming beaches along the lake. Guided walks, interpretive and educational programs are offered. Check the park office for a schedule of these changing events. There are also two natural areas within the park. The 161-acre Clark Island protects mature forests of white pine and hardwoods. Blackjack Swamp is a 725-acre wetlands.

Campsites, facilities: There are 93 sites for tents or RVs up to 40 feet: 49 have full hookups; 32 have water and electricity; two have electricity; 10 have no hookups. There are 20 pull-throughs. Picnic tables and fire rings are provided. Drinking water, restrooms with flush toilets, a dump station, showers, groceries, ice, LP gas, wood, a camp store, a rec hall, an arcade, a playground, basketball, horseshoes, badminton, volleyball, a sports field, and RV storage and supplies are available. Leashed pets are permitted. The campground has a traffic control gate for security.

Reservations, fees: Reservations are accepted. The rate is $19–21 per night for up to two people. Each additional person is $4. Major credit cards are accepted. Open mid-April through October.

Directions: From West Linesville, travel 3.75 miles west on U.S. 6, then turn left onto a paved road and travel 0.5 mile to the campground entrance on the left.

Contact: Mallards Landing Family Campground, 1525 Footsville Road, Linesville, PA 16424, 814/683-5870, mallardslandingcampground@stargate.net.

23 JAMESTOWN CAMPGROUND

Rating: 8

in Pymatuning State Park

BEST (

You have your choice of shaded or open sites at this spacious campground. Located in the southern half of Pymatuning State Park, the campground offers areas for hiking, swimming, and wildlife watching, as well as planned activities on weekends. The many kettle lakes in this area were formed over 14,000 years ago when the last glaciers melted. The bogs and wetlands surrounding the lakes soon came to support a great swamp forest noteworthy for their towering stands of white pines that attracted bears and wolves to the lake. The remnants of this forest are still a healthy food source for many types of animals, including the bald eagle. Several pairs nest on the Pennsylvania side. In addition to eagles, migratory waterfowl may be spotted here. The 725-acre Black Jack Swamp is a natural area that preserves emergent wetlands and an area of palustrine shrub-scrub wetlands. Typical deciduous plants in this region include blueberries, bottunbrush, meadowsweet, mountain holly, swamp rose, and winterberry. During the winter, ice fishing, iceboating, ice skating, sledding, snowmobiling, and cross-country skiing are favorite activities. Be advised that hunting is allowed seasonally in Pymatuning State Park.

Campsites, facilities: There are 331 sites for tents or RVs up to 30 feet: 165 have electricity; 166 have no hookups; no sites have full hookups. Picnic tables and fire rings are provided. Drinking water, restrooms with flush toilets, a dump station, showers, a laundry, a public phone, groceries, ice, wood, a camp store, a playground, and volleyball are available. Some sites are wheelchair accessible. Leashed pets are permitted.

Reservations, fees: Reservations are accepted at 888/PA-PARKS (888/727-2757). The rate is $14–19 per night for up to five people; a fee may apply for additional guests. Pets are $2 for up to two pets per night. Senior and Pennsylvania resident discounts are available. Open year-round.

Directions: From Jamestown, travel five miles west on U.S. 322 to the campground entrance.

Contact: Pymatuning State Park, 2660 Williams Field Road, Jamestown, PA 16134, 724/932-3141, pymatuningsp@state.pa.us.

24 BROOKDALE FAMILY CAMPGROUND

Rating: 7

near Meadville

At this 62-acre campground with seven ponds, you can enjoy catch-and-release fishing without a Pennsylvania license. If anglers would prefer a larger fishing ground, Tamarack Lake, a 562-acre reservoir, is just three miles south of Meadville. This stocked lake has species such as trout, sunfish, bluegill, smallmouth and largemouth bass, crappie, catfish, and perch. There are six boat launch areas for motorboats with electric motors only. With dams at both ends of the reservoir, the lake depth is only about 13 feet. If you prefer to partake in the campground's on-site entertainment, check out the hiking trails, pedal boat rentals, and weekend planned activities.

Campsites, facilities: There are 169 sites for tents or RVs up to 60 feet: 37 have full hookups; 110 have water and electricity; 22 have no hookups. There are 32 pull-throughs. Picnic tables and fire rings are provided. Drinking water, restrooms with flush toilets, a dump station, a portable dump, showers, a laundry, modem access, a phone hookup, a public phone, groceries, ice, LP gas, wood, a camp store, a pavilion, a rec room, an arcade, a rec hall, a swimming pool, a playground, horseshoes, volleyball, basketball, a sports field, and RV supplies are available. Some sites are wheelchair accessible. Leashed pets are permitted. The campground has a traffic control gate for security.

Reservations, fees: Reservations are accepted at 888/789-9186. The rate is $23–36 per night for up to two people. Each additional person is $5. Weekly, monthly, seasonal, and group rates are available. Major credit cards are accepted. Open mid-April through mid-October.

Directions: From the junction of Highway 77 and Highway 27, travel 5.5 miles east on Highway 27 to the campground entrance on the left.

Contact: Brookdale Family Campground, 25164 State Highway 27, Meadville, PA 16335, 814/789-3251, www.brookdalecampground.com.

25 OIL CREEK FAMILY CAMPGROUND

Rating: 8

near Oil Creek State Park

Most sites at Oil Creek Family Campground are open. You can fish for sunfish, bluegill, or perch in the on-site pond or take advantage of the hiking trail that runs around the perimeter of the wooded property and connects to trails at Oil Creek State Park. There are 52 miles of hiking trails in the state park. Among them is Girard Hiking Trail, a 36-mile trail with five connecting loops. You can also check out the three self-guided interpretive trails: Delzell Trail, Blood Farm Interpretive Trail, and Petroleum Centre Walking Tour. If you prefer to partake in the entertainment back at the campground, there are planned activities there on weekends.

Campsites, facilities: There are 91 sites for tents or RVs up to 27 feet: 47 have full hookups; 26 have water and electricity; 18 have no hookups. There are 55 pull-throughs. Picnic tables and fire rings are provided. Drinking water, restrooms with flush toilets, a dump station, a portable dump, showers, a public phone, ice, groceries, wood, a camp store, a pavilion, a swimming pool, a playground, badminton, horseshoes, volleyball, and a sports field are available. Some sites are wheelchair accessible. Leashed pets are permitted.

Reservations, fees: Reservations are accepted at 800/395-2045. The rate is $19–23 per night for up to two people. Each additional person is $7. Weekly, monthly, seasonal rates, and group discounts are available. Open mid-April through beginning of November.

Directions: From the junction of Highway 27 and South Highway 8, travel four miles south on Highway 8, then 0.75 mile east on an unnamed paved road, then one mile south on an unnamed gravel road to the campground entrance on the left.

Contact: Oil Creek Family Campground, 340 Shreve Road, Titusville, PA 16354, 814/827-1023, www.oilcreekcampground.com.

26 MINISTER CREEK CAMPGROUND

Rating: 8

in Allegheny National Forest

Minister Creek Campground is Allegheny National Forest's smallest campground. It is located along Minister Creek. Aside from the good trout and brookie fishing in the creek itself, there is also the Minister Creek Hiking Trail. It is a 6.6 mile looping trail which begins and ends at the campground and passes through the Minister Creek Undeveloped Area. This trail can be challenging because it ascends to a plateau within the Undeveloped Area. Part of the trail traverses an old railroad grade from its former logging days. At one point as the trail heads south, you can connect to the North Country National Scenic Trail and continue east or continue south on the loop back to the campground. Horseback riding is not permitted on the trail, but it is open to foot traffic even in the winter. In the older forested section of the Minister Creek Undeveloped Area, you have opportunities for wildlife viewing. Among the possible sightings are raccoons, chipmunks, red and gray squirrels, white-tailed deer, opossums, and woodchucks. The birders in your group could glimpse red-tailed hawks, blue jays, woodpeckers, ravens, and turkey buzzards.

Campsites, facilities: There are six sites for tents or RVs up to 30 feet. No sites have hookups. Picnic tables and fire rings are provided. Vault toilets and hand pumps for drinking water are available, though the Forest Service recommends boiling water before consumption. Leashed pets are permitted.

Reservations, fees: Reservations are not accepted. The rate is $9 per night for up to eight people; a fee may apply for additional guests. Major credit cards are accepted. Open mid-April through mid-December.

Directions: From Sheffield, travel west 14.75 miles on Highway 666 to the campground entrance.

Contact: Allegheny National Forest, P.O. Box 847, Warren, PA 16365, www.fs.fed.us/r9/forests/allegheny.

27 FOOTE REST CAMPGROUND

Rating: 6

near Allegheny National Forest

This mostly wooded campground offers shaded sites as well as an open lawn and a duck pond; be sure to look for the tame rabbits on the property. Water sports abound at nearby Kinzua Dam and East Branch Lake. There is no limit to horsepower in the 1,160-acre lake, so it's great for waterskiing, tubing, or just floating on a big old pontoon boat with the family. Please note that there are no beaches, and swimming is not permitted in the lake. Both the lake and nearby streams are stocked with cold-water and warm-water fish, including muskie, walleye, smallmouth bass, and brook, rainbow, brown, and lake trout. Nearby Five Mile, Seven Mile, Straight, Middle Fork and Crooked Creeks are all stocked as well. Abundant native brook trout can be found in many of the area's smaller streams. It should be noted that the entire park is open to hunting, trapping, and dog training during the appropriate seasons. The campground offers hiking trails and has planned activities like bingo, hayrides, fire truck rides, and potluck dinners on weekends.

Campsites, facilities: There are 162 sites for tents or RVs up to 28 feet: 25 have full hookups; 117 have water and electricity; 20 have no hookups. There are 135 pull-throughs. Picnic tables and fire rings are provided. Drinking water, restrooms with flush toilets, a dump station, a portable dump, showers, a laundry, groceries, ice, LP gas, wood, a camp store, a pavilion, a rec hall, a game room, a swimming pool, a playground, two shuffleboard courts, miniature golf, horseshoes, volleyball, and a sports field are available. Some sites are wheelchair accessible. Leashed pets are permitted.

Reservations, fees: Reservations are accepted. The rate is $24–26 per night for up to two people. Each additional person is $5. Open year-round.

Directions: From the junction of U.S. 6 and Highway 321, travel east 7.5 miles on U.S. 6, then north 0.5 mile on U.S. 219 to the campground entrance on the left.

Contact: Foote Rest Campground, 3183 Route 219, Kane, PA 16735, 814/778-5336, cardinal@penn.com.

28 TWIN LAKES CAMPGROUND

🏃🚴🏊🎣🛶❄🐕🚣♿🚐⛺

Rating: 10

in Allegheny National Forest

This campground is divided into upper and lower sites. The lower sites were built in 1936 and are closer to the lake. The upper sites were built in 1970 and have electricity. As part of Allegheny National Forest, Twin Lakes Recreation Area offers hiking, biking, and fishing. Among the many trails that run through the property are Black Cherry National Recreation Interpretive Trail, Twin Lakes Trail, Mill Creek Trail, and the Brush Hollow Trail System. The 1.6-mile Black Cherry National Interpretive Trail begins at the lower part of the campground and meanders through the surrounding forest. Twin Lakes Trail shoots off from Black Cherry and

travels a challenging 15 miles over varied terrain, eventually connecting to the gentler 6.5-mile Mill Creek Trail. Mill Creek, in turn, connects to the Brush Hollow Trail System and its three loops totaling 7.7 miles. All trails are for hiking, biking, or cross-country skiing, except for Black Cherry, which sustains foot traffic only. No motorized vehicles such as ATVs or snowmobiles are permitted on the trails.

Campsites, facilities: There are 50 sites for tents or RVs up to 28 feet: 27 have electricity; 23 have no hookups. Picnic tables and fire rings are provided. Drinking water, restrooms with flush toilets, a dump station, showers, hand pumps, a bathhouse, pavilions, a playground, and a fishing pier are available. Some sites are wheelchair accessible. Leashed pets are permitted.

Reservations, fees: Reservations are accepted at 877/444-6777. The rate is $16–21 per night for up to eight people; a fee may apply for additional guests. Major credit cards are accepted. Open mid-April through mid-December.

Directions: From Kane, travel eight miles south on Highway 321, then 1.5 miles west on FR 191. The campground entrance road has a railroad underpass with a 10-foot clearance.

Contact: Allegheny National Forest, P.O. Box 847, Warren, PA 16365, 814/723-5150, www.fs.fed.us/r9/forests/allegheny.

29 SIZERVILLE STATE PARK

🏃🏊🎣❄🚣♿🚐⛺

Rating: 9

in Elk State Forest

BEST (

This 386-acre park is in the middle of Elk State Forest. Some of the campground's wooded sites are streamside. The shade comes from a mix of hardwoods such as oak and maple as well as white pine and hemlock. Among the many outdoor activities available are picnicking, hiking, and fishing. You can walk any of the five loop trails contained within the park or hit the trailhead of the Bucktail Path Trail, which continues through Elk State Forest. The Sizerville Nature

Trail is an easy three miles with interpretive stops along the way. Also labeled easy are the Bottomlands Trail, Campground Trail, and North Slope Trail. The Nady Hollow Trail is more difficult due to a steep climb up the mountainside. The campground has planned activities on the weekends as well as interpretive and educational programs. You can check for a schedule of these activities at the park office. During the winter, snowmobiling and cross-country skiing are favorite activities. Be advised that hunting is allowed seasonally at Sizerville State Park.

Campsites, facilities: There are 23 sites for tents or RVs up to 25 feet: 18 have electricity; five have no hookups; no sites have full hookups. Picnic tables and fire rings are provided. Drinking water, restrooms with flush toilets, a dump station, showers, a public phone, a pavilion, a playground, an amphitheater, a swimming pool, and horseshoes are available. Some sites are wheelchair accessible. No pets are permitted.

Reservations, fees: Reservations are accepted at 888/PA-PARKS (888/727-2757). The rate is $14–19 per night for up to five people; a fee may apply for additional guests. Senior and Pennsylvania resident discounts are available. Open April through December.

Directions: From Emporium, travel north six miles on Highway 155 to the campground entrance on the right.

Contact: Sizerville State Park, 199 East Cowley Run Road, Emporium, PA 15834-9608, 814/486-5605, sizervillesp@state.pa.us.

30 SHENANGO RECREATION AREA CAMPGROUND

Rating: 9

at Shenango River Lake

This campground is run by the U.S. Army Corps of Engineers. Among the many activities to enjoy on the lake are swimming, boating, waterskiing, and fishing. Anglers can cast their lines for smallmouth, largemouth, and striped bass, walleye, crappie, bluegill, muskie, catfish, and sunfish. There are many trails that run throughout the area specific to hiking, biking, and ATV riding. The three hiking trails are Seth Myers Trail, Coonie Trail, and Shenango Trail. Seth Myers and Coonie Trails are both 0.5-mile self-guided nature walks. Shenango Trail is 8 miles long and follows the old towpath of the Erie Extension Canal. For birders there are two known nesting sites for bald eagles, a great heron rookery, and opportunities to spot warbler, osprey, egrets, and red-tailed hawks throughout the area. Be advised that hunting is allowed seasonally in the Golden Run Wildlife Area of Shenango River Lake. The campground offers planned activities like live music on weekends.

Campsites, facilities: There are 330 sites for tents or RVs up to 12 feet: 85 have electricity; 245 have no hookups. There are no full hookups. Picnic tables and fire rings are provided. Drinking water, restrooms with flush toilets, a dump station, showers, a laundry, a public phone, a pavilion, horseshoes, volleyball, and a playground are available. Some sites are wheelchair accessible. Leashed pets are permitted.

Reservations, fees: Reservations are accepted at 877/444-6777. The rates are $15–30 per night for up to two people. Open mid-May through end of September.

Directions: From the junction of I-80 and Highway 18, travel 6.5 miles north on Highway 18 to the campground entrance on the left.

Contact: Shenango River Lake, Resource Manager, 2442 Kelly Road, Hermitage, PA 16148-7308, 724/962-7746, www.lrp.usace.army.mil/rec/lakes/shenango.htm.

31 SHENANGO VALLEY RV PARK

Rating: 6

near Shenango River Lake

BEST (

You have your choice of shaded or open sites at this campground. You can use the hiking and biking trails here, or visit nearby eight-mile Shenango Trail, which travels along the Shenango River and the Erie Extension Canal. You can swim, boat, or fish at Shenango River Lake, managed by the U.S. Army Corps of Engineers. The boat launch is just 10 minutes from the campground. You can cast for muskie, walleye, smallmouth and largemouth bass, striped bass, catfish, bluegill, crappie, and sunfish. There are also hiking, biking, and ATV trails that run along the lake and into the surrounding forest area. Within the forest you have a chance to view wildlife such as raccoons, white-tailed deer, opossums, chipmunks, red and gray squirrels, cottontail rabbits, and skunks. Birders will be interested in the great heron rookery at Shenango River Lake. Back at the campground, you can join in planned activities on weekends.

Campsites, facilities: There are 142 sites for tents or RVs up to 30 feet: 47 have full hookups; 55 have water and electricity; 40 have no hookups. There are six pull-throughs. Picnic tables and fire rings are provided. Drinking water, restrooms with flush toilets, a dump station, showers, wood, a rec hall, a swimming pool, a playground, horseshoes, volleyball, and a sports field are available. Leashed pets are permitted.

Reservations, fees: Reservations are accepted. The rate is $22 per night for up to two people. Each additional person is $3. Seasonal rates are available. Open May through mid-October.

Directions: From the junction of I-80 and Highway 18 Exit 4B, travel nine miles north on Highway 18, then 0.5 mile east on Reynolds Industrial Park Road, then two miles southeast on Crestview Drive to the campground entrance on the left.

Contact: Shenango Valley RV Park, 559 East Crestview Drive, Transfer, PA 16154, 724/962-9800, www.shenangovalleyrvpark.com.

32 FARMA TRAVEL TRAILER PARK

Rating: 7

near Maurice K. Goddard State Park

BEST (

This 110-acre campground is located near Maurice K. Goddard State Park, home to Lake Wilhelm. The lake is popular with anglers and boaters and has a 241-slip marina and a 48-space dry land mooring area available from May 1 to October 31. A paved bicycle trail runs 12 miles from Dugan's Run to the marina and continues onto Boat Launch Four. Observant visitors may spot eagles, osprey, and other wildlife along the lake's shore, or in the park's abundant wetlands, mature forests, or old fields. Please note that hunting and trapping are permissible within the park in season. Winter activities include ice fishing, iceboating, ice skating, cross-country skiing, and snowmobiling. Back at Farma, families can enjoy many scheduled activities, such as bingo, dances, and talent shows, or take advantage of the hiking trails and lake fishing.

Campsites, facilities: There are 250 sites for tents or RVs up to 35 feet: 235 have full hookups; 15 have no hookups. There are two pull-throughs. Picnic tables and fire rings are provided. Drinking water, restrooms with flush toilets, a dump station, showers, a laundry, groceries, ice, wood, a camp store, a playground, a swimming pool, a rec hall, a sand volleyball court, a basketball court, a softball field, a bocce court, a snack bar, horseshoes, a shuffleboard court, and a ceramic shop are available. Leashed pets are permitted.

Reservations, fees: Reservations are accepted. The rate is $18 per night for up to four people. Each additional person is $3. Weekly rates are available. Open May through beginning of October.

Directions: From I-79 Exit 130, travel west six miles to the campground entrance.

Contact: Farma Travel Trailer Park, 87 Hughey Road, Greenville, PA 16125, 724/253-4535, www.farmaparks.com.

33 GODDARD PARK VACATIONLAND CAMPGROUND

Rating: 6

near Maurice K. Goddard State Park

Named after the nearby Maurice K. Goddard Sate Park, this campground offers short hiking trails on its property and planned activities like bingo, ceramics, and music on the weekends. The state park also has several trails for biking and hiking. The paved bicycle trail to Dugan's Run is 12 miles long and can be accessed at Boat Launch Four. Foot traffic is also welcome on this run. Falling Run Nature Trail is for hikers only. This 0.7-mile loop is a self-guided nature trail that will take you into Falling Run Ravine and its cascading waterfall. Goddard McKeever Hiking Trail connects Maurice K. Goddard State Park to McKeever Environmental Learning Center. The 1.25-mile trail is labeled difficult due to its steepness. There is a sealed coal mine shaft that is visible in the hillside near the hill's crest. The state park also offers fishing, boating, and swimming on Lake Wilhelm.

Campsites, facilities: There are 602 sites for tents or RVs up to 40 feet: 514 have full hookups; 49 have water and electricity; 39 have no hookups. There are 248 pull-throughs. Picnic tables and fire rings are provided. Drinking water, restrooms with flush toilets, a dump station, showers, a laundry, modem access, a phone hookup, TV hookup, groceries, ice, wood, a camp store, a pavilion, two swimming pools, three shuffleboard courts, a rec hall, a game room, a playground, miniature golf, tennis, badminton, volleyball, horseshoes, and a sports field are available. Some sites are wheelchair accessible. Leashed pets are permitted.

Reservations, fees: Reservations are accepted. The rate is $25–27 per night for up to two people. Each additional person is $6. Open mid-April through mid-October.

Directions: From the junction of I-79 Exit 130/34 and Highway 358, travel 0.2 mile west on Highway 358, then four miles on an unnamed paved road. Follow signs to the campground entrance on the right.

Contact: Goddard Park Vacationland Campground, 867 Georgetown Road, Sandy Lake, PA 16145, 724/253-4645.

34 CAMP WILHELM

Rating: 3

near Maurice K. Goddard State Park

At Camp Wilhelm, named for 1,860-acre Lake Wilhelm, you can bet there will be lots of recreational activities available on the water. If you don't have your own boat for the 241 slips available, you can rent a rowboat, paddleboat, pontoon boat, kayak, or canoe from the marina. Anglers will enjoy casting into this warm water fishery. Among the native and stocked species in these waters are walleye, largemouth and smallmouth bass, northern pike, bluegill, crappie, perch, muskie, catfish, and sunfish. There is a fishing pier at the marina called Rounded Point. The four boat launch areas have picnicking facilities. If you'd prefer to stay on land, you can bike or hike the many miles of trails in nearby Maurice K. Goddard State Park. The campground also has planned activities on weekends.

Campsites, facilities: There are 222 sites for tents or RVs up to 40 feet: 131 have full hookups; 30 have water and electricity; 61 have no hookups. There are four pull-throughs. Picnic tables and fire rings are provided. Drinking water, restrooms with flush toilets, a dump station, showers, groceries, ice, LP gas, wood, a camp store, a pavilion, a swimming pool, a rec room, an arcade, a playground, basketball, volleyball, horseshoes, and RV rentals and supplies are available. Leashed pets are permitted.

Reservations, fees: Reservations are accepted. The rate is $18–22 per night for up to four people. Each additional person is $4. Major credit cards are accepted. Open April through October.

Directions: From the junction of I-79 Exit 130/34 and Highway 358, travel 0.25 mile west on Highway 358, then 2.5 miles on a paved road. Follow the signs to a gravel road, then travel 0.75 mile to the campground entrance on the left.

Contact: Camp Wilhelm, 1401 Creek Road, Clarks Mills, PA 16114, 724/253-2886, camp-wilhelm@certainty.net.

35 TWO MILE RUN COUNTY PARK

🧍‍♀️ 🚲 🏊 🚣 🛥️ 🐕 🚗 ⛺

Rating: 10

near Oil Creek State Park

BEST (

This unique site has a plethora of inventive and progressive features. Most notable is the Treehouse Village, a $4.5-million project that was in its first phase of construction as of press time. Visitors can stay at the prototype, Aerie, which was built using green construction practices. A Murphy bed sleeps two, and there is a full bath and a kitchenette. When completed, the village will have 30 treehouses, an amphitheater, and an environmental conference center. The park's focus is Justus Lake, which is a Big Bass Lake and a Special Trout Stocking Lake, and special regulations apply. There are lakeside sites available, some with access to their own boat dock. In the summer, all attention is focused on Crosby Beach, which has lifeguards on duty to watch swimmers. There's even a special toddler beach where the little ones can splash without worry and whoop it up on their own miniature slide. There's a snack bar, water volleyball, and an inflatable slide. On summer weekends, the park offers "Movies under the Stars" and organized video game tournaments. The park claims to have the world's largest sandbox. This 600-acre, forested park has a 23-mile trail system for hiking and biking. Please note that hunting is permitted in season.

Campsites, facilities: There are 70 sites for tents or RVs up to 25 feet: 12 have full hookups; 28 have electricity; 30 have no hookups. There are three pull-throughs. Picnic tables and fire rings are provided. Drinking water, restrooms with flush toilets, a dump station, showers, a public phone, groceries, ice, LP gas, wood, a camp store, a pavilion, a rec hall, an arcade, a playground, miniature golf, badminton, horseshoes, volleyball, a sports field, and RV supplies are available. Leashed pets are permitted.

Reservations, fees: Reservations are accepted. The rate is $12–19 per night for up to six people; a fee may apply for additional guests. Major credit cards are accepted. Open year-round.

Directions: From the junction of Highway 8 and Highway 322, travel west 0.5 mile on Highway 322, then north six miles on Highway 417, then turn right onto Baker Road and follow signs to the campground entrance on the right.

Contact: Two Mile Run County Park, 471 Beach Road, Franklin, PA 16323, 814/676-6116, www.twomile.org.

36 TIONESTA RECREATION AREA CAMPGROUND

🧍‍♀️ 🚲 🏊 🚣 🛥️ 🐕 🚗 ⛺

Rating: 8

at Lake Tionesta

This campground is managed by the U.S. Army Corps of Engineers. Sites overlook the lake or the surrounding woodlands. You have your pick of sunny or shady sites. You can choose from many recreational activities on and off the water. The lake offers swimming, boating, and fishing. Among the fish you can cast for are striped and smallmouth bass, crappie, bluegill, trout, sunfish, catfish, walleye, northern pike, and muskie. A boat launch is on-site. Motorized boats, canoes, and kayaks are welcome. There are several short, self-guided nature trails as well as part of the North Country National Scenic Trail and the Kellettville-Nebraska Trace Trail. The 0.25-mile Information Center Loop Trail is located near the Damsite Area. From the campground area you can hike uphill on the Damsite Trail then connect to Mill Race Trail. The Summit Trail is 0.5 mile long and runs past the dam control tower. Plantation Trail starts at the park office and takes you through a wildlife area where you're likely to see white-tailed deer, chipmunks, red and gray squirrels, cottontail rabbits, and opossums. Bikes are welcome on roadways and some trails. The campground also has planned activities on weekends.

Campsites, facilities: There are 125 full-hookup sites for tents or RVs up to 66 feet. Picnic tables and fire rings are provided. Drinking water, restrooms with flush toilets, a dump station, showers, a public phone, groceries, wood, a general store, a pavilion, a playground, and volleyball are available. Leashed pets are permitted.

Reservations, fees: Reservations are accepted at 877/444-6777. The rate is $25 per night for up to two people; a fee may apply for additional guests. Open end of May through the end of September.

Directions: From Tionesta, travel one mile south on Highway 36. Follow signs to the campground entrance on the left.

Contact: Tionesta Lake Recreation Area, c/o U.S. Army Corps of Engineers, 1 Tionesta Lake, Tionesta, PA 16353, 814/755-3512.

37 FOREST RIDGE CAMPGROUND

Rating: 9

near Cook Forest State Park

You have your choice of wooded or open sites at Forest Ridge. The anglers in your group will enjoy the onsite stream fishing, as well as access nearby to Cook Forest State Park and the Clarion River. You can cast for trout, northern pike, catfish, crappie, sunfish, perch, bass, and bluegill. Canoeing is also popular on the river. If you don't have your own boat, there are several commercial outfitters that offer rentals. There are also hiking, biking, cross-country skiing, and horseback riding trails in the park. The 27 hiking-only trails extend through 29 miles of old-growth forest, over gentle hills, and into scenic valleys. The Bicycle Route offers 11.5 miles of roads and trails for bikers. Portions of the Brown's Run Trail and two designated bridle trails give horseback riders 4.5 miles of riding paths.

Campsites, facilities: There are 63 sites for tents or RVs up to 30 feet: 45 have full hookups; 12 have water and electricity; six have no hookups. There are three pull-throughs. Picnic tables and fire rings are provided. Drinking water, restrooms with flush toilets, showers, groceries, ice, LP gas, wood, a general store, a pavilion, a playground, basketball, horseshoes, volleyball, and a sports field are available. Leashed pets are permitted.

Reservations, fees: Reservations are accepted. The rate is $19–26 per night for up to two people. Each additional person is $1.50. Major credit cards are accepted. Open May through mid-December.

Directions: From the junction of Highway 899 and Highway 66, travel one mile north on Highway 66, then turn right onto a paved road and travel 2.25 miles to the campground entrance on the right.

Contact: Forest Ridge Campground, South Forest Street, Marienville, PA 16239, 814/927-8340, www.forestridgecabins.com.

38 BEAVER MEADOWS CAMPGROUND

Rating: 5

in Allegheny National Forest

The sites here are divided into upper and lower loops. The many pine trees surrounding both loops offer ample shade for all sites; the upper loop is closest to the lake. The Beaver Meadows Area of 517,000-acre Allegheny National Forest is adjacent to the Allegheny Wild and Scenic River. There are over 71 different species of fish in the 34-acre Beaver Meadows Lake, including bullhead, yellow perch, largemouth and smallmouth bass, bluegill, and pumpkinseed. Though the lake is not stocked, the populations are healthy and plentiful. If you're looking specifically for trout, try Salmon Creek. The impoundment has a boat launch and serves as a wildlife sanctuary for geese, ducks, and heron. The area's namesake, beavers, can be seen around the lake as well. Five interconnecting trails run through Beaver Meadows Recreation Area, totaling 7.1 miles. Three of these trails are loops. The 3.1-mile Beaver Meadows Loop goes south of the lake and passes through a grassy meadow with the occasional spruce and pine, through a blueberry patch, over the lake itself on a floating boardwalk, then ascends to a red maple and black cherry forest before returning to the meadow. The other two loop trails are much shorter, Salmon Creek Loop at 1.3 miles and Lakeside Loop at 0.5 mile.

Campsites, facilities: There are 38 sites for tents or RVs up to 72 feet. There are no hookups. Vault toilets and hand pumps for drinking water are available. The Forest Service recommends boiling water before consumption. Leashed pets are permitted.

Reservations, fees: Reservations are accepted at 877/444-6777. The rate is $10 per night; a fee may apply for additional guests. Major credit cards are accepted. Open end of May through beginning of October.

Directions: From Marienville, travel four miles north on FR 128, then follow signs to the campground entrance.

Contact: Allegheny National Forest, P.O. Box 847, Warren, PA 16365, 814/723-5150, www.fs.fed.us/r9/forests/allegheny.

39 LOLETA CAMPGROUND

Rating: 10

in Allegheny National Forest

BEST (

The campground is divided into two loops. The upper loop is recommended for small RVs and tents, while the lower loop has room for larger RVs. Both loops provide sunny and shaded sites. This part of Allegheny National Forest has several swimming beaches and trout fishing in Millstone Creek. A three-mile loop trail for hikers begins and ends at Loleta and takes you past a scenic overlook for the Millstone Valley. Head just four miles south of the campground to the Clarion River for canoeing or fishing. Among the species found in this body of water are perch, trout, bluegill, catfish, crappie, sunfish, largemouth and smallmouth bass, and walleye. Go five miles north of Loleta Campground to Buzzard Swamp Wildlife Management Area, run by the Forest Service in cooperation with the State Game Commission. It contains a 9.6-mile trail system for hiking, biking, and cross-country skiing that includes Songbird Sojourn Interpretive Trail. This 1.5-mile trail is self-guided and will take you through forested and swampy areas. Near the swamps you might see osprey, bald eagles, beavers, or snapping turtles.

Campsites, facilities: There are 38 sites for tents or RVs up to 50 feet: 20 have electricity; 18 have no hookups. Picnic tables and fire rings are provided. Drinking water, vault toilets, restrooms with flush toilets, showers, a volleyball court, a picnic area, and an amphitheater are available. Some sites are wheelchair accessible. Leashed pets are permitted.

Reservations, fees: Reservations are accepted at 877/444-6777. The rate is $12–15 per night for up to eight people; a fee may apply for additional guests. Major credit cards are accepted. Open end of May through beginning of October.

Directions: From Marienville, travel south six miles on Highway 27027 to the campground entrance.

Contact: Allegheny National Forest, P.O. Box 847, Warren, PA 16365, 814/723-5150, www.fs.fed.us/r9/forests/allegheny.

40 SINNEMAHONING STATE PARK

Rating: 5

on Sinnemahoning Creek

BEST

Located on the First Fork of the Sinnemahoning Creek, the state park offers many outdoor activities. Boating and fishing can be enjoyed on the 142-acre George B. Stevenson Reservoir. In this cold outflow from George B. Stevenson Dam, you can fish for crappie, bluegill, catfish, perch, tiger muskie, smallmouth and largemouth bass, brook, rainbow, and brown trout, pickerel, and sunfish. Motorized boats on the reservoir must have electric motors. There are five miles of hiking trails. The one-mile Red Spruce Trail begins at the campground and ends at Forty Maples Picnic Area. Occasional rattlesnakes may be encountered along this path so use caution. Other wildlife you may see include chipmunks, red and gray squirrels, elk, raccoons, opossums, cottontail rabbits, white-tailed deer, osprey, warblers, red-tailed hawks, and eagles. During the winter, ice fishing and snowmobiling are favorite activities. Be advised that hunting is allowed seasonally in Sinnemahoning State Park.

Campsites, facilities: There are 35 sites for RVs up to 30 feet and tents: 22 have electricity; 13 have no hookups. Drinking water, restrooms with flush toilets, a dump station, showers, a pavilion, a playground, and a public phone are available. Picnic tables and fire rings are provided. Some sites are wheelchair accessible. Leashed pets are permitted.

Reservations, fees: Reservations are accepted at 888/PA-PARKS (888/727-2757). The rate is $14–19 per night for up to five people; a fee may apply for additional guests. Pets are $2 for up to two pets per night. Senior and Pennsylvania resident discounts are available. Open April through December.

Directions: From the junction of Highway 120 and Highway 872, travel eight miles north on Highway 872 to the campground entrance on the right.

Contact: Sinnemahoning State Park, 8288 First Fork Road, Austin, PA 16720-9302, 814/647-8401, sinnemahoningsp@state.pa.us.

41 KOA MERCER/GROVE CITY CAMPGROUND

Rating: 5

near Shenango River Lake

This property is spacious, but the trees give it an intimate feel. It's conveniently located for visitors heading to Shenango River Lake for boating or fishing. Most visitors begin their explorations from the Mahaney, Clark, or Shenango Day Use Areas, open sunrise to sunset. The boat launches at Shenango and Clark are open 24 hours a day, but cars left in the lot overnight are subject to towing and fines. Areas on the lake are designated for waterskiing and unlimited horsepower operation. Anglers will enjoy fishing for bass, muskie, and pan fish. In the spring anglers head to the dam's outflow to fish for trout. Those who'd prefer to dip a paddle can try the Shenango River just upstream from the lake, and Pymatuning Creek, which is both quiet and scenic. Hiking trails near the lake include the Seth Myers and Coonie Trails, both of which are short, interpretive nature hikes. In May 2005, the Bayview ORV Area at Shenango River Lake opened for ATV riders. Back at the KOA you can enjoy your wooded campsite or head out to one of the many planned weekend activities like bingo or ceramics. Those wishing to remain on the property can fish and hike there as well.

Campsites, facilities: There are 175 sites for tents or RVs up to 90 feet: 117 have full hookups; 45 have water and electricity; 13 have no hookups. There are 31 pull-throughs. Picnic tables and fire rings are provided. Drinking water, restrooms with flush toilets, a dump station, a portable dump, showers, a laundry, groceries, ice, LP gas, wood, a general store, a pavilion, modem access, a rec room, a playground, a swimming pool, badminton, horseshoes, volleyball, and a sports field are available. Leashed pets are permitted.

Reservations, fees: Reservations are accepted at 800/KOA-2802 (800/562-2802). The rate is $25–55 per night for up to two people. Each additional person is $5. Major credit cards are accepted. Open April through October.

Directions: From the junction of I-80 and I-79, travel south three miles on I-79 to Exit 113/31, then north three miles on Highway 258 to the campground entrance on the right.

Contact: KOA Mercer/Grove City Campground, 1337 Butler Pike, Mercer, PA 16137, 724/748-3160, www.koakampgrounds.com/where/pa/38103/index.htm.

42 RV VILLAGE CAMPING RESORT

🏃‍♂️ 🌊 ⛵ 🎣 🐴 🚐 ⛺

Rating: 3

near Maurice K. Goddard State Park

This pleasantly open and wooded campground offers visitors spacious sites, a fishing pond, hiking trails, and planned activities on weekends. Just a short jaunt away is 2,856-acre Maurice K. Goddard State Park, which has 21 miles of hiking trails. At 11 miles,

the main trail that circles Lake Wilhelm might be a bit long for a day hike. If two vehicles are available it is possible to set up many shorter hikes via shuttle. Sandy Creek flows into Lake Wilhelm, a manmade lake that makes up approximately one half of the park's total acreage.

Campsites, facilities: There are 500 sites for tents or RVs up to 90 feet: 250 have full hookups; 150 have water and electricity; 100 have no hookups. There are 10 pull-throughs. Picnic tables and fire rings are provided. Drinking water, restrooms with flush toilets, a dump station, showers, a laundry, groceries, ice, LP gas, wood, a camp store, a pavilion, a rec room, an arcade, a playground, a swimming pool, miniature golf, two shuffle board courts, basketball, tennis, badminton, horseshoes, volleyball, a sports field, and RV storage and supplies are available. Leashed pets are permitted.

Reservations, fees: Reservations are accepted at 866/978-2267. The rate is $15–22 per night for up to two people. Each additional person is $4. Weekly and seasonal rates are available. Major credit cards are accepted. Open April through October.

Directions: From I-80, take the Mercer Exit, then travel two miles north on U.S. 19, then three miles north on Highway 258, then left onto Skyline Drive to the campground entrance.

Contact: RV Village Camping Resort, Mercer, PA 16137, 724/662-4560, www.rvvillages.com.

43 ROCKY SPRINGS CAMPGROUND

🏃‍♂️ 🌊 ⛵ 🎣 🐴 🚐 ⛺

Rating: 7

near Shenango River Lake

Located near Shenango River Lake, this quaint campground provides plenty of distractions for the weary traveler. Fishing is possible in a small pond located on the property, and hiking trails lead visitors away from the trappings of civilization. The staff plans a variety of weekend activities for their visitors. Some guests may sleep better at night knowing that the campground has a traffic control gate for security. Nearby attractions include Shenango River Lake, which has 3,550 acres of surface area for boating, fishing, waterskiing, and tubing. Recently built is the Bayview ORV Area, where visitors may bring ATVs to ride in a safe, controlled environment. For non-motorized pursuits, try canoeing on the scenic Shenango River from Kidd's Mill to New Hamburg or Big Bend. A 7.5-mile hiking trail follows this route as well.

Campsites, facilities: There are 132 sites for tents or RVs up to 25 feet: 102 have full hookups; 15 have water and electricity; 15 have no hookups. There are five pull-throughs. Picnic tables and fire rings are provided. Drinking water, restrooms with flush toilets, a dump station, showers, a laundry, a public phone, groceries, ice, LP gas, wood, a camp store, a playground, a rec hall, an arcade, a swimming pool, miniature golf, basketball, horseshoes, volleyball, a sports field, and RV supplies are available. Leashed pets are permitted.

Reservations, fees: Reservations are accepted. The rate is $21–23 per night for up to two people. Each additional person is $5. Open mid-April through mid-October.

Directions: From the junction of I-80 Exit 15/2 and U.S. 19, travel 2.75 miles north on U.S. 19, then five miles west on Highway 318, then turn left onto a gravel road and travel 0.5 mile to the campground entrance on the right.

Contact: Rocky Springs Campground, 84 Rocky Springs Road, Mercer, PA 16137, 724/662-4415, rockysprings@nowonline.net.

44 JUNCTION 19-80 CAMPGROUND

Rating: 5

near Shenango River Lake

Beginning at Big Bend, just north of the Junction 19-80 Campground, is the trailhead for the 7.5-mile Shenango Trail. This scenic trail follows the Shenango River and the historic Erie Extension Canal. White blazes take hikers to Kidd's Mill Covered Bridge. This was the footpath used by mules to drag barges along the Shenango River. You can still see canal channels, locks, loading bays, and out buildings from this area's past. Due south is Shenango River Lake, where visitors can go waterskiing or tubing. Back at the campground you can fish in the well-stocked lake or nearby streams. There are a variety of planned activities to choose from on most weekends. The well-shaded sites are near some short, pleasant hiking trails.

Campsites, facilities: There are 161 sites for tents or RVs up to 50 feet: 88 have full hookups; 61 have water and electricity; 12 have no hookups. There are 40 pull-throughs. Picnic tables and fire rings are provided. Drinking water, restrooms with flush toilets, a dump station, showers, a laundry, groceries, ice, wood, a camp store, a pavilion, a rec area, an arcade, a swimming pool, a playground, a shuffleboard court, a putting green, basketball, badminton, horseshoes, volleyball, a sports field, and RV storage are available. Some sites are wheelchair accessible. Leashed pets are permitted.

Reservations, fees: Reservations are accepted. The rate is $18–30.50 per night for up to two people. Each additional person is $4. Weekly and seasonal rates are available. Open May through beginning of October.

Directions: From the junction of I-80 Exit 15/2 and U.S. 19, travel 0.2 mile south on U.S. 19, then 0.2 mile east to the campground entrance on the left.

Contact: Junction 19-80 Campground, 1266 Old Mercer Road, Mercer, PA 16137, 724/748-4174, www.junction19-80campground.com.

45 GASLIGHT CAMPGROUND

🚶 🚴 🏊 🛶 🚤 ⛷ 🐕 🏇 ♿ 🚐 ⛺

Rating: 6

near Allegheny National Forest

Just north of I-80 along the Clarion River, Gaslight Campground is a great jumping-off point for trips into Allegheny National Forest and to the Wild and Scenic Clarion River. Highlights in Allegheny National Forest include the Kinzua Reservoir (which has over 100 miles of shoreline), over 600 miles of trails, scenic overlooks, plentiful wildlife, and the Longhouse National Scenic Drive. Backpackers can check out Morrison Trail, and 96 miles of the North Country Trail, a national scenic trail that can be accessed near Willow Bay Recreation Area; the trail then meanders south through the Tionesta Scenic Area before winding up at Seldom Seen Corners. There are also designated trails for bicycle and ATV use. Snowmobile riding is a popular winter pastime, since the national forest sports over 360 miles of groomed trails. You can fish in the on-site pond or in the nearby Clarion River. Gaslight provides planned activities like bingo and hayrides on weekends.

Campsites, facilities: There are 120 sites for tents or RVs up to 29 feet: 75 have full hookups; 45 have water and electricity. There are 100 pull-throughs. Picnic tables and fire rings are provided. Drinking water, restrooms with flush toilets, a dump station, showers, a laundry, groceries, ice, LP gas, wood, a camp store, a rec hall, a playground, a swimming pool, miniature golf, badminton, volleyball, horseshoes, and a sports field are available. Some sites are wheelchair accessible. Leashed pets are permitted.

Reservations, fees: Reservations are accepted. The rate is $25–29 for up to four people

per night. Each additional person is $6. Open mid-April through mid-October.

Directions: From the junction of I-80 Exit 42/5 and Highway 38, travel 100 yards north on Highway 38, then 0.25 mile west on Highway 208 to the campground entrance on the right.

Contact: Gaslight Campground, RD2 Box 10, Emlenton, PA 16373, 724/867-6981.

46 WOLF'S CAMPING RESORT

🏊 🛶 🚤 🐕 🏇 ♿ 🚐 ⛺

Rating: 6

near Knox

This property's large lake provides a wide range of water activities, though only non-motorized boats are permitted on the lake. If you don't have your own craft, you can rent a canoe, rowboat, or pedal boat during your stay. The lake also provides good fishing for bluegill, crappie, catfish, bass, sunfish, and perch. For smallmouth, largemouth, and striped bass, muskie, northern pike, and trout, anglers can check out nearby Kahle Lake. Wolf's has fire truck rides, dances, bingo, ceramics, game tournaments, and movies on large, outdoor screens under the stars.

Campsites, facilities: There are 667 sites for tents or RVs up to 30 feet: 594 have full hookups; 19 have water and electricity; 54 have no hookups. There are 80 pull-throughs. Picnic tables and fire rings are provided. Drinking water, restrooms with flush toilets, a dump station, showers, a laundry, cable hookup, modem access, a phone hookup, groceries, ice, LP gas wood, a camp store, two pavilions, a playground, a rec hall, an arcade, a swimming pool, a wading pool, a whirlpool, miniature golf, six shuffleboard courts, basketball, horseshoes, badminton, volleyball, a sports field, RV rentals, storage, and supplies are available. Some sites are wheelchair accessible. Leashed pets are permitted. The campground has a traffic control gate for security.

Reservations, fees: Reservations are accepted.

The rate is $22.25–33 per night for up to four people. Each additional person is $4.50. Major credit cards are accepted. Open year-round.

Directions: From the junction of I-80 Exit 53/7 and Highway 338, travel north 0.2 mile on Highway 338 to the campground entrance on the right.

Contact: Wolf's Camping Resort, 308 Timberwolf Run, Knox, PA 16232, 814/797-1103, www.wolfscampingresort.com.

47 COLWELL'S CAMPGROUND

🚶 🚴 🏊 🛶 🐴 ⛷ 🚐 ⛺

Rating: 4

near Knox

At Colwell's Campground, most sites are wooded and spacious. Located about halfway between Oil Creek State Park and Cook Forest State Park, the campground is a good base camp for exploring these areas. Once known as the "Black Forest," Cook Forest is famous for its stands of old-growth trees. The Clarion River, part of the National Wild and Scenic Rivers System, borders the eastern edge of the park. Canoeing is a popular pursuit here, and the narrow green valley is both beautiful and rugged. Scenic views can be found within the park at the rock ledges of Seneca Point Overlook and at #9 Fire Tower. It should be noted that there is an 80-foot climb to the top of the fire tower. There are 29 miles of trails within the park for exploring the cool stream valleys and rolling terrain. The North Country National Scenic Trail passes through the forest on its route from New York's Adirondacks to North Dakota's Missouri River. Biking is permitted on all one-way, dirt roads in the park, but not on hiking trails. The 11.5-mile Bicycle Route follows part of Heffern Run Trail and other lightly traveled roads. It takes riders through the scenic Tom's Run Valley and old pine plantations.

Campsites, facilities: There are 80 sites for tents or RVs up to 27 feet: four have full hookups; 66 have water and electricity; 10 have no hookups. Picnic tables and fire rings are provided. Drinking water, restrooms with flush toilets, a dump station, a portable dump, showers, ice, wood, a pavilion, a playground, a rec room, and horseshoes are available. Leashed pets are permitted.

Reservations, fees: Reservations are accepted. The rate is $17 per night for up to two people. Each additional person is $5. Open May through September.

Directions: From the junction of Highway 338 and Highway 208, travel 1.5 miles east on Highway 208, then turn right onto Huckleberry Ridge Road and travel 0.5 mile to the campground entrance on the right.

Contact: Colwell's Campground, Legislative Route, Knox, PA 16232, 814/797-1621.

48 RUSTIC ACRES CAMPGROUNDS

🚶 🚴 🏊 🛶 🐴 ⛷ ♿ 🚐 ⛺

Rating: 8

near Cook Forest State Park

At Rustic Acres, you have your choice of open or shaded sites. If you're ready to stretch your legs, the campground has its own hiking trails. At nearby Cook Forest State Park, you can enjoy the beautiful scenery of old growth trees on 29 miles of trails. There are 27 trails contained within Cook Forest as well as two through-trails: Baker Trail and North Country National Scenic Trail. Biking is welcome on state park roadways and the 11.5-mile Bicycle Route. You can also go horseback riding on 4.5 miles of bridle trails, including part of Brown's Run Trail. The Clarion River, which is the eastern border of the park, provides opportunities for canoeing and fishing for trout or bass. Among the wildlife that can be observed in the park are black bear, red and gray squirrels, porcupines, chipmunks, white-tailed deer, opossums, cottontail rabbits, skunks, and raccoons. The campground has planned activities like bingo, ceramics, and hayrides on weekends.

Campsites, facilities: There are 128 sites for tents or RVs up to 30 feet: 98 have full hook-ups; 10 have water and electricity; 20 have no hookups. There are 10 pull-throughs. Picnic tables and fire rings are provided. Drinking water, restrooms with flush toilets, a dump station, showers, a public phone, groceries, ice, LP gas, wood, a camp store, a pavilion, a rec hall, a playground, badminton, two shuffleboard courts, and volleyball are available. Some sites are wheelchair accessible. Leashed pets are permitted.

Reservations, fees: Reservations are accepted. The rate is $15 per night for up to four people. Each additional person is $5. Open April through October.

Directions: From the junction of I-80 Exit 60/8 and Highway 66, travel north three miles on Highway 66, then turn left onto Pine Terrace Road and travel 0.5 mile to the campground entrance on the left.

Contact: Rustic Acres Campgrounds, 634 Pine Terrace Road, Shippenville, PA 16254, 814/226-9850.

49 KALYUMET CAMPGROUND

🚶 🚴 ⛵ 🎣 🛶 🏕 🐎 ♿ 🚐 ⛺

Rating: 6

near Cook Forest State Park

The sites here are wooded and spacious. You can enjoy pond fishing or hiking one of the campground's trails, or participate in the planned activities on the weekends. There are more outdoor recreational opportunities awaiting you at nearby Cook Forest State Park. Among the many activities in this old-growth park are picnicking,

hiking, biking, and horseback riding. The 27 hiking trails total 29 miles. Bikers are welcome on state park roadways and the 11.5-mile Bicycle Route, which follows Heffern Run Trail. There are two bridle paths, and horseback riding is welcome on parts of Brown's Run Trail. On the Clarion River, which runs through the park, you can fish or canoe.

Campsites, facilities: There are 150 sites for tents or RVs up to 30 feet: 100 have full hookups; 26 have water and electricity; 24 have no hookups. There are 19 pull-throughs. Picnic tables and fire rings are provided. Drinking water, restrooms with flush toilets, a dump station, a portable dump, showers, a laundry, a public phone, groceries, ice, LP gas, wood, a camp store, a pavilion, a playground, a rec hall, a swimming pool, sand boxes, badminton, horseshoes, ping-pong, a community campfire, basketball, volleyball, and a sports field are available. Some sites are wheelchair accessible. Leashed pets are permitted.

Reservations, fees: Reservations are accepted. The rate is $21–28 per night for up to two people. Each additional person is $5. Weekly, monthly, and seasonal rates are available. Major credit cards are accepted. Open May through October.

Directions: From I-80 West Exit 62 (Clarion), make a right toward Clarion and continue straight 11.5 miles to the campground entrance.

Contact: Kalyumet Campground, 8630 Miola Road, Lucinda, PA 16235, 814/744-9622, www.kalyumet.com.

50 RIDGE CAMPGROUND

🚶 🚴 ⛵ 🎣 🛶 🎿 🏕 🐎 ♿ 🚐 ⛺

Rating: 9

in Cook Forest State Park

BEST (

You have your choice of shaded or open sites at this picturesque campground in the heart of Cook Forest State Park, home to the Sawmill Craft Center and Theater. Demonstrations of traditional crafts where classes conducted by master craftsmen are presented at the craft center. If you're not up to participating, you can meander through the many displays and the gift shop. The theater part of the Sawmill seats 180 people for plays and musicals. The campground has planned activities like bingo and hayrides on the weekends. During the winter, snowmobiling, cross-country skiing, sledding, and ice skating are favorite activities. Be advised that hunting is allowed seasonally in Cook Forest State Park. The Wild and Scenic Clarion River makes up the eastern border of the 7,182-acre park. It's great for trout fishing and canoeing. There are many trails for hiking, biking, and horseback riding. Bicycles are not permitted on the 27 hiking trails, except for a portion of Heffern Trail, which is part of the 11.5-mile Bicycle Route.

Campsites, facilities: There are 226 sites for tents or RVs up to 40 feet: 60 have electricity; 166 have no hookups. There are four pull-throughs. No sites have full hookups. Picnic tables and fire rings are provided. Drinking water, restrooms with flush toilets, a dump station, showers, a laundry, a public phone, wood, a pavilion, a swimming pool, a playground, and a sports field are located on this property. Some sites are wheelchair accessible. Leashed pets are permitted.

Reservations, fees: Reservations are accepted at 888/PA-PARKS (888/727-2757). The rate is $14–19 per night for up to five people; a fee may apply for additional guests. Pets are $2 for up to two pets per night. Senior and Pennsylvania resident discounts are available. Open year-round.

Directions: From the Clarion River Bridge in Cooksburg, travel one mile northwest on Highway 36 to the campground entrance on the right.

Contact: Cook Forest State Park, P.O. Box 120, Cooksburg, PA 16217-0120, 814/744-8407, cookforestsp@state.pa.us.

51 DEER MEADOW CAMPGROUND

Rating: 8

near Cook Forest State Park

There are both open and shaded sites in this spacious campground, which offers hiking trails and planned activities like bingo, theme dinners, and hayrides on weekends. For more trails, visit nearby Cook Forest State Park. It has trails for hiking, biking, and horseback riding. A portion of Brown's Run Trail plus two bridle trails allow for 4.5 miles on horseback. The Bicycle Route is a moderately difficult trail that runs 11.5 miles on park roadways and on part of the Heffern Run Trail. For foot traffic there are 27 trails totaling 29 miles. Also running through the park are portions of the North Country National Scenic Trail, which connects the Missouri River in North Dakota with New York's Adirondack Mountains, and the Baker Trail, which travels 140 miles from Freeport, Pennsylvania, to Allegheny National Forest. The Clarion River flows through Cook Forest and also provides fishing and canoeing opportunities.

Campsites, facilities: There are 504 sites for tents or RVs up to 29 feet: 265 have full hookups; 186 have water and electricity; 53 have no hookups. Picnic tables and fire rings are provided. Drinking water, restrooms with flush toilets, a dump station, showers, a public phone, groceries, ice, LP gas, wood, a camp store, a pavilion, a rec room, a swimming pool, a playground, miniature golf, a shuffleboard court, badminton, horseshoes, and volleyball are available. Some sites are wheelchair accessible. Leashed pets are permitted.

Reservations, fees: Reservations are accepted at 866/4DM-CAMP (866/436-2267). The rate is $21–29 per night for up to two people. Each additional person is $5. Seasonal rates are available. Major credit cards are accepted. Open May through October.

Directions: From the junction of Highway 36 and Clarion River Bridge, travel 0.2 mile northwest on Highway 36, then three miles north on Forest Road to the campground entrance on the left.

Contact: Deer Meadow Campground, 2761 Forest Road, Cooksburg, PA 16217, 814/927-8125, www.dearmeadow.com.

52 CLEAR CREEK STATE PARK

Rating: 9

near Sigel

This 1,676-acre park is part of the Clear Creek Valley and home to the Clarion River. Water activities abound here. A 180-foot sand beach allows swimming at your own risk. You can rent a canoe from a commercial outfitter or, if you have your own, use the park's launch area. For a full canoeing experience try the 10-mile trip from Clear Creek to Cook Forest State Park. If water levels are normal, you should finish the trip in about 4.5 hours. Anglers can fish the Clarion River for sunfish, bluegill, trout, smallmouth bass, and other panfish, or try Clear Creek for stocked and native brook trout. The park offers 25 miles of hiking trails that travel through various environments from mountain laurel and rhododendron thickets to stands of pine and oak. During the winter, sledding, tobogganing, and cross-country skiing are favorite activities. Be advised that hunting is allowed seasonally in Clear Creek State Park.

Campsites, facilities: There are 53 sites for tents or RVs up to 20 feet: 30 have electricity; 23 have no hookups: There are five pull-throughs. Picnic tables and fire rings are provided. Non-flush toilets, a dump station, a public phone, a pavilion, and a playground are available. Some sites are wheelchair accessible. Leashed pets are permitted.

Reservations, fees: Reservations are accepted at 888/PA-PARKS (888/727-2757). The rate is $14–19 per night for up to five people; a fee may apply for additional guests. Pets are $2 for up to two pets per night. Senior and Pennsylvania resident discounts are available. Open mid-April through late December.

Directions: From Route 36 travel 10 miles north to Route 949, then travel four miles north on Route 949 to the campground entrance on the left.

Contact: Clear Creek State Park, 38 Clear Creek State Park Road, Sigel, PA 15860-9502, 814/752-2368, clearcreeksp@state.pa.us.

53 CAMPER'S PARADISE CAMPGROUND & CABINS

Rating: 8

near Clear Creek State Park

The wooded sites at this campground offer shade and space. Centrally located near Clear Creek State Park, Cook Forest State Park, Allegheny National Forest, and the Clarion River, Camper's Paradise allows you quick access to many outdoor activities. At Clear Creek State Park you can fish for stocked and native trout in Clear Creek or hike one of the 25 miles of trails. Cook Forest State Park also has stocked trout in Tom's Run, as well as 29 miles of hiking trails, 11.5 miles of biking trails and 4.5 miles of horseback riding trails. Both state parks offer canoeing and fishing on the Clarion River. Allegheny National Forest provides hiking, fishing, wildlife and bird watching. The campground offers planned activities on weekends such as hayrides or games of checkers on a life-size checkerboard.

Campsites, facilities: There are 112 sites for tents or RVs up to 26 feet: 66 have full hookups; 30 have water and electricity; 16 have no hookups. Picnic tables and fire rings are provided. Drinking water, restrooms with flush toilets, a dump station, showers, groceries, ice, LP gas, wood, a general store, a pavilion, a swimming pool, a rec room, an arcade, a playground, volleyball, badminton, horseshoes, croquet, and a sports field are available. Leashed pets are permitted.

Reservations, fees: Reservations are accepted at 888/756-7567. The rate is $20–24 per night for up to two people. Each additional person is $4. Weekly, monthly, and seasonal rates are available. Major credit cards are accepted. Open year-round.

Directions: From the junction of Highway 36 and Highway 949, travel three miles north on Highway 949 to the campground entrance on the right.

Contact: Camper's Paradise Campground & Cabins, RD 1 Box 76B, Sigel, PA 15860, 814/752-2393, www.campersparadise.net.

54 CLEARVIEW CAMPGROUND
👥 🚴 🏇 🚐 ⛺

Rating: 4

near Moshannon State Forest

This mid-sized campground offers mostly open sites. Du Bois, Clearview's home, sits in the heart of a major part of Pennsylvania's public land. The Commonwealth owns 1.5 million acres in this area; almost all of it sits on the Appalachian Plateau. In the 19th and 20th centuries this area was heavily logged. Valuable white pine was removed via "splash dams," structures that could release a slug of water to float the logs to an awaiting mill downstream. Eventually railroad lines were built to make hauling timber easier, and even the most isolated stands quickly fell. What today's visitor sees is second and third growth, yet still the area is considered by some to be the most beautiful between New York City and the Rocky Mountains. Visitors can experience this beauty firsthand on the Rockton Mountain Trails, just to the northeast of Du Bois in the Moshannon State Forest. Here a 16-mile system forms several loops of varying difficulty for hikers and bikers.

Campsites, facilities: There are 70 sites for tents or RVs up to 26 feet: 41 have full hookups; 29 have water and electricity: There are four pull-throughs. Picnic tables and fire rings are provided. Drinking water, restrooms with flush toilets, a dump station, showers, a laundry, modem access, a phone hookup, a public phone, a pavilion, ice, wood, basketball, badminton, volleyball, and RV rentals are available. Leashed pets are permitted.

Reservations, fees: Reservations are accepted. The rate is $15–17 per night for up to two people. Open May through October.

Directions: From the junction of I-80 Exit 101/17 and Highway 255, travel 1.25 miles north on Highway 255, then one mile on a paved road. Follow signs to the campground entrance on the left.

Contact: Clearview Campground, RR 2, Box 355, Du Bois, PA 15801, 814/371-9947.

55 PARKER DAM STATE PARK
👥 🏊 🚣 � 🎣 🏇 🚶 🚐 ⛺

Rating: 10

near Penfield

BEST (

The campground here overlooks the eastern edge of Parker Lake. You have your choice of forested, partially shaded, and grassy sites. A sand beach offers swimming access to the 20-acre lake. You can also go boating or fishing for largemouth bass, sunfish, brook trout, and brown bullhead. If you don't have your own electric-powered or non-motorized boat, you can rent paddleboats, canoes, or rowboats from the park's concession. Several trails run through the park for hiking and backpacking. The eight easy trails are Stumpfield, Tornado Alley, Souder's, Skunk, Snow, Logside, Beaver Dam, and Abbott Hollow Trail. The moderate trails are Sullivan Ridge, Spurline, Trail of New Giants, and Laurel Run Trail. For backpacking, you can catch the western trailhead for the Quehanna Trail System here in the park. This 73-mile trail eventually connects with the Susquehannock Trail System. During the winter, ice skating, ice fishing, sledding, tobogganing, and snowmobiling are favorite activities. Be advised that hunting is allowed seasonally in Parker Dam State Park.

Campsites, facilities: There are 110 sites for tents or RVs up to 30 feet: 80 have water and electricity; 30 have no hookups. No sites have full hookups. Drinking water, restrooms with flush toilets, a dump station, showers, a public phone, ice, wood, a pavilion, a playground, and a sports field are available. Leashed pets are permitted.

Reservations, fees: Reservations are accepted at 888/PA-PARKS (888/727-2757). The rate is $14–19 per night for up to five people; a fee may apply for additional guests. Pets are $2 for up to two pets per night. Senior and Pennsylvania resident discounts are available. Open April through December.

Directions: From Penfield, travel south two miles on Highway 153, then east 2.5 miles to the campground entrance.

Contact: Parker Dam State Park, 28 Fairview Road, Penfield, PA 15849-9799, 814/765-0630, parkerdamsp@state.pa.us.

56 B-BAR-M CAMPGROUND

Rating: 2

near S. B. Elliott State Park

This small campground has an intimate feel, and the surrounding trees shade most of the sites. In nearby Benezette, you can view elk. Be sure to have your camera ready, as they can appear anywhere at any time. Just a mile down the road is Moshannon State Forest and its 318-acre S. B. Elliott State Park. For the anglers in your group, there are several small mountain streams with stocked and native

trout. If hiking is more to your tastes then try the three miles of trails within the park or use them to connect to the 85-mile Susquehannock Trail System or the 75-mile Quehanna Trail System. The Quehanna Trail System is within the 55,000-acre Quehanna Wild Area of Moshannon State Forest. This area has special regulations on activities because it has been set aside to allow forest regeneration. Adjacent to the Quehanna Wild Area is The Marion Brooks Natural Area. Its 975 acres has an old-growth stand of white birch and is also preserved in a natural state.

Campsites, facilities: There are 30 sites for tents or RVs up to 25 feet: 25 have full hookups; five have water and electricity. There are eight pull-throughs. Picnic tables and fire rings are provided. Drinking water, a dump station, restrooms with flush toilets, showers, cable TV, ice, wood, LP gas, a pavilion, a rec area, an arcade, a pool table, and a playground are available. Leashed pets are permitted.

Reservations, fees: Reservations are accepted. The rate is $12–19 per night for up to two people. Each additional person is $3. Open mid-April through mid-December.

Directions: From the junction of I-80 Exit 111/18 and Highway 153, travel north eight miles on Highway 153, then west 0.25 mile on a paved road to the campground entrance on the left.

Contact: B-Bar-M Campground, P.O. Box 2, Penfield, PA 15849, 814/637-5440, webpages.charter.net/bbarm/index.html.

57 S. B. ELLIOTT STATE PARK

Rating: 9

near Clearfield

BEST (

This 318-acre state park is part of the Moshannon State Forest. You have your choice of recreational opportunities here, such as fishing, picnicking, hiking, and backpacking. The local streams have stocked and native trout. The beautiful picnicking area is nestled among pine and oak trees. The three miles of trails within the park make for easy and scenic hiking. Among the wildlife that you may observe are red and gray squirrels, raccoons, chipmunks, cottontail rabbits, skunks, grouse, white-tailed deer, wild turkey, porcupines, and opossums. Backpackers have the choice of Quehanna Trail or Susquehannock Trail. Quehanna Trail is accessed by way of the Central Pennsylvania Lumber Company Trail. This 75-mile trail offers various degrees of difficulty and a variety of eco-systems. You can access Susquehannock Trail from part of Quehanna. This trail passes by Sinnemahoning State Park and through Susquehannock State Park. During the winter cross-country skiing and snowmobiling are favorite activities. Be advised that hunting is allowed seasonally in S. B. Elliott State Park.

Campsites, facilities: There are 25 sites for tents or RVs up to 30 feet. No sites have hookups. Picnic tables and fire rings are provided. Drinking water, restrooms with flush toilets, a dump station, a pavilion, and a playground are available. Some sites are wheelchair accessible. Leashed pets are permitted.

Reservations, fees: Reservations are accepted at 888/PA-PARKS (888/727-2757). The rate is $14–19 per night for up to five people; a fee may apply for additional guests. Pets are $2 for up to two pets per night. Senior and Pennsylvania resident discounts are available. Open April through December.

Directions: From Clearfield, travel north seven miles on Highway 153 to the campground entrance.

Contact: S. B. Elliott State Park, c/o Parker Dam, Penfield, PA 15849-9799, 814/765-0630, parkerdamsp@state.pa.us.

58 KOZY REST KAMPGROUND

Rating: 5

near Moraine State Park

Choose from shaded or open sites at this campground. It has hiking trails and planned activities like bingo, ceramics, and live music on the weekends. For more outdoor recreational options, try nearby Moraine State Park. The park is home to 3,225-acre Lake Arthur. You can enjoy it in many types of watercraft. If you don't have your own, sailboats, paddleboats, rowboats, canoes, kayaks, motorboats, and pontoon boats are available for rent. Windsurfing is also quite popular on the lake. The Pleasant Valley Day Beach on the South Shore and Lakeview Beach on the North Shore both allow swimming. You can also cast for stocked muskie, hybrid striped bass, channel catfish, and walleye, as well as native black crappie, northern pike, largemouth bass, and bluegill. Land activities include hiking and biking.

Campsites, facilities: There are 170 sites for tents or RVs up to 27 feet: 140 have full hookups; 26 have water and electricity; two have electricity; two have no hookups. There are 12 pull-throughs. Picnic tables and fire rings are provided. Drinking water, restrooms with flush toilets, a dump station, showers, modem access, a phone hookup, a public phone, groceries, ice, LP gas, wood, a camp store, a pavilion, a rec hall, a playground, a swimming pool, a game room, a shuffleboard court, badminton, horseshoes, volleyball, and a sports field are available. Some sites are wheelchair accessible. Leashed pets are permitted.

Reservations, fees: Reservations are accepted. The rate is $20–25 per night for up to two people. Each additional person is $4. Weekly and monthly rates are available. Major credit cards are accepted. Open mid-April through October.

Directions: From the junction of Highway 8 and Highway 58, travel 0.5 mile east on Highway 58, then turn left onto a paved road and travel two miles to the campground entrance on the left.

Contact: Kozy Rest Kampground, 449 Campground Road, Harrisville, PA 16038, 724/735-2417, www.kozyrestkampground.com.

59 ROSE POINT PARK

Rating: 8

near McConnells Mill State Park

Nearby McConnells Mill State Park offers climbing and rappelling, fishing, hiking, and whitewater boating on Slippery Rock Creek. Because Slippery Rock Creek is a narrow canyon with rapids, there is no swimming allowed here. The creek is stocked with trout and also has smallmouth and striped bass. Among the many miles of hiking trails is the 1.5-mile Alpha Pass, which is part of the North Country National Scenic Trail. It follows the eastern bank of Slippery Rock Creek to the Old Mill. Back at Rose Point Park, you can enjoy hiking trails, stream fishing, or planned activities like bingo and theme dinners.

Campsites, facilities: There are 211 sites for tents or RVs up to 30 feet: 119 have full hookups; 11 have water and electricity; 81 have no hookups. There are 15 pull-throughs. Picnic tables and fire rings are provided. Drinking water, restrooms with flush toilets, a dump station, showers, a laundry, a public phone, modem access, phone hookups, ice, groceries, LP gas, wood, a general store, a pavilion, a rec hall, an arcade, a playground, basketball, volleyball, a sports field, a swimming pool, tent and RV rentals, storage, and supplies are available. Some sites are wheelchair accessible. Leashed pets are permitted. The campground has a traffic control gate for security.

Reservations, fees: Reservations are accepted

at 800/459-1561. The rate is $20–25 per night for up to two people. Each additional person is $5. Weekly, monthly, and seasonal rates are available. Major credit cards are accepted. Open year-round.

Directions: From the junction of I-79 Exit 99/29 and U.S. 422, travel west three miles on U.S. 422, then north 0.25 mile on Rose Point Road to the campground entrance on the left.

Contact: Rose Point Park Campground, 314 Rose Point Road, New Castle, PA 16101, 724/924-2415, www.rosepointpark.com.

60 COOPER'S LAKE CAMPGROUND

Rating: 6

near McConnells Mill State Park

You have your choice of open, shaded, or lakeview sites on this campground's 500 scenic acres. The lake, which covers 10 acres, is not suitable for swimming, but you are welcome to fish here for perch, catfish, bluegill, and bass. The campground offers planned activities like bingo and hayrides as well. At nearby McConnells Mill State Park there are 11 miles of trails. Hells Hollow is the easiest hike. It travels 0.5 mile to Hells Hollow Falls. Kildoo and Alpha Pass are both moderate. Kildoo is a two-mile loop that runs along Slippery Rock Creek. Alpha Pass is part of the North Country National Scenic Trail. The most difficult hike is the 6.2-mile Slippery Rock Gorge Trail. It also is part of the North Country National Scenic Trail and ascends into Hell Run Valley and the steepest part of the gorge. Kayaking and canoeing are favorite sports on Slippery Rock Creek's rapids.

Campsites, facilities: There are 96 sites for tents or RVs up to 27 feet: 16 have full hookups; 44 have water and electricity; 24 have electricity; 12 have no hookups. There are

24 pull-throughs. Picnic tables and fire rings are provided. Drinking water, restrooms with flush toilets, a dump station, showers, a laundry, a public phone, a camp store, a pavilion, a playground, a rec hall, an arcade, basketball, ping-pong, and RV storage are available. Some sites are wheelchair accessible. Leashed pets are permitted.

Reservations, fees: Reservations are only accepted for holidays or by clubs. The rate is $8–18 per person per night. Weekly, monthly, and seasonal rates are available. Major credit cards are accepted. Open March through beginning of November.

Directions: From the junction of I-79 Exit 99/29 and U.S. 422, travel west 0.5 mile on U.S. 422, then turn right onto Currie Road and travel one mile to the campground entrance on the right.

Contact: Cooper's Lake Campground, 205 Corrie Road, Slippery Rock, PA 16057, 724/368-8710, www.cooperslake.com.

61 LAKE ARTHUR FAMILY CAMPGROUND

Rating: 8

near Moraine State Park

BEST (

This family-oriented campground offers views of its namesake, Lake Arthur in nearby Moraine State Park. You can choose from shaded or open sites. The 3,222-acre lake has many species of fish, such as largemouth and striped bass, muskie, northern pike, channel catfish, walleye, black crappie, bluegill, and sunfish. Motorboats, sailboats, canoes, kayaks, paddleboats, and pontoon boats are welcome. If you don't have your own, then you can rent one. Windsurfing is also a popular sport on the lake. There are two beaches where swimming is permitted along Lake Arthur: Pleasant Valley Day Beach and Lakeview Beach. Several trails for hiking

and biking run throughout the state park. The campground's hiking trail connects to North Country Trail. There are also planned activities like theme weekends and potluck dinners for your entertainment.

Campsites, facilities: There are 105 sites for tents or RVs up to 30 feet: 28 have full hookups; 62 have water and electricity; 15 have no hookups. There are two pull-throughs. Picnic tables and fire rings are provided. Drinking water, restrooms with flush toilets, a dump station, showers, ice, groceries, wood, a general store, a playground, a rec area, a game room, modem access, badminton, horseshoes, volleyball, and a sports field are available. Leashed pets are permitted.

Reservations, fees: Reservations are accepted. The rate is $17–22 per night for up to three people. Each additional person is $3. Weekly, monthly, and seasonal rates are available. Open May through mid-October.

Directions: From the junction of Highway 108 and Highway 173, travel 4.5 miles southeast on Highway 173, then 50 yards south on Highway 8, then 2.25 miles southwest on Highway 528, and finally one mile east on Liberty Road to the campground entrance on the left.

Contact: Lake Arthur Family Campground, 243 West Liberty Road, Slippery Rock, PA 16057, 724/794-9901, www.lakearthurfamilycampground.com.

62 PEACEFUL VALLEY FAMILY CAMPGROUND

Rating: 7

near Moraine State Park

At this spacious campground, you have your choice of open or shaded sites. Moraine State Park and Lake Arthur are a naturalist's delight. One can look for glacial features left over when the continental ice cap receded over 14,000 years ago. Moraines, eskers, and kettle lakes are just some of the features present in the area. Lake Arthur itself is a delightful warm-water fishery, home to a variety of stocked fish. Travelers should visit the Frank Preston Conservation Area where ospreys were recently reintroduced to the park. Nearby is a seven-mile bicycle trail that meanders around the north shore of Lake Arthur. The lake is perfect for boating and sailing, and there are hiking trails within the park as well. On the south shore, unguarded Pleasant Beach is open for swimming. On the north shore, Lakeview Beach has a lifeguard posted 11 A.M.–7 P.M. daily.

Campsites, facilities: There are 125 sites for tents or RVs up to 35 feet: 60 have full hookups; 50 have water and electricity; 15 have no hookups. Picnic tables and fire rings are provided. Drinking water, restrooms with flush toilets, a dump station, showers, a laundry, a public phone, ice, wood, a snack bar, a pavilion, a rec hall, a playground, a swimming pool, horseback riding, and volleyball are available. Some sites are wheelchair accessible. Leashed pets are permitted.

Reservations, fees: Reservations are accepted at 800/922-9644. The rate is $18–26 per night for up to two people. Each additional person is $4. Major credit cards are accepted. Open May through mid-November.

Directions: From the junction of Highway 38 and Highway 138, travel 0.5 mile southwest on Highway 138, then 0.5 mile north on Calico Road, then 0.25 mile east on Peaceful Valley Road to the campground entrance on the right.

Contact: Peaceful Valley Family Campground, 236 Peaceful Valley Road, West Sunbury, PA 16061, 724/894-2421.

63 BEAR RUN CAMPGROUND

Rating: 9

near Moraine State Park

This large, family-oriented campground offers both shaded and open sites. Because it borders Moraine State Park and is only five minutes from McConnells Mill State Park, outdoor activities abound. If you'd prefer to stay on-site for entertainment, the campground offers planned weekend activities like hayrides and bingo. The 16,000-acre Moraine State Park has areas for picnicking and Lake Arthur for boating, fishing, windsurfing, and swimming. There are also numerous trails for biking, hiking, and horseback riding. The 2,500-acre McConnells Mill State Park has climbing, rappelling, grist mill tours, whitewater rafting, kayaking, and canoeing. Also here is Slippery Rock Creek, which has wonderful trout fishing.

Campsites, facilities: There are 316 sites for tents or RVs up to 35 feet: 194 have full hookups; 53 have water and electricity; 67 have no hookups. There are 20 pull-throughs. Picnic tables and fire rings are provided. Drinking water, restrooms with flush toilets, a dump station, a portable dump, showers, a laundry, modem access, a phone hookup, a public phone, a rec room, a full-service store, ice, wood, LP gas, a swimming pool, a playground, badminton, basketball, volleyball, horseshoes, a sports field, an arcade, and RV rentals and storage are available. Some sites are wheelchair accessible. Leashed pets are permitted.

Reservations, fees: Reservations are accepted at 888/737-2605. The rate is $25 per night for up to two people. Each additional person is $5. Weekly, monthly, and seasonal rates are available. Major credit cards are accepted. Open mid-April through October.

Directions: From the junction of I-79 Exit 96/28 and Highway 488, travel 50 yards east on Highway 488, then turn left onto Badger Hill Road and travel 0.5 mile to the campground entrance on the right.

Contact: Bear Run Campground, 184 Badger Hill Road, Portersville, PA 16051, 724/368-3564, www.bearruncampground.com.

64 WOODLAND CAMPGROUND

🥾 ≈ 🛶 🚤 🐴 ♿ 🚐 ⛺

Rating: 7

near Woodland

You have your choice of spacious open or wooded sites here. The campground offers pond fishing for species like sunfish and bluegill, as well as a lake for swimming or boating. You can rent a pedal or rowboat, launch your own motorized boat with an electric motor, or go canoeing. There are also hiking trails. On the weekends you can participate in planned activities like scavenger hunts and campfires. Nearby are three different caves to explore: Penn's Cave, Indian Caverns, and Lincoln Caverns. Penn's Cave offers a guided one-hour motorboat tour of the limestone caverns on an underground stream. There is also a 1.5-hour motorized wildlife tour on the property. Among the animals you will see are wolves and bison. Indian Caverns has guided walking tours and Lincoln Caverns also has tours.

Campsites, facilities: There are 122 sites for tents or RVs up to 26 feet: 37 have full hookups; 73 have water and electricity; 12 have no hookups. There are 67 pull-throughs. Picnic tables and fire rings are provided. Drinking water, restrooms with flush toilets, a dump station, a portable dump, showers, a laundry, a modem hookup, a public phone, ice, groceries, LP gas, wood, a general store, a gift store, a chapel, a pavilion, a swimming pool, a playground, a rec room, horseshoes, volleyball, and RV storage are available. Some sites are wheelchair accessible. Leashed pets are permitted.

Reservations, fees: Reservations are accepted at 800/589-1674. The rate is $18–26 per night for up to two people. Each additional person is $3. Weekly, monthly, and seasonal rates are available. Major credit cards are accepted. Open April through end of December.

Directions: From the junction of I-80 Exit 123/20 and Highway 970, travel 0.75 mile north on Highway 970, then 0.25 mile east on a paved road to the campground entrance on the right.

Contact: Woodland Campground, 314 Egypt Road, Woodland, PA 16881, 814/857-5388, www.woodlandpa.com.

65 BUTTERCUP WOODLANDS CAMPGROUND

🥾 ≈ 🐴 🚴 ♿ 🚐 ⛺

Rating: 6

near Moraine State Park

This large campground is conveniently located close to several parks and recreational areas, including Alameda Park, Highfield Park, Butler Memorial Park, Butler Township Park, and Connoquenessing Park. Nearby Connoquenessing Creek offers kayaking and fishing. Just a few miles further north is Moraine State Park, which has scenic hiking trails. The two easiest trails are Five Points Trail and Pleasant Valley Trail, a 2.6-mile mowed trail through the South Shore valley. The 1.5-mile loop of Five Points Trail is near Lakeview Beach. There are also two moderate trails, a moderate-to-difficult trail, and one difficult trail. If you prefer to partake in the entertainment back at the campground, planned activities like bingo are offered on weekends.

Campsites, facilities: There are 330 sites for tents or RVs up to 35 feet: 300 have full hookups; 30 have no hookups. Picnic tables and fire rings are provided. Drinking water, restrooms with flush toilets, a dump station, showers, a laundry, cable TV, modem access, phone hookup, public phones, groceries, ice, wood, LP gas, a general store, a playground, a pavilion, a rec room, an equipped pavilion, an arcade, a swimming pool, basketball, volleyball, badminton, horseshoes, a sports field, two shuffleboard courts, and RV rentals and storage are available. Some sites are wheelchair accessible. Leashed pets are permitted. The campground has a traffic control gate for security.

Reservations, fees: Reservations are accepted. The rate is $27 per night for up to four people. Each additional person is $6. Major credit cards are accepted. Open year-round.

Directions: From the junction of I-79 Exit 83/26 and Highway 528, travel 1.5 miles east on Highway 528, then 8 miles east on Highway 68 to the campground entrance on the left.

Contact: Buttercup Woodlands Campground, 854 Evans City Road, Renfrew, PA 16053, 724/789-9340, buttcup@zbzoom.net.

66 WHEEL-IN CAMPGROUND

Rating: 3

near Clear Creek State Park

Among the water activities you can enjoy at the campground's lake are stream fishing for trout and perch, canoeing, and boating. Only non-motorized boats are allowed. Wheel-In offers pedal boat rentals and planned activities on the weekends. The Clarion River also offers canoeing and fishing at nearby Clear Creek State Park. Many visitors paddle a 10-mile trip from Clear Creek to Cook Forest State Park. At normal water levels you can expect to make the trip in about 4.5 hours. Among the fish you can cast for are trout, smallmouth bass, sunfish, crappie, and bluegill. Clear Creek has stocked and native brook trout. The park also has a 180-foot sand beach for swimming and 25 miles of hiking trails. During the summer, the park offers environmental and interpretive programs, including guided walks, campfire programs, and hands-on activities. Check the park office for a schedule of these changing events. Be advised that hunting is allowed seasonally in Clear Creek State Park.

Campsites, facilities: There are 100 sites for tents or RVs up to 45 feet: eight have full hookups; 92 have water and electricity. There are 10 pull-throughs. Picnic tables and fire rings are provided. Drinking water, restrooms with flush toilets, a dump station, a portable dump, showers, ice, wood, a pavilion, a rec hall, a playground, two shuffleboard courts, horseshoes, a volleyball court, and a sports field are available. Leashed pets are permitted.

Reservations, fees: Reservations are accepted. The rate is $21–23 per night for up to four people. Each additional person is $5. Open April through October.

Directions: From the junction of Business U.S. 422 and U.S. 422, travel eight miles west on U.S. 422, then 0.75 mile on a paved road. Follow signs to the campground entrance on the left.

Contact: Wheel-In Campground, RD 2 Box 147, Shelocta, PA 15774, 724/354-3693, wheelin@yourinter.net.

NORTH CENTRAL

© JASON MILLER

BEST CAMPGROUNDS

Pennsylvania's north-central mountains lie in a

section of the state known to geologists as the Deep Valleys Section. In some of these steep-sloped valleys, streams can lie more than 1,000 feet below the relatively flat uplands. Some of these valleys have a stair-step appearance due to the differences in the durability of the sandstones and less resistant shales that form the valley walls.

Day-trippers and campers in this area will note an abundance of scenic overlooks and outstanding geological features. Photo opportunities are plentiful at vistas such as Kettle Creek Gorge and Slate Run Gorge along Route 44, and at Hyner View State Park and Benson Ridge. Exploration can really pay off with rewards such as Algerine Swamp Bog, Angel Falls, Big Trail Vista, Dry Run Falls, Fox Mountain, Ice Mine, Loyalsock Creek Gorge, Rimrock Overlook, and Sharp Top Vista. The Route 44 Scenic Highway provides easy access to features that include Benson Ridge Vista, Cherry Springs Scenic Area, Longtoe Vista, and Pine Mountain Vista.

No guide to this region would be complete without encouraging visitors to stop at Pine Creek Gorge and Ricketts Glen State Park; these attractions exemplify this part of the state and are what every traveler hopes to find at the end of a long drive.

Pine Creek Gorge is a National Natural Landmark located in 160,000-acre Tioga State Forest. Known as "Pennsylvania's Grand Canyon," this geological feature is 1,000 feet deep and 4,000 feet wide. The gorge was formed more than 20,000 years ago when northerly flowing Pine Creek was greeted by a southerly advancing wall of ice and debris. Today visitors can hike the gorge's many trails, accessible from a pair of state parks on either side. Leonard Harrison and Colton Point State Parks are joined by three-mile Turkey Path Trail, which drops 1,000 feet to the bottom of the gorge. At the bottom is 42-mile Pine Creek Trail, which runs from Ansonia to Waterville. The Seneca used this route to link the Great Shamokin Path along the Susquehanna to the Iroquois villages along the Genesee River in New York. Visitors will easily see why in 2001 *USA Today* named Pine Creek Trail one of the top 10 places in the country to bike tour: among the sights are rock outcrops, waterfalls, spruce plantations, old growth hemlock, and wildlife such as deer, coyote, eagles, osprey, and otter. Rafting and kayaking are possible on Pine Creek's Class II and III rapids, and the creek and many of its surrounding streams are favorites for fly-fishing. There are many privately owned campgrounds within a few miles of these natural attractions, and Leonard Harrison and Colton Point State Parks have several campgrounds that range from rustic to modern to suit your tastes.

Ricketts Glen State Park is the other must-see in this part of the state. Several campgrounds in and around Ricketts Glen provide comfortable, temporary homes while you enjoy all the area has to offer. The 13,000-acre park is home to Red Rock Mountain and Glens Natural Area, another National Natural Landmark. A five-mile loop trail takes hikers through Ganoga Glen and Glen Leigh, home to 21 of the park's named waterfalls. At Waters Meet, where the two branches of Kitchen Creek join before plunging into Ricketts Glen, visitors will find the remainder of the park's waterfalls and a moist, cool microclimate created by the mist. Because of its accessibility, most visitors prefer Ganoga Glen, whose lush old-growth forest is home to hemlocks, pines, and oaks, some almost 1,000 years old, and 94-foot Ganoga Falls, the highest falls in the park.

Backpackers should take note of the area's long trails. The West Rim Trail, from Ansonia to Blackwell along the West Rim of Pine Creek Gorge was picked by *Outside* magazine as the best hike in Pennsylvania in 1996. The Susquehannock Trail is an 8.5-mile loop that takes hikers through wetlands, virgin hemlocks, and a variety of other types of forest. Rugged Black Forest Trail is a 45-mile loop in northwest Lycoming County that rewards hikers with many scenic views. Even longer hikes can be found on the 160 miles of the Mid State Trail that run from the West Rim Trail to the town of Water Street.

Rugged beauty is the theme in this part of Pennsylvania, and campers often find unexpected rewards. Here, even a casual trip from the campground can reveal covered bridges or old-time amusement parks, sights easily overlooked when speeding past on an interstate. Back roads often end at overlooks, farms, or scenic streams that aren't in any guidebook.

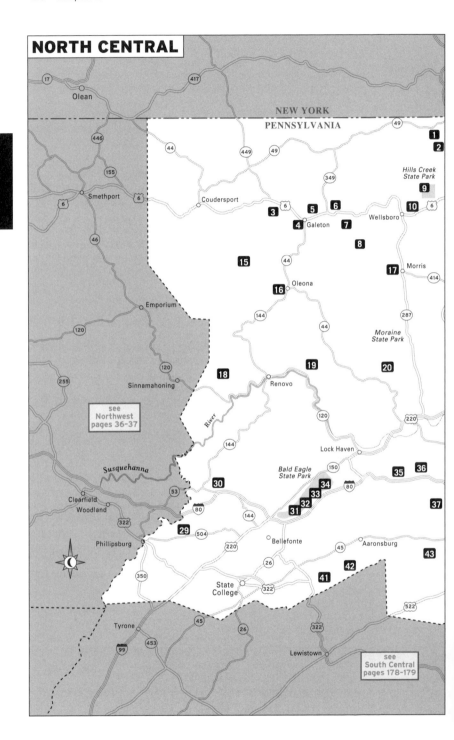

NORTH CENTRAL

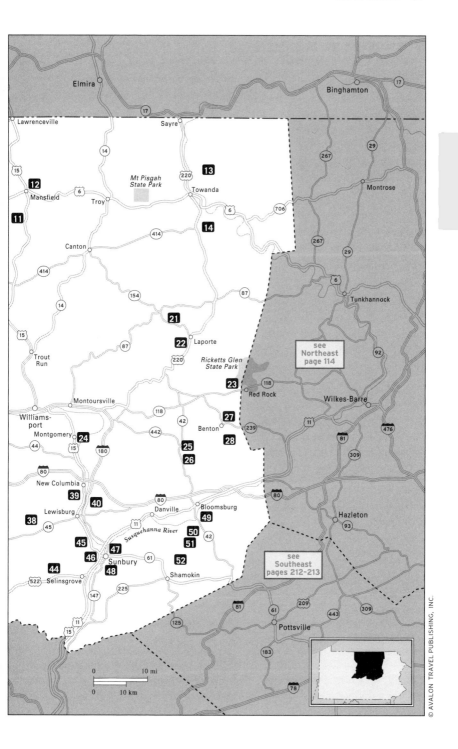

Elmira

Binghamton

17

Lawrenceville

Sayre

17

14

15

12

Mansfield

11

6

Troy

Mt Pisgah
State Park

220

13

Towanda

Montrose

29

267

6

706

14

414

Canton

267

29

414

6

154

87

Tunkhannock

14

21

15

87

22 Laporte

220

Ricketts Glen
State Park

92

see
Northeast
page 114

Trout
Run

Montoursville

23

118

Red Rock

Wilkes-Barre

Williams-
port

118

42

27

239

11

476

Montgomery

24

442

Benton

28

81

309

44

15

180

25

26

80

80

New Columbia

39

40

Danville

Bloomsburg

Hazleton

Lewisburg

49

93

38

45

11

50

42

Susquehanna River

45

51

see
Southeast
pages 212-213

46

47

61

52

44

48

Sunbury

Shamokin

81

61

209

443

309

522

Selinsgrove

147

225

Pottsville

125

11

15

183

0   10 mi

78

0   10 km

© AVALON TRAVEL PUBLISHING, INC.

1 TOMPKINS RECREATION AREA CAMPGROUND
🥾 ≈ 🛶 🚤 🏕 🐎 ♿ 🚐 ⛺

Rating: 9

at Cowanesque Lake

Tompkins Recreation Area and its campground are located along the northern shore of Cowanesque Lake. You have your choice of wooded or open sites. Cowanesque Lake is a 1,085-acre reservoir that serves as water storage and for flood control. It also offers many recreational opportunities. Since there is no limit on horsepower, most types of watercraft are welcome on the lake. You can use the five boat launches or any of the numerous mooring slips. Waterskiing and windsurfing are popular activities on the lake. Anglers from your group can cast for stocked walleye, largemouth and hybrid striped bass, white crappie, lake and rainbow trout, muskie, channel catfish, bluegill, and sunfish. You can also swim from a grass beach. If you prefer to stay on dry land, you can hop onto one of the numerous hiking trails, including the Mid State Trail, which connects Cowanesque Lake to Hammond Lake. Be advised that hunting is allowed seasonally in the area.

Campsites, facilities: There are 126 sites for tents or RVs up to 68 feet: 68 have water and electricity; 58 have no hookups. There are 16 walk-in sites. Picnic tables and fire rings are provided. Drinking water, restrooms with flush toilets, a dump station, showers, a public phone, groceries, ice, wood, a camp store, a pavilion, a playground, volleyball, a sports field, and an amphitheater are available. Some sites are wheelchair accessible. Leashed pets are permitted.

Reservations, fees: Reservations are accepted at 877/444-6777. The rate is $18–22 per night for up to two people. Each additional person is $3. Open mid-May through September.

Directions: From the junction of Highway 49 and U.S. 15, travel 0.25 mile north on U.S. 15, then turn left onto Bliss Road and travel three miles to the campground entrance on the left.

Contact: Cowanesque/Tioga-Hammond Lakes, Corps of Engineers, RD 1 Box 65, Tioga, PA 16946-9733, 570/835-5281, CowanesqueLakeWEB@usace.army.mil.

2 IVES RUN RECREATION AREA CAMPGROUND
🥾 ≈ 🛶 🚤 🏕 🐎 ♿ 🚐 ⛺

Rating: 9

at Hammond Lake

The Ives Run Recreation Area offers hiking and interpretive trails, as well as a portion of the 261-mile Mid State Trail System. Hammond Lake provides many recreational opportunities on the water. Motorboats, canoes, kayaks, rowboats, pedal boats, paddleboats, and wind surfboards are welcome on the lake. You have your choice of five boat launches and several mooring slips. The anglers in your group will appreciate the variety of stocked fish, including tiger and purebred muskie, walleye, largemouth and hybrid striped bass, channel catfish, white and black crappie, and lake and rainbow trout. A grass beach is located along the shore for swimming. You can also take advantage of several picnicking facilities. Birders can get the binoculars out for sightings of osprey, eagles, mallard and wood ducks, Canada geese, grouse, warblers, and other migratory birds. Be advised that hunting is allowed seasonally in the area.

Campsites, facilities: There are 187 sites for tents or RVs up to 70 feet: 45 have full hookups; 63 have water and electricity; 76 have electricity; three have no hookups. There is one pull-through. Picnic tables and fire rings are provided. Drinking water, restrooms with flush toilets, non-flush toilets, a dump station, showers, a public phone, groceries, ice, wood, a camp store, a pavilion, a playground, volleyball, and a sports field are available. Some sites are wheelchair accessible. Leashed pets are permitted.

Reservations, fees: Reservations are accepted at 877/444-6777. The rate is $18–24 per night for up to two people; a fee may apply for additional guests. Open mid-April through mid-October.

Directions: From the junction of U.S. 15 and Highway 287, travel two miles south to Tioga, turn west, then four miles south on Highway 287 to the campground entrance on the left.

Contact: Ives Run Recreation Area, c/o U.S. Army Corps of Engineers, RR 1 Box 65, Tioga, PA 16946, 570/835-5281.

3 LYMAN RUN STATE PARK

Rating: 9

near Galeton

The campsites in this 595-acre state park are divided into two sections, Daggett Run and Lower Campground. The centerpiece of Lyman Run is 45-acre Lyman Run Lake. If you have an electric motor or non-powered boat, you can use the launch, dock, and mooring spaces at the lake. Along the shore is a 300-foot guarded sand beach. Anglers can cast for stocked palomino and rainbow trout. Six miles of hiking trails link with other trails within the Susquehannock State Forest. In the northern section are Spur Line, Beehive, and Wildcat Trails. Lyman Run Trail starts at the dam and runs along the lake until it meets Fish Trail. The state park is also an access point for 43 miles of ATV trails. During the winter, Lyman Run is the trailhead for a 43-mile snowmobiling trail that loops through the Susquehannock State Forest. Other favorite winter activities are ice fishing and ice skating. Be advised that hunting is allowed seasonally in Lyman Run State Park.

Campsites, facilities: There are 35 sites for tents or RVs up to 30 feet: 29 have electricity; six have no hookups. There are five pull-throughs. Picnic tables and fire rings are provided. Non-flush toilets, a dump station, water hydrants, a public phone, ice, wood, a pavilion, and a playground are available. Some sites are wheelchair accessible. Leashed pets are permitted.

Reservations, fees: Reservations are accepted at 888/PA-PARKS (888/727-2757). The rate is $14–19 per night for up to five people; a fee may apply for additional guests. Pets are $2 for up to two pets per night. Senior and Pennsylvania resident discounts are available. Open mid-April through mid-December.

Directions: From Galeton, travel seven miles west on West Branch Road to the campground entrance on the right.

Contact: Lyman Run State Park, 454 Lyman Run Road, Galeton, PA 16922, 814/435-5010, lymanrunsp@state.pa.us.

4 PINE CREEK VISTA CAMPGROUNDS

Rating: 7

near Colton Point State Park

Pine Creek Vista is conveniently located next to its namesake, Pine Creek Gorge. Stream fishing is available right on the property, but most campers head to Colton Point State Park to hit the trails or check out the stunning views from a park overlook. The park has four miles of rugged trails within its boundaries, most notably the Rim Trail. It's a one-mile hike that connects to all the overlooks. The terrain is relatively flat. Turkey Path Trail is the lung-buster. Its three miles take hikers and anglers down to the floor of the canyon. Even those who don't make it to the bottom are rewarded with a 70-foot cascading waterfall less than 0.5 mile down. Note that there is no bridge across Pine Creek. Visitors should take caution and always remain behind fences and in protected areas. At the bottom of the canyon is the 42-mile Pine Creek Trail, a multi-use trail for biking, hiking, and in winter, cross-country skiing. Horseback riding is permitted only on the dirt access road on the nine miles from Ansonia to Tiadaghton. Visitors can see waterfalls, rock outcrops, spruce plantations, and wildlife such as deer, coyote, eagle, osprey, turkey, otter, and black bear.

Campsites, facilities: There are 109 sites for tents or RVs up to 25 feet: 84 have water and electricity; 25 have no hookups. There are 16 pull-throughs. Picnic tables and fire rings are provided. Drinking water, restrooms with flush toilets, a dump station, showers, a laundry, a public phone, groceries, ice, wood, a camp store, a pavilion, a playground, a rec room, and volleyball are available. Some sites are wheelchair accessible. Leashed pets are permitted.

Reservations, fees: Reservations are accepted. The rate is $17 per night for up to four people. Each additional person is $5. Seasonal rates are available. Open year-round.

Directions: From the junction of Highway 349 and U.S. 6, travel west 1.25 miles on U.S. 6, then one mile on a paved road. Follow signs to the campground entrance on the right.

Contact: Pine Creek Vista Campgrounds, RR 1 Box 124, Gaines, PA 16921, 814/435-6398.

⑤ KEARSE CAMPGROUND
🧍‍♂️🏊‍♀️🚣‍♀️🚻🐴🚐🏕️

Rating: 5

near Colton Point State Park

Electric motorboats and non-powered craft are permitted on Kearse Campground's stocked lake. Rowboat rentals are available, and anglers can fish in the lake or wet a line in Pine Creek. Most visitors, however, come to see Pine Creek Gorge, Pennsylvania's very own Grand Canyon. It was formed almost 20,000 years ago when southerly creeping glaciers blocked Pine Creek's northerly route to the sea. Water began to back up behind a dam of debris and ice, and eventually levels got so high that it began to flow south, carving the 1,000-foot gorge out of the sedimentary rock. Visitors can access the gorge at Colton Point State Park, where trailheads for hiking and horseback

riding can be found. Anglers can take a steep trail to the bottom to fish where most others don't bother to go. When water levels permit, Pine Creek can become a nice Class II run, suitable for beginners or other casual paddlers.

Campsites, facilities: There are 150 sites for tents or RVs up to 27 feet: four have full hookups; 126 have water and electricity; 20 have no hookups. Picnic tables and fire rings are provided. Drinking water, restrooms with flush toilets, a dump station, a portable dump, showers, a public phone, ice, LP gas, wood, a pavilion, a playground, badminton, and volleyball are available. Leashed pets are permitted.

Reservations, fees: Reservations are accepted. The rate is $15 per night for up to four people. Seasonal rates are available. Open year-round.

Directions: From the junction of Highway 349 and U.S. 6, travel one mile west on U.S. 6 to the campground entrance on the left.

Contact: Kearse Campground, P.O. Box 74, Gaines, PA 16921, 814/435-2550, kearse@penn.com.

⑥ KENSHIRE KAMPSITE
🧍‍♂️🏊‍♀️🚣‍♀️🚻🦌🚐🏕️

Rating: 7

near Colton Point State Park

Hiking is king at Colton Point State Park, which is just a short distance from Kenshire Kampsite. Most visitors come to view Pine Creek Gorge, considered the jewel in the crown of the state's park system. The scenic 1,000-foot-deep gorge, which is often referred to as Pennsylvania's Grand Canyon, was carved by the reverse flows of a glacial lake as it began to flow south rather than north. Autumn is particularly beautiful, when purples and reds and oranges fill the vista with chlorophyll-less fire. Anglers with sturdy legs will find trails that lead to the bottom, where fishing can be enjoyed in the relative solitude of well-shaded banks. Some trails are open for equestrian purposes and primitive camping. When water levels are generous, white-water boaters can paddle Pine Creek's class II rapids. Kenshire Kampsite has river swimming and stream fishing, and canoeing and kayaking for its campers.

Campsites, facilities: There are 129 sites for tents or RVs up to 26 feet: six have full hookups; 118 have water and electricity; five have no hookups. Picnic tables and fire rings are provided. Drinking water, restrooms with flush toilets, a dump station, a laundry, cable TV hookup, a public phone, groceries, ice, wood, a camp store, a pavilion, a rec room, an arcade, basketball, volleyball, and RV storage and rentals are available. Leashed pets are permitted.

Reservations, fees: Reservations are accepted. The rate is $16–18 per family per night. Seasonal and group rates are available. Open April through mid-December.

Directions: From the junction of Highway 349 and U.S. 6, travel 0.5 mile west on U.S. 6 to the campground entrance on the left.

Contact: Kenshire Kampsite, RR 1 Box 31, Gaines, PA 16921, 814/435-6764, http://pavisnet.com/kenshirekampsite.

7 COLTON POINT STATE PARK

Rating: 10

near Wellsboro

BEST (

Colton Point is on the rim of Pine Creek Gorge across from Leonard Harrison State Park. Pine Creek Gorge is one of Pennsylvania's most scenic places. No visitor should leave disappointed. A series of trails crisscross the gorge and surrounding state forest. Wild Turkey is a three-mile jaunt straight to the bottom, but visitors should check their stamina before starting; once down, it's a long way to the top. But there are other ways down. The 42-mile Pine Creek Trail allows bikers, hikers, and anglers a chance to view the gorge from an otter's point of view. The trail is a great way to see waterfalls, stands of old-growth trees, and rock outcrops along the river's rocky

banks. The cold water of Pine Creek attracts eagle, osprey, bear, and other critters, including whitewater paddlers from March to June. Be advised that hunting is allowed seasonally in Colton Point State Park.

Campsites, facilities: There are 25 sites for tents or RVs up to 20 feet. No sites have hookups. Picnic tables and fire rings are provided. Drinking water, non-flush toilets, a dump station, grills, a pavilion, a playground, and a sports field are available. Leashed pets are permitted.

Reservations, fees: Reservations are not accepted. The rate is $14–19 per night for up to five people. Pets are $2 for up to two pets per night. Senior and Pennsylvania resident discounts are available. Open mid-April through mid-October.

Directions: From Wellsboro, travel 11 miles west on U.S. 6, then turn left onto Colton Point Road and travel six miles to the campground entrance.

Contact: Colton Point State Park, c/o Leonard Harrison, Wellsboro, PA 16901-8970, 570/724-3061, leonardharrisonsp@state.pa.us.

8 LEONARD HARRISON STATE PARK

Rating: 10

near Wellsboro

BEST (

Leonard Harrison State Park sits astride Pine Creek Gorge. The gorge, sometimes called Pennsylvania's Grand Canyon, is one of the state's most famous attractions. The 1,000-foot gorge was formed almost 20,000 years ago when Pine Creek's northerly flow was impeded by the encroaching glaciers and their moraines of rock and uprooted trees. As water levels rose, a lake formed next to the wall of ice, eventually getting so high that the creek reversed its flow. As it rushed south Pine Creek Gorge was carved. Most visitors to the park are content to drive to an overlook, take a few photos, and return to their road trip. But it should be noted that there are a variety of recreational activities to be had in the park. Hiking, biking, fishing, and hunting are permitted here, as well as at Colton Point State Park, Leonard Harrison's twin on the opposite side. Turkey Path Trail is the steep footpath that connects the parks. It's a three-mile drop to the bottom like an acorn through a downspout, so hikers should take a moment to consider their stamina before departing. Like the saying goes, what goes down must come up. Or something like that.

Campsites, facilities: There are 30 sites for RVs up to 35 feet and tents; 9 have electricity; 21 have no hookups. No sites have full hookups. Picnic tables and fire rings are provided. Drinking water, non-flush toilets, a dump station, a public phone, grills, a pavilion, and a playground are available. Leashed pets are permitted.

Reservations, fees: Reservations are accepted at 888/PA-PARKS (888/727-2757). The rate is $14–19 per night for up to five people; a fee may apply for additional guests. Pets are $2 for up to two pets per night. Senior and Pennsylvania resident discounts are available. Open mid-April through mid-October.

Directions: From Wellsboro, travel 10 miles southwest on Highway 660 to the campground entrance.

Contact: Leonard Harrison State Park, Wellsboro, PA 16901-8970, 570/724-3061, leonardharrisonsp@state.pa.us.

⁹ HILLS CREEK STATE PARK

🏃 🏊 🛶 🚐 🐕 🛶 🚙 ⛺

Rating: 8

near Wellsboro

You have your choice of sites that are grassy and open or nestled among giant Hemlock trees. The centerpiece of this 407-acre park is Hills Creek Lake, where anglers can cast for walleye, smallmouth and largemouth bass, yellow perch, black crappie, muskie, bluegill, and sunfish. Ice fishing is a popular winter activity. There are three

mooring areas, two of which have boat launch ramps. If you're into sailing, Hills Creek Lake is a perfect spot. You can also go motorboating as long as it is an electric motor. The park rents rowboats, kayaks, canoes, and paddleboats. Sand and grass beaches are available along the shore. Those who prefer to stay on land can take advantage of five miles of hiking trails. Lake Side and Tauschers Trails are 1.5 miles each, and Yellow Birch is only one mile. Among the wildlife you might view while hiking are white-tailed deer, red and gray squirrels, raccoons, minks, and chipmunks.

Campsites, facilities: There are 102 sites for tents or RVs up to 20 feet: 26 have electricity; 76 have no hookups. Picnic tables and fire rings are provided. Drinking water, restrooms with flush toilets, a dump station, showers, a public phone, a pavilion, and a playground are available. Leashed pets are permitted.

Reservations, fees: Reservations are accepted at 888/PA-PARKS (888/727-2757). The rate is $14–19 per night for up to five people; a fee may apply for additional guests. Pets are $2 for up to two pets per night. Senior and Pennsylvania resident discounts are available. Open April through October.

Directions: From the junction of Highway 660 and U.S. 6, travel four miles east on U.S. 6, then north on an access road to the campground entrance.

Contact: Hills Creek State Park, 111 Spillway Road, Wellsboro, PA 16901-9676, 570/724-4246, hillscreeksp@state.pa.us.

¹⁰ CANYON COUNTRY CAMPGROUND

🏃 🏊 🛶 🚐 🐕 🛶 🚙 ⛺

Rating: 7

near Hills Creek State Park

All sites at Canyon Country are wooded and hiking trails run throughout the property. At nearby Hills Creek State Park, you have five more miles of trails to roam. The one-mile Yellow Birch Trail is the shortest. It begins in the hardwood and hemlock forests and moves into the marsh areas of the park. Tauschers and Lake Side Trails are both 1.5 miles long. Tauschers runs through the pine plantations in the park's northeastern section. Lake Side follows the shoreline of Hills Creek Lake. A sand and grass swimming beach is open from late May to mid-September. You can cast a line from shore or from a boat. Electric motor and non-powered boats are welcome on the lake.

Campsites, facilities: There are 68 sites for tents or RVs up to 27 feet 30 have full hookups; 16 have water and electricity; 8 have electricity; 14 have no hookups. There are 17 pull-throughs. Picnic tables and fire rings are provided. Drinking water, restrooms with flush toilets, a dump station, showers, a laundry, modem access, a phone hookup, a public phone, groceries, ice, LP gas, wood, a general store, a pavilion, a playground, a rec hall, an arcade, basketball, badminton, horseshoes, volleyball, a sports field, a library, and RV rentals and supplies are available. Leashed pets are permitted.

Reservations, fees: Reservations are accepted. The rate is $20–27 per night for up to two people. Each additional person is $5. Major credit cards are accepted. Open mid-April through October.

Directions: From the junction of U.S. 6 and Highway 660, travel nine miles west on Highway 660, then 0.25 mile southwest on a gravel road to the campground entrance on the right.

Contact: Canyon Country Campground, 130 Wilson Road, Wellsboro, PA 16901, 570/724-3818, www.campinpa.com.

11 TANGLEWOOD CAMPING
🚶‍♀️🏊🛶🚐🏠🎣🚌⛺

Rating: 8

near Hills Creek State Park

Tanglewood is situated around a five-acre spring-fed lake, which is perfect for swimming and non-motorized boating. You can rent pedal boats and canoes or just swim from the sand and grass beach. The campground offers a variety of planned activities, such as ice cream socials, beach parties, and a cardboard boat regatta. Nearby Hills Creek State Park offers chances to see loons, osprey, and other waterfowl. Its 137-acre lake is a popular sailing destination, and kayaks, canoes, rowboats, and paddleboats can be rented onsite. Boats with electric motors are also allowed. Swimmers can enjoy the lake's sand beach, and anglers can fish for a variety of warm-water species. The state park also offers five miles of hiking trails.

Campsites, facilities: There are 80 sites for tents or RVs up to 30 feet: 60 have water and electricity; 20 have water. There are 10 pull-throughs. Picnic tables and fire rings are provided. Drinking water, restrooms with flush toilets, a dump station, a portable dump, showers, a public phone, groceries, ice, wood, a camp store, a pavilion, a playground, a rec hall, badminton, volleyball, and a sports field are available. Leashed pets are permitted.

Reservations, fees: Reservations are accepted. The rate is $21–28 per night for up to two people. Each additional person is $3. Weekly, monthly, and seasonal rates are available. Major credit cards are accepted. Open end of April through mid-November.

Directions: From the junction of Highway 660 and U.S. 15, travel south one mile on U.S. 15, then turn left onto State Street and travel 3.5 miles, then turn right onto a gravel road and travel 1.5 miles to the campground entrance at the end. The last 0.5 mile is a steep grade.

Contact: Tanglewood Camping, P.O. Box 35, Covington, PA 16917, 570/549-8299, www.tanglewoodcamping.com.

12 BUCKTAIL FAMILY FUN PARK CAMPING RESORT
🚶‍♀️🏊🛶🚐🏠🎣♿🚌⛺

Rating: 6

near Hills Creek State Park

This 100-acre campground with wooded and open sites is located near Hills Creek State

Park and the Tioga Reservoir. You can take advantage of the property's fishing pond and hiking trails, as well as participate in weekend activities such as fireworks, pumpkin hunts, and dances. The campground also has train rides. At Hills Creek State Park, you can boat and fish in 137-acre Hills Creek Lake. A sand and grass beach is also available for swimming. If you prefer hiking and wild-life watching, take the five miles of trails that run throughout the park. Among the fauna you might see are white-tailed deer, raccoons, skunks, red and gray squirrels, woodchucks, cottontail rabbits, minks, and chipmunks. Birders can be on the lookout for osprey, eagles, herons, warblers, and migratory songbirds.

Campsites, facilities: There are 200 sites for tents or RVs up to 25 feet: 26 have full hookups; 174 have water and electricity. There are 12 pull-throughs. Picnic tables and fire rings are provided. Drinking water, restrooms with flush toilets, a dump station, a laundry, a public phone, groceries, ice, wood, a camp store, a pavilion, two playgrounds, a rec hall, a swimming pool, miniature golf, basketball, batting cages, a Frisbee golf course, and volleyball are available. Some sites are wheelchair accessible. Leashed pets are permitted.

Reservations, fees: Reservations are accepted. The rate is $34.75–44.75 per night for up to four people. Each additional person is $7–10. Weekly, seasonal, and group rates are available. Major credit cards are accepted. Open mid-April through October.

Directions: From the junction of U.S. 15 and U.S. 6, travel 0.5 mile east on U.S. 6, then turn left onto Lambs Creek Road and travel 1.5 miles, then turn left again onto Mann Creek Road and travel one mile to the campground entrance on the left.

Contact: Bucktail Camping Resort, 1029 Mann Creek Road, Mansfield, PA 16933, 570/662-2923, www.bucktailcamping.com.

13 PINE CRADLE LAKE FAMILY CAMPGROUND

Rating: 7

near the Susquehanna River

Located way up north near the New York State border, Pine Cradle Lake Family Campground is a spot ideally suited for rest and relaxation in the relative isolation of Pennsylvania's northern mountains. Try boating (electric motors only) or canoeing on the campground's lake. There is a dock to fish from, or you can rent rowboats and pedal boats. The campground offers a variety of planned activities, and hiking trails all around the property help you get out to see wildflowers or wildlife such as deer, heron, black bear, or coyote. The Susquehanna is nearby for those wishing to paddle and fish the largest American river that empties into the Atlantic.

Campsites, facilities: There are 114 sites for tents or RVs up to 28 feet: 58 have full hookups; 46 have water and electricity; 10 have no hookups. Picnic tables and fire rings are provided. Drinking water, restrooms with flush toilets, a dump station, a portable dump, showers, a laundry, a public phone, groceries, ice, wood, a camp store, a pavilion, a playground, a rec room, a swimming pool, miniature golf, a shuffleboard court, badminton, horseshoes, and volleyball are available. Some sites are wheelchair accessible. Leashed pets are permitted.

Reservations, fees: Reservations are accepted at 800/362-6973. The rate is $20–25 per night for up to four people. Each additional person is $4. Weekly and group rates are available. No pets are permitted. Major credit cards are accepted. Open year-round.

Directions: From the junction of Highway 6 and Highway 187, travel seven miles north on Highway 187 to Rome, then turn left onto a paved road and travel 3.25 miles, and then

1.25 miles on a gravel road. Follow signs to the campground entrance on the left.
Contact: Pine Cradle Lake Family Campground, P.O. Box 113, Rome, PA 18837, 570/247-2424, www.pclake.com.

14 RIVERSIDE ACRES CAMPGROUND

Rating: 8

near the Susquehanna River

Riverside Acres is ideally located for a variety of water-related activities, most notably boating and fishing. With no limits for engine sizes on the nearby Susquehanna River, waterskiing and tubing are possible. The campground rents rowboats and canoes for downriver floats. A variety of wooded and open sites invite campers to enjoy the cool evening breezes that blow up the wide river valley. The nearly full activities calendar at Riverside Acres will keep you busy. Mt. Pisgah State Park is located just down the road in Pennsylvania's Endless Mountains. This 1,302-acre park sits at the base of 2,260-foot-tall Mt. Pisgah. A small lake provides opportunities for boating and fishing for perch, smallmouth and hybrid striped bass, sunfish, bluegill, and catfish. During the winter, ice skating is a popular activity.

Campsites, facilities: There are 41 sites for tents or RVs up to 30 feet: 12 have full hookups; 24 have water and electricity; five have no hookups. Picnic tables and fire rings are provided. Drinking water, restrooms with flush toilets, a dump station, a laundry, a public phone, groceries, ice, wood, grills, a camp store, a pavilion, a playground, and horseshoes are available. Leashed pets are permitted.

Reservations, fees: Reservations are accepted. The rate is $24–26 per night for up to two people. Each additional person is $5. Weekly and monthly rates are available. Open year-round.

Directions: From the junction of U.S. 6 and Highway 187, travel 0.75 mile south on Highway 187, then turn left onto Echo Beach Road and travel 1.5 miles to the campground entrance on the left.
Contact: Riverside Acres Campground, RR 2 Box 211, Towanda, PA 18848, 570/265-3235, www.riversideacres.com.

15 CHERRY SPRINGS STATE PARK

Rating: 8

near Susquehannock State Forest

Cherry Springs State Park gets its name from the large cherry trees that populate the park. This Civilian Conservation Corps park covers only 48 acres of Susquehannock State Forest's 262,000 acres. Hikers and backpackers will want to hop onto Susquehanna Trail. Part of its 85 miles runs nearby and loops through hardwood and hemlock forests into the valleys. Mountain bikers have a 15-mile single-track trail that travels to Denton Hill. Susquehannock State Forest offers more trails for hiking, backpacking, biking, ATV riding, cross-country skiing, and snowmobiling. Horseback riding is allowed on state forest, timber, and pipeline roads. Several streams, such as Cross Fork Creek and Hammersley Fork, offer trout fishing and Kettle Creek has fly-fishing. Among the wildlife you may see are white-tailed deer, black bears, bobcats, raccoons, red and gray squirrels, porcupines, woodchucks, minks, and chipmunks. Birders can spy grouse, eagles, osprey, warblers, herons, red-tailed hawks, and migratory songbirds. Be advised that hunting is allowed seasonally in Susquehannock State Forest.

Campsites, facilities: There are 30 sites for tents or RVs up to 30 feet. No sites have hookups. Picnic tables and fire rings are provided. Drinking water, non-flush toilets, a dump station, wood, grills, and a pavilion are available. Leashed pets are permitted.

Reservations, fees: Reservations are accepted at 888/PA-PARKS (888/727-2757). The rate is $14–19 per night for up to five people; a fee may apply for additional guests. Pets are $2 for up to two pets per night. Senior and Pennsylvania resident discounts are available. Open April through December.

Directions: From Coudersport, travel 12 miles south on Highway 44 to the campground entrance.

Contact: Cherry Springs State Park, c/o Lyman Run, Galeton, PA 16922, 814/435-5010, lymanrunsp@state.pa.us.

16 OLE BULL STATE PARK

Rating: 9

near Cross Fork

The campground is divided into two sections along Kettle Creek. You can choose from sunny or shaded spots. Three trails run through the park, totaling two miles. The 0.75-mile Beaver Dam Nature Trail starts at the concrete fordway and follows Kettle Creek. This trail is easy and flat. You can also hop onto a section of the 85-mile Susquehannock Trail System that passes through the state park. Anglers in your group can fish for brown, brook, and rainbow trout in Kettle Creek. There is also a 150-foot sand swimming beach along its shore. You can participate in environmental and interpretive programs during the summer. These include guided walks, hand-on activities, and campfire talks. Check the park office for a schedule of these changing events. During the winter, cross-country skiing, snowshoeing, and snowmobile riding are favorite activities. Be advised that hunting is allowed seasonally in Ole Bull Sate Park.

Campsites, facilities: There are 45 sites for tents or RVs up to 36 feet; all sites have elec-

tricity. Picnic tables and fire rings are provided. Drinking water, restrooms with flush toilets, a dump station, a public phone, wood, grills, a pavilion, a playground, and a sports field are available. Some sites are wheelchair accessible. No pets are permitted.

Reservations, fees: Reservations are accepted at 888/PA-PARKS (888/727-2757). The rate is $14–19 per night for up to five people. Senior and Pennsylvania resident discounts are available. Open year-round.

Directions: From the junction of U.S. 6 and Highway 144, travel south 20 miles on Highway 144, then follow signs to the campground entrance on the right.

Contact: Ole Bull State Park, HCR 62 Box 9, Cross Fork, PA 17729-9701, 814/435-5000, olebullsp@state.pa.us.

17 TWIN STREAMS CAMPGROUND

Rating: 8

near Leonard Harrison State Park

Twin Streams is located near scenic Leonard Harrison State Park, which overlooks Pennsylvania's Grand Canyon, Pine Creek Gorge. At this scenic park, visitors can hike from overlook to overlook on a series of trails, or take Wild Turkey Trail 1,000 feet down to the stream below. You should pause before starting this trail and note that many who go all the way down lack the energy to make it back to the top. As it follows the scenic stream through the gorge, 42-mile Pine Creek Trail passes among spruce plantations and virgin hemlock. It provides great access for anglers and gives bikers and hikers the opportunity to spot eagles and otters. Back at Twin Streams, visitors have a choice between open or creek-side sites.

Campsites, facilities: There are 135 sites for tents or RVs up to 27 feet: 76 have full hookups; 34 have water and electricity; 25

have no hookups. Picnic tables and fire rings are provided. Drinking water, restrooms with flush toilets, a dump station, showers, a laundry, modem access, a phone hookup, cable TV hookup, groceries, ice, LP gas, wood, a general store, a pavilion, a playground, a rec hall, an arcade, basketball, a shuffleboard court, volleyball, and RV rentals and supplies are available. Some sites are wheelchair accessible. Leashed pets are permitted.

Reservations, fees: Reservations are accepted. The rate is $17–27 per night for up to two people. Each additional person is $5. Group rates are available. Major credit cards are accepted. Open mid-April through mid-December.

Directions: From the junction of Highway 414 and North Highway 287, travel 0.25 mile north on Highway 287 to the campground entrance on the left.

Contact: Twin Streams Campground, 2143 Route 287, Morris, PA 16938, 570/353-7251, www.wellsboropa.com/twinstreams.html.

18 KETTLE CREEK STATE PARK

Rating: 9

near Sproul State Forest

BEST (

This campground is divided into an upper and lower section. Both areas have waterfront sites. The anglers in your group can cast a line into 167-acre Kettle Creek Reservoir, 7-acre Kettle Creek Lake, or any of the numerous streams on property. Among the species inhabiting these waters are brown, brook, and rainbow trout, catfish, yellow perch, black crappie, sucker, bluegill, sunfish, carp, and brown bullhead. The reservoir has a boat launch and moorings, and is a favorite spot for sailboats and sailboards. Electric motor and non-powered boats are welcome. On the northern end of the reservoir is a 250-foot sandy swimming beach.

For land-based pursuits, try horseback riding, hiking, or biking. The equestrian trail loops 22 miles into Sproul State Forest and back. During the winter, sledding, tobogganing, ice fishing, snowmobiling, and cross-country skiing are favorite activities. Be advised that hunting is allowed seasonally in Kettle Creek State Park.

Campsites, facilities: There are 71 sites for tents or RVs up to 36 feet: 50 have electricity; 21 have no hookups. Picnic tables and fire rings are provided. Drinking water, non-flush toilets, a dump station, a public phone, a pavilion, a playground, horseshoes, and a sports field are available. Leashed pets are permitted.

Reservations, fees: Reservations are accepted at 888/PA-PARKS (888/727-2757). The rate is $14–19 per night for up to five people. Pets are $2 for up to two pets per night. Senior and Pennsylvania resident discounts are available. Open April through December.

Directions: From Renovo, travel west six miles on Highway 120 to Westport, then north seven miles on SR 4001. Follow signs to the campground entrance.

Contact: Kettle Creek State Park, 97 Kettle Creek Park Lane, Renovo, PA 17764-9708, 570/923-6004, kettlecreeksp@state.pa.us.

19 HYNER RUN STATE PARK

Rating: 9

in Sproul State Forest

BEST (

Right in the heart of the 276,764-acre Sproul State Forest, Hyner Run State Park offers many outdoor recreational activities. Known for its excellent trout fishing, Hyner Run has native brook trout and stocked brown and brook trout. Flyfishing is welcome in Young Woman's Creek. Backpackers and day hikers can hop onto the 50-mile Donut Hole Trail System at its eastern trailhead here in the park. There is a seven-acre picnicking facility that offers mostly shaded or partially shaded tables and pavilions. Hyner Run's sister park is nearby Hyner View State Park. Here you can hang glide over the West Branch of the Susquehanna River and its beautiful valley. The take-off point for hang-gliding is at the scenic vista. Snowmobiling is a favorite winter activity on the 64-mile Hyner Mountain Snowmobile Trail. Be advised that hunting is allowed seasonally in Hyner Run State Park. Other state parks in the area are Ole Bull, Bald Eagle, Kettle Creek, and Little Pine.

Campsites, facilities: There are 30 sites for tents or RVs up to 30 feet. No sites have hookups. Picnic tables and fire rings are provided. Drinking water, non-flush toilets, a dump station, a public phone, a pavilion, a playground, and a swimming pool are available. Leashed pets are permitted.

Reservations, fees: Reservations are accepted at 888/PA-PARKS (888/727-2757). The rate is $14–19 per night for up to five people. Pets are $2 for up to two pets per night. Senior and Pennsylvania resident discounts are available. Open mid-April through mid-December.

Directions: From Renovo, travel east six miles on Highway 120 to the Hyner Intersection, then turn left and travel north three miles to the campground entrance.

Contact: Hyner Run State Park, P.O. Box 46, Hyner, PA 17738-0046, 570/923-6000, hynerrunsp@state.pa.us.

20 LITTLE PINE STATE PARK

Rating: 9

in Tiadaghton State Forest

You have your choice of shaded and open sites along a stream. Located in the mountainous section of Tiadaghton State Forest, 2,158-acre Little Pine State Park has plenty of recreational opportunities on and off the water. Little Pine Lake has a launch area and mooring spaces for electric motor and non-powered boats. If you don't have your own boat, you can rent paddleboats, canoes, and rowboats from the park's concession. The 94-acre lake has 3.3 miles of shoreline that include a sand and grass swimming beach. There are also 4.2 miles of streams flowing into and out of the lake. Anglers have their choice of warm-water and cold-water fisheries. Among the species you can fish for are smallmouth bass, stocked and native brown, rainbow, and brook trout, catfish, black crappie, sunfish, bluegill, pickerel, and perch. Hikers have 14 miles of trails, and bikers can ride on 42.6-mile Pine Creek Rail Trail. During the winter, cross-country skiing, sledding, tobogganing, ice fishing, and snowmobiling are favorite activities. Be advised that hunting is allowed seasonally in Little Pine State Park.

Campsites, facilities: There are 104 sites for tents or RVs up to 30 feet: 66 have electricity; 38 have no hookups. There are six walk-in sites. Picnic tables and fire rings are provided. Drinking water, restrooms with flush toilets, a dump station, showers, a public phone, a pavilion, a playground, and volleyball are available. No pets are permitted.

Reservations, fees: Reservations are accepted at 888/PA-PARKS (888/727-2757). The rate is $14–19 per night for up to five people; a fee may apply for additional guests. Senior and Pennsylvania resident discounts are available. Open beginning of April through mid-December.

Directions: From the junction of Highway 44 and LR 4001, travel four miles north on LR 4001 to the campground entrance.

Contact: Little Pine State Park, 4205 Little Pine Creek Road, Waterville, PA 17776-9705, 570/753-6000, littlepinesp@state.pa.us.

21 WORLDS END STATE PARK

Rating: 10

near Forksville

BEST (

Loyalsock Creek runs through the valley of Worlds End State Park. Kayakers will love the whitewater, especially during the spring. Open canoes are not allowed on Loyalsock Creek. There is a small dammed swimming area that is unguarded. The creek is a cold water fishery and stocked with trout. The park also has 20 miles of hiking trails most of which are moderate or difficult due to steep and rocky slopes. The most popular is 3.5-mile Canyon Vista Trail. At an elevation of 1,750 feet, it offers a wonderful view into Loyalsock Creek Gorge. At one point this trail parallels Cold Run Road. You can make a shorter loop by hopping onto part of the larger Loyalsock Trail about halfway through. The easiest trail is Double Run Nature Trail, a 1.2-mile loop that runs along the West Branch of Double Run. This cold-water fishery has native trout. During the winter, cross-country skiing and snowmobiling are favorite activities. Be advised that hunting is allowed seasonally in Worlds End State Park.

Campsites, facilities: There are 70 sites for tents or RVs up to 15 feet: 32 have electricity; 38 have no hookups; 1 is a pull-through. No sites have full hookups. Picnic tables and fire rings are provided. Drinking water, restrooms with flush toilets, a dump station, showers, a public phone, a snack bar, a pavilion, and a sports field are available. Some sites are wheelchair accessible. No pets are permitted.

Reservations, fees: Reservations are accepted at 888/PA-PARKS (888/727-2757). The rate is $14–19 per night for up to five people; a fee may apply for additional guests. Senior and Pennsylvania resident discounts are available. Open year-round.

Directions: From Forksville, travel south two miles on Highway 154 to the campground entrance on the right.

Contact: Worlds End State Park, P.O. Box 62, Forksville, PA 18616-0062, 570/924-3287, worldsendsp@state.pa.us.

22 PIONEER CAMPGROUND

Rating: 7

near Worlds End State Park

All of the sites here are wooded and spacious. Among the activities you can enjoy at the campground are hiking and fishing in Lake Mokoma. There are planned activities on weekends such as hayrides and fire truck rides. At nearby Worlds End State Park, you have more outdoor recreational opportunities at your disposal. Loyalsock Creek has a dammed swimming area and also offers fishing and whitewater boating. Hikers have their choice of six trails totaling 20 miles. Most of these are moderate to difficult hikes over rocky and steep areas. Double Run Nature Trail is the easiest. This loop travels 1.2 miles along Double Run. Part of the 60-mile Loyalsock Trail passes through the park, as well. Be advised that hunting is allowed seasonally in Worlds End State Park.

Campsites, facilities: There are 100 sites for tents or RVs up to 31 feet: 70 have water and electricity; 30 have no hookups. Picnic tables and fire rings are provided. Drinking water, restrooms with flush toilets, a dump station, a portable dump, showers, a laundry, modem access, phone hookup, cable TV hookup, a public phone, groceries, ice, LP gas, wood, a camp store, a pavilion, a playground, a rec hall, a swimming pool, badminton, volleyball, and a sports field are available. Some sites are wheelchair accessible. Leashed pets are permitted.

Reservations, fees: Reservations are accepted. The rate is $22–28 per night for up to two people. Each additional person is $5. Weekly rates are available. Major credit cards are accepted. Open mid-April through mid-October.

Directions: From South Laporte, travel two miles south on U.S. 220, then turn right onto a gravel road and travel 0.5 mile to the campground entrance at the end.

Contact: Pioneer Campground, P.O. Box 185, Laporte, PA 18626, 570/946-9971, www.pioneercampground.com.

23 ACORN ACRES CAMPGROUND

Rating: 8

near Ricketts Glen State Park

Acorn Acres is conveniently located near two of Pennsylvania's most scenic state parks, Worlds End and Ricketts Glen. Worlds End is home to spectacular scenery and tremendous views of the S-shaped valley of Loyalsock Creek. It's particularly beautiful in October when fall foliage season is at its peak. Nearby Ricketts Glen is another natural delight and hosts Glens Natural Area, a National Natural Historic Landmark. The Glens, located along the Falls Trail, is a group of wildly cascading waterfalls, 22 in all. The highest is the 94-foot Ganoga Falls. Back at Acorn Acres, wet a line for smallmouth bass, trout, sunfish, catfish, or bluegill in two stocked ponds. On weekends, the campground offers live music, dances, and other planned activities. The spacious, wooded property is crossed by hiking and snowmobile trails and surrounded by hills. Be advised that hunting is allowed seasonally in Worlds End and Ricketts Glen State Parks.

Campsites, facilities: There are 111 sites for tents or RVs up to 30 feet: 57 have full hookups; 37 have water and electricity; 17 have no hookups. Picnic tables and fire rings are provided. Drinking water, restrooms with flush toilets, a dump station, showers, a laundry, a public phone, groceries, ice, wood, a camp store, a restaurant, a pavilion, a playground, a rec room, an arcade, a basketball court, horseshoes, RV rentals and storage are available. Leashed pets are permitted.

Reservations, fees: Reservations are accepted. The rate is $20–26 per night for up to four people. Each additional person is $5. Seasonal and group rates are available. Major credit cards are accepted. Open April through October.

Directions: From the junction of Highway 239 and Highway 487, travel 6.5 miles north on Highway 239, then 0.75 mile east on Highway 118, then turn left onto a gravel road and travel 0.5 mile to the campground entrance on the left.

Contact: Acorn Acres Campground, 1334 State Route 118, Benton, PA 17814, 570/925-2656, www.acornacres.net.

24 RIVERSIDE CAMPGROUND

Rating: 8

near the Susquehanna River

BEST (

Riverside Campground is located right on the banks of the Susquehanna. Access to boating and canoeing is as easy as walking down to Riverside's very own dock. Canoe rentals are available for river trips of varying lengths, making fishing an easy task. Riverside boasts six well-stocked trout streams nearby: Blackhole Creek, Spring Creek, South Creek, Loyalsock Creek, Lycoming Creek, and Muncy Creek. Riverside offers float trips down the Susquehanna. They take you to various points along the river, depending on how long of a float you'd like, and let the current bring you back to the campground. Wildlife spottings are frequent here. Waterfowl, birds of prey, and even black bear have been spotted. The campground also offers planned activities such as covered dish socials and barbecues.

Campsites, facilities: There are 135 sites for tents or RVs up to 30 feet: 98 have full hookups; 30 have water and electricity; seven have no hookups. There are seven pull-throughs. Picnic tables and fire rings are provided. Drinking water, restrooms with flush toilets, a dump station, a portable dump, showers, a laundry, modem access, cable TV hookups, a public phone, a restaurant, ice, LP gas, wood, patios, three pavilions, a rec hall, a swimming pool, miniature golf, horseshoes, volleyball, and RV storage are available. Leashed pets are permitted.

Reservations, fees: Reservations are recommended. The rate is $25–36 per night for up to two people. Each additional person is $5. Weekly, monthly, seasonal, and group rates are available. Open year-round.

Directions: From the junction of U.S. 15 and Highway 54, travel east three miles on Highway 54, then east 0.25 mile on South Main Street to the campground entrance at the end.

Contact: Riverside Campground, 125 South Main Street, Montgomery, PA 17752, 570/547-6289, www.riverside-campground.com.

25 TURNER'S HIGH VIEW CAMPING AREA

Rating: 8

on the Susquehanna River

Turner's High View Camping Area is located midway between Ricketts Glen and Tuscarora State Parks along the banks of the Susquehanna. But campers looking for outdoor recreation should head south to Tuscarora State Park. The scenic picnic area here is a popular fishing spot and day-trip destination for families. At Tuscarora Lake electric motors are permitted, and you can rent rowboats, canoes, and pedal boats from a concession at either park. Swimming is permitted from Memorial Day to Labor Day. Anglers can wet a line for bass, muskie, catfish, yellow perch, and sunfish. Night fishing as well as ice fishing is permitted here. Please note that hunting is permitted seasonally in Tuscarora State Park. Hiking trails take visitors through a variety of habitats, including wetlands, meadows, and deciduous forest, and rangers lead environmental education programs.

Campsites, facilities: There are 92 sites for tents or RVs up to 27 feet: 74 have water and electricity; 18 have no hookups. Picnic tables and fire rings are provided. Drinking water, restrooms with flush toilets, a dump station, a portable dump, showers, a public phone, groceries, ice, wood, a camp store, a pavilion, a playground, and volleyball are available. Leashed pets are permitted.

Reservations, fees: Reservations are accepted. The rate is $20 per night for up to four people. Each additional person is $5. Seasonal rates are available. Open April through November.

Directions: From the junction of I-80 Exit 232/34 and Highway 42, travel one mile north on Highway 42, then 2.25 miles on a paved road. Follow the signs to the campground entrance at the end.

Contact: Turner's High View Camping Area, 119 Turner's High View Road, Bloomsburg, PA 17815, 570/784-6940.

26 SHADY REST CAMPGROUND

Rating: 7

near the Susquehanna River

Located about halfway between Ricketts Glen State Park and the Susquehanna, Shady Rest is ideally suited for explorations of each. Ricketts Glen is more accessible to the casual visitor, and its 22 waterfalls are easily located off of the park's main trail. Most of the waterfalls are located above Waters End, where the two branches of Kitchen Creek combine. Hikers should take caution on the trails, which are rocky and frequently wet. In the winter, cross-country skiers will find the spectacle of frozen falls so amazing that even photos won't do them justice. There are plenty of opportunities for fishing in nearby lakes and streams. Canoeists and kayakers can launch along the banks of the Susquehanna and paddle to one of the many islands downstream for camping or viewing wildlife such as osprey, eagles, otter, deer, or coyote.

Campsites, facilities: There are 100 sites for tents or RVs up to 27 feet: all have water and electricity. Picnic tables and fire rings are provided. Drinking water, restrooms with flush toilets, a dump station, showers, groceries, ice, wood, a camp store, a pavilion, a playground, and volleyball are available. Leashed pets are permitted.

Reservations, fees: Reservations are accepted. The rate is $12–13 per night for up to four people. Seasonal rates are available. Open May through October.

Directions: From the junction of I-80 Exit 232/34 and Highway 42, travel north 6.5 miles on Highway 42, then turn left onto Eyers Grove Road and travel 0.5 mile to the campground entrance on the left.

Contact: Shady Rest Campground, RR 1, Box 335A, Millville, PA 17846, 570/458-6327.

27 MILL RACE GOLF & CAMPING RESORT

🚶 🚴 🏊 ⚓ 🏕 🚐 ⛰

Rating: 7

near Ricketts Glen State Park

Located in scenic Benton, Mill Race is an uncommon mixture of camping and golf. It's a great place to stay if you'd like to chase balls down scenic fairways on a championship 18-hole course. There are plenty of other on-site activities beside golf, a list that includes boating, canoeing, and fishing for rainbow trout in surrounding lakes and streams, and feeding rainbow trout from a wooden bridge. There are plenty of opportunities for hiking and biking nearby, most notably at Ricketts Glen State Park, which has 22 waterfalls. Wildlife abounds in the region, and visitors have many chances to see eagles, deer, and turkey. If you decide to linger around the property there are also plenty of chances to see red and gray squirrels and other small animals.

Campsites, facilities: There are 110 sites for tents or RVs up to 30 feet. All sites have full hookups. Picnic tables and fire rings are provided. Drinking water, restrooms with flush toilets, a dump station, showers, a public phone, a pavilion, a golf course, a driving range, a putting area, a pro shop, and a sports field are available. Leashed pets are permitted.

Reservations, fees: Reservations are accepted at 877/297-0320. The rate is $35 per night for up to four people. Each additional person is $6. Open April through November.

Directions: From the junction of Highway 239 and Highway 487, travel north 0.75 mile on Highway 487 to the campground entrance on the right.

Contact: Mill Race Golf & Camping Resort, 4585 Red Rock Road, Benton, PA 17814, 570/925-2040, www.millracegolf.com.

28 WHISPERING PINES CAMPING ESTATES

🚶 🏊 🏕 ⚓ ♿ 🚐 ⛰

Rating: 7

near Ricketts Glen State Park

Whispering Pines Camping Estates is located in Pennsylvania's scenic Red Rock Mountains amidst rich farm country and rolling hills. Using Whispering Pines as a base camp, visitors can hunt, hike, and fish some of the finest trout streams in the county among picturesque mountains. Whispering Pines has a small pond for fishing and hiking trails on its property. In nearby Ricketts Glen, visitors can visit the National Natural Area's 22 waterfalls. Knoebels pay-as-you-go amusement park is nearby, as is Pine Creek Gorge. As it retreated from advancing glaciers, Pine Creek carved the 1,000-foot canyon. This geologic feature is a must-see for any visitor to the area.

Campsites, facilities: There are 58 sites for tents or RVs up to 35 feet: 42 have full hookups; five have water and electricity; 11 have no hookups. Picnic tables and fire rings are provided. Drinking water, restrooms with flush toilets, a dump station, a laundry, a public phone, wood, a pavilion, a playground, basketball, horseshoes, and a sports field are available. Some sites are wheelchair accessible. Leashed pets are permitted.

Reservations, fees: Reservations are accepted at 877/925-6810. The rate is $18–30 per night for up to four people. Each additional person is $6. Seasonal rates are available. Major credit cards are accepted. Open May through October.

Directions: From the junction of Highway 487 and Highway 239, travel four miles southeast on Highway 239, then one mile south on a paved road to the entrance on the right.

Contact: Whispering Pines Camping Estates, 1557 North Bendertown Road, Stillwater, PA 17878, 570/925-6810, www.wpce.com.

29 BLACK MOSHANNON STATE PARK

Rating: 10

near Philipsburg

BEST (

The 3,394-acre Black Moshannon State Park covers a diversity of ecosystems from forest and lake to wetland and bog. Anglers have their choice of Black Moshannon Creek, Six Mile Run, Black Bear Run, and 250-acre Black Moshannon Lake. The lake welcomes motorboats and non-powered boats, or you can swim from a sand beach. Several gentle hiking trails run through the park. Bog Trail is a wheelchair-accessible, elevated boardwalk that loops 0.5 mile through a wetland area. Other loops include Moss-Hanne, Star Mill, Ski Slope, Shingle Mill, and Sleepy Hollow. Dry Hollow and Snowmobile are the only trails open for biking, but biking is also allowed on state park roads. During the

winter, ice skating, ice fishing, iceboating, cross-country skiing, and snowmobiling are favorite activities. Be advised that hunting is allowed seasonally in Black Moshannon State Park.

Campsites, facilities: There are 80 sites for tents or RVs up to 30 feet: 55 have electricity; 25 have no hookups; 3 are pull-throughs. No sites have full hookups. Picnic tables and fire rings are provided. Drinking water, restrooms with flush toilets, a dump station, a public phone, groceries, ice, wood, a camp store, a pavilion, and a playground are available. Some sites are wheelchair accessible. Leashed pets are permitted.

Reservations, fees: Reservations are accepted at 888/PA-PARKS (888/727-2757). The rate is $14–19 per night for up to five people; a fee may apply for additional guests. Pets are $2 for up to two pets per night. Senior and Pennsylvania resident discounts are available. Open April through end of December.

Directions: From Philipsburg, travel east nine miles on Highway 504 to the park entrance, then north 0.5 mile on Cassanova-Munson Road to the campground entrance on the right.

Contact: Black Moshannon State Park, 4216 Beaver Road, Phillipsburg, PA 16866-9519, 814/342-5960, blackmoshannonsp@state.pa.us.

30 SNOW SHOE PARK

Rating: 9

near Bald Eagle State Park

Snow Shoe Park is located just west of Bald Eagle State Park, a large site with over 5,900 acres of land. At the boundary of two distinct geological provinces, Snow Shoe makes an exceptionally pretty spot to hike or boat. Located within this park are a variety of habitats, including wetlands, riparian, forests, meadows, and grassy fields that are home to woodcocks. The mature hardwood forest provides habitat for turkey and porcupine. Anglers will find crappie, smallmouth and largemouth bass, and other warm-water species in the lake. Swimming is possible from Memorial Day to Labor Day at a 1,200-foot-long guarded beach. Water enthusiasts will enjoy the 1,730-acre lake, which permits boating with no limit on engine size. Please note that seasonal hunting is permitted. Over 11 miles of trails are available for hiking and cross-country skiing. Other winter activities include ice skating, sledding and tobogganing, and ice fishing when the ice on the lake is at least four inches thick.

Campsites, facilities: There are 94 sites for tents or RVs up to 22 feet; all have full hookups. Picnic tables and fire rings are provided. Drinking water, restrooms with flush toilets, a dump station, showers, ice, grills, a pavilion, a playground, a swimming pool, and tennis courts are available. Some sites are wheelchair accessible. Leashed pets are permitted.

Reservations, fees: Reservations are accepted. The rate is $18–24 per night for up to two people. Each additional person is $6. Open mid-April through mid-October.

Directions: From the junction of I-80 Exit 147 and Highway 144, travel 0.5 mile north on Highway 144 to the campground entrance.

Contact: Snow Shoe Park, P.O. Box 231, Snow Shoe, PA 16874, 814/387-6299.

31 FORT BELLEFONTE CAMPGROUND

Rating: 7

near Bald Eagle State Park

Fort Bellefonte Campground is situated near Bald Eagle State Park, 5,900 acres of scenic beauty at the border of two distinct geologic provinces. To the north and the west are the smooth, rolling uplands of the Allegheny Plateau. To the south and east are the long, narrow, parallel ridges of the Ridge and Valley Province. Lakes, forests, streams, wetlands, and fields provide habitat for animals downy woodpeckers, bluebirds, porcupines, turkeys, white-tailed deer, and woodcock. The alkaline lake is a great habitat for smallmouth and largemouth bass, black crappie, and yellow perch, and many animals can be spotted near the shore. Snapping turtles, great blue heron, and bald eagles come for the fish that feast on the aquatic insects, crayfish, and minnows that thrive here. Back at Fort Bellefonte, campers can enjoy planned activities on weekends. A series of hiking trails and terraced sites provide campers with a view of the Bald Eagle Valley.

Campsites, facilities: There are 100 sites for tents or RVs up to 35 feet: 48 have full hookups; 22 have water and electricity; 30 have no hookups. There are 36 pull-throughs. Picnic tables and fire rings are provided. Drinking water, restrooms with flush toilets, a dump station, showers, laundry, modem access, a phone hookup, groceries, ice, wood, a camp store, a pavilion, a playground, a rec hall, miniature golf, two shuffleboard courts, badminton, volleyball, and a sports field are available. Some sites are wheelchair accessible. Leashed pets are permitted.

Reservations, fees: Reservations are accepted at 800/487-9067. The rate is $23–34 per night for up to two people. Each additional person is $5. Open April through November.

Directions: From the junction of I-80 Exit 161/24 and Highway 220, travel one mile north on Highway 220/Jacksonville Road to the campground entrance on the left.

Contact: Fort Bellefonte Campground, 2023 Jacksonville Road, Bellefonte, PA 16823, 814/355-9820.

32 KOA BELLEFONTE/ STATE COLLEGE

Rating: 7

near Bald Eagle State Park

Located near 5,900-acre Bald Eagle State Park, KOA Bellefonte/State College is as close to scenic beauty as it is to Penn State football. The area around this KOA is famous for its alkaline fisheries, and Bald Eagle is a great place to fish for crappie, smallmouth and largemouth bass, and other warm-water species. Fly-fishing is a hit at many nearby streams. On Saturdays, the KOA is a great place to purchase fresh fruit and vegetables. Local Amish families set up a farmers market and sell a variety of goods. Hiking trails are plentiful in the Bald Eagle Mountain area, and the Appalachian Trail is just 10 miles away. The property has a catch-and-release pond and planned activities such as hayrides, movies, pizza on Fridays, ice cream on Saturdays, and pancakes on Sundays. There are bikes available for rent.

Campsites, facilities: There are 163 sites for tents or RVs up to 70 feet: 65 have full hookups; 58 have water and electricity; 40 have no hookups. There are 26 pull-throughs. Picnic tables and fire rings are available. Drinking water, restrooms with flush toilets, a dump station, a portable dump, showers, a laundry, modem access, a phone hookup, cable TV hookup, a public phone, groceries, ice, LP gas, wood, a general store, a snack bar, a pavilion, two playgrounds, a rec hall, a swimming pool, a wading pool, badminton, horseshoes, volleyball, and a sports field are available. Some sites are wheelchair accessible. Leashed pets are permitted.

Reservations, fees: Reservations are accepted at 800/KOA-8127 (800/562-8127). The rate is $22–42 per night for up to two people. Each additional person is $6. Open April through November.

Directions: From the junction of I-80 Exit 161/24 and Highway 26, travel two miles north on Highway 26 to the campground entrance on the left.

Contact: KOA Bellefonte/State College, 2481 Jacksonville Road, Bellefonte, PA 16823, 814/355-7912, www.koa.com/where/pa/38117/index.htm.

33 BALD EAGLE STATE PARK

Rating: 9

near Howard

The state park has six boat launches for the Foster Joseph Sayers Reservoir and Lake. Both motorized and non-powered boats are welcome. You can also fish or swim from the sand beach. For land lovers, there is hiking and biking. All of the trails in the 11-mile network are easy or moderate. The 1.5-mile Butterfly Trail takes you into a butterfly conservation area and past a pond. Skyline Drive Trail travels two miles through hardwood forest to Skyline Drive Road. Lakeside Trail breaks into a 2.9-mile loop and a 5.4-mile loop. The Hunter Run Trails each go two miles in opposite directions. West Trail heads to the West Boat Launch, while East Trail leads to Hunter Run Cove. Biking is welcome on state park roads. During the winter, sledding, tobogganing, ice fishing, ice skating, and cross-country skiing are favorite activities. Be advised that hunting is allowed seasonally in Bald Eagle State Park.

Campsites, facilities: There are 70 sites for tents or RVs up to 35 feet. No sites have hookups. There are three pull-throughs and 35 walk-in sites. Picnic tables and fire rings are provided. Drinking water, non-flush toilets, a dump station, a playground, a snack bar, a marina, and an amphitheater are available. No pets are permitted.

Reservations, fees: Reservations are accepted at 888/PA-PARKS (888/727-2757). The rate is $14–19 per night for up to five people. Senior and Pennsylvania resident discounts are available. Open mid-April through mid-December.

Directions: From the junction of I-80 Exit 158 and Highway 150, travel eight miles north on Highway 150 to Route 26, then turn right and travel 1.5 miles to the campground entrance on the left.

Contact: Bald Eagle State Park, 149 Main Park Road, Howard, PA 16841, 814/625-2775, baldeaglesp@state.pa.us.

34 RUSSELL P. LETTERMAN CAMPGROUND

Rating: 9

in Bald Eagle State Park

Both motor boats and non-powered boats are welcome on the 1,730-acre Foster Joseph Sayers Reservoir and Lake. With Hunter Run West Launch nearby, you have boat access from the campground. Anglers can go warm-water fishing for tiger muskie, smallmouth and largemouth bass, sunfish, channel catfish, bluegill, yellow perch, and black crappie. There is also a 1,200-foot sand and grass swimming beach. The park offers four picnic areas. The park has an 11-mile network of easy to moderate trails. Bikers are welcome on state park roads. The park offers environmental and interpretive programs in the summer, and activities such as campfires and guided walks. Check the park office for a schedule of these changing events. During the winter, ice skating, ice fishing, cross-country skiing, sledding, and tobogganing are favorite activities. Be advised that hunting is allowed seasonally in Bald Eagle State Park.

Campsites, facilities: There are 99 sites for tents or RVs up to 45 feet: 84 have electricity; 15 have no hookups. Picnic tables and fire rings are provided. Drinking water, restrooms with flush toilets, a dump station, showers, a public phone, wood, a pavilion, a playground, horseshoes, two volleyball courts,

a marina, and an amphitheater are available. Some sites are wheelchair accessible. No pets are permitted.

Reservations, fees: Reservations are accepted at 888/PA-PARKS (888/727-2757). The rate is $14–19 per night for up to five people. Senior and Pennsylvania resident discounts are available. Open mid-April through mid-December.

Directions: From the junction of I-80 Exit 158 and Highway 150, travel north nine miles on Highway 150 to the campground entrance on the right.

Contact: Bald Eagle State Park, 149 Main Park Road, Howard, PA 16841, 814/625-2775, baldeaglesp@state.pa.us.

35 HOLIDAY PINES CAMPGROUND

Rating: 8

near McCalls Dam State Park

Holiday Pines has its own hiking trails, and the three state parks nearby also provide plenty of choices for outdoor recreation. McCalls Dam State Park, named after Johnny McCall, the 1850s builder of the original dam, offers picnicking and wildlife watching in the midst of Bald Eagle State Forest. Ravensburg State Park also has picnicking, as well as fishing for brown and brook trout in the cold waters of Rauchtown Run. The one-mile Ravens Trail follows Rauchtown Run. The larger R. B. Winter State Park has fishing and swimming in Halfway Lake. Bikers can use most trails in this park, and roadways in all the state parks. Be advised that hunting is allowed seasonally in R. B. Winter State Park.

Campsites, facilities: There are 85 sites for tents or RVs up to 28 feet: 18 have full hookups; 51 have water and electricity; 16 have no hookups. There are 38 pull-throughs. Picnic tables and fire rings are provided. Drinking water, restrooms with flush toilets, a dump station, a portable dump, showers, a laundry, groceries, ice, LP gas, wood, a general store, a pavilion, a playground, a rec hall, a swimming pool, two shuffleboard courts, badminton, horseshoes, volleyball, and a sports field are available. Some sites are wheelchair accessible. Leashed pets are permitted.

Reservations, fees: Reservations are accepted. The rate is $24–27 per night for up to four people. Each additional person is $5. Seasonal rates are available. Open March through December.

Directions: From the junction of I-80 Exit 185/27 and Highway 477, travel north 0.25 mile on Highway 477, then turn right onto Rockey Road and travel two miles to the campground entrance on the right.

Contact: Holiday Pines Campground, 16 Pine Tree Lane, Loganton, PA 17747, 570/725-2267.

36 RAVENSBURG STATE PARK

Rating: 8

in Tiadaghton State Forest

The 78-acre Ravensburg State Park is in a Nippenose Mountain gorge. Rauchtown Run flows through it and offers great fishing opportunities for native brook and brown trout. The one-mile Raven Trail follows Rauchtown Run and runs the entire length of the park. Other hiking trails are available in the surrounding 215,000-acre Tiadaghton State Forest. Among them is a portion of the 250-mile Mid State Trail. From this trail at the southern end of the park you can see Castle Rocks, the most interesting geologic feature of Ravensburg State Park. These tall spires are remnants of eroded sandstone. Within the Tiadaghton State Forest are other long trails. Pine Creek Trail stretches 62 miles north to Tioga State Forest. Black Forest Trail travels 42 miles along old railroad grades and logging roads. The Loyalsock Trail has 14 of its 59 miles in the state forest. The 27-mile Old Loggers

Path also utilizes old logging roads and railroad grades. Also nearby are Mt. Logan and Rosecrans Bog Natural Areas.

Campsites, facilities: There are 21 sites for tents. No sites have hookups. Picnic tables and fire rings are provided. Non-flush toilets, a public phone, grills, a pavilion, a playground, horseshoes, and a sports field are available. Leashed pets are permitted.

Reservations, fees: Reservations are accepted at 888/PA-PARKS (888/727-2757). The rate is $14–19 per night for up to five people; a fee may apply for additional guests. Pets are $2 for up to two pets per night. Senior and Pennsylvania resident discounts are available. Open mid-April through end of October.

Directions: From the junction of Highway 44 and Highway 880, travel 12 miles south on Highway 44 to the campground entrance on the left.

Contact: Ravensburg State Park, c/o R. B. Winter, Mifflinburg, PA 17844-9656, 570/966-1455, rbwintersp@state.pa.us.

37 R. B. WINTER STATE PARK

Rating: 8

in Bald Eagle State Forest

This 695-acre park is located within the Bald Eagle State Forest, and the campground's sites are all shade by oak and pine. Biking and hiking trails run throughout the park and into the state forest. You can find access points for 25 off-road mountain bike trails. Hikers can traverse seven trails totaling 6.3 miles: Rapid Run, Old Boundary, and Boiling Spring Trails are the easiest; Brush Hollow and Overlook Trails are both rated moderate; the most difficult trails are Bake Oven and West Boundary. A section of the 250-mile Mid State Trail also runs through the park. A sand swimming beach is open from Memorial Day to Labor Day. Anglers can cast for brown, rainbow, or brook trout in stocked streams. Cross-country skiing, ice fishing, and snowmobiling are favorite winter activities. Be advised that hunting is allowed seasonally in R. B. Winter State Park.

Campsites, facilities: There are 59 sites for tents or RVs up to 30 feet: 21 have electricity; 38 have no hookups. There is one pull-through. No sites have full hookups. Picnic tables and fire rings are provided. Drinking water, restrooms with flush toilets, non-flush toilets, a dump station, showers, a public phone, grills, a pavilion, a playground, horseshoes, volleyball, a sports field, and an amphitheater are available. Leashed pets are permitted.

Reservations, fees: Reservations are accepted at 877/PA-PARKS (888/727-2757). The rate is $14–19 per night for up to five people; a fee may apply for additional guests. Pets are $2 for up to two pets per night. Senior and Pennsylvania resident discounts are available. Open mid-April through mid-December.

Directions: From the junction of U.S. 15 and Highway 192, travel 18 miles west on Highway 192 to the campground entrance.

Contact: R. B. Winter State Park, RR 2 Box 314, Mifflinburg, PA 17844-9656, 570/966-1455.

38 HIDDEN VALLEY CAMPING RESORT

Rating: 9

near R. B. Winter State Park

BEST (

The lake in the middle of Hidden Valley offers a nice spot for fishing and boating. You can rent pedal boats from the campground. With its proximity to R. B. Winter State Park and the Susquehanna River, there are plenty of other outdoor recreational activities to try. Several hiking and biking trails run throughout the state park. Hikers

can choose from among easy, moderate, and difficult trails. Mountain bikers can also make use of state park roadways. The park also has large picnicking facilities. Hidden Valley has hiking trails of its own and planned activities on weekends like horse-drawn hayrides, fireworks, live music, and pony rides.

Campsites, facilities: There are 395 sites for tents or RVs up to 26 feet: 150 have full hookups; 225 have water and electricity; 20 have no hookups. There are 40 pull-throughs. Picnic tables, restrooms with flush toilets, a dump station, a portable dump, showers, a laundry, modem access, a phone hookup, cable TV hookups, a public phone, groceries, ice, LP gas, wood, a general store, a pavilion, a playground, a rec hall, an arcade, a swimming pool, miniature golf, basketball, two shuffleboard courts, badminton, a sand volleyball court, a sports field, a petting farm, and RV storage and supplies are available. Some sites are wheelchair accessible. Leashed pets are permitted.

Reservations, fees: Reservations are accepted. The rate is $24–32 per night for up to two people. Each additional person is $3. Group rates are available. Major credit cards are accepted. Open mid-April through mid-October.

Directions: From the junction of U.S. 15 and Highway 192, travel nine miles west on Highway 192 to the entrance on the left.

Contact: Hidden Valley Camping Resort, 162 Hidden Valley Lane, Mifflinburg, PA 17844, 570/966-1330, hvcamp@ptd.net.

39 NITTANY MOUNTAIN CAMPGROUND

Rating: 8

near Milton State Park

Located in the heart of Pennsylvania's mountains amidst a variety of state parks and other recreational opportunities, Nittany Mountain is a family-friendly site with plenty to keep kids busy. Families can fish in a pond on the property, or participate in a variety of planned activities like ceramics, bingo, and hayrides. Short hiking trails give campers a chance to stretch their legs and see some wildlife or wildflowers. Nittany Mountain's proximity to the Susquehanna River makes it easy to get wet or drop a line in the wide, slow river. Paddlers will like being able to have easy access to put-ins and take-outs that make trips of any length available.

Campsites, facilities: There are 347 sites for tents or RVs up to 35 feet: 30 have full hookups; 310 have water and electricity; seven have no hookups; 30 are pull-throughs. Picnic tables and fire rings are provided. Drinking water, restrooms with flush toilets, a dump station, a portable dump, showers, a laundry, modem access, a phone hookup, cable TV hookup, a public phone, groceries, ice, LP gas, wood, a camp store, a pavilion, a playground, a rec hall, an arcade, a swimming pool, a wading pool, miniature golf, basketball, two shuffleboard courts, volleyball, a sports field, and RV rentals, storage, and supplies are available. Some sites are wheelchair accessible. Leashed pets are permitted.

Reservations, fees: Reservations are accepted. The rate is $24–35 per night for up to two people. Each additional person is $5. Pets are $1 per pet per night. Weekly and monthly rates are available. Major credit cards are accepted. Open year-round.

Directions: From the junction of I-80 Exit 210A/30A and U.S. 15, travel 0.25 mile south on U.S. 15, then turn right onto New Columbia Road and travel 4.25 miles, then turn right onto Miller's Bottom Road and travel 0.25 mile to the campground entrance on the right.

Contact: Nittany Mountain Campground, 2751 Millers Bottom Road, New Columbia, PA 17856, 570/568-5541, www.fun-camping.com.

40 SHANGRI-LA ON THE CREEK

Rating: 10

near Shikellamy State Park

BEST (

Shangri-La is located along the Chillisquaque Creek at the foot of Montour Ridge. You have your choice of wooded, partially shaded, and creekside sites. There are two catch-and-release ponds for fishing, as well as hiking and biking trails. If you don't have your own equipment for these activities, you can rent fishing poles, bikes, and helmets. The campground has planned activities on weekends like bingo, dances, and ceramics classes. For more outdoor recreational activities, visit nearby Shikellamy State Park and the Susquehanna River for boating, fishing, and hiking.

Campsites, facilities: There are 167 sites for tents or RVs up to 30 feet: 60 have full hookups; 90 have water and electricity; 17 have no hookups. There are 35 pull-throughs. Picnic tables and fire rings are provided. Drinking water, restrooms with flush toilets, a dump station, a portable dump, a laundry, cable TV hookups, Internet access, a public phone, groceries, ice, LP gas, wood, fishing supplies, a general store, a snack bar, grills, a pavilion, an equipped pavilion, a playground, a rec room, an arcade, a swimming pool, a wading pool, badminton, horseshoes, basketball, volleyball, a sports field, Frisbee golf, and RV storage and supplies are available. Some sites are wheelchair accessible. Leashed pets are permitted.

Reservations, fees: Reservations are recommended at 800/445-6660. The rate is $27–39 per night for up to two people. Each additional person is $3. Weekly and monthly rates are available. Major credit cards are accepted. Open year-round.

Directions: From the junction of I-80 Exit 212A/31A and Highway 147, travel eight miles south on Highway 147, then 0.25 mile northwest on Highway 405, then 0.75 mile east on Hidden Paradise Road to the campground entrance at the end.

Contact: Shangri-La on the Creek, 670 Hidden Paradise Road, Milton, PA 17847, 570/524-4561, www.slcreek.com.

41 PENN AVON CAMPGROUND

🚶 🚴 🛶 🚐 🎣 🏇 ♿ 🚍 ⛺

Rating: 7

near Shikellamy State Park

The campground offers stream fishing and canoeing. Lake August, at nearby Shikellamy State Park also offers opportunities for fishing and canoeing. The lake is a portion of the Susquehanna River that was created by the world's largest inflatable dam. You can cast for walleye, muskie, largemouth and small-mouth bass, black crappie, northern pike, and catfish or launch a boat from the marina. Unlimited horsepower and non-powered boats are welcome. There are also courtesy docks at the marina. If you don't have your own, you can rent a boat. The park also has picnic and pavilion areas, and trails for biking and hiking. A one-mile nature trail leads to Shikellamy Overlook, 360 feet above the river, and bikers and hikers alike can enjoy a one-mile paved trail that encircles the marina. Bike rentals are available at the marina.

Campsites, facilities: There are 48 sites for tents or RVs up to 30 feet: 32 have full hookups; four have water and electricity; 12 have no hookups. Picnic tables and fire rings are provided. Drinking water, restrooms with flush toilets, a dump station, showers, modem access, a phone hookup, cable TV hookups, ice, wood, a pavilion, a playground, badminton, volleyball, and a sports field are available. Some sites are wheelchair accessible. Leashed pets are permitted.

Reservations, fees: Reservations are accepted. The rate is $20–24 per night for up to four people. Each additional person is $5. Seasonal and group rates are available. Open April through October.

Directions: From the junction of U.S. 522 and Highway 204, travel 1.5 miles north on Highway 204 to the campground entrance on the right.

Contact: Penn Avon Campground, RR 1 Box 366D, Selinsgrove, PA 17870, 570/374-9468, pennavon@ptdprolog.net.

42 POE PADDY STATE PARK

🚶 🏊 🛶 🚐 ❄ 🏇 🚍 ⛺

Rating: 8

in Bald Eagle State Forest

BEST (

In the middle of the Bald Eagle State Forest, Poe Paddy has wonderful wildlife-viewing opportunities. Among the animals you may spot are white-tailed deer, woodchucks, red and gray squirrels, raccoons, porcupines, minks, bobcats, and chipmunks. Penn's Creek flows right by the campground, so anglers can cast their lines for brook and brown trout before breakfast. During the winter, snowmobiling is a favorite activity. Hikers can walk part of the Mid State Trail as it passes through the park. This section, leftover from the area's heyday in lumbering, leads to the Paddy Mountain Railroad Tunnel. Poe Paddy's sister park, Poe Valley, offers additional recreational activities. On 25-acre Poe Lake, you can boat and fish for catfish, pickerel, rainbow and brown trout, sunfish, and perch. A sand beach offers swimming from shore. There are three miles of hiking trails. During the winter, you can cross-country ski, ice fish, ice skate, and snowmobile. Be advised that hunting is allowed seasonally in Poe Valley State Park.

Campsites, facilities: There are 41 sites for tents or RVs up to 30 feet. No sites have hookups. There are two walk-in sites. Picnic tables and fire rings are provided. Drinking water, non-flush toilets, a dump station, a public phone, and a pavilion are available. Leashed pets are permitted.

Reservations, fees: Reservations are accepted at 888/PA-PARKS (888/727-2757). The rate is $14–19 per night for up to five people; a fee may apply for additional guests. Pets are $2 for up to two pets per night. Senior and Pennsylvania resident discounts are available. Open mid-April through mid-December.

Directions: From Potters Mills, travel south 1.5 miles on U.S. 322 to Sand Mountain Road (unpaved), then 10 miles to the park, and finally 3.5 miles on paved and unpaved roads to the campground entrance.

Contact: Poe Paddy State Park, c/o Reeds Gap, Milroy, PA 17063-9735, 717/667-3622, reedsgapsp@state.pa.us.

43 PENN'S CREEK CAMPGROUND

Rating: 6

near R. B. Winter State Park

You can fish or canoe on the campground's namesake, Penn's Creek, or take advantage of the property's hiking trails. At nearby R. B. Winter State Park, you can cast a line in Halfway Lake. This cold-water fishery is stocked with brown, brook, and rainbow trout. There is a 300-foot white-sand swimming beach along the shore. The state park is a mountain biker's haven; there are 25 biking trails to choose from, totaling 48 miles. There are also 100 miles of interconnecting state park roadways. Among the wildlife you may spot within the area are white-tailed deer, red and gray squirrels, raccoons, woodchucks, porcupines, mink, skunks, and chipmunks. Birders can view osprey, eagles, red-tailed hawks, woodpeckers, vireos, warblers, Canada geese, teal and mallard ducks, and migratory songbirds. You can participate in environmental and interpretive programs such as campfires and guided nature walks. Check the park office for these changing events. Be advised that hunting is allowed seasonally in R. B. Winter State Park.

Campsites, facilities: There are 87 sites for tents or RVs up to 29 feet: 65 have full hookups; 12 have water and electricity; 10 have no hookups. There are 10 pull-throughs. Picnic tables and fire rings are provided. Drinking water, restrooms with flush toilets, a dump station, showers, ice, wood, a pavilion, a playground, volleyball, and a sports field are available. Leashed pets are permitted.

Reservations, fees: Reservations are accepted. The rate is $20–25 per night for up to four people. Each additional person is $5. Seasonal rates are available. Open mid-April through mid-October.

Directions: From the junction of Highway 45 and Highway 235, travel three miles south on Highway 235, then turn right onto Creek Road and travel 2.75 miles to the campground entrance on the right.

Contact: Penn's Creek Campground, RR1, Millmont, PA 17845, 570/922-1371.

44 SEVEN MOUNTAINS CAMPGROUND

Rating: 7

near Poe Valley State Park

This campground, which offers shaded and open sites, is conveniently situated near two natural points of interest. Poe Valley State Park is a good place for fishing and boating with electric motors or non-powered boats. A 25-acre lake is surrounded by 620 acres of state park and 198,000 acres of the Bald Eagle State Forest. Nearby is Bear Meadows Natural Area, an 890-acre bog left over from the last ice age that is home to plants typical to areas much further north. Black spruce and balsam fir are the dominant species of trees here, rather than the hemlock and white pine found dominating nearby. Rare orchids and carnivorous pitcher and sundew plants are found in this unique environment. Birders will enjoy the observation platform and may glimpse red-tailed hawks, ospreys, egrets, herons, vireos, or warblers. Hikers will have plenty to explore along the trails.

Campsites, facilities: There are 70 sites for tents or RVs up to 22 feet: 28 have full hook-ups; 42 have water and electricity. There are four pull-throughs. Picnic tables and fire rings are provided. Drinking water, restrooms with flush toilets, a dump station, a portable dump, showers, a laundry, modem access, cable TV hookup, a public phone, wood, a pavilion, and horseshoes are available. Leashed pets are permitted.

Reservations, fees: Reservations are accepted at 888/468-2556. The rate is $14–22 per night for up to two people. Each additional person is $4. Weekly, monthly, and seasonal rates and senior discounts are available. Open April through mid-December.

Directions: From the junction of Highway 144 and U.S. 322, travel east 2.5 miles on U.S. 322 to the campground entrance on the right.

Contact: Seven Mountains Campground, 101 Seven Mountains Campground Road, Spring Mills, PA 16875, 814/364-1910, www.geoci-ties.com/sevenmountainscampground.

45 LITTLE MEXICO CAMPGROUND

🥾 🚴 🏊 🛶 🚤 🐴 🎣 🚐 ⛺

Rating: 7

near Shikellamy State Park

Anglers have three fishing ponds available to them, as well as Penns Creek, which runs through the campground property. Among the species to cast for are bass, pickerel, carp, catfish, perch, and bluegill. The campground has planned activities on weekends, such as candy bar bingo, mini carnivals, and ice cream socials. At nearby Shikellamy State Park, you can fish in 3,060-acre Lake August or go boating on a section of the Susquehanna River. Hikers and bikers can use a one-mile

paved trail that encircles the Shikellamy Marina. Another one-mile nature trail leads to Shikellamy Overlook and is open only to foot traffic.

Campsites, facilities: There are 264 sites for tents or RVs up to 26 feet: 30 have full hook-ups; 234 have water and electricity. There are 20 pull-throughs. Picnic tables and fire rings are provided. Drinking water, restrooms with flush toilets, a dump station, a protable dump, showers, a laundry, cable TV hookups, a public phone, groceries, ice, LP gas, wood, a general store, a pavilion, a playground, a rec hall, a swimming pool, miniature golf, horseshoes, and a sports field are available. Leashed pets are permitted.

Reservations, fees: Reservations are accepted. The rate is $25–28 per night for up to four people. Each additional person is $4. Weekly, monthly, and seasonal rates are available. Senior and military discounts are available. Major credit cards are accepted. Open mid-April through mid-October.

Directions: From the junction of Highway 45 and U.S. 15, travel south four miles on U.S. 15, then west six miles on Highway 304, then turn left onto Little Mexico Road and travel one mile to the campground entrance on the left.

Contact: Little Mexico Campground, RR1 Box 188 Little Mexico Road, Winfield, PA 17889, 570/374-9742, www.littlemexico.net.

46 RIVER EDGE RV CAMP & MARINA

🥾 🏊 🚤 🐴 🎣 ♿ 🚐 ⛺

Rating: 8

near the Susquehanna River

On the West Branch of the Susquehanna lies River Edge RV Camp and Marina, a great place for water-related activities. River fishing for bass, muskie, catfish, and other warm-water species is as easy as strolling down to one of the camp's floating docks or riverbank from a shaded or open site. Kayaks and canoes rented onsite can be launched from the camp's ramp. On weekends, stay close to River Edge for a variety of planned activities such as hayrides and bingo. Shikellamy State Park is just a few river miles away. Hiking trails lead to a dramatic overlook of the park's main island, located between two branches of the Susquehanna.

Campsites, facilities: There are 140 sites for tents or RVs up to 70 feet two have full hookups; 124 have water and electricity; seven have electricity; seven have no hookups. There are eight pull-throughs. Picnic tables and fire rings are provided. Drinking water, restrooms with flush toilets, a dump station, a portable dump, showers, a laundry, modem access, a phone hookup, a public phone, groceries, ice, LP gas, wood, fishing supplies, a general store, a library, a pavilion, a playground, a rec hall, an arcade, basketball, a shuffleboard court, badminton, horseshoes, volleyball, a sports field, and RV rentals, storage, and supplies are available. Some sites are wheelchair accessible. Leashed pets are permitted.

Reservations, fees: Reservations are accepted. The rate is $22–30 per night for up to two people. Each additional person is $5. Weekly, monthly, and group rates are available. Major credit cards are accepted. Open April through October.

Directions: From the junction of Highway 45 and U.S. 15, travel four miles south on U.S. 15, then one mile on a paved road. Follow signs to the entrance at the end.

Contact: River Edge RV Camp & Marina, 443 River Edge Lane, Winfield, PA 17889, 570/524-0453, www.riveredgervcamp.com.

47 YOGI-ON-THE-RIVER

🚶 🚲 🏊 🛶 ⛵ 🏕️ 🐕 ♿ 🚐 ⛺

Rating: 8

on the Susquehanna River

BEST (

This campground is all about water sports. With a ramp and dock on the property, you can go boating or canoeing. If you don't have your own, the campground rents rowboats, canoes, and pedal boats. Anglers will enjoy the lake and stream fishing for bass, trout, perch, sunfish, bluegill, and catfish. Adults and kids alike will love the bumper boats. If you prefer to stay dry, walk the trails or rent a bike or golf cart to explore the grounds. You have your choice of wooded, open, and creekside sites. There are also planned activities like bingo and ceramics. Yogi-on-the-River borders the Susquehanna and is near Shikellamy State Park.

Campsites, facilities: There are 180 sites for tents or RVs up to 26 feet: 170 have full hookups; 10 have water and electricity. There are 60 pull-throughs. Picnic tables and fire rings are provided. Drinking water, restrooms with flush toilets, a dump station, a portable dump, showers, a laundry, modem access, a public phone, groceries, ice, LP gas, wood, a general store, a pavilion, an equipped pavilion, a playground, a rec hall, a swimming pool, miniature golf, badminton, basketball, volleyball, a sports field, and an outdoor movie theater are available. Some sites are wheelchair accessible. Leashed pets are permitted.

Reservations, fees: Reservations are accepted at 800/496-4320. The rate is $31–43 per night for up to two people. Each additional person is $5. Major credit cards are accepted. Open mid-April through mid-October.

Directions: From the junction of I-80 Exit 224/33 and Highway 54, travel two miles on Highway 54, then 7.5 miles south on U.S. 11, then turn left onto a paved road and travel 0.25 mile to the campground entrance at the end.

Contact: Yogi-on-the-River, RR 1 Box 116, Northumberland, PA 17857, 570/473-8021, www.riverandfun.com.

48 FANTASY ISLAND CAMPGROUND

🚶 🏊 🛶 🚐 🏕️ 🐕 ♿

Rating: 7

near the Susquehanna River

With its proximity to the Susquehanna River,

the campground offers boating, canoeing, a dock, and fishing. Among the species you can cast for are walleye, smallmouth and largemouth bass, muskie, white and black crappie, sunfish, carp, catfish, suckers, and bluegill. There are several popular spots for fly-fishing. You can also motorboat, canoe, kayak, and windsurf on the river. Swimming areas are located along part of the shoreline. While hiking in nearby woods and along the shore, you may spot white-tailed deer, raccoons, beaver, otters, skunks, woodchucks, muskrats, red and gray squirrels, coyotes, chipmunks, or fox. Among the birdlife present are gadwall, teal, and mallard ducks, ringnecks, herons, egrets, scaup, flycatchers, warblers, thrushes, vireos, orioles, tanagers, tree swallows, gulls, Canada geese, and cormorants. Fantasy Island Campground also has planned activities like bingo and ice cream socials.

Campsites, facilities: There are 98 sites for RVs up to 30 feet; all have water and electricity. There are 10 pull-throughs. Picnic tables and fire rings are provided. Drinking water, restrooms with flush toilets, a dump station, a portable dump, a laundry, ice, LP gas, wood, patios, a playground, a rec hall, a shuffleboard court, badminton, volleyball, and a sports field are available. Leashed pets are permitted.

Reservations, fees: Reservations are accepted. The rate is $23–30 per night for up to two people. Each additional person is $4. Weekly and seasonal rates are available. Open mid-April through mid-October.

Directions: From the junction of U.S. 11 and Highway 147, travel 0.25 mile south on Highway 147, then turn left onto Park Drive and travel 100 yards to the campground entrance on the left.

Contact: Fantasy Island Campground, 401 Park Drive, Sunbury, PA 17801, 866/882-1307, www.fantasyislandcampground.com.

49 INDIAN HEAD CAMPGROUND

Rating: 8

near the Susquehanna River

Indian Head Campground is located along its very own stretch of the Susquehanna River, allowing campers ample opportunities for boating, canoeing, and river and creek fishing for muskie, catfish, bass, and a variety of other fish. There's a boat ramp and plenty of hiking trails on the shaded, level property. Grassy sites encourage campers to gather on their way to the planned bike trail utilizing old railroad grades. Indian Head is within walking distance of the Bloomsburg Fairgrounds, home of the Bloomsburg Fair held each September. Knoebels and Ricketts Glen are also nearby.

Campsites, facilities: There are 229 sites for tents or RVs up to 70 feet: 24 have full hookups; 163 have water and electricity; 42 have no hookups. There are 62 pull-throughs. Picnic tables and fire rings are provided. Drinking water, restrooms with flush toilets, a dump station, a portable dump, showers, modem access, a phone hookup, a public phone, groceries, ice, wood, fishing supplies, a camp store, a pavilion, a playground, an arcade, a rec hall, basketball, volleyball, a sports field, and RV storage and supplies are available. Some sites are wheelchair accessible. Leashed pets are permitted.

Reservations, fees: Reservations are accepted. The rate is $25–31 per night for up to two people. Each additional person is $5. Seasonal and group rates are available. Major credit cards are accepted. Open May through November.

Directions: From the junction of I-80 Exit 232/34 and Highway 42, travel south three miles on Highway 42, then turn left onto a paved road and travel 0.5 mile to the campground entrance on the left.

Contact: Indian Head Campground, 340 Reading Street, Bloomsburg, PA 17815,

570/784-6150, www.indianheadcamp-ground.com.

50 J & D CAMPGROUND

🚶 🚵 ⛱ 🛶 🚐 ❄ 🐕 🎠 ♿ 🚙

Rating: 7

near the Susquehanna River

Located near Locust Lake State Park and Tuscarora State Park, J & D Campground is well-situated for campers desiring a chance to stretch their legs. At Tuscarora, there are plenty of trails through a variety of environments to keep hikers busy. Crow Trail passes through deciduous forest, a plantation of larch and pine, and grassy meadows. Edge Trail is a grass-covered trail that leads to the park office. Hill Trail is the most direct path to the beach. Other activities at these nearby state parks include boating (electric motors only), fishing, boat rental, hunting, swimming, biking, and winter activities such as skating and ice fishing. J & D has a pond for fishing located on the property. Among the waterfowl you may see are egrets, herons, eagles, teal and mallard ducks, and Canada geese.

Campsites, facilities: There are 250 sites for RVs up to 31 feet: 240 have full hookups; 10 have water and electricity. Picnic tables and fire rings are provided. Drinking water, restrooms with flush toilets, a dump station, a portable dump, showers, cable TV hookups, a public phone, ice, LP gas, wood, a pavilion, a playground, a rec hall, a swimming pool, miniature golf, a basketball court, two shuffleboard courts, volleyball, a sports field, and RV storage are available. No tents can be accommodated. Some sites are wheelchair accessible. Leashed pets are permitted.

Reservations, fees: Reservations are accepted. The rate is $29–33 per night for up to five people. Each additional person is $6. Seasonal and group rates are available. Major credit cards are accepted. Open May through October.

Directions: From the junction of Highway 42 north and Highway 487, travel five miles south on Highway 487 to the campground entrance on the right.

Contact: J & D Campground, 973 Southern Drive, Catawissa, PA 17820, 570/356-770, jdcampground@aol.com.

51 KNOEBELS AMUSEMENT RESORT AND CAMPGROUND

🚶 ⛱ 🛶 🚐 ❄ 🐕 🎠 ♿ 🚙 ⛰

Rating: 7

near the Susquehanna River

BEST (

Knoebels Amusement Resort and Campground is a destination for families with kids that need perpetual excitement. The massive property, nestled in pines and hemlocks, is famous for an amusement park that draws the crowds. The free-entry park boasts two world-class roller coasters and a multitude of other family and kiddie rides. A 750,000-gallon pool with four waterslides, open from Memorial Day to Labor Day, is also on the property. The campground has its own pool, as well as a beautiful lake for catch-and-release fishing, all situated on 160 wooded acres. Many visitors come to the area to view the scenic covered bridges, 24 in all. Visitors seeking a natural retreat flock to Ricketts Glen, a scenic area composed of 13,050 acres, for hiking to beautiful waterfalls, boating, hunting, fishing, swimming, cross-country and downhill skiing, ice fishing, and snowmobile trails.

Campsites, facilities: There are 500 sites for tents or RVs up to 25 feet: 475 have electricity; 25 have no hookups. Picnic tables and fire rings are provided. Drinking water, restrooms with flush toilets, a dump station, showers, a public phone, groceries, ice, wood, a camp store, a pavilion, a playground, a rec hall, two swimming pools, miniature golf, volleyball, and an amusement park are available. Some sites are wheelchair accessible. Leashed pets are permitted.

Reservations, fees: Reservations are accepted at 800/487-4386. The rate is $32–34 per night for up to four people. Weekly rates are available. Major credit cards are accepted. Open mid-April through mid-October.

Directions: From the junction of Highway 487 and Highway 54, travel north two miles on Highway 487, then turn right onto a paved road and travel for 0.5 mile to the campground entrance on the right.

Contact: Knoebels Amusement Resort and Campground, P.O. Box 487, Elysburg, PA 17824, 570/672-9555, www.knoebels.com.

52 LAKE GLORY CAMPGROUND

🧗 🏊 🛶 🚤 ❄️ 🐕 ♿ 🚐 ⛺

Rating: 9

near the Susquehanna River

Lake Glory Campground is part of the Knoebels Amusement Park property, and provides accessibility for campers wishing to ride roller coasters or soak in a 750,000-gallon pool. The site's 160 acres provide access to stream fishing and a scenic pond, but many visitors will want to check out the attractions; Knoebels boasts two world-class roller coasters, family rides, and kiddie rides, all on a pay-as-you-go basis. Admission to the park is free, but taking a spin on the merry-go-round will cost you. The massive pool has four waterslides and a large sunning area, all just a short distance from Lake Glory. Hikers will want to head to nearby Ricketts Glen, a Natural Area with waterfalls cascading from all angles. After a heavy rain the park is especially beautiful. The park is littered with hiking trails, which become cross-country trails in the winter when the frozen falls slumber. Fishing and boating are activities that can be found in the park's lake.

Campsites, facilities: There are 210 sites for tents or RVs up to 60 feet: 52 are full hookups; 66 have water and electricity; 60 have no hookups; 32 are tents only. Picnic tables and fire rings are provided. Drinking water, restrooms with flush toilets, a dump station, showers, a public phone, groceries, ice, wood, a camp store, a pavilion, a playground, a rec hall, two swimming pools, miniature golf, volleyball, and an amusement park are available. Some sites are wheelchair accessible. Leashed pets are permitted.

Reservations, fees: Reservations are accepted at 800/487-4386. The rate is $30–34 per night for up to two people. Weekly rates are available. Major credit cards are accepted. Open mid-April through mid-October.

Directions: From the junction of Highway 487 and Highway 54, travel north two miles on Highway 487, then turn right onto a paved road and travel for 0.5 mile to the campground entrance on the right.

Contact: Lake Glory Campground, 96 Eisenhower Road, Catawissa, PA 17820, 570/356-7392, www.knoebels.com.

NORTHEAST

© JASON MILLER

BEST CAMPGROUNDS

◖ Best for Leisure Hiking
Lackawanna State Park, **page 118**.
Keen Lake Camping & Cottage Resort, **page 119**.
Lower Lake Campground, **page 128**.
Foxwood Family Campground, **page 138**.
Blue Ridge Campground, **page 140**.

◖ Best for Mountain Hiking
Frances Slocum State Park, **page 125**.
Tobyhanna State Park, **page 130**.
Hickory Run State Park, **page 134**.

◖ Best Historic-Area Campgrounds
Sunrise Lake Family Campground, **page 117**.

◖ Best Swimming Beaches
Ricketts Glen State Park, **page 124**.
Pickerel Point Campground, **page 127**.
Otter Lake Camp Resort, **page 136**.

◖ Most Pet-Friendly
The Pines Campground, **page 126**.
81-80 RV Park & Campground, **page 132**.

◖ Most Scenic
Lake Moc A Tek Campground, **page 124**.
Mount Pocono Campground, **page 131**.

The northeast corner of Pennsylvania is one of the

most-visited parts of the state – not necessarily because it's the most scenic or has the most activities, but because it's within easy reach of New York City and other major population centers. Millions of people reside within 90 miles of this part of Pennsylvania, and they come here in droves to hike, bike, ski, raft, and fish. With numbers like these, you're bound to rub elbows. But given the abundance of campgrounds near the interstates and the state parks and forests, you'll be surprised how isolated this beautiful area can feel at times. There are still isolated views, secluded groves, and secret spots for those willing to hike or bike even a few miles. With 18 state parks and the Delaware Water Gap National Recreation Area in this region, finding room to stretch isn't too difficult.

Lehigh Gorge is a popular camping destination. The Lehigh's Class III rapids have introduced many a paddler to whitewater, and many visitors get their first glimpses of the deep gorge, cascading waterfalls, and rock outcrops from the comfort of an inflated raft. Lehigh Gorge Trail is a 26-mile stretch of abandoned railroad grade. As it follows the Lehigh, it provides anglers with stream access and gives hikers, bikers, and photographers the opportunity to view streamside wildlife and vistas.

Hickory Run State Park, in the western foothills of the Poconos, has 43 miles of rhododendron-lined trails, some that are open to cross-country skiing and snowmobiling. The 15,500-acre park is known for its boulder field area, a geological oddity left over from the last ice age.

Beltzville State Park's 949-acre lake is a great place to water-ski, jet ski, or just watch all of the action from a pontoon boat. At the lake's edge, beachcombers can find fossils of trilobites, clams, brachiopods, crinoids, coral, bryozoans, and snails. Hiking trails lead through creek valleys to an old gristmill raceway, dam and gateways, and a Colonial-era slate quarry.

If big views are your thing, then Big Pocono State Park is a must-see. From Camelback Mountain views include a large portion of Pennsylvania, and parts of New York and New Jersey. Seven miles of trails on the rugged terrain include a scenic loop around the mountain that provides nearly 360-degree views. In the winter, Camelback transforms into one of the best snow parks in the Poconos, with 33 trails, two terrain parks, and a half-pipe.

Promised Land State Park, one of Pennsylvania's oldest, lies in Delaware State Forest. The 12,464-acre park rests on the Pocono Plateau at an elevation of 1,800 feet. More than 50 miles of hiking trails wind through beech, oak, maple, and hemlock forest. Small streams, waterfalls, two glacial lakes, laurel and rhododendron blooms, and fall foliage add to the scenery.

Delaware State Forest contains six other areas of geological, scenic, or ecological interest. Little Mud Swamp Natural Area is a glacial bog with plants typically found much further north. Pine Lake Natural Area, another bog, has habitats that range from open water to woods. Mixed oaks surround the high mountain swamp at Buckhorn Natural Area. Nearby Pennel Run Natural Area sits amidst a mixture of scrub and other mixed oaks, gray birch, and aspen. Stillwater Natural Area, home to Union deserters during the Civil War, is popular for canoeing. Last is 2,845-acre Bruce Lake Natural Area, home to a spring-fed glacial lake.

Delaware State Forest is a natural boundary to the Delaware Water Gap National Recreation Area and Upper Delaware Scenic and Recreational River. On its long route to the sea, this 73-mile section of pristine mountain stream passes thick vegetation, waterfalls plunging over rocky cliffs, and the world's oldest existing suspension bridge. The National Recreation Area begins where the Delaware passes through the Appalachian Mountains. Visitors come to canoe, hike, bike, swim, ski, and ride horses past waterfalls, geologic formations, and rural scenery. Northbound Appalachian Trail through-hikers arrive at Totts Gap before climbing Mount Minsi and crossing the Delaware next to I-80. This rocky section is notorious for shredding boots and making hikers wonder if they have what it takes to make it to Maine.

Though this part of the state is popular with people fleeing the urban jungle, visitors should take comfort in the fact that finding a patch of forest to call their own is as easy hiking another half-mile or staying a little longer.

NORTHEAST

❶ EAST LAKE CAMPGROUND

🏃 🏊 ⛵ 🎣 🏕️ 🐕 ♿ 🚐 ⛺

Rating: 7

near the Susquehanna River

This campground offers lake swimming, boating, canoeing, and fishing. If you don't have your own boat, you can rent rowboats, canoes, and pedal boats. The Susquehanna River also offers boating, including waterskiing and personal watercraft riding. The anglers in your group can cast for smallmouth bass, muskie, walleye, catfish, crappie, sunfish, carp, and bluegill. Hiking along the shore and in the surrounding woodlands offer great opportunities for wildlife viewing and bird watching. Among the animals you may spot are river otters, beavers, muskrats, minks, snapping turtles, white-tailed deer, foxes, woodchucks, red and gray squirrels, cottontail rabbits, raccoons, skunks, and chipmunks. Birders should get out their binoculars for heron, cormorants, osprey, eagles, gulls, turkey vultures, wild turkeys, pheasants, and woodcocks. Back at the campground you can participate in planned weekend activities like bingo.

Campsites, facilities: There are 91 sites for tents or RVs up 70 feet: 77 have full hookups; 14 have water and electricity. There are 14 pull-throughs. Picnic tables and fire rings are provided. Drinking water, restrooms with flush toilets, a dump station, showers, a laundry, a public phone, groceries, ice, LP gas, wood, a rec hall, a pavilion, a playground, two shuffleboard courts, badminton, miniature golf, volleyball, and RV storage and supplies are available. Some sites are wheelchair accessible. Leashed pets are permitted.

Reservations, fees: Reservations are accepted at 800/226-7688. The rate is $16–22.50 per night for up to two people. Each additional person is $3. Group discounts and weekly, monthly, and seasonal rates are available. Open April through mid-December.

Directions: From the junction of I-81 Exit 223/67 and Highway 492, travel east 0.5 mile on Highway 492, then turn left onto East Lake Road and travel three miles to the campground entrance on the left.

Contact: East Lake Campground, RR 2 Box 131P, New Milford, PA 18834, 570/465-2267, www.campingateastlake.com.

❷ SHORE FOREST CAMPGROUND

🏃 🚵 🏊 🎣 ⛵ 🏕️ 🐕 ♿ 🚐 ⛺

Rating: 9

near Lackawanna State Park

At this property's lake, you can rent rowboats, canoes, and pedal boats or cast a line for bass, sunfish, catfish, and bluegill. Campers can also take advantage of outdoor recreational activities at nearby Lackawanna State Park. Lake Lackawanna is a 198-acre warm- and cold-water fishery with stocked and native muskie, walleye, brown, brook, and rainbow trout, channel catfish, brown bullhead, and largemouth bass. Electric motorboats, canoes, rowboats, inflatables, and other non-powered boats are welcome on the lake. There is also a network of looping hiking trails totaling five miles that runs throughout the park; 3.5-mile multi-use Abington Trail also allows biking and horseback riding. Back at the campground you can participate in planned activities like theme weekends.

Campsites, facilities: There are 167 sites for tents or RVs up to 28 feet: 150 have full hookups, 17 have water and electricity. There are seven pull-throughs. Picnic tables and fire rings are provided. Drinking water, restrooms with flush toilets, a dump station, showers, a laundry, a public phone, groceries, ice, LP gas, wood, a general store, a rec hall, a swimming pool, a playground, badminton, volleyball and RV storage and supplies are available. Some sites are wheelchair accessible. Leashed pets are permitted.

Reservations, fees: Reservations are accepted. The rate is $22–28 per night for up to two people. Each additional person is $5. Monthly rates are available. Major credit cards are accepted. Open mid-April through October.

Directions: From the junction of I-81 Exit 211/64 and Highway 106, travel 1.5 miles west on Highway 106, then 4.5 miles on a paved road. Follow signs to the campground entrance on the right.

Contact: Shore Forest Campground, P.O. Box 366, Hop Bottom, PA 18824, 570/289-4666.

3 SHADY REST CAMPGROUND

Rating: 7

near Lackawanna State Park

The campground offers stream fishing, but serious anglers can head to nearby Lackawanna State Park to cast for stocked and native fish in 198-acre Lake Lackawanna. Among the warm- and cold-water species are walleye, brown, rainbow, and brook trout, channel catfish, bluegill, largemouth bass, muskie, pickerel, bullhead, and sunfish. There are three boat launches for electric motorboats and non-powered craft. If you don't have your own boat, you can rent one from the park's concession. A five-mile network of looping trails includes Abington Trail, a 3.5-mile multi-use trail that allows mountain bikes and horseback riders in addition to foot traffic. The trails are your best bet for wildlife viewing and bird watching. Among the animals you may see are white-tailed deer, minks, cottontail rabbits, red and gray squirrels, chipmunks, skunks, turtles, heron, gulls, eagles, osprey, and turkey vultures. Be advised that hunting is allowed seasonally in Lackawanna State Park.

Campsites, facilities: There are 35 sites for tents or RVs up to 25 feet: 10 have full hookups; 20 have water and electricity; five have no hookups. Picnic tables and fire rings are provided. Drinking water, restrooms with flush toilets, a dump station, ice, wood, a playground, horseshoes, a sports field, and RV storage and supplies are available. Leashed pets are permitted.

Reservations, fees: Reservations are accepted. The rate is $10–15 per night for up to four people. Each additional person is $4. Open May through October.

Directions: From the junction of I-81 Exit 211/64 and Highway 92, travel three miles north on Highway 92, then turn right onto a paved road and travel 0.2 mile to the campground entrance on the left.

Contact: Shady Rest Campground, RR 92, South Gibson, PA 18842, 570/222-3383.

4 DAY'S END CAMPGROUND

Rating: 6

near the Susquehanna River

With its proximity to the Susquehanna River, you can count on lots of water sports at Day's End Campground. If you have your own boat, you'll be happy to note the many access points along the river, including ramps and launches. Motorboats, canoes, kayaks, personal watercraft, inflatables, water skis, pedal boats, paddleboats, and other non-powered craft are welcome on the Susquehanna. The anglers in your group can cast for smallmouth bass, muskie, carp, catfish, walleye, sunfish, and bluegill. Fly-fishing is a favorite on the river. Day's End Campground also has pond fishing and offers rowboat rentals. On land, you can hike along the shoreline or in the surrounding woodlands. Birders should have their binoculars ready to spot red-tailed hawks, eagles, osprey, turkey buzzards, cormorant, gulls, warblers, bluebirds, vireos, pheasants, woodcocks, and flycatchers.

Campsites, facilities: There are 55 sites for tents or RVs up to 25 feet: 45 have water and electricity; 10 have no hookups. There are three pull-throughs. No sites have full hookups. Picnic tables and fire rings are provided. Drinking water and restrooms with flush toilets, a dump station, showers, groceries, ice, wood, a camp store, a rec hall, a pavilion, a sports field, and RV storage and supplies are available. Leashed pets are permitted.

Reservations, fees: Reservations are accepted. The rate is $18 per night for up to two people. Each additional person is $4. Open May through mid-October.

Directions: From the junction of U.S. 6 and Highway 267, travel 8.75 miles north on Highway 267, then turn right onto a paved road and travel two miles, then turn left onto a gravel road and travel 0.5 mile to the campground entrance on the right.

Contact: Day's End Campground, RR 3 Box 118D, Meshoppen, PA 18630, 570/965-2144.

5 SLUMBER VALLEY CAMPGROUND

Rating: 6

near the Susquehanna River

This campground offers pond and stream fishing and hiking trails. At the nearby Susquehanna River you can enjoy other water- and land-based activities. Anglers can cast for muskie, walleye, carp, smallmouth bass, catfish, bluegill, suckers, and sunfish. Though canoeing is the favorite activity on the river, motorboats and other non-powered boats are also welcome. If you don't have your own boat, there are outfitters who can rent you one. Hiking along the shore or in the surrounding woodlands is the best way to view birds and other wildlife. Among the animals you may see are heron, eagles, cormorants, osprey, gulls, teal, wood, and mallard ducks, Canada geese, pheasants, woodcocks, vireos, red-tailed hawks, warblers, turtles, minks,

muskrats, otters, beavers, white-tailed deer, red and gray squirrels, skunks, raccoons, opossums, chipmunks, woodchucks, brown bats, and eastern coyotes.

Campsites, facilities: There are 70 sites for RVs up to 25 feet: one has a full hookup; 49 have water and electricity, 20 have no hookups. There are 10 pull-throughs. Picnic tables and fire rings are provided. Drinking water, restrooms with flush toilets, a dump station, showers, a laundry, ice, wood, a rec area, a pavilion, a swimming pool, a playground, badminton, horseshoes, a sports field, volleyball, and RV storage and supplies are available. Leashed pets are permitted.

Reservations, fees: Reservations are accepted. The rate is $20–25 per night for up to two people. Each additional person is $5. Open mid-April through mid-October.

Directions: From the junction of Highway 267 and U.S. 6, travel one mile east on U.S. 6, then turn left onto a paved road and travel one mile to the campground entrance on the left.

Contact: Slumber Valley Campground, RR 4 Box 4211, Meshoppen, PA 18630, 570/833-5208.

6 SUNRISE LAKE FAMILY CAMPGROUND

Rating: 7

near Lackawanna State Park

BEST (

Sunrise Lake Family Campground is a perfect base camp for local historical and outdoor attractions. From here you can visit Steamtown National Historic Site, Wyoming County Historical Society, Nicholson Viaduct, Lackawanna Coal Mine Tour, and Electric Trolley Museum and Excursion Rides. At nearby Lackawanna State Park you can take advantage of 198-acre Lackawanna Lake for fishing and boating. There are also five miles of looping trails that run throughout the state park. Abington Trail, a 3.5-mile multi-use trail in the northeastern section of the park. welcomes hikers, bikers, and horseback riders. Back at the campground you can enjoy hayrides, bass fishing, or renting a paddleboat for the lake. You have your choice of sunny and shaded sites.

Campsites, facilities: There are 96 sites for tents or RVs up to 70 feet: 43 have full hookups; 53 have water and electricity. There are eight pull-throughs. Picnic tables and fire rings are provided. Drinking water, restrooms with flush toilets, a dump station, a laundry, showers, cable TV hookup, groceries, ice, LP gas, wood, a camp store, a pavilion, a sport field, a playground, a swimming pool, badminton, basketball, Frisbee golf, horseshoes, shuffleboard, volleyball, and a sports field are available. Leashed pets are permitted.

Reservations, fees: Reservations are accepted at 888/556-3219. The rate is $23–24 per night for up to two people. Each additional person is $5. Senior discounts and weekly and seasonal rates are available. Major credit cards are accepted. Open April through the beginning of November.

Directions: From the junction of Pennsylvania Turnpike Exit 39 and Route 11, travel north on Route 11 to the junction with Route 92, then south 2.5 miles on Route 92 to the campground entrance on the right.

Contact: Sunrise Lake Family Campground, Box 275S, Rt. 92 South, Nicholson, PA 18446, 570/942-6421, www.sunriselakefamily.com.

7 LACKAWANNA STATE PARK

🏃 ♨ 🚣 🛶 ❄ 🐕 🚴 ♿ 🚐 ⛺

Rating: 10

near Dalton

BEST (

This mostly wooded campground embodies the tranquility and playful quality of the state park. The 198-acre Lake Lackawanna offers boating and fishing for stocked rainbow, brook, and brown trout, muskie, walleye, channel catfish, pickerel, largemouth bass, and bullhead. If you have your own sailboat, rowboat, canoe, motorboat with electric motor, or other non-powered craft, you can use the park's three launch areas. Rental boats are also available at the concession. The park has a five-mile network of looping hiking trails. Among the favorites is the nature trail leading from Little Fern Loop and Grouse Trail, which runs along Fairground Hill and Woodland Ponds Trail and leads to a number of small fishing ponds. The 3.5-mile Abington multi-use trail allows biking and horseback riding. During the winter, cross-country skiing, sledding, tobogganing, ice skating, and ice fishing are favorite activities. Be advised that hunting is allowed seasonally in Lackawanna State Park.

Campsites, facilities: There are 96 sites for tents or RVs up to 48 feet: 61 have water and electricity; 35 have no hookups. There are 19 walk-in sites. No sites have full hookups. Picnic tables and fire rings are provided. Drinking water, restrooms with flush toilets, showers, a public phone, wood, a snack bar, a pavilion, a playground, a swimming pool, and an amphitheater are available. Some sites are wheelchair accessible. Leashed pets are permitted.

Reservations, fees: Reservations are accepted at 888/PA-PARKS (888/727-2757). The rate is $14–19 per night for up to five people; a fee may apply to additional guests. Pets are $2 for up to two pets. Senior and Pennsylvania resident discounts are available. Open mid-April through mid-October.

Directions: From I-81 Exit 199, travel west three miles on Highway 524, then north on Highway 407 to the campground entrance on the left.

Contact: Lackawanna State Park, RR 1 Box 230, Dalton, PA 18414-9785, 570/945-3239, lackawannasp@state.pa.us.

8 VALLEYVIEW FARM AND CAMPGROUND

🚶 🚲 🏊 ⛵ 🐕 🏕 ♿ 🚐 ⛰

Rating: 6

near Dyberry Creek

You can take advantage of the on-property fishing pond or go to nearby Dyberry Creek. The anglers in your group can cast for stocked brook, brown, and rainbow trout, catfish, bluegill, and sunfish. The creek is also a favorite for fly-fishing. Hiking along the shore or in the surrounding woodlands will give you wonderful opportunities for bird watching and wildlife viewing. Birders should have their binoculars ready for red-tailed hawks, pheasants, woodcocks, wild turkeys, teal, wood, and mallard ducks, Canada geese, warblers, vireos, tanagers, and flycatchers. Among the animals you may see are white-tailed deer, red and gray squirrels, chipmunks, cottontail rabbits, muskrats, skunks, opossums, raccoons, salamanders, and turtles. Bikers will enjoy the challenge of four tracks that run in and around Dyberry Creek. Yellow Track goes by Honesdale and offers a view of Jadwin Dry Dam. Red Track moves in and out of the valley and is the most difficult.

Campsites, facilities: There are 74 sites for tents or RVs up to 26 feet: 55 have full hookups; 19 have no hookups. Picnic tables and fire rings are provided. Drinking water, restrooms with flush toilets, a dump station, a laundry, a public phone, groceries, ice, wood, a camp store, a rec hall, a swimming pool, miniature golf, and a playground are available. Some sites are wheelchair accessible. Leashed pets are permitted.

Reservations, fees: Reservations are accepted. The rate is $18 per night for up to two people. Each additional person is $4. Open mid-May through mid-October.

Directions: From the junction of U.S. 6 and Highway 296, travel seven miles north on Highway 296, then 0.5 mile on a paved road. Follow signs to the campground entrance on the left.

Contact: Valleyview Farm and Campground, RD 1 Box 1348, Waymart, PA 18472, 570/448-2268, rvcamp@nep.net.

9 KEEN LAKE CAMPING & COTTAGE RESORT

🚶 🏊 ⛵ 🚿 🏕 🏔 🚐 ⛰

Rating: 9

near Dyberry Creek

BEST (

There are three walking paths on this property's 90 acres; Hearth, Haven, and Meadow Paths will take you on leisurely hikes through wooded and meadowland areas. As its name suggests, the campground is located on Keen Lake. There is a boat ramp and dock available, as well as a swimming area roped off from boat traffic. If you don't have your own boat, you can rent rowboats, canoes, kayaks, or pedal boats. Among the species of fish you can catch and release are pickerel, perch, calico, bass, catfish, sunfish, and bluegill. There is also stream fishing for trout. Fly-fishing is a favorite activity at Dyberry Creek. The campground has planned activities like theme weekends.

Campsites, facilities: There are 315 sites for tents or RVs up to 25 feet: 164 have full hookups; 105 have water and electricity; 46 have no hookups. There are four pull-throughs. Picnic tables and fire rings are provided. Drinking water, restrooms with flush toilets, a dump station, showers, a laundry, modem access, a phone hookup, cable TV hookup, a public phone, groceries, ice, LP gas, wood, fishing supplies, a camp store, a rec area, a pavilion, an arcade, a swimming pool, basketball, a playground, two shuffleboard courts, badminton, horseshoes, a sports field, volleyball, and RV storage and supplies are available. Leashed pets are permitted.

Reservations, fees: Reservations are accepted. The rate is $25–40 per night for up to two people. Each additional person is $3–5. Weekly and monthly rates are available. Open end of April through mid-October.

Directions: From the junction of U.S. 6 and Highway 296, travel 1.5 miles east on U.S. 6 to the campground entrance on the right.
Contact: Keen Lake Camping and Cottage Resort, RR 3 Box 1976, Waymart, PA 18472, 570/488-5522 or 800/443-0412, www.keen-lake.com.

10 PONDEROSA PINES CAMPGROUND

Rating: 8

near Dyberry Creek

With its proximity to Dyberry Creek, you can expect lots of fun on the water while staying at Ponderosa Pines. You can head out on your motorboat, canoe, or kayak to do some fishing or just enjoy the scenery. If you don't have your own boat, you can rent canoes or pedal boats here. Dyberry is stocked with brook, rainbow, and brown trout, and you can also fish for bluegill and other panfish. Fly-fishing is a favorite on the creek. Bikers will find the Red and Blue Tracks a challenge, while hikers can view wildlife and watch birds from trails along the shoreline or in the surrounding woodlands. You can also participate in planned activities like theme weekends at the campground.

Campsites, facilities: There are 88 sites for tents or RVs up to 30 feet: five have full hookups; 83 have water and electricity. There are three pull-throughs. Picnic tables and fire rings are provided. Drinking water, restrooms with flush toilets, a dump station, showers, a laundry, groceries, ice, LP gas, wood, a camp store, a rec hall, a pavilion, an arcade, a swimming pool, a basketball court, a playground, horseshoes, miniature golf, a sports field, a volleyball court, and RV storage and supplies are available. Leashed pets are permitted.

Reservations, fees: Reservations are accepted. The rate is $25 per night for up to two people. Each additional person is $5. Major credit cards are accepted. Open May through mid-October.

Directions: From the junction of U.S. 6 and Route 170, travel 3.5 miles north on Route 170, then turn right onto Beech Grove and travel 1.5 miles east on Beech Grove, then turn left onto Alden Road and travel one mile to the campground entrance.
Contact: Ponderosa Pines Campground, RR 3, Honesdale, PA 18431, 570/253-2080.

11 COUNTRYSIDE FAMILY CAMPGROUND

Rating: 8

near Dyberry Creek

This campground, located in the northern Pocono Mountains, has sites that are partially wooded and shaded. On weekends you can partake in free coffee and planned activities such as hayrides and bingo. In the town of Honesdale, home of the first train ever built, you can visit the Stourbridge Train Museum for train rides on the weekends. If you need to stretch your legs after a long drive or a restful sleep, then hop on one of the hiking trails on the property. At nearby Dyberry Creek, you can cast for stocked rainbow, brook, and brown trout. For more fishing and boating options, visit nearby Lake Wallenpaupack.

Campsites, facilities: There are 70 sites for tents or RVs up to 30 feet: 62 have water and electricity; eight have no hookups. Picnic tables with fire rings are provided. Drinking water, restrooms with flush toilets, a dump station, showers, a laundry, a public phone, groceries, ice, LP gas, wood, a camp store, a rec hall, ping-pong, an arcade, a pavilion, a swimming pool, a playground, a basketball court, badminton, horseshoes, miniature golf, a sports field, a volleyball court, and RV storage and supplies are available. Some sites are wheelchair accessible. Leashed pets are permitted.

Reservations, fees: Reservations are accepted. The rate is $19–28 per night for up to two people. Each additional person is $5. Weekly, monthly, and seasonal rates are available. Major credit cards are accepted. Open year-round.

Directions: From the junction of U.S. 6 north and Highway 191, travel 0.5 mile north on Highway 191, then 6.25 miles north on Highway 670 to the campground entrance on the left.

Contact: Countryside Family Campground, P.O. Box 1165, Honesdale, PA 18431, 570/253-0424, www.countrysidefamily campground.com.

12 SOARING EAGLE CAMPGROUND

Rating: 9

on the Delaware River

You can choose from among open, wooded, riverside, and brookside sites at this campground. Because Soaring Eagle is located along the Upper Delaware River, you can expect lots of water-related activities. You can launch your own boat or a rented canoe, kayak, or tube right from the campground. The anglers in your group can cast a line for shad, smallmouth bass, walleye, muskie, sunfish, bluegill, and brook, brown, and rainbow trout. The hiking and biking trails are the best places to watch birds and view wildlife. Birders will want their binoculars for eagles, heron, gulls, osprey, teal, wood, and mallard ducks, cormorants, Canada geese, wild turkeys, warblers, vireos, eastern bluebirds, flycatchers, woodcocks, pheasants, turkey vultures, and red-tailed hawks. Among the wildlife you may see are white-tailed deer, foxes, coyotes, red and gray squirrels, skunks, raccoons, opossums, chipmunks, turtles, salamanders, woodchucks, and

cottontail rabbits. You can also visit nearby attractions such as Carousel Water Park and Fort Delaware.

Campsites, facilities: There are 40 sites for tents or RVs up to 35 feet: 10 have water and electricity; 30 have no hookups. Picnic tables and fire rings are provided. Drinking water, restrooms with flush toilets, showers, ice, and wood are available. Leashed pets are permitted.

Reservations, fees: Reservations are accepted at 877/278-8383. The rate is $10–32 per night for up to two people. Each additional person is $4. Major credit cards are accepted. Open year-round.

Directions: From Scranton, travel east on Route 6 to Route 191, then north to Route 1018/Brahman Road, and finally six miles to the campground entrance.

Contact: Soaring Eagle Campground, Brahman Road, Stalker, PA 18417, 570/224-4666, www.soaringeaglecampground.com.

13 CHERRY RIDGE CAMPSITES & LODGING

Rating: 7

near Dyberry Creek

This campground offers lake swimming and boating in nearby Paupackan Lake and Dyberry Creek. Motorboats, canoes, and other non-powered boats are welcome on the lake. Smaller, non-powered craft are best for Dyberry. If you don't have your own watercraft, you can rent a rowboat. The anglers in your group will appreciate the fly-fishing spots along Dyberry, which is stocked with brown, brook, and rainbow trout. Bikers can travel the roadways in the area, making loops or traveling to specific destinations like Tanner Falls or Lower Woods Pond. Shoreline and woodland hiking trails at the lake and creek provide excellent opportunities for bird watching and wildlife viewing. You may see white-tailed deer, woodchucks, cottontail rabbits, red and gray squirrels, red foxes, chipmunks, minks, muskrats, turtles, skunks, raccoons, opossums, and salamanders. Migratory and year-round bird species include wild turkeys, teal, wood, and mallard ducks, pheasants, red-tailed hawks, Canada geese, osprey, eagles, turkey buzzards, warblers, flycatchers, vireos, and woodcocks.

Campsites, facilities: There are 102 sites for tents or RVs up to 26 feet: 99 have full hookups; three have water and electricity. There are 25 pull-throughs. Picnic tables and fire rings are provided. Drinking water, restrooms with flush toilets, a dump station, showers, a laundry, ice, wood, and a playground are available. Leashed pets are permitted.

Reservations, fees: Reservations are accepted. The rate is $19–25 per night for up to two people. Each additional person is $4. Open mid-April through mid-October.

Directions: From the junction of U.S. 6 south and Highway 191, travel 3.5 miles south on Highway 191, turn right onto Owego Turnpike and travel 2.5 miles, then turn right onto a paved road and travel 1.5 miles to the campground entrance on the right.

Contact: Cherry Ridge Campsites & Lodging, RR 2 Box 500, Honesdale, PA 18431, 570/488-6654.

14 TUNKHANNOCK FAMILY CAMPGROUND

Rating: 8

near the Susquehanna River

Bordering Tunkhannock Creek, this campground offers canoeing, stream fishing, hiking trails, and planned activities like bingo and theme weekends. At the nearby Susquehanna River you can enjoy more outdoor recreational activities on and off the water. If you have your own motorboat, canoe, kayak, sailboat, or other craft you can choose from several launch areas along the river. If you need to rent a boat, there

are outfitters who can help you. The anglers in your group can cast for smallmouth bass, suckers, carp, catfish, muskie, walleye, sunfish, and bluegill. You can also hike along the river's shore or the surrounding woodlands. Be on the lookout for bird life and animals. Among the creatures you may see are cormorants, heron, osprey, eagles, gulls, swallows, flycatchers, vireos, warblers, red-tailed hawks, turkey vultures, mallard ducks, and Canada geese. Animals to look for are white-tailed deer, raccoons, cottontail rabbits, beavers, muskrats, otters, turtles, salamanders, minks, opossums, chipmunks, red and gray squirrels, and foxes.

Campsites, facilities: There are 217 sites for tents or RVs up to 32 feet: 158 have full hookups; 29 have water and electricity; 30 have no hookups. There are 63 pull-throughs. Picnic tables and fire rings are provided. Drinking water and restrooms with flush toilets, a dump station, a laundry, a public phone, LP gas, groceries, ice, grills, wood, a rec hall, a pavilion, a swimming pool, a playground, horseshoes, volleyball, and RV storage and supplies are available. Some sites are wheelchair accessible. Leashed pets are permitted.

Reservations, fees: Reservations are accepted. The rate is $24 per night for up to two people. Each additional person is $5. Open year-round.

Directions: From the junction of Highway 29 and U.S. 6, travel two miles east on U.S. 6, then 0.5 mile south on a gravel road to the campground entrance at the end.

Contact: Tunkhannock Family Campground, 30 Campground Road, Tunkhannock, PA 18657, 570/836-4122.

15 HIGHLAND CAMPGROUND

Rating: 8

near Lackawanna State Park

This spacious campground is nestled in a section of the Endless Mountains. It provides both shaded and sunny sites. The Pennsylvania state flower, mountain laurel, grows throughout the surrounding woodlands. At nearby 1,411-acre Lackawanna State Park you have numerous outdoor activities to keep you busy. The centerpiece of the park is the 198-acre Lackawanna Lake. Anglers can cast for a variety of species in this warm and cold water fishery, including brown, brook, and rainbow trout, walleye, channel catfish, bluegill, muskie, yellow and brown bullhead, pickerel, and largemouth bass. You can take advantage of the three boat launches for your canoe, rowboat, motorboat with electric motor, or sailboat. There is also a rental concession at the park. Hikers have five miles of trails, as well as the 3.5-mile multi-use Abington Trail, which welcomes biking and horseback riding. During the summer Lackawanna offers environmental and interpretive programs. Check the park office for a schedule of these changing events. The campground is also near Lake Winola.

Campsites, facilities: There are 70 sites for tents or RVs up to 27 feet: 30 have full hookups; 30 have water and electricity; 10 have no hookups. There are four pull-throughs. Picnic tables and fire rings are provided. Drinking water, restrooms with flush toilets, a dump station, a laundry, a public phone, groceries, ice, wood, a rec hall, a swimming pool, a playground, badminton, volleyball and RV storage and supplies are available. Leashed pets are permitted.

Reservations, fees: Reservations are accepted. The rate is $18–20 per night for up to four people. Open May through October.

Directions: From the junction of I-81 Exit 194/58 and US6, travel 1.5 miles west on U.S. 6/11, then six miles northwest on Highway 307, then turn right onto a paved road and travel 1.25 miles, and finally one mile on a gravel road. Follow signs to the campground entrance on the left.

Contact: Highland Campground, RR 2 Box 278, Dalton, PA 18414, 570/586-9972.

16 WILSONVILLE RECREATION AREA

Rating: 9

near Lake Wallenpaupack

Water activities abound at Wilsonville Recreation Area. The 5,700-acre Lake Wallenpaupack offers boating, fishing, and swimming. If you don't have your own motorboat or non-powered boat, there are concessions nearby with rentals for canoes, kayaks, and inflatables. If you brought your craft with you then you'll be happy with the ramp and dock facilities here. The anglers in your group can cast a line for smallmouth, largemouth, and striped bass, walleye, brown and rainbow trout, yellow perch, and panfish. For those who prefer to stay on dry land, there are many hiking trails along the shore and in the surrounding woodlands. These make perfect spots for wildlife viewing and bird watching. Among the species you may see are white-tailed deer, minks, muskrats, red and gray squirrels, cottontail rabbits, raccoons, opossums, chipmunks, woodchucks, foxes, skunks, eagles, osprey, turkey buzzards, cormorants, gulls, herons, Canada geese, teal, wood, and mallard ducks, warblers, vireos, tanagers, wild turkeys, and red-tailed hawks.

Campsites, facilities: There are 168 sites for RVs up to 25 feet: 160 have electricity; eight have no hookups. Picnic tables and fire rings are provided. Drinking water, restrooms with flush toilets, showers, a dump station, a laundry, a public phone, groceries, ice, wood, a camp store, a rec area, horseshoes, a playground, and RV storage and supplies are available. Some sites are wheelchair accessible. No pets are permitted.

Reservations, fees: Reservations are accepted. The rate is $20 per night for up to four people; a fee may apply for additional guests. No pets allowed. Open mid-April through mid-October.

Directions: From the junction of Highway

590 and U.S. 6, travel two miles east on U.S. 6 to the campground entrance on the right. **Contact:** Wilsonville Recreation Area, HC6 Box 6114; Hawley, PA 18428; 570/226-4382.

17 LAKE MOC A TEK CAMPGROUND

🚶 🚲 🛶 ⛴ 🎣 🐕 🏇 🚐 ⛺

Rating: 9

near Lake Wallenpaupack

BEST (

You have your choice of shaded, open, and lakefront sites on these 70 acres. Lake Moc A Tek offers fishing and boating. You can cast for smallmouth, largemouth, and rock bass in this 24-acre lake. There is a boat launch on the property for motorboats with electric motors, canoes, and other non-powered craft. If you don't have your own boat, you can rent a rowboat from the campground. On weekends you can participate in planned activities such as bingo, karaoke nights, and themed dinners. Nearby Lake Wallenpaupack offers swimming, fishing, boating, hiking, biking, bird watching, and wildlife viewing.

Campsites, facilities: There are 177 sites for tents or RVs up to 30 feet: 105 have full hookups; 62 have water and electricity; 10 have no hookups. Picnic tables and fire rings are provided. Drinking water, restrooms with flush toilets, a dump station, showers, a laundry, modem access, a phone hookup, cable TV hookup, groceries, ice, LP gas, wood, fishing supplies, a camp store, a rec area, a pavilion, an arcade, a swimming pool, a wading pool, a volleyball court, a basketball court, and a sports field are available. Leashed pets are permitted.

Reservations, fees: Reservations are accepted at 570/226-6877. The rate is $15–21 per night for up to two people. Each additional person is $5. Weekly, monthly, and seasonal rates are available. Open year-round.

Directions: From the junction of U.S. 6 and

Route 590, travel seven miles south on Route 590, then turn left onto Piefer Road and travel 0.25 mile to the campground entrance. **Contact:** Lake Moc A Tek Campground, P.O. Box 481, Hamlin, PA 18427, 570/226-3433, www.lakemocatekcampground.com.

18 RICKETTS GLEN STATE PARK

🚶 🚲 🛶 ⛴ 🎣 ❄ 🐕 ♿ 🚐 ⛺

Rating: 9

near Bloomsburg

BEST (

All of this campground's sites are shaded. The 245-acre Lake Jean offers boating and fishing. If you have a motorboat with an electric motor or a non-powered boat, you can take advantage of the launch area. You can also rent rowboats, kayaks, canoes, or paddleboats from the park concession. Since the lake is both a warm-water and cold-water fishery, you can cast for bass, trout, walleye, catfish, sucker, crappie, sunfish, and bluegill. Swimming is allowed at a 600-foot sand beach, but there is no lifeguard. There are 26 miles of hiking trails, as well as equestrian trails. Bikers can ride on the state park roadways. During the winter, you can go cross-country skiing, snowmobiling, ice fishing, and ice climbing. Be advised that hunting is allowed seasonally in Ricketts Glen State Park.

Campsites, facilities: There are 120 sites for tents or RVs up to 35 feet. No sites have hookups. Picnic tables and fire rings are provided. Drinking water, restrooms with flush toilets, a dump station, showers, grills, and a public phone are available. Some sites are wheelchair accessible. Leashed pets are permitted.

Reservations, fees: Reservations are accepted at 888/PA-PARKS (888/727-2757). The rate is $14–19 per night for up to five people; a fee may apply for additional guests. Pets are $2 for up to two pets. Senior and Pennsylvania resident discounts are available. Open year-round.

Directions: From Bloomsburg, travel 30 miles north on Highway 487. Because the section of Highway 487 from the town of Red Rock to the Lake Jean area of the park is very steep, heavy RVs should avoid this route and take Highway 487 south from Dushore.

Contact: Ricketts Glen State Park, 695 State Route 487, Benton, PA 17814, 570/477-5675, rickettsglensp@state.pa.us.

19 FRANCES SLOCUM STATE PARK

Rating: 10

near Wyoming

BEST (

This wooded campground lies in the heart of scenic Frances Slocum State Park, which has nine miles of hiking trails. Frances Slocum Trail is a 0.7-mile loop that takes you past a Native American rock shelter. Lakeshore Trail follows the lake for 1.4 miles. Deer Trail has three loops of 1.3, 2.5, and 3.8 miles. The two-mile Larch Tree Trail loops through the northeast. Part of the one-mile Campground Trail runs along Larch Tree Trail. You can also boat and fish on 165-acre Frances Slocum Lake. The park has rowboat, canoe, and pedal boat rentals. During the winter ice skating, ice fishing, sledding, tobogganing, and snowmobiling are favorite activities. Be advised that hunting is allowed seasonally in Frances Slocum State Park.

Campsites, facilities: There are 100 sites for tents or RVs up 35 feet: 54 have electricity; 46 have no hookups. There are 15 walk-in sites. Picnic tables and fire rings are provided. Drinking water, restrooms with flush toilets, a dump station, showers, a public phone, a snack bar, a pavilion, a swimming pool, a playground, and RV storage and supplies are available. Leashed pets are permitted.

Reservations, fees: Reservations are accepted at 888/PA-PARKS (888/727-2757). The rate is $14–19 per night for up to five people; a fee

may apply for additional guests. Pets are $2 for up to two pets. Senior and Pennsylvania resident discounts are available. Open April through October.

Directions: From the junction of I-81 Exit 170B and Highway 309, travel seven miles north on Highway 309, turn right onto Carverton Road and travel four miles, then turn left onto Eighth Street and travel one mile, and finally turn left onto Mount Olivet Road and travel one mile to the campground entrance.

Contact: Frances Slocum State Park, 565 Mount Olivet Road, Wyoming, PA 18644-9333, 570/696-3525, francesslocumsp@state.pa.us.

20 LEDGEDALE RECREATION AREA

Rating: 8

near Lake Wallenpaupack

With 5,700-acre Lake Wallenpaupack so close, you can expect to enjoy lots of water sports while staying at Ledgedale Recreation Area. The campground has a dock, a ramp, and two launches for boats or canoes. If you don't have your own, you can rent a rowboat or canoe. Anglers can cast for walleye, largemouth, smallmouth, and striped bass, yellow perch, brown and brook trout, pickerel, bluegill, and sunfish. The lake has six total recreation areas. There are also hiking trails that run on the property. From the trails or from the 52 miles of shoreline you may spot white-tailed deer, minks, muskrats, raccoons, opossums, red and gray squirrels, woodchucks, skunks, cottontail rabbits, and chipmunks. Birders can get out their binoculars for eagles, osprey, turkey vultures, Canada geese, gulls, cormorants, teal, wood, and mallard ducks, herons, red-tailed hawks, bluebirds, wrens, warblers, vireos, tanagers, and flycatchers.

Campsites, facilities: There are 70 sites for tents or RVs up to 30 feet: all sites have electricity; there are no full hookups. There are two pull-throughs. Picnic tables and fire rings are provided. Drinking water, restrooms with non-flush toilets, showers, a dump station, a laundry, groceries, ice, wood, a camp store, a rec area, horseshoes, and RV storage and supplies are available. Some sites are wheelchair accessible. Leashed pets are permitted.

Reservations, fees: Reservations are accepted. The rate is $20 per night for up to two people; a fee may apply for additional guests. Leashed pets are permitted. Open mid-April through mid-October.

Directions: From the junction of I-84 Exit 20/6 and Highway 507, travel 0.5 mile north on Highway 507, then turn left onto a paved road and travel two miles to the campground entrance on the right.

Contact: Ledgedale Recreation Area, RR 3 Box 379C, Greentown, PA 18426, 570/689-2181, ledgedal@ptd.net.

21 IRONWOOD POINT RECREATION AREA

🏃 🚣 ➰ 🐕 🚤 ♿ 🚐 ⛺

Rating: 8

on Lake Wallenpaupack

Campers can launch motorboats or canoes from this campground's dock and ramp right onto man-made Lake Wallenpaupack. Kayaks, water skis, personal watercraft, paddleboats, rowboats, and inflatables are also welcome on the lake. Anglers can cast a line for brown and brook trout, pickerel, smallmouth and largemouth bass, striped bass, and walleye. Hikers can choose from numerous trails along the 52 miles of shoreline or in the surrounding woodlands. There are wonderful opportunities for bird watching and wildlife viewing from the trails. Among the species of birds you may see are eagles, gulls, herons, cormorants, osprey, turkey buzzards, and red-tailed hawks. Wildlife in the area include white-tailed deer, minks, raccoons, red and gray squirrels, opossums, muskrats, cottontail rabbits, chipmunks, and woodchucks.

Campsites, facilities: There are 62 sites for tents or RVs up to 30 feet: 60 have full hookups; two have no hookups. Picnic tables and fire rings are provided. Drinking water, non-flush toilets, showers, a dump station, a laundry, a public phone, groceries, ice, wood, a camp store, a rec area, a pavilion, a playground, and RV storage and supplies are available. Some sites are wheelchair accessible. Leashed pets are permitted.

Reservations, fees: Reservations are accepted. The rate is $20 per night for up to four people. Each additional person is $3. Leashed pets are permitted. Major credit cards are accepted. Open end of April through mid-October.

Directions: From the junction of I-84 Exit 20/6 and Highway 507, travel north 2.25 miles on Highway 507, then turn left onto a paved road and travel 0.5 mile to the campground entrance at the end.

Contact: Ironwood Point Recreation Area, P.O. Box 344, Greentown, PA 18426, 570/857-0880, ironwood@ptd.net.

22 THE PINES CAMPGROUND

🏃 🚴 🏊 🚣 ➰ 🐕 🚤 ♿ 🚐 ⛺

Rating: 9

in Promised Land State Park

BEST (

The Pines Campground is one of four camping areas in Promised Land State Park; it is located in the northwest part of the property. A trail leads to a nearby picnic area and Main Beach for swimming. You can take out your boat on the park's two lakes, Lower Lake and Promised Land Lake. If you need to rent a craft, the concessions have rowboats, pedal boats, and canoes. Anglers have a choice of fishing spots and can cast for pickerel, muskie, smallmouth and largemouth bass, yellow perch, catfish, brook, brown, and rainbow trout, and sunfish. Over 50 miles of hiking trails run throughout the park, and there are trails for biking and horseback riding in the surrounding 12,464-acre Delaware State Forest. Be advised that hunting is allowed seasonally in Promised Land State Park.

Campsites, facilities: There are 63 sites for tents or RVs up to 87 feet. No sites have hookups. Picnic tables and fire rings are provided. Drinking water, restrooms with flush toilets, showers, a dump station, a public phone, grills, a pavilion, a playground, and a volleyball court are available. Some sites are wheelchair accessible. Leashed pets are permitted.

Reservations, fees: Reservations are accepted at 888/PA-PARKS (888/727-2757). The rate is $14–19 per night for up to five people; a fee may apply for additional guests. Pets are $2 for up to two pets. Senior and Pennsylvania resident discounts are available. Open from May to beginning of September.

Directions: From the junction of I-84 Exit 26 and Highway 309, travel five miles south on Highway 390 to the campground entrance.

Contact: Promised Land State Park, RR 1 Box 96, Greentown, PA 18426-9735, 570/676-3428, promisedlandsp@state.pa.us.

23 DEERFIELD CAMPGROUND

Rating: 8

in Promised Land State Park

Promised Land State Park is in the middle of 12,464-acre Delaware State Forest. Deerfield is the smallest of four camping areas within the park. It is located just south of 422-acre Promised Land Lake, which provides access to lake swimming from a sand beach. A boat ramp and dock for motorboats with electric motors, canoes, and other non-powered craft

is available as are rowboat, pedal boat, kayak, and canoe rentals. Anglers can drop a line for stocked rainbow, brook, and brown trout, or fish for muskie, smallmouth and largemouth bass, pickerel, yellow perch, catfish, and sunfish. Other outdoor activities at the park include hiking and biking, orienteering, picnicking, and wildlife viewing and bird watching. With 50 miles of trails to choose from, you'll want to hit highlights like the loop trail around Conservation Island and Little Fall Trails and its many waterfalls. Be advised that hunting is allowed seasonally in Promised Land State Park.

Campsites, facilities: There are 62 sites for tents or RVs up to 35 feet. No sites have hookups. Picnic tables and fire rings are provided. Drinking water, restrooms with flush toilets, showers, a dump station, a public phone, grills, a pavilion, a playground, a volleyball court, and an amphitheater are available. Some sites are wheelchair accessible. Leashed pets are permitted.

Reservations, fees: Reservations are accepted at 888/PA-PARKS (888/727-2757). The rate is $14–19 per night for up to five people; a fee may apply for additional guests. Pets are $2 for up to two pets. Senior and Pennsylvania resident discounts are available. Open May through beginning of September.

Directions: From the junction of I-84 Exit 26 and Highway 309, travel five miles south on Highway 390 to the campground entrance.

Contact: Promised Land State Park, RR 1 Box 96, Greentown, PA 18426-9735, 570/676-3428, promisedlandsp@state.pa.us.

24 PICKEREL POINT CAMPGROUND

Rating: 10

in Promised Land State Park

BEST (

One of four campgrounds in Promised Land State Park, Pickerel Point Campground is unique because of its location on a peninsula on the southern side of 422-acre Promised Land Lake. Water sports rule at this campground. You can go lake swimming, boating, canoeing, and fishing. There are two large sand beaches, Pickerel and Main Beach. If you don't have your own electric motorboat or other non-powered craft, you can rent rowboats, kayaks, canoes, or pedal boats from the park's concessions. You can cast for muskie, yellow perch, rainbow, brook, and brown trout, sunfish, smallmouth and largemouth bass, and catfish. There are 50 miles of trails to hike or bike. Or maybe you brought your compass and are ready for some orienteering. These activities give you the best opportunities for bird watching and wildlife viewing. During the winter, you can ice skate, ice fish, snowmobile, and cross-country ski, and snowshoe. Be advised that hunting is allowed seasonally in Promised Land State Park.

Campsites, facilities: There are 125 sites for tents or RVs up to 35 feet. No sites have hookups. There are 39 walk-in sites. Picnic tables, water, restrooms with flush toilets, showers, a dump station, a public phone, grills, a pavilion, a playground, a volleyball court, and an amphitheater are available. Leashed pets are permitted.

Reservations, fees: Reservations are accepted at 888/PA-PARKS (888/727-2757). The rate is $14–19 per night for up to five people; a fee may apply for additional guests. Pets are $2 for up to two pets. Senior and Pennsylvania resident discounts are available. Open year-round.

Directions: From the junction of I-84 Exit 26 and Highway 309, travel five miles south on Highway 390 to the campground entrance.

Contact: Promised Land State Park, RR 1 Box 96, Greentown, PA 18426-9735, 570/676-3428, promisedlandsp@state.pa.us.

25 LOWER LAKE CAMPGROUND

Rating: 10

in Promised Land State Park

BEST (

This campground is located at the western edge of Lower Lake in Promised Land State Park. There are three camping areas here: Beechwood, Rhododendron, and Northwoods. Only Beechwood Area has paved roads and electricity. Water sports are the draw: You can go lake swimming and fishing and there is a mooring area and boat launch near the campground. If you don't have your own motorboat or non-powered craft, you can rent rowboats, canoes, and pedal boats at the concessions. There are 50 miles of hiking trails in the park, including Little Falls Trail, which runs beside the campground. The surrounding Delaware State Forest offers other trails for horseback riding, biking, and hiking. Though trails range in difficulty, there are many easy leisure hikes for taking in the scenery and looking for wildlife. During the winter, you can go ice fishing, ice skating, snowmobiling, and cross-country skiing. Be advised that hunting is allowed seasonally in Promised Land State Park.

Campsites, facilities: There are 217 sites for tents or RVs up to 87 feet: 104 have electricity; 113 have no hookups. Picnic tables and fire rings are provided. Drinking water, restrooms with flush toilets, showers, a dump station, a public phone, grills, a pavilion, a playground, and a volleyball court are available. Leashed pets are permitted.

Reservations, fees: Reservations are accepted at 888/PA-PARKS (888/727-2757). The rate is $14–19 per night for up to five people; a fee may apply for additional guests. Pets are $2 for up to two pets. Senior and Pennsylvania resident discounts are available. Open mid-April through end of December.

Directions: From the junction of I-84 Exit 26 and Highway 309, travel five miles south on Highway 390 to the campground entrance.

Contact: Promised Land State Park, RR 1 Box

96, Greentown, PA 18426-9735, 570/676-3428, promisedlandsp@state.pa.us.

26 RIVER BEACH CAMPSITES
🚶 🏊 🛶 🚤 🎣 🐕 ♿ 🚐 ⛺

Rating: 9

near the Delaware River

This 18-acre campground is all about water recreation. With the Delaware River so close, you can go swimming, boating, canoeing, kayaking, and fishing. If you don't have your own craft, you can rent a canoe or kayak or sign up for a float trip. The anglers in your group can cast for shad, carp, smallmouth, largemouth, and rock bass, stripers, fall fish, herring, suckers, sunfish, brown, brook, and rainbow trout, bluegill, and walleye. Hikers have lots of shoreline and woodlands to explore, as well as portions of the Appalachian National Scenic Trail and the Delaware Canal Towpath. Along these trails, you might catch sight of white-tailed deer, opossums, raccoons, red and gray squirrels, cottontail rabbits, or chipmunks. Back at the campground, you have your choice of wooded, riverside, or creekside sites.

Campsites, facilities: There are 165 sites for tents or RVs up to 26 feet: 55 have water and electricity; 110 have no hookups. There are 11 pull-throughs. Picnic tables and fire rings are provided. Drinking water, a dump station, showers, a laundry, modem access, a phone hookup, cable TV hookup, a public phone, groceries, ice, LP gas, wood, a camp store, a rec hall, an arcade, and RV storage and supplies are available. Some sites are wheelchair accessible. Leashed pets are permitted.

Reservations, fees: Reservations are accepted at 800/356-2852. The rate is $11 per night for up to two people. Each additional person is $5. Seasonal rates are available. Major credit cards are accepted. Open April through beginning of December.

Directions: From the junction of I-84 Exit 53/11 and U.S. 209, travel three miles south on U.S. 209 to the campground entrance on the left.

Contact: River Beach Campsites, P.O. Box 382, Milford, PA 18337, 570/296-7421, www.kittatinny.com/pages/camping.php.

27 TRI-STATE RV PARK
🚶 🚲 🛶 🚤 🎣 🐕 🚐 ⛺

Rating: 5

near the Delaware River

As its name implies, this campground is at the border of Pennsylvania, New York, and New Jersey. It's also near the Delaware River and all of its water activities. You have a dock, ramp, and launch at your disposal for motorboats, canoes, kayaks, and other non-powered craft. If you need to rent a boat, the campground offers rowboats, canoes, and pedal boats. Anglers can cast for carp, herring, fall fish, smallmouth, largemouth, striped, and rock bass, suckers, sunfish, rainbow, brown, and brook trout, shad, and walleye. Many trails run through the Delaware Water Gap, including the 60-mile Delaware Canal Towpath, which is registered as a National Heritage Hiking Trail, and the Appalachian National Scenic Trail, which passes through on its way from Georgia to Maine. Bikers also have trails options as well as the roadways within the Delaware Water Gap National Recreation Area.

Campsites, facilities: There are 130 sites for tents or RVs up to 26 feet: 51 have full hookups; 20 have water and electricity; 59 have no hookups; There are 15 pull-throughs. Picnic tables and fire rings are provided. Drinking water, restrooms with flush toilets, a dump station, showers, a laundry, modem access, a phone hookup, cable TV hookup, a public phone, groceries, ice, LP gas, wood, a general store, a pavilion, and RV storage and supplies are available. Leashed pets are permitted.

Reservations, fees: Reservations are accepted.

The rate is $28–30 per night for up to four people. Each additional person is $6. Major credit cards are accepted. Open year-round.
Directions: From I-84 east Exit 53/11, travel straight through the stoplight and onto Rose Lane. Rose Lane turns into Shady Lane. Follow signs to the campground entrance at the end.
Contact: Tri-State RV Park, 400 Shady Lane, Matamoras, PA 18336, 570/491-4948, www .tristatervpark.com.

28 TOBYHANNA STATE PARK

Rating: 10

near Tobyhanna

BEST (

With 5,440 acres, including a 170-acre lake, there is lots to explore in Tobyhanna State Park. The park rests 2,000 feet above sea level so temperatures are usually cool here, especially at night. During the day you can take advantage of lake swimming from an unguarded sand beach. Motorboats with electric motors, canoes, kayaks, and other non-powered boats are welcome on the lake. There are several mooring spots, a ramp, and a dock here for your convenience. If you don't have your own craft, the park concession has rowboat, canoe, and pedal boat rentals. Anglers can fish Tobyhanna Lake for pickerel, yellow perch, catfish, smallmouth, largemouth, and rock bass, brook trout, and sunfish. There are several challenging mountain trails for hikers and bikers. During the winter, some trails are open to cross-country skiers and snowmobile riders. Ice fishing is also popular in the colder months. Be advised that hunting is allowed seasonally in Tobyhanna State Park.
Campsites, facilities: There are 140 sites for tents or RVs up to 25 feet. No sites have hookups. Picnic tables and fire rings are provided. Drinking water, non-flush toilets, a dump station, a public phone, a pavilion, a playground, and a sports field are available.

Some sites are wheelchair accessible. Leashed pets are permitted.
Reservations, fees: Reservations are accepted at 888/PA-PARKS (888/727-2757). The rate is $14–19 per night for up to five people; a fee may apply for additional guests. Pets are $2 for up to two pets. Senior and Pennsylvania resident discounts are available. Open April through December.
Directions: From the junction of I-380 Exit 8 and Highway 423, travel three miles north on Highway 423 to the campground entrance on the left.
Contact: Tobyhanna State Park, P.O. Box 387, Tobyhanna, PA 18466-0387, 570/894-8336, tobyhannasp@state.pa.us.

29 HEMLOCK CAMPGROUND & COTTAGES

Rating: 8

near Tobyhanna State Park

These wooded sites are located in the heart of the Pocono Mountains. At nearby 5,440-acre Tobyhanna State Park, you can go boating, fishing, and swimming at Tobyhanna Lake, or hiking on the many trails that run throughout park property. The 5.1-mile multi-use Lakeside Trail travels all the way around Tobyhanna Lake and welcomes bikers, cross-country skiers, and snowmobile riders. Yellow Trail is a difficult 3.3-mile hike through wetlands and boulder fields. Hemlock Campground & Cottages is also near Gouldsboro State Park. You can participate in the campground's planned activities such as dances and theme parties.
Campsites, facilities: There are 89 sites for tents or RVs up to 27 feet: 63 have full hookups; 18 have water and electricity; 8 have no hookups. There are two pull-throughs. Picnic tables and fire rings are provided. Drinking water, restrooms with flush toilets, a dump station, a laundry, modem access, a phone hookup, cable TV hookup, a public phone, groceries, ice, LP

gas, wood, a camp store, a rec area, a pavilion, an arcade, a swimming pool, basketball, a playground, badminton, volleyball, and RV storage and supplies are available. Leashed pets are permitted. The campground has a traffic control gate for security.

Reservations, fees: Reservations are accepted. The rate is $20–30 per night for up to two people. Each additional person is $3. Weekly, monthly, and seasonal rates are available, as are firefighter, police, and military discounts. Major credit cards are accepted. Open May through October.

Directions: From the junction of I-380 Exit 8 and Highway 611, travel 1.75 miles south on Highway 611, then 1.25 miles southeast on Hemlock Drive to the campground entrance on the left.

Contact: Hemlock Campground & Cottages, 362 Hemlock Drive, Tobyhanna, PA 18466, 570/894-4388, www.hemlockcampground.com.

30 MOUNT POCONO CAMPGROUND

🧍🏊🏕️🚣🚐⛺

Rating: 8

near Big Pocono State Park

BEST (

There are open, shaded, and wooded sites on this 42-acre campground, as well as views of New York and Mount Kittatinny. At nearby Big Pocono State Park you can explore the mountains on three interconnecting hiking trails totaling seven miles: North, South, and Indian Trails. South Trail is also an equestrian trail. Be advised that hunting is allowed seasonally in Big Pocono State Park. Mount Pocono Campground is also near Tobyhanna and Gouldsboro State Parks. The campground offers planned activities like bingo and theme weekends.

Campsites, facilities: There are 179 sites for tents or RVs up to 40 feet: 68 have full hookups; 41 have water and electricity, 70 have no

hookups. There are 16 pull-throughs. Picnic tables and fire rings are provided. Drinking water, restrooms with flush toilets, a dump station, a laundry, cable TV hookup, modem access, phone hookup, groceries, ice, LP gas, wood, a rec hall, a pavilion, an arcade, a swimming pool, a wading pool, a playground, badminton, horseshoes, a sports field, volleyball, and RV storage and supplies are available. Leashed pets are permitted.

Reservations, fees: Reservations are accepted. The rate is $20–40 per night for up to two people. Each additional person is $3–7. Weekly and monthly rates are available. Senior, police, firefighter, and military discounts are available. Major credit cards are accepted. Open May through October.

Directions: From the junction of Highway 611 and Highway 196, travel 0.75 mile north on Highway 196, then turn right onto Edgewood Road and travel 0.5 mile, then 0.25 mile on a paved road, and finally 0.25 mile on a gravel road to the campground entrance at the end.

Contact: Mount Pocono Campground, 30 Edgewood Road, Mount Pocono, PA 18344, 570/839-8950, www.mtpoconocampground.com.

31 PARADISE CAMPGROUND RESORT

🧍🚴🛶🚐🏕️🐕🚐⛺

Rating: 7

on the Susquehanna River

Water activities rule at this campground along the Susquehanna River. There are several launch areas at the river. If you don't have your own motorboat, canoe, kayak, sailboat, or other non-powered craft, you can rent rowboats and pedal boats right here. You can also fish for smallmouth bass, walleye, suckers, carp, catfish, sunfish, and bluegill. Hiking along the river's shoreline or in the surrounding woodlands is the best way to watch birds and view wildlife. You might spot heron, gulls, cormorants, eagles, osprey, swallows, warblers, red-tailed hawks, vireos, tanagers, flycatchers, teal, wood, and mallard ducks, Canada geese, and woodpeckers. Animal life in the area include white-tailed deer, eastern coyote, foxes, raccoons, opossums, red and gray squirrels, otters, minks, beavers, muskrats, turtles, and cottontail rabbits. Bikers can use the interconnecting roadways in the area. Be advised that hunting is allowed seasonally in the area.

Campsites, facilities: There are 55 sites for tents or RVs up to 30 feet: 30 have full hookups; 15 have water and electricity; 10 have no hookups. Picnic tables and fire rings are provided. Drinking water, restrooms with flush toilets, a dump station, showers, a public phone, ice, wood, a pavilion, and RV storage and supplies are available. Leashed pets are permitted.

Reservations, fees: Reservations are accepted. The rate is $20 per night for up to two people. Each additional person is $5. Open year-round.

Directions: From the junction of I-80 Exit 256/38 and Highway 93, travel 3.75 miles north on Highway 93, then 0.2 mile northeast on Highway 239, then three miles on a paved road. Follow signs to the campground entrance on the right.

Contact: Paradise Campground Resort, P.O. Box 514, Nescopeck, PA 18635, 570/379-3729.

32 MOYER'S GROVE CAMPGROUND

🥾 🏊 🛶 🚤 🐎 🚵 ♿ 🚐 ⛺

Rating: 8

near the Susquehanna River

This campground is set on 70 acres alongside a brook. You can go fishing in the stream or rent a canoe and fish in the pond. There are planned weekend activities like fishing derbies and car shows. At the nearby Susquehanna River, you can take out your motorboat or other watercraft or cast for muskie, walleye, smallmouth bass,

suckers, carp, catfish, sunfish, and bluegill. For hikers, the shore and surrounding woodlands offers wonderful scenery well as opportunities for bird watching and wildlife viewing. Among the creatures you may spot are heron, gulls, eagles, osprey, ducks, red-tailed hawks, turkey buzzards, white-tailed deer, raccoons, foxes, skunks, opossums, turtles, salamanders, cottontail rabbits, squirrels, and brown bats.

Campsites, facilities: There are 147 sites for tents or RVs up to 28 feet: 70 have full hookups; 70 have water and electricity; 7 have no hookups. Picnic tables and fire rings are provided. Drinking water, restrooms with flush toilets, a dump station, a laundry, showers, groceries, ice, LP gas, wood, a camp store, a rec area, a pavilion, volleyball, a swimming pool, a playground, miniature golf, two shuffleboard courts, and RV storage and supplies are available. Some sites are wheelchair accessible. Leashed pets are permitted.

Reservations, fees: Reservations are accepted at 800/722-1912. The rate is $25–32 per night for up to two people. Each additional person is $5. Weekly rates and group discounts are available. Major credit cards are accepted. Open year-round.

Directions: From the junction of I-80 Exit 256/38 and Highway 93, travel 3.75 miles north on Highway 93, then 0.75 mile northeast on Highway 239, then 3.5 miles on a paved road. Follow signs to the campground entrance on the right.

Contact: Moyer's Grove Campground, 309 Moyers Grove Road, Wapwallopen, PA 18660, 570/379-3375, www.moyercgrv.com.

33 81-80 RV PARK & CAMPGROUND

🥾 🏊 🛶 🎿 🐎 🚵 ♿ 🚐 ⛺

Rating: 6

near Nescopeck State Park

BEST (

The sites here are wooded. At nearby Nescopeck State Park, you have 19 miles of trails to hike. Most of the trails begin along Honey Hole Road and travel through forest, wetland, and meadow habitats. This provides a great opportunity for bird watching and wildlife viewing. Among the animals you may see are white-tailed deer, raccoons, opossums, red and gray squirrels, salamanders, and muskrats. Bird species include warblers, wrens, flycatchers, tanagers, vireos, ducks, and red-tailed hawks. Be advised that hunting is allowed seasonally in Nescopeck State Park. In the winter, some of the trails are used for cross-country skiing. The anglers in your group won't feel left out with nine-acre Lake Frances and Nescopeck Creek. The lake has bass, trout, and panfish. The creek has native brook and brown trout.

Campsites, facilities: There are 87 sites available for tents or RVs up 90 feet: 45 have full hookups; 28 have water and electricity; 14 have no hookups. There are 48 pull-throughs. Picnic tables and fire rings are provided. Drinking water, restrooms with flush toilets, a dump station, showers, a laundry, modem access, phone hookup, TV cable hookup, a public phone, groceries, ice, wood, a camp store, a gift shop, a rec area, a swimming pool, a playground, and RV storage and supplies are available. Some sites are wheelchair accessible. Leashed pets are permitted.

Reservations, fees: Reservations are accepted. The rate is $24–33 per night for up to four people. Each additional person is $5. Major credit cards are accepted. Open year-round.

Directions: From the junction of I-80 Exit 262 and Highway 309, travel north 0.75 mile on Highway 309, then turn left onto a gravel road for 0.25 mile to the campground entrance at the end.

Contact: 81-80 RV Park & Campground, 718 North Old Turnpike Road, Drums, PA 18222-2012, 570/788-3382, www.81-80rvpark.com.

34 LEHIGH GORGE FAMILY CAMPGROUND

Rating: 7

near Hickory Run State Park

During your stay you can take advantage of the campground's lake fishing and hiking trails. There are more outdoor recreational opportunities at nearby 15,500-acre Hickory Run State Park. The park's 43 miles of trails vary in difficulty from easy, leisurely walks to steep climbs over boulder fields. The most difficult hikes are Boulder Field, Fireline, Fourth Run, Ridge, and Shades of Death Trails. During the winter some of trails allow cross-country skiing and snowmobiling. Be advised that hunting is allowed seasonally in Hickory Run State Park. You can swim from a guarded sand beach along the Lehigh River from Memorial Day to Labor Day. The river is also one of the prime fishing spots in the park. Other fisheries include Fourth Run, Sand Spring Run, Mud Run, and Hickory Run. All of these streams are stocked with brook and brown trout. Lehigh Gorge Family Campground is also near Lehigh Gorge State Park and Nescopeck State Park. The campground offers planned activities like theme weekends, bingo, and hayrides.

Campsites, facilities: There are 190 sites for tents or RVs up 26 feet: 150 have full hookups; 40 have no hookups. There are 20 pull-throughs. Picnic tables and fire rings are provided. Drinking water, restrooms with flush toilets, a dump station, a laundry, LP gas, ice, wood, a rec area, a pavilion, a swimming pool, a playground, volleyball, and RV storage and supplies are available. Leashed pets are permitted.

Reservations, fees: Reservations are suggested. The rate is $24–28 per night for up to two people. Each additional person is $6. Weekly, monthly, and seasonal rates are available. Open year-round.

Directions: From the junction of I-80 Exit

274/41 and Highway 534, travel 0.5 mile west on Highway 534, then 0.25 mile west on Highway 940 to the campground entrance on the right.

Contact: Lehigh Gorge Family Campground, 4584 State Street, White Haven, PA 18661, 570/443-9191, www.lehighgorgerv.com.

35 SANDY VALLEY CAMPGROUND

🚶 🏊 ⛵ 🚣 🐎 👫 🚐 ⛺

Rating: 7

near Hickory Run State Park

You can take advantage of the campground's boating, canoeing, and lake fishing. There are also hiking trails and planned weekend activities. At nearby Hickory Run State Park, 43 miles of trails range from easy to difficult. If you're an experienced hiker and feeling adventurous, you may want to try Boulder Field Trail or Shades of Death Trail. In the winter, some trails allow cross-country skiing and snowmobiling. Be advised that hunting is allowed seasonally in Hickory Run State Park. Anglers can fish at Hickory Run, Lehigh River, Fourth Run, Mud Run, or Sand Spring Run, all of which are stocked with brook and brown trout. There is a guarded sand beach for swimming along the Lehigh River. Sandy Valley Campground is also near Lehigh Gorge State Park.

Campsites, facilities: There are 113 sites for tents or RVs up to 27 feet: 98 have water and electricity; 15 have no hookups. Picnic tables and fire rings are provided. Drinking water, restrooms with flush toilets, a dump station, showers, a laundry, groceries, ice, LP gas, wood, a camp store, a rec area, a swimming pool, a playground, volleyball, and RV storage and supplies are available. Leashed pets are permitted.

Reservations, fees: Reservations are accepted. The rate is $24 per night for up to two people. Each additional person is $5. Seasonal rates are available. Open year-round.

Directions: From the junction of I-80 Exit 273/40 and Highway 940, travel 0.75 mile west on Highway 940, then turn left onto Lehigh Gorge Drive and travel 0.25 mile, then turn right onto Sandy Valley Road and travel 3.75 miles to the campground entrance on the right.

Contact: Sandy Valley Campground, RR 1 Box 110, White Haven, PA 18661, 570/636-0206, www.sandyvalley.com.

36 HICKORY RUN STATE PARK

🚶 🏊 ⛵ ❄ 🐎 👫 🚐 ⛺

Rating: 10

near White Haven

BEST (

The campground sits in the heart of the state park and is surrounded by woodlands. You have your choice of wooded and grassy sites. Among the park's 43 miles of hiking trails, there are 11 easy trails, seven moderate trails, and five difficult trails. Experienced hikers may want to try the ominously named Boulder Field Trail and Shades of Death Trail. Several trails are under a mile, like the 0.3-mile Leonardsville Trail, the 0.5-mile Beach and Nature Trails, the 0.6-mile Deer and Lake Trails, and the 0.7-mile Hawk Falls Trail. These trails not only offer diverse scenery but also provide good opportunities for bird watching and wildlife viewing. The anglers in your group won't feel left out with four trout-stocked streams and the Lehigh River running through the park. There is a guarded sand beach for swimming along the river. It is open from Memorial Day to Labor Day. During the winter, you can go cross-country skiing, snowmobiling, and ice skating. Be advised that hunting is allowed seasonally in Hickory Run State Park.

Campsites, facilities: There are 381 sites for tents or RVs up to 10 feet: 64 have electricity; 317 have no hookups. Picnic tables and fire rings are available. Drinking water, restrooms with flush toilets, a dump station, a public phone, groceries, ice, wood, a camp store, a pavilion, and a playground are available. Leashed pets are permitted.

Reservations, fees: Reservations are accepted at 888/PA-PARKS (888/727-2757). The rate is $14–19 per night for up to five people; a fee may apply for additional guests. Pets are $2 for up to two pets. Senior and Pennsylvania resident discounts are available. Open April through December.

Directions: From the junction of I-80 Exit 274 and Highway 534, travel six miles east on Highway 534 to the campground entrance on the right.

Contact: Hickory Run State Park, RR 1 Box 81, White Haven, PA 18661-9712, 570/443-0400, hickoryrunsp@state.pa.us.

37 W T FAMILY CAMPING

Rating: 7

near Hickory Run State Park

The sites at this campground are wooded. You can walk the trails here or head over to 15,500-acre Hickory Run State Park, where there are 43 miles of trails. There are mostly easy and moderate trails, but Ridge, Boulder Field, Fourth Run, Fireline, and Shades of Death are all marked difficult and should be attempted only by experienced hikers. Along Hickory Run, you can fish or swim from a sand beach. Other fishing spots include Fourth Run, Mud Run, Sand Spring Run, and the Lehigh River which runs along the western border of the park. Be advised that hunting is allowed seasonally in Hickory Run State Park. W T Family is also near Pocono Lake. The campground offers planned activities like bingo and theme weekends.

Campsites, facilities: There are 110 sites for tents or RVs up to 28 feet: 42 have full hookups; 40 have water and electricity; 28 have no hookups; 7 are pull-throughs. Picnic tables

and fire rings are provided. Drinking water, restrooms with flush toilets, a dump station, a public phone, groceries, ice, wood, a rec hall, an arcade, a pavilion, a swimming pool, a wading pool, a playground, miniature golf, badminton, a sports field, volleyball, and RV storage and supplies are available. Leashed pets are permitted. There is a traffic control gate for security.

Reservations, fees: Reservations are accepted. The rate is $26–42 per night for up to two people. Each additional person is $7. Weekly, monthly, and seasonal rates are available. Major credit cards are accepted. Open year-round.

Directions: From the junction of I-80 Exit 284/43 and Highway 115, travel 5.5 miles south on Highway 115 to the campground entrance on the right.

Contact: W T Family Camping, Box 1486, Route 115, Blakeslee, PA 18610, 570/646-9255, www.wtfamily.com.

38 FOUR SEASONS CAMPGROUNDS

Rating: 8

near Big Pocono State Park

The views from this mountain campground can be glimpsed between the beautiful surrounding areas of woodlands. You have your choice of shaded or sunny sites here. At nearby Big Pocono State Park, you can go hiking on a seven-mile trail system. There are three interconnecting trails designated by color. North Trail is red; South Trail is yellow; and Indian Trail is orange. North Trail is the most difficult with steep grades and rough surfaces. Three-mile South Trail welcomes hikers and horseback riders. The trails are your best chances for spotting birds and wildlife. Those birding binoculars will come in handy for the view at Camelback Mountain's summit where you can see eastern Pennsylvania and parts of New York and New Jersey. Be advised that hunting is allowed seasonally in Big

Pocono State Park. Back at the campground, you can participate in planned activities on the weekends.

Campsites, facilities: There are 125 sites for RVs up to 30 feet: 100 have full hookups; 25 have water and electricity. There are 38 pull-throughs. Picnic tables and fire rings are provided. Drinking water, restrooms with flush toilets, a dump station, a laundry, groceries, ice, LP gas, wood, a general store, a rec area, a swimming pool, a playground, two shuffleboard courts, badminton, horseshoes, a sports field, a volleyball court, and RV storage and supplies are available. Some sites are wheelchair accessible. Leashed pets are permitted.

Reservations, fees: Reservations are accepted. The rate is $28–30 per night for up to two people. Open mid-April through mid-October.

Directions: From the junction of Highway 715 and Highway 611, travel one mile north on Highway 611, then turn left onto Scotrun Avenue and travel 0.25 mile, then turn left onto Babbling Brook Road and travel 0.75 mile to the campground entrance on the right.

Contact: Four Seasons Campgrounds, RD 1 Box 18, Babbling Brook Road, Scotrun, PA 18355, 570/629-2504, www.four seasonscampgounds.com.

39 OTTER LAKE CAMP RESORT

Rating: 10

near Delaware State Forest

BEST (

This 300-acre property lies in the midst of the Poconos; all of its campsites are wooded. Motorboats with electric motors, canoes, kayaks, and other non-powered craft are welcome on 60-acre Otter Lake. If you don't have your own, you can rent rowboats, canoes, and pedal boats from the resort. Among the species of fish you can cast for are bass, sucker,

catfish, sunfish, and bluegill. You can swim from the sand beach along the lake's shore. There are miles of hiking trails that double as snowmobiling trails in the winter. Ski trails are also nearby. Back at the campground, there are planned activities like bingo, ceramics, and archery.

Campsites, facilities: There are 300 sites for tents or RVs up to 33 feet: 250 have full hookups; 50 have water and electricity; 25 are pull-throughs. Picnic tables and fire rings are provided. Drinking water, restrooms with flush toilets, a dump station, showers, two laundries, modem access, phone hookup, cable TV hookup, a public phone, groceries, ice, LP gas, wood, a full service store, a pavilion, an equipped pavilion, a playground, a rec hall, an arcade, two swimming pools, a wading pool, two whirlpools, a sauna, a basketball court, two shuffleboard courts, four tennis courts, two racquetball courts, badminton, horseshoes, volleyball, a sports field, and RV supplies are available. Some sites are wheelchair accessible. Leashed pets are permitted.

Reservations, fees: Reservations are accepted at 800/345-1369. The rate is $32–50 per night for up to two people. Each additional person is $5. Weekly and seasonal rates and group discounts are available. Major credit cards are accepted. Open year-round.

Directions: From the junction of I-80 Exit 309/52 and U.S. 209, travel four miles north on U.S. 209, then 300 feet northwest on Highway 402, then 7.5 miles west on a paved road to the campground entrance on the left.

Contact: Otter Lake Camp Resort, P.O. Box 850, Marshalls Creek, PA 18335, 570/223-0123, www.otterlake@otterlake.com.

40 MOUNTAIN VISTA CAMPGROUND

Rating: 8

near the Delaware Water Gap

Mountain Vista lives up to its name with

a wonderful view of the surrounding valley. The sites here are large and wooded. You can enjoy the property's stocked trout pond or planned weekend activities like live entertainment, dances, bingo, and crafts. At the nearby Delaware Water Gap, you enjoy many recreational activities on and off the water including boating, canoeing, fishing, hiking, biking, bird watching, and wildlife viewing.

Campsites, facilities: There are 195 sites for tents or RVs up 40 feet; 170 have full hookups; 25 have water and electricity. There are 18 pull-throughs. Picnic tables and fire rings are provided. Drinking water, restrooms with flush toilets, a dump station, a public phone, cable TV hookup, modem access, a phone hookup, groceries, ice, wood, fishing supplies, a general store, a rec area, an equipped pavilion, an arcade, ping-pong, a swimming pool, a basketball court, a bocce court, a playground, a shuffleboard court, a tennis court, badminton, horseshoes, a sports field, a sand volleyball court, and RV storage and supplies are available. Some sites are wheelchair accessible. Leashed pets are permitted.

Reservations, fees: Reservations are accepted. The rate is $28–39.50 per night for up to two people. Each additional person is $5. Weekly, monthly, and seasonal rates are available. Open April through beginning of November.

Directions: From the junction of I-80 Exit 309/52 and U.S. 209, travel north 0.1 mile on U.S. 209, then northwest two miles on Highway 447, then north three miles on Business U.S. 209, then turn left onto Craig's Meadow Road and travel one mile, and finally turn left onto Taylor Drive and travel 500 feet to the campground entrance on the right.

Contact: Mountain Vista Campground, 50 Taylor Drive, East Stroudsburg, PA 18301, 570/223-0111, www.mtnvistacampground.com.

41 DELAWARE WATER GAP KOA

Rating: 9

near the Delaware Water Gap

You have your choice of grassy, wooded, and open sites. At the Delaware Water Gap you can find enjoyable activities on and off the water. Boating and fishing are popular activities here. There are several launch areas for your watercraft. You can rent a boat if you don't have your own. The anglers in your group can cast for herring, shad, smallmouth, largemouth, and rock bass, trout, sunfish, suckers, carp, fall fish, stripers, and walleye. Both the Appalachian National Scenic Trail and the Delaware Canal Towpath run through this recreation area. Back at KOA you can participate in planned weekend activities like hayrides, bingo, and miniature train rides. The campground has a traffic control gate for security.

Campsites, facilities: There are 166 sites for RVs up to 55 feet: 159 have water and electricity; seven have no hookups. There are 12 pull-throughs. Picnic tables and fire rings are provided. Drinking water, restrooms with flush toilets, a dump station, showers, a laundry, modem access, a phone hookup, cable TV hookup, a public phone, groceries, ice, LP gas, wood, a camp store, a snack bar, an equipped pavilion, a rec area, a swimming pool, a playground, badminton, a sports field, horseshoes, miniature golf, volleyball, and RV storage and supplies are available. Some sites are wheelchair accessible. Leashed pets are permitted.

Reservations, fees: Reservations are accepted at 800/562-0375. The rate is $33–37 per night for up to two people. Each additional person is $6. Open April through October.

Directions: From the junction of I-80 Exit 309/52 and U.S. 209, travel six miles north on U.S. 209, then turn right onto Hollow Road and travel one mile to the campground entrance on the left.

Contact: Delaware Water Gap KOA, 233 Hollow Road, East Stroudsburg, PA 18301, 570/223-8000, www.koa.com/where/pa/38101.

42 DINGMANS CAMPGROUND

🏃 🚴 🏊 🚣 🛥 🎿 🐕 🏇 ♿ 🚐 ⛺

Rating: 9

near the Delaware Water Gap

You have your choice of wooded, open, and riverside sites. The campground offers lake boating, fishing, and swimming from a sand beach. For drier pursuits, you can enjoy the hiking trails or participate in campfires. At nearby Delaware Water Gap National Recreation Area, you have more options on and off the water. Motorboats, canoes, kayaks, and other non-powered craft are welcome on the river. The anglers in your group can cast for smallmouth bass, muskie, walleye, catfish, bluegill, and sunfish. The area has several hiking trails, including part of the Appalachian National Scenic Trail. Dingman's Falls Boardwalk Trail is wheelchair accessible and leads to the base of the falls. Other hiking trails include Raymondskill Falls, Karamac, and Table Rock Spur. The McDade Recreational Trail is a multi-use trail open to bikers and cross-country skiers. You can go horseback riding on Conashaugh View and Upper Ridge Trails.

Campsites, facilities: There are 133 sites for tents or RVs up to 30 feet. No sites have hookups. There are eight walk-in sites. Picnic tables and fire rings are provided. Drinking water, restrooms with flush toilets, a dump station, showers, a sports field, a playground, volleyball, horseshoes, a Frisbee golf course, and RV storage and supplies are available. Some sites are wheelchair accessible. Leashed pets are permitted.

Reservations, fees: Reservations are accepted at 877/828-1551. The rate is $22–25 per night for up to two people. Each additional person

is $5. Group rates are available. Major credit cards are accepted. Open year-round.

Directions: From the junction of I-80 Exit 309 and Highway 209, travel 22.75 miles north on Highway 209, then follow signs to the campground entrance on the right.

Contact: Dingmans Campground, 1006 Route 209, Dingmans Ferry, PA 18328, 570/828-1551, www.dingmanscampground.com.

43 FOXWOOD FAMILY CAMPGROUND

🏃 🏊 🚣 🛥 🏇 🐕 ♿ 🚐 ⛺

Rating: 9

near the Delaware Water Gap

BEST (

This property's 170 acres have shaded and open sites, as well as a 0.5-acre stocked fishing pond. At the nearby Delaware River, you have many recreational opportunities on and off the water. You can boat on the river or fish for shad, smallmouth bass, black and white crappie, channel catfish, muskie, bluegill, brown, brook, and rainbow trout, and white sucker. There are also hiking trails along the shore and in the surrounding woodlands. Back at the campground, you can participate in planned activities on the weekends like campfires, movies, hayrides, and arts and crafts.

Campsites, facilities: There are 350 sites for tents or RVs up to 27 feet: 164 have full hookups; 186 have water and electricity. There are 12 pull-throughs. Picnic tables and fire rings are provided. Drinking water, restrooms with flush toilets, a dump station, showers, a laundry, modem access, a phone hookup, a public phone, groceries, ice, LP gas, wood, a camp store, a rec area, a swimming pool, a playground, miniature golf, badminton, a sports field, and volleyball are available. Some sites are wheelchair accessible. Leashed pets are permitted.

Reservations, fees: Reservations are accepted at 800/845-4938. The rate is

$27–30 per night for up to two people. Each additional person is $6. Weekly and seasonal rates and group discounts are available. Major credit cards are accepted. Open mid-April through October.

Directions: From the junction of I-80 Exit 309/52 and U.S. 209, travel 1.5 miles north on U.S. 209, then turn right onto Buttermilk Falls Road and travel 0.25 mile, then turn left onto Mount Nebo Road and travel one mile to the campground entrance on the left.

Contact: Foxwood Family Campground, 400 Mount Nebo Road, East Stroudsburg, PA 18301, 570/421-1424, www.foxwoodcamp-ground.com.

44 JIM THORPE CAMPING RESORT

🏃 ♨ 🛶 🚣 🐎 ⛳ ♿ 🚐 ⛺

Rating: 8

near the Lehigh River

If you're an angler, you'll love the proximity of this campground to the Lehigh River. Among the species you can cast a line for are trout, bluegill, crappie, and catfish. If you prefer to stay on dry land, check out the hiking trails at the campground. Jim Thorpe Camping Resort is also near 2,972-acre Beltzville State Park. The centerpiece of the park is 949-acre Beltzville Lake and its 19.8 miles of shoreline. Motorboats, rowboats, canoes, kayaks, inflatables, and other non-powered watercraft are welcome on the lake. Since it is a warm-water and cold-water fishery, you can fish for stocked trout, walleye, muskie, striped, largemouth, and smallmouth bass, and perch. There are 15 miles of hiking that traverse the park. Back at the campground you can enjoy planned weekend activities.

Campsites, facilities: There are 200 sites for tents or RVs up to 28 feet: 100 have full hookups, 70 have water and electricity; 30 have no hookups. There are 75 pull-throughs. Picnic tables and fire rings are provided. Drinking water and restrooms with flush toilets, a dump station, a laundry, a pubic phone, groceries, ice, LP gas, wood, a rec hall, a pavilion, a swimming pool, a playground, a shuffleboard court, badminton, volleyball, and RV storage and supplies are available. Some sites are wheelchair accessible. Leashed pets are permitted.

Reservations, fees: Reservations are accepted. The rate is $25–33 per night for up to two people. Each additional person is $5. Major credit cards are accepted. Open April through October.

Directions: From the junction of U.S. 209 and Highway 903, travel north 0.25 mile on U.S. 209, then turn left onto Broadway and travel 2.25 miles to the campground entrance on the left.

Contact: Jim Thorpe Camping Resort, P.O. Box 328, Jim Thorpe, PA 18229, 570/325-2644, www.jimthorpecamping.com.

45 SUNNY REST LODGE

🏃 ♨ 🛶 🚣 🐎 🚐 ⛺

Rating: 5

near Beltzville State Park

At this 190-acre nudist campground, clothes are optional in most areas, but nudism is required in the pool and spa. At nearby Beltzville State Park, you can choose from a wide variety of outdoor recreational options. Water activities abound on and around 949-acre Beltzville Lake. You can launch motorboats from two launch areas, Pine Run East Launch and Preacher's Camp. If you don't have your own craft, you can rent a paddleboat, canoe, rowboat, pontoon boat, or motorboat from the park's concession. Waterskiing is a favorite sport on the lake. You can also cast for trout, bass, walleye, muskie, and perch. For drier pursuits, check out the 15 miles of hiking trails that traverse the park. Be advised that hunting is allowed seasonally in Beltzville State Park.

Campsites, facilities: There are 121 sites for tents or RVs up to 60 feet: eight have full hookups; 38 have water and electricity; 75 are tents only; 15 are pull-throughs. Picnic tables and fire rings are provided. Drinking water, restrooms with flush toilets, a dump station, showers, a laundry, modem access, phone hookup, cable TV hookup, a public phone, groceries, ice, LP gas, wood, a camp store, a rec area, a playground, an arcade, a swimming pool, a spa, two tennis courts, a volleyball court, water volleyball, ping-pong, and a basketball court are available. No pets are permitted.

Reservations, fees: Reservations are required at 866/786-6950. The rate is $25–50 per night for up to two people. Each additional person is $5. Seasonal rates are available. Major credit cards are accepted. Open mid-May through mid-September.

Directions: From the junction of Pennsylvania Turnpike Exit 74/34 and U.S. 209, travel 150 feet north to the Bowmanstown sign, then turn right and travel three miles to the campground entrance on the left.

Contact: Sunny Rest Lodge, 425 Sunny Rest Drive, Palmerton, PA 18071, 610/377-2911, www.sunnyrestlodge.com.

46 BLUE MOUNTAIN RV & CAMPING RESORT

Rating: 7

near Beltzville State Park

You can enjoy stream fishing on this campground's property or head to nearby Beltzville State Park and 949-acre Beltzville Lake. The water is stocked with warm-water and cold-water species like brook, brown, and rainbow trout, walleye, muskie, smallmouth and largemouth bass, and perch. Anglers can cast from 19.8 miles of shoreline or take out a boat. Motorboats with unlimited horsepower, canoes, kayaks, inflatables, rowboats, pedal boats, and most other non-powered craft are welcome on the lake. There are two launching and mooring spots. Pine Run East Launch is on the north shore of the lake, and Preacher's Camp is on the south. Pohopoco Creek runs along the state park property. Waterskiing is a favorite activity in these waters. If you don't have your own boat, you can check out the rentals at the park concessions. Those of you who prefer to stay dry can hike 15 miles of trails within the park.

Campsites, facilities: There are 63 sites for tents or RVs up to 25 feet: 51 have full hookups, 12 have no hookups. Picnic tables and fire rings are provided. Drinking water, restrooms with flush toilets, a dump station, showers, a laundry, groceries, ice, LP gas, wood, a camp store, a rec area, a pavilion, a swimming pool, a playground, horseshoes, and RV storage and supplies are available. Leashed pets are permitted.

Reservations, fees: Reservations are accepted. The rate is $28.50 per night for up to two people. Each additional person is $6. Open year-round.

Directions: From the junction of Pennsylvania Turnpike Exit 74/34 and U.S. 209, travel 0.25 mile south on U.S. 209, then turn left onto Rock Street and travel 100 yards to the campground entrance on the right.

Contact: Blue Mountain RV & Camping Resort, 1500 Rock Street, Lehighton, PA 18235, 610/377-5313, dlh70@ptd.net.

47 BLUE RIDGE CAMPGROUND

Rating: 9

near Beltzville State Park

BEST (

Hikers will love this campground's proximity to the Appalachian National Scenic Trail and the Blue Ridge Mountains. A stream stocked by the state runs along the property, as do hiking trails. On the weekends, Blue

Ridge has planned activities, such as bingo, ceramics, and pig roasts. At nearby 2,972-acre Beltzville State Park, you can go boating and fishing in Beltzville Lake. The 949-acre lake has 19.8 miles of shoreline. There are 15 miles of hiking trails. Saw Mill Trail is the most interesting. Along its path you pass a gristmill raceway, a dam and gateways, several small ponds, a 1700s slate quarry, a stream, and wetlands. The campground is also near Jim Thorpe and the Lehigh River, a great spot for rafting, biking, and hiking.

Campsites, facilities: There are 120 sites for tents or RVs up to 50 feet: 100 have full hookups; 20 have water and electricity. Picnic tables and fire rings are provided. Drinking water, restrooms with flush toilets, a dump station, a portable dump, showers, a laundry, a public phone, groceries, ice, wood, a camp store, a pavilion, a playground, a rec room, an arcade, a swimming pool, a wading pool, badminton, volleyball, and a sports field are available. Some sites are wheelchair accessible. Leashed pets are permitted.

Reservations, fees: Reservations are accepted. The rate is $25–28.95 per night for up to two people. Each additional person is $5. Weekly and monthly rates are available. Open April through October.

Directions: From the junction of PA Turnpike Exit 74/34 and U.S. 209, travel 1.5 miles south on U.S. 209, then three miles southeast on Highway 248, and finally five miles west on Highway 895 to the campground entrance on the left.

Contact: Blue Ridge Campground, Route 895, P.O. Box 269, Ashfield, PA 18212, 570/386-2911, www.blueridgecamp.info.

48 DON LAINE CAMPGROUND

🚶 ⛵ 🛶 🚤 🦌 🚵 ♿ 🚐 ⛺

Rating: 6

near Beltzville State Park

At nearby Beltzville State Park you have a range of outdoor recreational activities at your disposal. The 949-acre Beltzville Lake has 19.8 miles of shoreline that includes a sand swimming beach. You can cast for brown and brook trout, muskie, smallmouth, largemouth, and striped bass, walleye, and perch. The park has two launching areas, Pine Run East and Preacher's Camp. Most motorized and non-powered watercraft are welcome on the lake, and waterskiing is a favorite activity. Motorboats, canoes, rowboats, pontoon boats, and paddleboats can be rented from the concession. For drier pursuits, you can enjoy the 15 miles of trails that run throughout the property or go for a picnic at the Pine Run West Day Use Area. Be advised that hunting is allowed seasonally within Beltzville State Park. Don Laine Campground is also near the Appalachian Trail. If you prefer to partake in the campground's entertainment offerings, there are planned weekend activities.

Campsites, facilities: There 166 sites for tents or RVs up to 27 feet: 100 have full hookups; 66 have water and electricity. Picnic tables and fire rings are provided. Drinking water, restrooms with flush toilets, a dump station, a laundry, a public phone, groceries, ice, LP gas, wood, a camp store, a pavilion, a playground, horseshoes, a rec area, a swimming pool, and a volleyball court are available. Some sites are wheelchair accessible. Leashed pets are permitted.

Reservations, fees: Reservations are accepted. The rate is $22–23 per night for up to four people. Each additional person is $5. Open mid-April through October.

Directions: From the junction of Pennsylvania Turnpike Exit 74/34 and U.S. 209, travel north nine miles to the Don Laine sign. Turn right onto a paved road and follow signs to the campground entrance at the end.

Contact: Don Laine Campground, 790 57 Drive, Palmerton, PA 18071, 610/381-3341 or 800/635-0152, www.donlaine.com.

49 CHESTNUT LAKE CAMPGROUND

Rating: 8

near Jacobsburg State Park

Fishing, boating, and canoeing are all welcome at this property's lake. If you don't have your own boat, you can rent a rowboat or canoe. At nearby Jacobsburg State Park, you can cast your line for stocked trout in Bushkill Creek or hike on 18.5 miles of trails. These multi-use trails are open to bikers and horseback riders. Among the wildlife you may spot along the way are white-tailed deer, red and gray squirrels, woodchucks, chipmunks, opossums, raccoons, and skunks. The park is also a favorite hangout for birders. Be advised that hunting is allowed seasonally in Jacobsburg State Park. The campground is also near Penn Forest Reservoir, Wild Creek Reservoir, and Minsi Lake. Chestnut Lake also has planned weekend activities.

Campsites, facilities: There are 285 sites for tents or RVs up to 30 feet: 100 have full hookups; 75 have water and electricity; 110 have no hookups. Picnic tables and fire rings are provided. Drinking water, restroom with flush toilets, a dump station, a laundry, a public phone, groceries, ice, LP gas, wood, a rec hall, a pavilion, a playground, badminton, horseshoes, a sports field, volleyball, and RV storage and supplies are available. Some sites are wheelchair accessible. Leashed pets are permitted.

Reservations, fees: Reservations are accepted. The rate is $25–27 for up to two people. Each additional person is $5. Open May through November.

Directions: From the junction of Highway 115 and U.S. 209, travel northeast 1.25 miles on U.S. 209, then turn right onto Frable Road and travel 0.25 mile, and finally turn right onto Frantz Road and travel 0.25 mile to the campground entrance on the right.

Contact: Chestnut Lake Campground,

P.O. Box 390, Brodheadsville, PA 18322, 570/992-6179.

50 SILVER VALLEY CAMPSITES

Rating: 7

near Big Pocono State Park

This campground offers pond fishing and planned activities on weekends. At nearby Big Pocono State Park you can hop onto a seven-mile trail system to explore the surrounding area. The three interconnecting trails that make up the system are Indian, North, and South Trails. North Trail is for seasoned hikers only. South Trail doubles as an equestrian trail. Be advised that hunting is allowed seasonally at Big Pocono State Park. Silver Valley is also near Jacobsburg State Park and Minsi Lake, which has a ramp and launch area for electric motorboats and non-powered craft. Anglers can cast for white perch, largemouth bass, or stocked rainbow trout and walleye.

Campsites, facilities: There are 125 sites for tents or RVs up to 30 feet: 77 have full hookups; 30 have water and electricity; 18 have no hookups. Picnic tables and fire rings are provided. Drinking water, restrooms with flush toilets, a dump station, a laundry, a public phone, modem access, a phone hookup, cable TV hookup, groceries, ice, LP gas, wood, a camp store, a rec hall, an arcade, two swimming pools, a playground, volleyball, and RV storage and supplies are available. Leashed pets are permitted.

Reservations, fees: Reservations are accepted at 888/CAMP-PA1 (888/ 226-7721). The rate is $34–40 per night for up to four people. Each additional person is $6. Major credit cards are accepted. Open April through October.

Directions: From the junction of Highway 115 and U.S. 209, travel one mile northeast on U.S. 209, then turn left onto Silver Valley

Road and travel 0.75 mile, then 0.5 mile on a paved road. Follow signs to the campground entrance on the right.

Contact: Silver Valley Campsites, RR 4, Box 4214, Saylorsburg, PA 18353, 570/992-4824, www.silvervalleycamp.com.

51 POCONO VACATION PARK

Rating: 9

near the Delaware Water Gap

At the Delaware Water Gap you can enjoy many outdoor recreational activities on and off the water. You can launch your own boat or rent one from an outfitter. Anglers can cast a line for shad, bluegill, smallmouth bass, channel catfish, muskie, black and white crappie, white sucker, and brook, brown, and rainbow trout. If you prefer to stay on dry land, there are 60 miles of trails in the Delaware Water Gap National Recreation Area. Back at the campground, you can participate in weekend activities such as hayrides and bingo.

Campsites, facilities: There are 325 sites for tents or RVs up to 90 feet: 315 have full hookups; 10 have water and electricity. There are 300 pull-throughs. Picnic tables and fire rings are provided. Drinking water, restrooms with flush toilets, a dump station, showers, a laundry, modem access, a phone hookup, cable TV hookup, a public phone, groceries, ice, LP gas, wood, a camp store, a pavilion, a playground, a rec hall, an arcade, a swimming pool, a wading pool, a putting green, a basketball court, a shuffleboard court, horseshoes, a volleyball court, a sports field, and RV storage are available. Leashed pets are permitted.

Reservations, fees: Reservations are accepted. The rate is $24.25–29 per night for up to two people. Each additional person is $5. Weekly, monthly, and seasonal rates are available. Major credit cards are accepted. Open year-round.

Directions: From the junction of I-80 Exit 305/48 and Business U.S. 209, travel two miles south on Business U.S. 209, then turn right onto Shafer School House Road and travel 0.5 mile to the campground entrance on the left.

Contact: Pocono Vacation Park, Shafer School House Road, RD5 Box 5214, Stroudsburg, PA 18360, 570/424-2587, www.poconovacationpark.com.

52 CAMP CHARLES CAMPGROUNDS

Rating: 8

near the Delaware Water Gap

Anglers and boaters can enjoy nearby Minsi Lake. Among the species of fish you can cast for are stocked rainbow trout and walleye, largemouth bass, white perch, and panfish. The state record for a white perch was set here in 1991. You are welcome to launch electric motorboats and non-powered craft on the lake. For more outdoor recreational opportunities, check out Delaware Water Gap National Recreation Area. River activities include canoeing, kayaking, tubing, and fishing. The 37-mile McDade Recreation Trail is open to hikers and bikers. If you're looking to do part of the Appalachian Trail, then you'll be happy to know 25 miles of it run through the Delaware Water Gap. There are also shared equestrian and hiking trails. You will have wonderful opportunities for bird watching and wildlife viewing while on the trails. Back at the campground you can participate in planned weekend activities.

Campsites, facilities: There are 155 sites for tents or RVs up to 27 feet: 120 have water and electricity; 35 have no hookups. Picnic tables and fire rings are provided. Drinking water, restrooms with flush toilets, a dump station, a portable dump, showers, a laundry, a public phone, groceries, ice, LP gas, wood, a camp store, a rec hall, a swimming pool, badminton, and volleyball are available. Leashed pets are permitted.

Reservations, fees: The rate is $22 per night for up to two people. Each additional person is $5. Open April through October.

Directions: From the junction of Highway 512 and Highway 191, travel 2.5 miles north on Highway 191, then turn right onto Lake Minsi Drive and travel 2.5 miles, then turn left onto Blue Mountain Drive and travel 1.75 miles to the campground entrance on the right.

Contact: Camp Charles Campgrounds, 1077 Blue Mountain Drive, Bangor, PA 18013, 610/588-0553, www.campcharles.com.

53 DRIFTSTONE ON THE DELAWARE

🏃‍♂️🏊‍♂️🛶🚣🐕🎣🚐⛺

Rating: 9

on the Delaware River

This campground is located on 140 acres along the Delaware River, near Minsi Lake. Anglers can cast for smallmouth and rock bass, walleye, pickerel, channel catfish, muskie, bluegill, and eels. You can use the boat ramp and dock for motorboats or non-powered craft. If you don't have your own boat, you can rent canoes and kayaks at the campground. The river is a favorite for canoeing, kayaking, and float trips. If you prefer to hike, the campground has 20 acres to explore. The area is great for wildlife viewing and bird watching. Back at the campground you can enjoy planned activities on the weekends like live entertainment, various sporting competitions, and a river festival.

Campsites, facilities: There are 190 sites for tents or RVs up to 45 feet; 184 have water and electricity, 6 have no hookups. No sites have full hookups. Picnic tables and fire rings are provided. Drinking water, restrooms with flush toilets, a dump station, a laundry, a public phone, modem access, phone hookup, groceries, ice, LP gas, wood, a general store, a rec area, an arcade, a swimming pool, a wading pool, a basketball court, a playground, badminton, a sports field, a volleyball court, and RV storage and supplies are available. Leashed pets are permitted. The campground has a traffic control gate for security.

Reservations, fees: Reservations are recommended at 888/355-6859. The rate is $31–39 per night for up to two people. Each additional person is $5. Some weekly and monthly rates are available. Open mid-May through mid-September.

Directions: From the junction of Highway 611 and Portland-Columbia Bridge/River Road, travel 3.75 miles south on River Road to the campground entrance on the left.

Contact: Driftstone on the Delaware, 2731 River Road, Mt. Bethel, PA 18343, 570/897-6859, www.driftstone.com.

54 EVERGREEN LAKE CAMPGROUND

🏃‍♂️🏊‍♂️🛶🚣❄️🐕🎣🚐⛺

Rating: 8

near Jacobsburg State Park

This campground has lake swimming, fishing, and boating. If you don't have your own non-powered boat, you can rent rowboats and pedal boats here. There are hiking trails and planned activities on weekends as well. At nearby Jacobsburg State Park, you have more outdoor recreational opportunities. Bushkill Creek is stocked with trout and an 18-mile network of multi-use trails welcomes hikers, bikers, horseback riders, and cross-country skiers. The 1.9-mile Henry's Woods Loop Trail is one of the best places for wildlife viewing. Be on the lookout for white-tailed deer especially. Be advised that hunting is allowed seasonally in Jacobsburg State Park.

Campsites, facilities: There are 275 sites for tents or RVs up to 28 feet: 100 have full hookups; 175 have water and electricity. There are 10 pull-throughs. Picnic tables and fire rings are provided. Drinking water, restrooms with flush toilets, a dump station, a portable dump, showers, a laundry, modem access, a phone hookup, cable TV hookup, a public phone, groceries, ice, LP gas, wood, fishing supplies, a general store, a pavilion, a playground, a rec hall, an arcade, a basketball court, and a sports field are available. Leashed pets are permitted.

Reservations, fees: The rates are $26–33 per night for up to four people. Each additional person is $6. Open April through October.

Directions: From the junction of U.S. 22 and SR 512, travel 8.5 miles north on Route 512 to Route 946 at the Moorestown signal, then 0.5 mile west on SR 946 to Copella Road, then turn right onto Benders Drive and travel 2.75 miles, and finally turn right and travel 0.25 mile to the campground entrance on the left.

Contact: Evergreen Lake Campground, 2375 Benders Drive, Bath, PA 18014, 610/837-6401.

SOUTHWEST

© JASON MILLER

BEST CAMPGROUNDS

In Pennsylvania's southwest region, you have a large

offering of family-friendly campgrounds thanks to the area's spectacular waterfalls, historic battlefields, and inspiring museums. This area's natural and historic sites are mostly in and around Uniontown, Johnstown, and Pittsburgh.

Scenic Ohiopyle State Park, just east of Uniontown in the Laurel Highlands, is one the state's largest and most popular parks. The Youghiogheny River has made Ohiopyle a nationally known rafting destination. The river travels right through the park, so you can watch rafters and kayakers on the Lower Yough's Class III and IV rapids or take your own ride on nature's roller coaster on a guided rafting trip. The Middle Yough's Class I and II rapids are perfect for taking in the scenery at a slower pace on a float or canoe.

The National Road (U.S. 40) runs through Uniontown into the highlands. Along the way to Ohiopyle, it passes Braddock's Grave and Mount Washington Tavern at Fort Necessity Battlefield. A restored fort marks the location where George Washington surrendered to the French on July 4, 1754.

Frank Lloyd Wright's Fallingwater, which is only 10 miles from Ohiopyle State Park, has been called the greatest work of art produced by an American. Its cantilevered ledges jut out over Bear Run in a dramatic fashion. Laurels and native sandstone help the house appear as if it has been there since the coal-forming times of the Carboniferous.

East of Greensburg, the historic Lincoln Highway roughly follows Forbes Trail, which was the main route between Fort Bedford and Fort Ligonier in the 1700s. Latrobe Brewing Company, the producer of Rolling Rock beer, can be found near scenic Saint Vincent's College in Latrobe. Further east is Idlewild Amusement Park, one of America's oldest theme parks, home to classic wooden coasters and Storybook Forest. Every September it hosts the Ligonier Highlands Games, where guests can toss the caber or enjoy some locally brewed stout.

In Johnstown you can ride the world's steepest vehicular inclined plane to the top of a mountain for views and souvenirs, or visit the

Allegheny Portage Railroad National Historic Site to see one of the greatest engineering feats of the 19th century. Lakemont Park, north of Altoona, has over 30 rides and attractions, including wooden roller coasters and a water park.

Unfortunately many of the attractions in the area take on a more somber tone. Of historical significance is the Johnstown Flood Museum, which memorializes the 2,209 people killed on May 31, 1889, when an earthen dam burst while the town slept. The site of the Flight 93 crash is popular with people wishing to pay respects to the passengers and crew members who perished in the skies above Western Pennsylvania on September 11, 2001.

Southeast of Johnstown, original inns and other examples of unique architecture can be seen along the road and in small settlements such as Schellsburg. Old Bedford Village, on old U.S. 220 just north of Bedford, is a complex of historical buildings collected from all over the county. Arranged in the manner of a typical colonial settlement, the buildings were reconstructed and contain demonstrations of early American crafts.

The City of Bedford Historic District includes the oldest courthouse in use in Pennsylvania and the Espy House, where President George Washington headquartered in 1794. A walking tour of 51 buildings in the historic district is available in the Bedford County Travel Guide.

In southwest Pennsylvania, all roads eventually lead to Pittsburgh. The Carnegie Museum of Natural History, the Carnegie Museum of Art, Carnegie Science Center, and the Andy Warhol Museum are cosmopolitan retreats in this part of the state, and new stadiums, walkways, restaurants, and shopping districts have popped up in areas once inhabited by steel mills and iron works. Those with ample time can see some of the area's more obscure locales, such as Meadowcroft Rockshelter, one of the oldest occupations in the Americas.

Let the back roads steer you to a farmer's market or an unnamed waterfall. Either way, southwest Pennsylvania's surprises aren't limited to what can be found along the road.

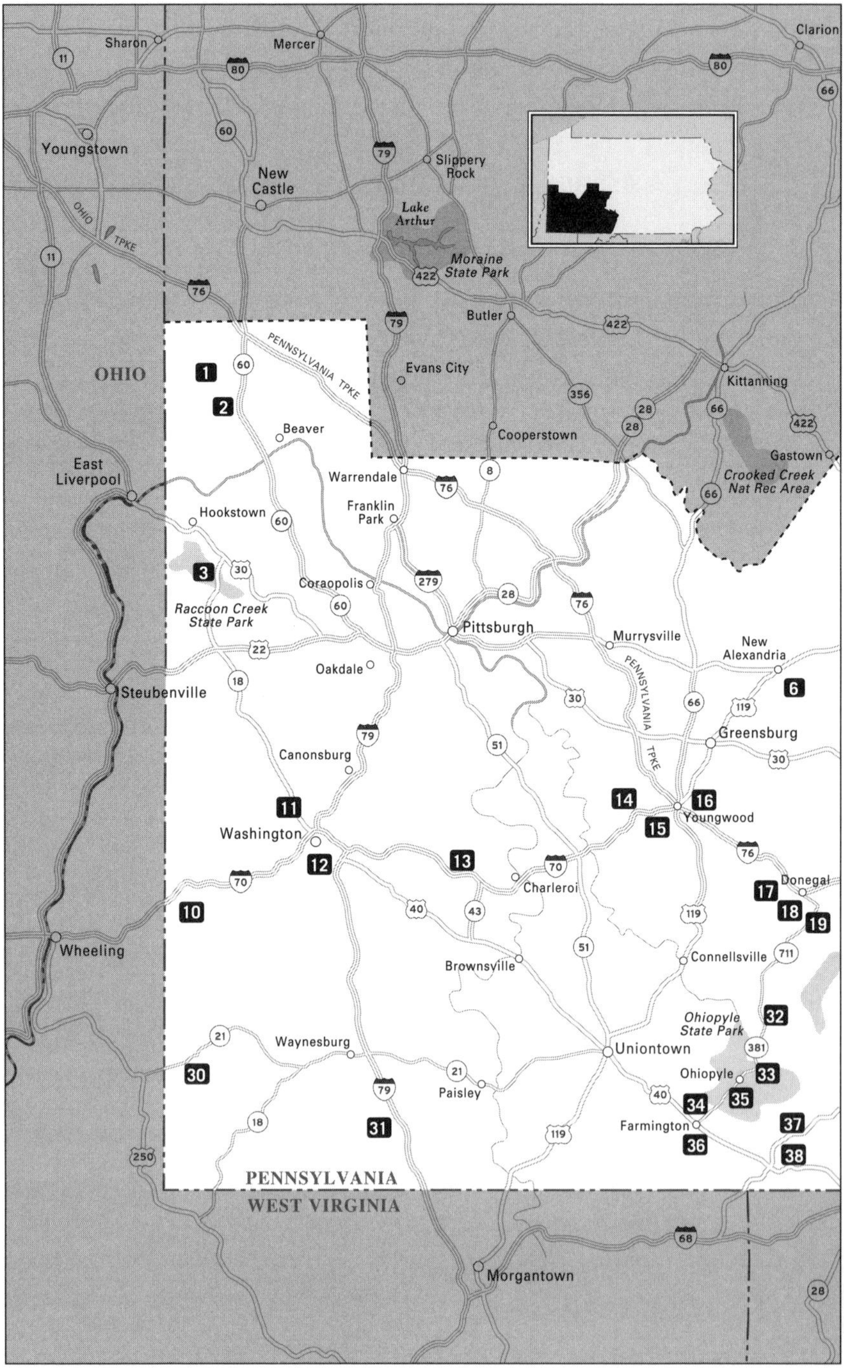

Sharon
Mercer
Clarion
Youngstown
New Castle
Slippery Rock
Lake Arthur
Moraine State Park
OHIO TPKE
Butler
Evans City
Kittanning
Cooperstown
Gastown
Crooked Creek Nat Rec Area
OHIO
PENNSYLVANIA TPKE
Beaver
East Liverpool
Warrendale
Franklin Park
Hookstown
Raccoon Creek State Park
Coraopolis
Pittsburgh
Murrysville
New Alexandria
Oakdale
Steubenville
Greensburg
Canonsburg
Youngwood
Washington
Charleroi
Donegal
Wheeling
Brownsville
Connellsville
Ohiopyle State Park
Waynesburg
Uniontown
Ohiopyle
Paisley
Farmington
PENNSYLVANIA
WEST VIRGINIA
Morgantown

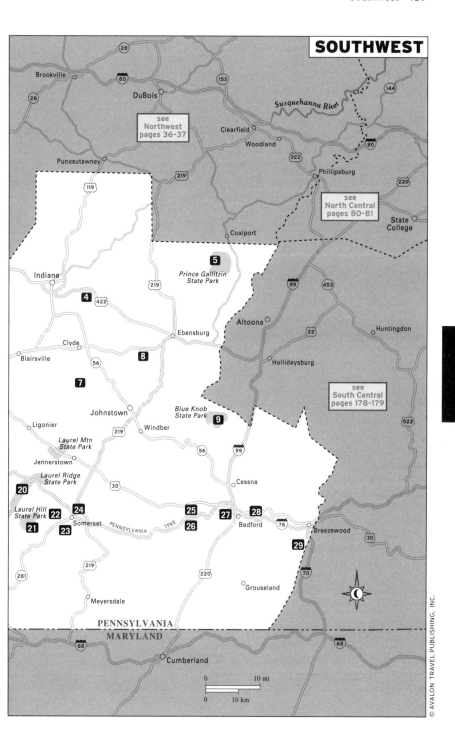

SOUTHWEST

Susquehanna River

28
Brookville
80
153
144
28
DuBois
see
Northwest
pages 36-37
Clearfield
Woodland
80
322
Punxsutawney
Phillipsburg
220
119
219
see
North Central
pages 80-81
State
College
Coalport
5
Prince Gallitzin
State Park
219
99
453
Indiana
Altoona
Huntingdon
4 422
Ebensburg
22
Clyde
Hollidaysburg
Blairsville
56
8
7
see
South Central
pages 178-179
Johnstown
Blue Knob
State Park
522
Ligonier
219
Windber
9
Laurel Mtn
State Park
56
99
Jennerstown
Cessna
Laurel Ridge
State Park
30
20
25 **27** **28**
Laurel Hill
State Park
22
24
Somerset
26
Bedford
76
Breezewood
21
23
PENNSYLVANIA TPKE
30
29
219
220
70
281
Grouseland
Meyersdale

PENNSYLVANIA
MARYLAND
68
68
Cumberland

0   10 mi
0   10 km

© AVALON TRAVEL PUBLISHING, INC.

① CRAWFORD'S CAMPING PARK

🏊 ⛴ 🏠 🎣 🚐 ⛺

Rating: 5

near Darlington

At this family-friendly campground, you can enjoy your evening under a shade tree after a beautiful drive through the Pennsylvania countryside. A climb to any of the three "B" hilltops (Beatty, Booth, and Bliss) gives a wonderful view of the Beaver County landscape. For a more moderate hike, try Fisherman's Trail. If you're an angler yourself, cast your rod on-site at Miskita Lake or make the short four-mile drive to Darlington Lake. The campground also has planned activities like bingo and hayrides on the weekends.

Campsites, facilities: There are 125 sites for tents or RVs up to 28 feet: 25 have full hookups; 80 have water and electricity; 20 have no hookups. There are 15 pull-throughs. Fire rings are provided. Drinking water, a dumping station, restrooms with flush toilets, showers, a fishing pond, a swimming pool, a sports field, a pavilion, a playground, ice, and wood are available. Leashed pets are permitted.

Reservations, fees: Reservations are accepted. The rate is $20–23 per night for up to two people. Each additional person is $3. Open mid-April through September.

Directions: From the junction of Highway 51 and Highway 168, travel one mile south on Highway 168, then right onto Hodgson Road for 0.75 mile to the campground entrance on the left.

Contact: Crawford's Camping Park, 273 Hodgson Road, Darlington, PA 16115, 724/846-5964.

② ORCHARD GROVE CAMPSITES

🥾 🏊 🏠 🎣 🚐

Rating: 4

near New Castle

As its name implies, you'll be surrounded by trees at Orchard Grove. For the active travelers among you, hikes up Steffen's Hill and Booth Hill offer views of Beaver and Allegheny Counties as well as their many lakes and rivers. You may be able to spot eagles, turkey vultures, red-tailed hawks, warblers, woodpeckers, and cardinals along the way. Among the animals you might see are white-tailed deer, raccoons, red and gray squirrels, cottontail rabbits, chipmunks, woodchucks, and opossums. With Pittsburgh only 30 minutes away, you can choose from many cultural and historical attractions, as well as water sports like boating and waterskiing. The Carnegie Museums are open year-round, as is the Andy Warhol Museum. The tourist boats of the Gateway Clipper Fleet offer trips down the Allegheny and Monongahela Rivers seasonally, and if you happen to be there in June, you can attend the Pittsburgh Regatta, a celebration of the Allegheny, Ohio, and Monongahela Rivers, which converge at Point State Park downtown. If you'd prefer activities nearer the campground, you can check out Wolf Run, Six Mile Run, or Warrior's Point for good hiking, bird watching, and wildlife viewing opportunities.

Campsites, facilities: There are 40 full hookup sites for RVs up to 30 feet. There are 20 pull-throughs. No tents are permitted. Picnic tables and fire rings are provided. Drinking water, a swimming pool, a playground, LP gas, and wood are available. Leashed pets are permitted.

Reservations, fees: Reservations are accepted. The rate is $18–20 per night for up to two people. Each additional person is $5. Open May through November.

Directions: From the junction of Highway 68 and Highway 60 Brighton Exit, travel north two miles on Highway 60, then turn left onto Tuscarawas Road for 4.5 miles to the campground entrance on the right.

Contact: Orchard Groves Campsites, 6138 Tuscarawas Road, Industry, PA 15052, 724/495-7828.

❸ RACCOON CREEK STATE PARK

Rating: 8

near Hookstown

BEST (

With 44 miles of hiking trails, 19.5 of which are backcountry and perfect for backpacking, 17 for mountain biking, Raccoon Creek offers many opportunities to get out and view the park's namesake raccoons. They visit at night, whether you're in a tent or in one of the park's 10 cabins. There are also deer, muskrat, mink, fox, and opossum. Among the many bird species are warblers and wild turkeys. A 314-acre wildflower reserve contains a diversity of plant life typifying Western Pennsylvania forest types, such as oak-hickory and pine, with over 500 species of plants identified within the reserve. You can fish in 101-acre Raccoon Lake, or swim at an 800-foot-long sand beach. The lake has walleye, yellow perch, bluegill, largemouth and smallmouth bass, sauger, crappie, sunfish, muskie, and bullhead catfish. During the winter, ice fishing and ice skating are permitted on the lake, and some trails are open to cross-country skiing. Snowmobiling is not permitted, but sledding is. Be advised that hunting is allowed seasonally in Raccoon Creek.

Campsites, facilities: There are 172 sites for tents or RVs up to 78 feet: 65 have electricity; 107 have no hookups. Picnic tables and fire rings are provided. Drinking water, restrooms with flush toilets, a dump station, hot showers, and a playground are available. Some sites are wheelchair accessible. Leashed pets are permitted in designated sites.

Reservations, fees: Reservations are accepted at 888/PA-PARKS (888/727-2757). The rate is $14–19 per night for up to five people; a fee may apply for additional guests. Pets are $2 for up to two pets per night. Weekly rates and discounts for seniors and Pennsylvania residents are available. Open mid-April through mid-October.

Directions: From Frankfort Springs, travel one mile north on Route 18, then turn right onto Main Park Road for one mile to the campground entrance on the left.

Contact: Raccoon Creek State Park, 3000 State Route 18, Hookstown, PA 15050-9416, 724/899-2200, raccooncreeksp@state.pa.us.

❹ L & M CAMPGROUNDS

Rating: 5

near Yellow Creek State Park

L & M draws outdoors enthusiasts of all sorts. The property's tall deciduous and evergreen trees hint at what can be found at nearby Yellow Creek State Park. Fishing and boating are popular activities on the 720-acre lake at Yellow Creek. The warm-water fishery has walleye, largemouth and smallmouth bass, pike, muskie and tiger muskie, bluegill, perch, and catfish. You can rent canoes, motor craft, or pontoon boats, or just opt for a swim. Marked trails make hiking enticing. The easiest trail is 0.5-mile Laurel Run, which loops from the park office. The more challenging two-mile Ridgetop Trail begins at the beach and heads upward on the ridge, but it doesn't loop back. For a great view of Yellow Creek Dam, take the 2.5-mile Damsite Trail. For less active pursuits, check out the horseshoes pit or the bird-watching tower. You can even take in an educational or interpretive workshop during your stay. Schedules are posted at the park office and change on a regular basis. Be advised that hunting is allowed seasonally in Yellow Creek State Park.

Campsites, facilities: There are 239 sites for tents or RVs up to 30 feet: 199 have full hookups; 10 have water and electricity; 30 have no hookups. There are four pull-throughs. Some sites are seasonal. Picnic tables and fire rings are provided. Drinking water, a dump station, a portable dump, restrooms with flush toilets, a laundry, miniature golf, groceries, a pavilion, playground equipment, ice, basketball, volleyball, shuffleboard, badminton, a sports field, wood, a public phone, and RV storage are available. Leashed pets are permitted.

Reservations, fees: Reservations are accepted. The rate is $12–15 per night for up to two people; a fee may apply for additional guests. Open mid-April through mid-October.

Directions: From the junction of U.S. 119 and U.S. 422, travel east 9.5 miles on U.S. 422, then south three miles on Highway 259, then west one mile on Campground Road to the campground entrance on the left.

Contact: L & M Campgrounds, 2743 Campground Road, Penn Run, PA 15765, 724/479-3264.

5 PRINCE GALLITZIN STATE PARK

🚶 🚴 🏊 🛶 🎣 🚐 ❄️ 🐕 ♿ 🚌 ⛺

Rating: 10

near Patton

BEST (

Located on the Allegheny Plateau, this state park offers beautiful views and an abundance of wildlife. The 6,249-acre park has a lake and wetlands, which provide excellent spots to see waterfowl such as mallard and wood ducks, warblers, and vireos. Glendale Lake has 26 miles of shoreline to explore by boat or on foot. Some sections of the sandy beaches are watched by lifeguards during the day, but most are secluded. Boating (in craft with up to 20-hp motors) and fishing are favorite activities. Since the lake is a warm-water fishery,

you'll find populations of muskie, pike, bass, trout, crappy, perch, and bluegill. A horseback riding area called Bridle Trail is in the southeast corner of the park. There are also cycling and hiking trails. During the winter, a 20-mile mountain bike path becomes a snowmobile and cross-country skiing trail. You can also try iceboating on the lake. Be alert that this park allows hunting seasonally.

Campsites, facilities: There are 437 sites for tents or RVs up to 30 feet: 80 have electricity; 357 have no hookups. Drinking water, restrooms with flush toilets, showers, laundry, a playground, camp store, boat rental and mooring, and a guarded swimming beach are available. Some sites are wheelchair accessible. Leashed pets are permitted in designated campsites.

Reservations, fees: Reservations are accepted at 888/PA-PARKS (888/727-2757). The rate is $14–19 for up to five people; a fee may apply for additional guests. Pets are $2 for up to two pets per night. Senior and PA resident discounts are available. Open April through mid-December.

Directions: From the junction of Highway 53 and Highway 253, travel south 1.75 miles on Highway 53, then turn right onto Beaver Valley Road for three miles to the campground entrance on the right.

Contact: Prince Gallitzin State Park, 966 Marina Road, Patton, PA 16668-6317, 814/674-1000, princegallitzinsp@state.pa.us.

6 KEYSTONE STATE PARK

🚶 🚴 🏊 🛶 🎣 🚐 ❄️ 🐕 ♿ 🚌 ⛺

Rating: 9

near Derry

This 1,200-acre park near Pittsburgh has a 78-acre lake that was constructed in the 1900s by the Keystone Coal and Coke Company. Swimming is permitted at the lake's sand beach, but no pets, smoking, food, or beverages are allowed on the beach proper.

There are also a plethora of trails for hiking, including McCune Run Trail, which is less than a mile long and leads to a beaver pond, and Davis Run, which travels 2.5 miles to wetlands and upland forests near the lake. Three of the trails loop. Lake Side Trail loops around the lake, and is over 2.5 miles long. Pine Trail is a short loop through a white and red pine plantation. Stone Lodge Trail is a more challenging 1.4-mile loop that starts and ends at the visitor center; it becomes steep as it moves from deciduous hardwoods to conifers at the ridge top. Lake Side Trail is the only park trail available for biking, but park roads are open to bikes. The campsites are divided into hillside and lakeside areas. During the winter, cross-country skiing, ice skating, and sledding are favorite activities. Be advised that hunting is allowed seasonally in Keystone State Park.

Campsites, facilities: There are 100 sites for tents or RVs up to 55 feet: 39 have electricity; 61 have no hookups. A dump station, restrooms with flush toilets, and showers are available. Drinking water is not available. Some sites are wheelchair accessible. Leashed pets are permitted in designated sites.

Reservations, fees: Reservations are accepted at 888/PA-PARKS (888/727-2757). The rate is $14–19 per night for up to five people; a fee may apply for additional guests. Pets are $2 for up to two pets. Senior and Pennsylvania resident discounts are available. Open April through December.

Directions: From the junction of U.S. 22 and Highway 981, travel 0.25 mile south on Highway 981, then turn left onto Derry Street and travel 0.7 mile. Derry Street becomes Keystone Park Road, which you follow for 1.5 miles until it becomes Manitto Road. Travel 0.4 mile on Manitto Road and follow signs to the campground entrance.

Contact: Keystone State Park, 1150 Keystone Park Road, Derry, PA 15627-3633, 724/668-2939, keystonesp@state.pa.us.

7 MIRROR LAKE RV CAMPING AND FISHING
🏕️ 🛶 🐕 🚐

Rating: 3

near Linn Run State Park

This campground's name comes from Mirror Lake, an on-property five-acre fishing lake that is stocked and permit accessible. Even if you're not an angler, you can appreciate the beautiful reflective water. Tall pines surround the lake and provide shade for many of the camping sites. A trout stream runs through the property as well. Nearby Linn Run State Park offers fishing, horseback riding, and hiking. Mountain bikes are not permitted on the six miles of trails, but foot traffic is welcome. Two of the trails loop. Adams Falls travels one mile through rhododendron and hemlock trees and takes you past a waterfall. Grove Run Trail's four miles begin quite easily, then climb steeper as the trail follows Grove Run. Flat Rock Trail is only 0.5 mile long; its terminus at the Linn Run stream has many large, slippery rocks. Iscrupe Trail is just a little longer at 0.75 mile, but is much easier going as it follows the original Linn Run Road. If you need a change from natural scenery, Idlewild Park, a family amusement park, is just a few miles from the campground. There is a water park at Idlewild, as well as many activities for families with young children.

Campsites, facilities: There are 85 sites for RVs up to 30 feet: 10 have full hookups; 75 have water and electricity. Drinking water, restrooms with flush toilets, a snack bar, and LP gas are available. Laundry facilities are nearby. Leashed pets are permitted.

Reservations, fees: Reservations are accepted. The rate is $20–24 per night for up to two people. Each additional person is $6. Seasonal rates are available. Major credit cards are accepted. Open mid-April through October.

Directions: From the junction of Route 56 and Route 711, travel eight miles south on Route 711 to the campground entrance.

Contact: Mirror Lake RV Camping and Fishing, 112 Trout Run Drive, New Florence,

PA 15944, 724/235-9983, http://users.adel-
phia.net/~mirrorlakellc.

8 WOODLAND PARK, INC.
🏃 🛶 🏠 🐕 🎣 🚐 ⛺

Rating: 3

near Gallitzin State Forest

Set on 72 acres of wooded grounds, this
campground gives you privacy and a natural
setting with modern amenities. You can fish
on six different ponds or hike one of the
many trails on the property. If you want local
history, visit the Johnstown Flood National
Memorial or the Johnstown Flood Museum.
The museum offers an award-winning movie
about this terrible tragedy that affected the
area in the early 1900s. You can also go to the
Johnstown Inclined Plane or the Allegheny
Portage Railroad National Historic Site. For
a more natural excursion, try nearby Gallitzin
State Forest and its 15,336 acres. If you're not
up to the 11.3-mile main trail in the Babcock
Division of the state forest or the 17.3-mile
John P. Saylor Memorial Trail, you might
enjoy the six-mile loop through the Clear
Shade Wild Area.

Campsites, facilities: There are 230 shaded
sites for tents or RVs up to 26 feet: 185 have
full hookups; 15 have water and electricity; 30 have no hookups. There are seven
pull-throughs. Picnic tables are provided.
Drinking water, a dump station, restrooms
with flush toilets, showers, a playground, basketball and volleyball courts, a softball field,
a pavilion, and fishing ponds are available. A
supply store sells groceries, ice, propane, and
firewood. Leashed pets are permitted.

Reservations, fees: Reservations are accepted. The rate is $12–18 per night for up to two
people. Each additional person is $1. Weekly,
monthly, and seasonal rates are available.
Major credit cards are accepted. Open mid-
April through mid-October.

Directions: From the junction of U.S. 219 West

and U.S. 22, travel 1.25 miles west on U.S. 22
to the campground entrance on the left.

Contact: Woodland Park, Inc., 220 Campground Road, Ebensburg, PA 15931, 814/472-
9857, woodlandparkinc@paonline.com.

9 BLUE KNOB STATE PARK
🏃 🚴 🏊 🛶 🎣 🏠 🐕 🎣 🚐 ⛺

Rating: 9

near Imler

Blue Knob Mountain reaches 3,146 feet above
sea level, making it the second-highest mountain in Pennsylvania. Its dome stands out from
the rest of the Allegheny Front and provides
wonderful views in every direction. With 5,874
acres of woodlands, Blue Knob State Park has
numerous trails, most of which are multi-use.
Three Springs Trail and Chappell's Field
Trail allow mountain biking and horseback
riding, and Mountain View Trail, Rock 'N'
Ridge Trail, and Crist Ridge Trail are suitable for
experienced bikers. The 26-mile Lost Turkey
Trail weaves through state park and state forest
land and is popular with backpackers. There are
several streams for swimming and fishing.
Brook trout as well as stocked trout are abundant. Blue Knob is home to many wildlife and
bird species. Among them are white-tailed deer,
raccoons, squirrels, red-tailed hawks, vireos, and
warblers. The campsites are available in both
open fields and wooded areas. Environmental
and interpretive programs are presented at the
amphitheater. You can check the schedules
posted at the park office for these changing
events. During the winter, snowmobiling,
downhill and cross-country skiing, and snow-
tubing are favorite activities. Be advised that
hunting is allowed seasonally in Blue Knob.

Campsites, facilities: There are 45 sites for
tents or RVs up to 40 feet: 25 have electricity;
20 have no hookups. There are two walk-in
sites. Drinking water, a dump station, restrooms with flush toilets, picnic pavilions and
tables, a swimming pool, and a playground

are available. Leashed pets are allowed in designated areas.

Reservations, fees: Reservations are accepted at 888/PA-PARKS (888/727-2757). The rate is $14–19 per night for up to five people. Pets are $2 for up to two pets per night. Weekly rates are available. Senior and Pennsylvania discounts are available. Open April through October.

Directions: From the junction of I-99 Exit 23 and U.S. 220, turn right onto Highway 164 West, then turn left onto Blue Knob Road and travel five miles to the campground entrance on the left.

Contact: Blue Knob State Park, 124 Park Road, Imler, PA 16655-9207, 814/276-3576, blueknobsp@state.pa.us.

10 FOUR SEASONS CAMPING RESORT

🚶 🚴 🏊 🎣 🐕 🚐 ⛺

Rating: 7

near West Finley

At 2,500 feet in elevation, this resort campground is surrounded by beautiful mountains and forest and borders state game lands. The resort property covers 700 acres and offers a choice of open and wooded sites. The campground is very family oriented and asks that campers adhere to resort rules about pets, trash, and use of facilities. The campground has three fishing ponds with species such as bluegill, sunfish, and catfish. There are also on-property trails for hiking and ATVs. Among the nearby attractions are Meadows Race Track, which features harness racing every night, the Pennsylvania Motor Speedway, and Capitol Music Hall.

Campsites, facilities: There are 90 sites for tents or RVs up to 30 feet: 30 have full hookups; 60 have water and electricity. All sites are pull-throughs. Drinking water, restrooms with flush toilets, showers, a laundry, a clubhouse, a general store, a snack bar, a restaurant, a TV lounge, indoor and outdoor pools,

picnic areas, a pavilion, a game room, a basketball court, and a sand volleyball court are available. Leashed pets are permitted.

Reservations, fees: Reservations are required at 877/660-4407. The rate is $27–29 per night for up to two people. Each additional person is $6. Open year-round.

Directions: From the junction of I-70 Exit 6/2 and U.S. 40, travel 0.75 mile east on U.S. 40, then 3.5 miles south on Highway 231, then turn right onto Burnsville Ridge Road and travel eight miles, then follow signs for 2.25 miles to the campground entrance.

Contact: Four Seasons Camping Resort, 69 Four Seasons Road, West Finley, PA 15377, 724/428-4407, www.campfourseasonsresort.com.

11 WHISPERING PINES FAMILY CAMPGROUND

🚶 🏊 🐕 🏇 🚐 ⛺

Rating: 2

near Washington

If the many planned activities at the campground, such as bingo and hayrides, aren't enough, you can take in the harness races at Meadows Race Track. Races at the huge venue are normally in the evenings. Choose from indoor seating or standing outside along the rail. There are fast-food vendors in addition to a sit-down restaurant. You could also visit the nearby Pennsylvania Trolley Museum and take a ride. Nature lovers can visit nearby 464-acre Cedar Creek Park, an access point for the Youghiogheny River Trail. Hikers and bikers can follow this trail for scenic views of the river or to prime fishing spots. You can go 21 miles north to McKeesport or 79 miles south to Meyersdale. Among the many species of fish found in the Youghiogheny are perch, bluegill, sunfish, catfish, and bass. The Gorge Trail offers views into the steep gorge cut into the northern section of the park by Cedar Creek, providing a chance to see natural cascades as the creek runs over shale steps.

Be advised that hunting is allowed seasonally in portions of the park.

Campsites, facilities: There are 42 sites for tents or RVs up to 30 feet: 11 have full hookups; 12 have water and electricity; 19 have no hookups. Drinking water, restrooms with flush toilets, a dump station, public phone, modem hookup, a pavilion, a swimming pool, a playground, and a sports field are available. Leashed pets are permitted.

Reservations, fees: Reservations are accepted. The rate is $20–24 per night for up to two people. Each additional person is $5. Major credit cards are accepted. Open mid-April through October.

Directions: From the junction of I-70 Exit 17/6 and Highway 18, travel 4.5 miles north on Highway 18 to the campground entrance on the left.

Contact: Whispering Pines Family Campground, 1969 Henderson Avenue, Washington, PA 15301, 724/222-9830.

12 WASHINGTON/ PITTSBURGH SW KOA

Rating: 7

near Washington

At this campground you have a choice between open and wooded sites. There is a catch-and-release pond on the property for fishing. You can also take the many trails on foot or on horseback to explore the wooded landscape. At the Pennsylvania Trolley Museum in Washington, you can browse displays or take a 90-minute guided tour. The museum also offers scenic trolley rides that travel about four miles round-trip. The campground is also within range of Pittsburgh, where you'll find the Carnegie and Andy Warhol Museums, baseball games at PNC Park, and boating on the Ohio, Allegheny, and Monongahela Rivers. At the north end of Washington County, Meadowcroft Rockshelter has a museum and archaeological displays. Native Americans lived here over 14,000 years ago, making this one of the oldest inhabited sites in North America. If you'd prefer to partake in the campground's entertainment, you have your choice of hayrides, bonfires, and special events celebrations.

Campsites, facilities: There are 94 sites for tents or RVs up to 80 feet: 67 have full hookups; 20 have water and electricity; 7 have no hookups; 35 are pull-throughs. Fire rings are provided. Drinking water, a dump station, restrooms with flush toilets, laundry, a public phone, a rec room, a pavilion, a swimming pool, badminton, ice, volleyball courts, LP gas, and a general store are available. Leashed pets are permitted.

Reservations, fees: Reservations are accepted. The rate is $20–36 per night for up to two people. Each additional person is $6. Open year-round.

Directions: From the junction of east I-70 and I-79, travel 0.75 mile south on I-79 Exit 33/7, then 0.5 mile west on U.S. 40, then turn right onto Vance Station Road for one mile to the campground entrance on the left.

Contact: Washington/Pittsburgh SW KOA, 7 KOA Road, Washington, PA 15301, 724/225-7590, www.koa.com/where/pa/38146.

13 CAMPGROUND 70

Rating: 2

near Washington

This campground in the Mon Valley is close to the Monongahela River, where boating is popular. If you don't have your own craft, there are several companies that offer rentals. The scenery at this campground is more urbanized than at other campgrounds in the area, but it has better access to main highways, like its namesake I-70. Nearby are Mingo Creek Park and Cross Creek County Park. Mingo Creek has 11 miles of trails for horseback riding or hiking. Many of these trails loop and are rated easy. The one-mile Hemlock Trail is an interpretive nature trail that can be enjoyed on foot. Cross Creek have a picnic area and a small 1.5-mile hiking trail.

Along Wheeling Creek is the Enlow Fork Natural Area. It is part of State Game Lands that have been protected by the Western Pennsylvania Conservatory. Several hiking trails follow the stream or venture into more forested areas. They vary by length and difficulty.

Campsites, facilities: There are 35 full hook-up sites for RVs up to 30 feet. There are 33 pull-throughs. Picnic tables and fire rings are provided. Drinking water, a dump station, restrooms with flush toilets, laundry, and LP gas are available. Leashed pets are permitted.

Reservations, fees: Reservations are accepted at 800/327-6053. The rate is $18 per night for up to four people. Each additional person is $5. Open mid-April through October.

Directions: From the junction of I-70 and Highway 917 Exit 32B, travel 0.25 mile north on Highway 917, turn left at the T, then 0.75 mile to the campground entrance on the right.

Contact: Campground 70, 824 Bentleyville Road, Charleroi, PA 15022, 724/239-2737, dperun@bentcom.net.

14 MADISON/PITTSBURGH KOA

🏃 ⛵ 🚣 🐾 🚐 ⛺

Rating: 3

near Ruffs Dale

The large trees at this KOA provide wonderful shade for the campsites. An on-property pond provides entertainment for the anglers in your group. The campground's central location is perhaps its best attribute, however. You are within 45 minutes of Pittsburgh to the north and within 30 minutes of Ohiopyle State Park and the Youghiogheny River to the east. One day you may experience museums and incline rides in the city and the next horseback riding and rafting in the Laurel Highlands. Pittsburgh also has the Monongahela, Allegheny, and Ohio Rivers for motorboating and waterskiing. Ohiopyle has numerous hiking and biking trails, such as 3.8-mile Sugarloaf Trail, which goes from Sugarloaf Mountain down to the Middle Youghiogheny. Sugarloaf Mountain is inside Ohiopyle State Park and has another 9.4 miles of horseback riding and snowmobiling trails that can be biked. If you're on foot, Ferncliff Peninsula is a must. The main trail, Ferncliff Trail is an easy 1.7-mile loop that branches three other short trails; 0.1-mile Buffalo Nut trail, 0.5-mile Fernwood Trail, and 0.5-mile Oakwoods Trail. Spelunkers can go deep at Laurel Caverns Geologic Park, one of Pennsylvania's largest caves. If you'd prefer to stay on-site, the campground offers organized activities like bingo and live music.

Campsites, facilities: There are 110 sites for tents or RVs up to 45 feet: 105 have full hookups; five have no hookups. There are 80 pull-throughs. Drinking water, a dump station, restrooms with flush toilets, showers, laundry, modem hookup, a game room, boat rentals, and LP gas are available. Leashed pets are permitted.

Reservations, fees: Reservations are accepted at 800/562-4034. The rate is $23–41 per night for up to two people. Each additional person is $5. Major credit cards are accepted. Open year-round.

Directions: From the junction of I-70 Exit 54/25A and Madison Road, travel north 0.75 mile on Madison Road to the campground entrance on the right.

Contact: Madison/Pittsburgh KOA, RR 2 Box 560, Ruffs Dale, PA 15679, 724/722-4444, kampkoa@infionline.net.

15 BUFFALO RUN RV PARK

🏃 🚴 ⛵ 🐾 🚐

Rating: 5

near Laurel Summit State Park

Buffalo Run is a creek that flows on the campground's property. Its name comes from the buffalo that lived here when the first Europeans arrived. Buffalo, wolves, and cougar are no longer present, but there's a circa-1840s barn with the original advertisements still visible, as well as a quirky general store. The laid-back country feel and surrounding woods make this campground the perfect place to return to after a day at Idlewild Amusement Park or Laurel Summit State Park, which are only about 30 minutes away. Laurel Summit is a six-acre park located in the mountains at 2,739 feet in elevation. It has picnicking areas with tables and pavilions, as well as restrooms and drinking water. Trailheads for Spruce Flats Bog and Wolf Rocks Trail are also located here. Back at the campground, you can visit two mine entrances, see a coal seam, and learn of the history of coal and coke in the area; you can also fish in Buffalo Run or take a ride on the nearby bike trail.

Campsites, facilities: There are 24 sites for RVs up to 30 feet. All of the sites have water and electricity. No tents are permitted. Picnic tables and fire rings are provided. Drinking water, a dump station, restrooms with flush toilets, wood, and ice are available.

Reservations, fees: Reservations are accepted. The rate is $20 per night for up to two people. Each additional person is $4. Weekly, monthly, and seasonal rates are available. Major credit cards are accepted. Open year-round.

Directions: From the junction of Pennsylvania Turnpike Exit 75/8 and I-70, travel 0.5 mile west on I-70 Hunker Exit, then two miles south on an unnamed paved road to the campground entrance on the right.

Contact: Buffalo Run RV Park, RR 2 Box 845, Ruffsdale, PA 15679, 724/925-1540, www.buffalorunrvpark.freeservers.com.

16 FOX DEN ACRES CAMPGROUND

Rating: 6

near New Stanton

Located at the foothills of the Laurel Highlands, this campground offers wonderful wooded views. The property's lake is not only scenic, but it also provides fishing, swimming, and boating opportunities. Fox Den Acres also has a wildlife museum and trading post that are open to guests. Some campsites take advantage of the surrounding woods' shade, but most are open. For wonderful hiking opportunities, visit nearby Beechwood Farms Nature Reserve and the Youghiogheny River Trail. Beechwood Farms, operated by the Audubon Society, has five miles of hiking trails. Of its 134 acres, 40 are set aside for a native plant sanctuary. The Youghiogheny River Trail is a 43-mile Pennsylvania rails-to-trails project. You can pick up part of this well-maintained hiking and biking trail anywhere from Pittsburgh to Confluence. If you'd prefer to partake of the on-site activities, the campground has organized weekend events like bingo, ceramics, and hayrides.

Campsites, facilities: There are 350 sites for tents or RVs up to 120 feet: 200 have full hookups; 80 have water and electricity; 20 have electricity; 50 have no hookups. There are 105 pull-throughs. Picnic tables and fire rings are provided. Drinking water, a dump station, restrooms with flush toilets, showers, modem hookups, a pavilion, wading and swimming pools, a playground, horseshoes, ice, a sports field, volleyball, basketball, LP gas, and RV supplies are available. Leashed pets are permitted.

Reservations, fees: Reservations are accepted. The rate is $20–25 per night for up to two people. Each additional person is $5. Weekly and monthly rates are available. Open May through October.

Directions: From the junction of Pennsylvania Turnpike Exit 75/8 and I-70 and U.S. 119, travel 0.5 mile north on U.S. 119, then one mile north on Highway 66 Exit 1/2, then bear to the right and travel 0.5 mile on an unnamed paved road. Follow signs to the campground entrance on the left.

Contact: Fox Den Acres Campground, Wilson Fox Road, New Stanton, PA 15672, 724/925-7054, www.foxdenacres.com.

17 DONEGAL CAMPGROUND

Rating: 2

near Kooser State Park

You have your choice of two ski resorts nearby: Hidden Valley has an intimate setting, while Seven Springs offers more slopes and more people. The 70-mile Laurel Highlands Hiking Trail begins at Ohiopyle State Park and goes to Johnstown. You can pick up sections of the trail for day hikes at Seven Springs or Kooser State Park. For fishing, visit Kooser Lake in Kooser State Park. This warm-water fishery has bluegill, bass, and trout. Be advised that neither night fishing nor boating are permitted at the lake. Swimming along the 350-foot beach on the lake is at your own risk. You can also hike the easy 1.5-mile Kooser Trail or the one-mile Kincora Trail, which was named after an Irish priest. There are more hiking trails at Kooser's sister park, Linn Run. Grove Run Trail, a four-mile loop with some steep sections, is the longest.

Campsites, facilities: There are 45 sites for tents or RVs up to 30 feet: 36 have full hookups; four have water and electricity; five have no hookups. There are 38 pull-throughs. Picnic tables and fire rings are provided. Drinking water, a dump station, restrooms with flush toilets, a modem hookup, a public phone, a pavilion, a swimming pool, a rec hall, wood, playground equipment, groceries, ice, and a general store are available. Groceries, ice, and wood are sold. Leashed pets are permitted.

Reservations, fees: Reservations are accepted. The rate is $22 per night for up to two people. Each additional person is $6. Major credit cards are accepted. Open year-round.

Directions: From the junction of Pennsylvania Turnpike Exit 91/9 and Highway 31, travel west 0.5 mile on Highway 31 to the campground entrance on the left.

Contact: Donegal Campground, P.O. Box 104, Donegal, PA 15628, 724/593-7717.

18 LAUREL HIGHLANDS CAMPLAND

Rating: 7

near Laurel Hill State Park

These open sites sit in a shallow valley surrounded by woodlands. The quaint outbuildings give this large campground a down-home feel. You can fish at the little pond on the property, but save the swimming for the pool. You can also fish at nearby Laurel Hill Lake for crappie, sunfish, bluegill, perch, largemouth and smallmouth bass, trout, and sucker. The lake allows swimming from a 1,200-foot sand beach. The maximum depth is five feet. Canoes, paddleboat, and rowboat rentals are available and if you have an electric motorboat, you can use one of two launch areas or 30 mooring areas along the 63-acre lake. There are also 12 miles of hiking trails within the 3,935 acres of Laurel Hill State Park. Among them are the easy Pumphouse and Martz Trails, the moderate Tram Road, Waterline, Hemlock, and Ridge Trails, and the difficult Bobcat and Lake Trails. Winter activities include ice fishing, snowmobiling, cross-country skiing, and iceboating. If you'd prefer to participate in the on-site entertainment, Laurel Highlands Campland has organized activities like bingo, ceramics, and live music.

Campsites, facilities: There are 400 full hookup sites for tents or RVs up to 30 feet. There are 200 pull-throughs. Drinking water, a dump station, restrooms with flush toilets, a laundry, a game room, a rec hall, a snack bar, a pool, and LP gas are available. Cable hookups are an additional charge. All areas are wheelchair accessible. Leashed pets are permitted.

Reservations, fees: Reservations are accepted at 724/593-6325. The rate is $28 per night for up to six people. Each additional person is $5. Open year-round.

Directions: From the junction of Pennsylvania Turnpike Exit 91/9 and Highway 31, travel 0.75 mile east on Highway 31 to the campground entrance on the right.

Contact: Laurel Highlands Campland, P.O. Box 188, Donegal, PA 15628, 724/593-6326.

19 MOUNTAIN PINES CAMPING RESORT

Rating: 6

near Laurel Hill State Park

The sites here are shaded, and Mountain Pines provides 24-hour security. The trout stream that runs on the property is stocked, but requires a locally available Pennsylvania fishing license Even if you're not after the "big one," this stream adds nice ambience to the campground. You can sit and listen to its murmuring or you can head out for some hiking and biking on the nearby rails-to-trails on part of the Great Allegheny Passage. Laurel Hill State Park offers wildlife and bird watching. Among the most frequently seen animals are chipmunks, woodchucks, white-tailed deer, red, gray, and fox squirrels, skunks, opossums, raccoons, and cottontail rabbits. Birders will enjoy bluebirds, tree swallows, and red-tailed hawks. Just remember that feeding wildlife is not permitted. The old-growth stand of hemlock trees within the park can be visited by way of Hemlock Trail. Upon your return to Mt. Pines, enjoy an evening hayride and roast some marshmallows before turning in for the night.

Campsites, facilities: There are 823 sites for tents or RVs up to 38 feet: 800 have full hookups; 23 have no hookups. Drinking water, a dump station, restrooms with flush toilets, cable TV, a camp store, miniature golf, concession stands, lighted tennis courts, an indoor pool, an outdoor pool, a wading pool, a playground, steam and exercise rooms, and shuffleboard are available. Leashed pets are permitted.

Reservations, fees: Reservations are accepted. The rate is $18–30 per night for up to two people. Each additional person is $6. Weekly rates are available. Open year-round.

Directions: From the junction of PA Turnpike Exit 9 and Route 31, travel east two miles on Route 31 to Route 711, then south two miles on Route 711 to the campground entrance on the left side.

Contact: Mountain Pines Camping Resort, RD1 Box 715, Champion, PA 15622, 724/455-7414.

20 KOOSER STATE PARK

Rating: 9

near Somerset

This state park offers 250 forested acres at an elevation of 2,600 feet. It is named for John Kooser, who settled part of the area near Kooser Spring in 1867. Almost 60 years later, the property was acquired by the Commonwealth of Pennsylvania. It was turned into a Civilian Conservation Corps project in the 1930s. The CCC built the lake, along with many of the cabins. The 350-foot beach allows swimming at your own risk and has a concession, changing facilities, and a restroom area. A trout stream runs through the park, and also carries bluegill and bass. Kincora and Kooser Trails are the most popular for hiking. In the winter, Kooser is perfect for cross-country skiing. If you're looking for something outside of this small state park, a stopover area for the 70-mile Laurel Highlands Hiking Trail is near Kooser State Park, and 51,000-acre Forbes State Forest and 3,213-foot Mount Davis are right down the road.

Campsites, facilities: There are 47 sites for tents or RVs up to 40 feet: 14 have electricity; 33 have no hookups. Picnic tables and pavilions are available. Drinking water and a dump station are nearby. Some sites are wheelchair accessible. Leashed pets are permitted.

Reservations, fees: Reservations are accepted at 888/PA-PARKS (888/727-2757). The rate is $14–19 per night for up to five people; a fee may apply for additional guests. Pets are $2 for up to two pets. Senior and Pennsylvania resident discounts are available. Open April through December.

Directions: From the junction of I-70/76 and Highway 31, travel southeast nine miles on Highway 31 to the campground entrance on the right.

Contact: Kooser State Park, 943 Glades Pike, Somerset, PA 15501-8509, 814/445-8673, koosersp@state.pa.us.

21 LAUREL HILL STATE PARK

Rating: 9

near Somerset

This mostly mountainous park was a Civilian Conservation Corps project that started in 1935. The corps built the first roads, trails, camps, and recreational facilities. Laurel Hill Lake comprises 63 of the park's 3,935 acres. Its warm-water fishery has trout, largemouth and smallmouth bass, sunfish, perch, crappie, catfish, sucker, and bluegill. Lifeguards attend the 1,200-foot sand beach along the lake. Two trout streams, Laurel Hill Creek and Jones Mill Run, flow on park property. You can enjoy activities on and along the lake or hike and bike the many scenic trails. The most spectacular trail is Hemlock Trail, which meanders through an old-growth stand of hemlock trees. Laurel Hill also offers several educational and interpretive programs. Check the schedule at the park office for these changing events. During the winter, snowmobiling, cross-country skiing, ice fishing, and ice boating are favorite activities. Be advised that hunting is allowed seasonally in Laurel Hill. The Flight 93 site is within driving distance. You can obtain directions from the park office.

Campsites, facilities: There are 262 sites for tents or RVs up to 40 feet: 149 have electricity; 113 have no hookups. Drinking water, a dump station, restrooms with flush toilets, and showers are available. Some sites are wheelchair accessible. No pets are permitted.

Reservations, fees: Reservations are accepted at 888/PA-PARKS (888/727-2757). The rate is $14–19 per night for up to five people; a fee may apply for additional guests. Weekly rates are available. Senior and Pennsylvania resident discounts are available. Open April through October.

Directions: From the junction of I-70/76 Exit 110 and Highway 31, travel 10 miles west on Highway 31, then two miles south on Highway 31. Follow signs to the campground entrance on the right.

Contact: Laurel Hill State Park, 1454 Laurel Hill Park Road, Somerset, PA 15501-5629, 814/445-7725, laurelhillsp@state.pa.us.

22 PIONEER PARK CAMPGROUND

Rating: 8

near Forbes State Forest

Pioneer Park has 185 acres of recreational area, comprising the campground and a wooded area, and 50 acres of lakes. Located in the foothills of the Laurel Ridge Mountains, the beautifully maintained campground offers grassy sites and specializes in trout fishing. Only permits, not licenses, are required to fish these stocked lakes, and for children it's free. You can also take a paddleboat out on one of the lakes. At nearby Forbes State Forest, you can check out Becks Springs along the Jones Mill Run or hike to the Jones Mill Run Dam. You also can hike easy, 2.5-mile Fish Run Trail to the remains of an old railroad grade and bridge; take Wolf Rock Trail two miles to the Wolf Rocks Overlook for an open view of the Linn Run Valley; or walk 1.5-mile Spruce Flats Bog Trail to the 28-acre bog at an elevation of 2,660 feet. If you'd prefer to remain on-site, the campground offers organized activities like bingo and ceramics.

Campsites, facilities: There are 345 sites for tents or RVs up to 40 feet: 229 have full hookups; 20 have electricity and water; 96 have no hookups. There are 107 pull-throughs. Drinking water, restrooms with flush toilets, a laundry, cable TV, modem access, a rec hall, a swimming pool, a game room, miniature golf, and LP gas are available. Some sites are wheelchair accessible. Leashed pets are permitted.

Reservations, fees: Reservations are accepted. The rate is $20–31 per night for up to two people. Each additional person is $3. Weekly, monthly, and seasonal rates are available. Major credit cards are accepted. Open year-round.

Directions: From the junction of Pennsylvania Turnpike Exit 110/10 and Highway 601, travel 0.5 mile south on Highway 601, then seven miles west on Highway 31, then turn right onto Trent Road for 0.25 mile to the campground entrance on the right.

Contact: Pioneer Park Campground, 273 Trent Road, Somerset, PA 15501, 814/445-6348, www.pioneerparkcampground.com.

23 SCOTTYLAND CAMPING RESORT

Rating: 6

near Laurel Hill State Park

Adjacent to Laurel Hill Creek in the Laurel Highlands, Scottyland sits on 311 acres. The woodlands surrounding the park almost give you the feel of being in a valley all your own. The atmosphere varies in different parts of the property. When you're by the creek or on the hiking trails, the rest of the world seems to melts away; when you're near the activities area, however, you may find yourself wanting join in a game or take a dip in the pool.

Among the fish stocked at nearby Laurel Hill State Park are perch, bass, trout, bluegill, and catfish. The park's 12 miles of trails offer easy, moderate, and difficult hikes. From the Pumphouse Trail parking lot, you can follow the moderate 0.6-mile Waterline Trail uphill to view some of the park's large lepidodendron fossils or take the easier 1.6-mile Pumphouse Trail to the Jones Mill Run Dam. If you're feeling really adventurous, try the difficult one-mile Bobcat Trail, the most remote and least-used trail in the entire park.

Campsites, facilities: There are 566 sites for tents or RVs up to 48 feet: 14 have full hookups; 31 have water and electricity; 521 have no hookups. There are 450 pull-throughs. Drinking water, a dump station, restrooms with flush toilets, showers, a laundry, pavilions, a rec hall/game room, a skating rink, a snack bar, miniature golf, a baseball field, tennis and basketball courts, and a playground are available. Leashed pets are permitted.

Reservations, fees: Reservations are accepted at 800/242-CAMP (800/242-2267). The rate is $23–25 per night for up to three people. Each additional person is $2. Open year-round.

Directions: From the junction of Pennsylvania Turnpike Exit 110/10 and Highway 601, travel 0.5 mile south on Highway 601, then 10 miles south on Highway 281, then one mile west on Highway 653 to the campground entrance on the right.

Contact: Scottyland Camping Resort, 1618 Barron Church Road, Rockwood, PA 15557, 814/926-3200.

24 WOODLAND CAMPSITES

Rating: 5

near Laurel Hill State Park

Nestled at the foot of the Laurel Highlands, this campground offers great views of the surrounding woods and glimpses of Mount Davis, the highest mountain in Pennsylvania. The nearby streams and lakes of Laurel Hill State Park make fishing and boating very accessible. Jones Mill Run and Laurel Hill Creek are excellent for trout fishing and 63-acre Laurel Hill Lake is stocked with crappie, bluegill, perch, sucker, bass, and catfish. You can rent a paddleboat, canoe, or rowboat at the 1,200-foot beach. Electric motorboats are welcome at the launch area. The state park offers 12 miles of trails, ranging from easy to difficult. Not to be missed are Martz Trail for the trees, Hemlock Trail for the stands of old-growth forest, and Lake Trail for its fantastic views of Laurel Hill Lake. If you'd prefer to partake of the on-site entertainment, the campground offers many organized activities throughout the week. Some campground sites are shaded, but most are open and grassy. If you stay over on a weekend you're likely to catch a number of musical performances.

Campsites, facilities: There are 105 sites for tents or RVs up to 23 feet: 65 have full hookups; 40 have electricity and water. There are three pull-throughs. Drinking water, restrooms with flush toilets, laundry, a rec hall, miniature golf, a game room, and a swimming pool are available. Leashed pets are permitted.

Reservations, fees: Reservations are accepted. The rate is $20–25 per night for up to two people. Each additional person is $6. Open April through October.

Directions: From the junction of Pennsylvania Turnpike Exit 110/10 and Highway 601, travel 1.75 miles north on Highway 601, then turn right onto Gilmour Road and travel 0.5 mile to the campground entrance on the right.

Contact: Woodland Campsites, 291 Gilmour Road, Somerset, PA 15501, 814/445-8860.

25 SHAWNEE STATE PARK

Rating: 10

near Schellsburg

This 3,983-acre park, named for the Shawnee tribe that lived here in the early 1700s, has numerous nature trails as well as 451-acre Shawnee Lake. This warm-water fishery is stocked with bluegill, crappie, yellow perch, sunfish, largemouth and smallmouth bass, pike, pickerel, muskie, walleye, sucker, bullhead, and carp. Among the hiking trails are 3.8-mile Forbes Trail, 3.4-mile Lake Shore Trail, 2-mile Field and 2-mile Felton Trails, 1.7-mile Pigeon Hills Trail, 1.5-mile Shawnee Trail, 0.9-mile Tiday Trail, 0.8-mile Lost Antler Trail, and 0.4-mile Colvin Trail. Lake Shore is the easiest of the 7.5 miles of biking trails. You can also visit remnants of the original Forbes Trail in the park. In 1758 General Forbes and his army stayed here on their way to Fort Duquesne in Pittsburgh to fight in the French and Indian War. During the winter, snowmobiling, sledding, ice fishing, ice skating, and tobogganing are favorite activities. Be advised that hunting is allowed seasonally in Shawnee State Park.

Campsites, facilities: There are 293 sites for tents or RVs up to 40 feet: 65 have electricity; 228 have no hookups. Drinking water, a dump station, restrooms with flush toilets, showers, a laundry, picnic tables, pavilions, a camp store, wood, and charcoal are available. Some sites are wheelchair accessible. Leashed pets are permitted in designated campsites.

Reservations, fees: Reservations are accepted at 888/PA-PARKS (888/727-2757). The rate is $14–19 per night for up to five people; a fee may apply for additional guests. Pets are $2 for up to two pets per night. Senior and Pennsylvania resident discounts are available. Open April through December.

Directions: From Schellsburg, travel two miles south on Highway 96 to the campground entrance on the left.

Contact: Shawnee State Park, 132 State Park Road, Schellsburg, PA 15559-7300, 814/733-4218, shawneesp@state.pa.us.

26 CHOICE CAMPING COURT

🧗 🏊 🚣 ❄️ 🐕 🐎 ♿ 🚐 ⛺

Rating: 3

near Cowans Gap State Park

These open sites are clean and comfortable. With a stream running on the property, this is a good spot for casual anglers and kids. If you're looking for a nice weekend stopover, Choice Camping Court provides planned activities on Friday night, and all day on Saturday and Sunday. At nearby Cowans Gap State Park, you can take a picnic lunch or buy something to eat from the concession stand. Cowans Gap Lake has perch, smallmouth and largemouth bass, panfish, and trout. Its 500-foot sand beach is good for swimming and has lifeguards present most days between Memorial Day and Labor Day. You can also get a great feel for the scenic lake by traveling around it on the popular 1.5-mile Lakeside Trail, which is an easy, level hike. During the winter, cross-country skiing, ice fishing, and ice skating are favorite activities. Be advised that hunting is allowed seasonally in Cowans Gap State Park.

Campsites, facilities: There are 200 sites for tents or RVs up to 30 feet: 150 have full hookups; 50 have water and electricity. Picnic tables and fire rings are provided. Drinking water, restrooms with flush toilets, a dump station, a laundry, a public phone, ice, wood, horseshoes, a sports field, and RV rentals are available. Some facilities are wheelchair accessible. Leashed pets are permitted.

Reservations, fees: Reservations are accepted. The rate is $23–25 per night for up to four people. Each additional person is $5. Open April through October.

Directions: From the junction of U.S. 220 and U.S. 30, travel five miles west on U.S. 30, then 2.5 miles southwest on Highway 31, then 0.25 mile west on Watson Road to the campground entrance on the left.

Contact: Choice Camping Court, 209 Choice Camping Road, Manns Choice, PA 15550, 814/623-9272.

27 FRIENDSHIP VILLAGE CAMPGROUND & RV PARK

🧗 🏊 🚣 🚐 🐕 ♿ 🚐 ⛺

Rating: 7

near Laurel Hill State Park

Many visitors to Friendship Village come for the nearby fort, built by the British to feign off attacks by Native Americans. The family-oriented campground offers a variety of daily activities and special events such as the Kids' Olympics in June and Hawaiian New Year in July. You have your choice of shaded or sunny sites. With a lake fringing some sites, water sports like fishing and paddle boating are easily accessible. There are also some hiking paths available for use in this country setting, but if you're looking for more of a hiking challenge, visit nearby Laurel Hill State Park. The park has 12 miles of hiking trails, including Pumphouse Trail, an easy 1.6-mile hike that leads to the picturesque Jones Mill Run Dam.

Campsites, facilities: There are 200 sites for tents or RVs up to 75 feet: 157 have full hookups; 33 have electricity; 10 have no hookups. Drinking water, restrooms with flush toilets, a dump station, showers, a laundry, cable TV, a swimming pool, a village store, a rec hall, a game room, miniature golf, a pavilion, boat rentals, wood, ice, LP gas, and RV rentals are available. Some sites are wheelchair accessible. Leashed pets are permitted.

Reservations, fees: Reservations are accepted at 800/992-3528. The rate is $20–31 per night for up to four people. Each additional person is $2 per night. Major credit cards are accepted. Open April through November.

Directions: From the junction of PA Turnpike Exit 146/11 and I-99/US 220, travel south three miles on U.S. 220, then west two miles on U.S. 30, then north 0.5 mile to the end of Friendship Village Road to the campground entrance.

Contact: Friendship Village Campground,

348 Friendship Village Road, Bedford, PA 15522, 814/623-1677, friendship@adelphia.net.

28 SHAWNEE SLEEPY HOLLOW CAMPGROUND

Rating: 7

near Shawnee State Park

BEST (

This campground takes its name from nearby Shawnee State Park, located in the Allegheny Mountains. The Shawnee Sleepy Hollow Camp office resides in a stone and log building that is over 230 years old and was originally used as a stagecoach stop on the Forbes Trail. The area offers two lakes, Shawnee Lake and Raystown Lake, where you can rent a boat or go fishing. The warm-water fisheries offer up largemouth and smallmouth bass, yellow perch, muskie, bluegill, sucker, catfish, sunfish, pike, crappie, walleye, carp, bullhead, and pickerel. Shawnee State Park also offers educational and interpretive programs, which include nature walks, evening campfire tales, and movie screenings. Nearby Bedford also has many historic spots to explore, including Old Bedford Village, Fort Bedford Museum, and Historic Downtown Bedford. Old Bedford Village has craftspeople who wear authentic period clothing and give demonstrations of their craft. On your way to the attractions, you might cross one of the many covered bridges. If you prefer to stay on-site, the campground provides organized activities like bingo and hayrides.

Campsites, facilities: There are 74 sites for tents or RVs up to 26 feet: 67 have electricity and water; seven have no hookups. There are four pull-throughs. Drinking water, a pump-out service, restrooms with flush toilets, showers, laundry, a game room, a heated pool, a camp store, and trailer rentals are available. Boat rentals are available nearby. Leashed pets are permitted.

Reservations, fees: Reservations are accepted. The rate is $19–26 per night for up to four people. Pets are $2 per pet for up to two pets per night. Weekly, monthly, and seasonal discounts are available. Major credit cards are accepted. Open April through October.

Directions: From the junction of U.S. 220 and U.S. 30, travel seven miles west on U.S. 30 to the campground entrance on the right.

Contact: Shawnee Sleepy Hollow Campground, 147 Sleepy Hollow Road, Schellsburg, PA 15559, 814/733-4380, stauffer@bedford.net.

29 BRUSH CREEK CAMPGROUND

Rating: 6

near Cowans Gap State Park

Brush Creek Campground offers shaded and open sites on this small, quiet property. At nearby 1,085-acre Cowans Gap State Park, you can fish for trout, panfish, or bass in 42-acre Cowans Gap Lake or in the South Branch of Little Aughwick Creek. There is also a 500-foot sand beach along the lake for swimming. You can rent rowboats and paddle boats, or moor your own motorboat. Only motorboats with electric motors are permitted on the lake. There are several environmental and educational programs held at the park; they range from guided walking tours to hands-on activities. Check the park office for details on the changing events. The park's 10 hiking trails cover almost 10 miles total. The easiest trails are Ski Trail, One Mile Trail, Lakeside Trail, and Logging Road Trail. The three moderate trails are Plessinger Trail, Three Mile Trail, and Knobsville Road Trail. There are two difficult hikes, Geyer Trail and Cameron Trail. There is also one trail rated very difficult: Horseshoe Trail. Not only is this trail steep, but it also traverses loose stone as it winds its way up to the top of Cove Mountain.

Campsites, facilities: There are 35 sites for

tents or RVs up to 30 feet: 15 have full hookups; 10 have water and electricity; 10 have no hookups. Picnic tables and fire rings are provided. Drinking water, restrooms with flush toilets, a dumping station, a laundry, playground equipment, horseshoes, and a sports field are available. Leashed pets are permitted.

Reservations, fees: Reservations are accepted. The rate is $20 for up to four people. Each additional person is $5. Open April through October.

Directions: From the junction of Pennsylvania Turnpike Exit 161/12 and I-70, travel four miles east on I-70 Exit 151/30, then 0.5 mile west on Gapsville Road to the campground entrance on the left.

Contact: Brush Creek Campground, 2118 South Breezewood Road, Breezewood, PA 15533, 814/735-4035.

30 McNAY RIDGE CAMPGROUND

🚶 🏊 🛶 🎣 ♿ 🚗 ⛰️

Rating: 8

at Ryerson Station State Park

Named for Fort Ryerson, which was constructed in 1792, this 1,164-acre area became a state park in 1958. The campsites sit on McNay Ridge, which overlooks the rest of Ryerson Station State Park. A stream provides fishing within the park. Trout is stocked and there are also warm-water fish such as bluegill, catfish, sunfish, crappie, and perch. There are 11 miles of hiking trails; among them is Fox Feather Trail, which offers wonderful views of the surrounding woodlands. Other popular trails include Lazear Trail and Pine Box Trail. Guided hikes are sometimes offered during the summer, and there are educational and interpretive programs during evenings and weekends. Check the park office for current programs. During the winter, sledding, tobogganing, snowmobiling, ice fishing, and cross-country skiing are favorite activities. Be

advised that hunting is allowed seasonally in Ryerson Station State Park.

Campsites, facilities: There are 50 sites for tents or RVs up to 30 feet: 16 have electricity; 34 have no hookups. Picnic tables and fire rings are provided. Drinking water, a dump station, rustic toilets, a pool, pavilions, a concession stand, and a play area are available. Some sites are wheelchair accessible. No pets are permitted.

Reservations, fees: Reservations are accepted at 888/PA-PARKS (888/727-2757). The rate is $10–14 per night for up to five people; a fee may apply for additional guests. Weekly rates and discounts for seniors and Pennsylvania residents are available. Open mid-April through mid-December.

Directions: From Wind Ridge, travel two miles southwest on Highway 21, then turn left onto Bristoria Road for two miles, then left onto McNay Ridge Road for 0.5 mile to the campground entrance on the left.

Contact: Ryerson Station State Park, 361 Bristoria Road, Wind Ridge, PA 15380-1258, 724/428-4254, ryersonstationsp@ state.pa.us.

31 MT. MORRIS TRAVEL TRAILER PARK

🚶 🚴 🏕️ 🚗 ⛰️

Rating: 5

near Mount Morris

The large pine trees that encompass this rural site with gently rolling hills certainly give you the feeling of living outdoors. There are sunny and shady sites available. You have several choices for hiking nearby. The 30-mile Catawba Trail begins in Rice's Landing and ends at the Mason-Dixon Historical Park, never straying too far from the Mason-Dixon Line itself. Warrior Trail is a 68-mile trail that was originally established by Native Americans in the area as a route to Flint Ridge, Ohio, to trade for flint. This trail begins in

Greensboro and ends in Moundsville, West Virginia. Friendship Hill Historic Site was Albert Gallatin's residence. Gallatin was Thomas Jefferson's Secretary of State, and one of the people responsible for finding funding for the Louisiana Purchase. His beautifully restored home graces this wooded property, which has a 3.5-mile hiking trail that moves through meadows and a forested area with 200–300-year-old oak, pine, and beech trees. In Star City, West Virginia, only eight miles away, you have access to the Monongahela River and water sports like boating, canoeing, kayaking, fishing, and water skiing.

Campsites, facilities: There are 40 sites for tents or RVs up to 30 feet: 20 have full hookups; 20 have water and electricity. There are seven pull-throughs. Drinking water, a dump station, restrooms with flush toilets, hot showers, a laundry, a picnic area, and firewood are available. Leashed pets are permitted.

Reservations, fees: Reservations are accepted. The rate is $22 per night for up to two people. Each additional person is $5. Open year-round.

Directions: From I-79 Exit 1, travel 0.5 mile west on Locust Avenue, then one mile north on U.S. 19 to the campground entrance on the left.

Contact: Mt. Morris Travel Trailer Park, Route 19, Mount Morris, PA 15349, 724/324-2432.

32 YOGI BEAR'S JELLYSTONE PARK CAMP-RESORT

🚶 🚵 ⛵ 🎣 🚐 🏕 🏄 ♿ 🚙 ⛺

Rating: 8

near Ohiopyle State Park

BEST (

This campground has the feel of an old-time amusement park, without all the noisy coasters. From pool slides to a carousel, there are a staggering array of activities. You can also take train rides, fire-truck rides, and wagon rides around the beautiful property, and there are even visits from the resort's mascot, Yogi the Bear, and his

friends. This fun-filled atmosphere makes the campground a destination all its own, but its proximity to Ohiopyle State Park makes your stay even more special. You can take guided rafting and canoe trips down the Youghiogheny River or simply rent a boat for the day on your own. Trout fishing is seasonal at the park. There are also numerous hiking and biking trails. Old Mitchell Trail is a 1.8-mile moderate foot trail that loops to and from Old Mitchell Place Parking Area and winds through forest and meadow habitats. Sugar Run Trail, a 1.6-mile moderate trail, connects to Old Mitchell from Jonathan Run Trail.

Campsites, facilities: There are 150 sites for tents or RVs up to 40 feet: 108 have full hookups; 10 have water and electricity; 32 have no hookups. There is one pull-through. Drinking water, restrooms with flush toilets, a pump-out service, a laundry, cable and modem hookups, a snack bar, a game room, a swimming pool with two water slides, miniature golf, and LP gas are available. The facilities are wheelchair accessible. Leashed pets are permitted.

Reservations, fees: Reservations are accepted at 800/439-9644. The rate is $28–46 per night for up to four people. Each additional person is $6. Group rates are available. Major credit cards are accepted. Open year-round.

Directions: From Mill Run, travel 0.25 mile south on Highway 381 to the campground entrance on the right.

Contact: Yogi Bear's Jellystone Park Camp-Resort, 839 Mill Run Road, Mill Run, PA 15464, 724/455-2929, www.jellystonemillrun.com.

33 SCARLETT KNOB CAMPGROUND

🚶 🚵 🎣 🚐 🐕 🚙 ⛺

Rating: 10

near Ohiopyle State Park

BEST (

Scarlett Knob adjoins breathtaking Ohiopyle State Park, home of the Lower Youghiogheny River. Youghiogheny Bike Trail is one of several hiking, biking, and horseback riding trails within the park. Many visitors to the campground are boaters, and there's even a special area for kayakers and canoeists where quiet time begins a little earlier than at the other sites. If you don't have your own boat, there are many whitewater rafting companies in Ohiopyle that offer rentals and guided tours. You can raft the Class III/IV Lower section of the river through rapids like Cucumber, Dimple, and Railroad. The Middle Yough has gentler Class I/II rapids. Both sections have fishing, and a fishing lake on the property has species such as bluegill and sunfish. The wooded sites at Scarlett Knob make you feel like a part of the state park. Its convenient location makes it easy to take advantage of all the activities that the park and the town of Ohiopyle have to offer.

Campsites, facilities: There are 110 sites for RVs up to 40 feet: 18 have electricity and water; 92 have no hookups. There is one pull-through. Picnic tables and fire rings are provided. Drinking water, restrooms with flush toilets, a dump station, pit toilets, and a coin-operated laundry are available. Boat rentals are nearby. Leashed pets are permitted.

Reservations, fees: Reservations are strongly suggested. The rate is $19–21 per night for up to two people. Each additional person is $9.50. Major credit cards are accepted. Open mid-April through mid-October.

Directions: From Ohiopyle, travel two miles north on Highway 381 to the campground entrance on the left.

Contact: Scarlett Knob Campground, Route 381 North, Box 44, Ohiopyle, PA 15470, 724/329-5200, scarlettknobcampground.com.

34 BENNER'S MEADOW RUN CAMPING & CABINS

Rating: 9

near Ohiopyle State Park

BEST

Situated only a few miles from Ohiopyle State Park in the Laurel Highlands of southwestern

The Middle Youghiogheny River offers gentle Class I and II rapids for rafting.

© JASON MILLER

Pennsylvania, Benner's takes advantage of the surrounding woodlands for atmosphere and shade. A small fishing pond and big trees give this campground a natural feel. You have your choice of outdoor activities at Benner's or nearby, including caving at Laurel Caverns, horseback riding at Nemacolin Resort, biking at Ohiopyle, and boating on the Youghiogheny River. There is also trout fishing at the river and hiking trails to view its beauty from close and far. The best view of the Youghiogheny River Gorge is from the overlook at Baughman Rock. You can either drive there or take a challenging hike up steep, 3.4-mile Baughman Trail. If historic sites are more your taste, you can visit Braddock's Grave, Washington Tavern, or Fort Necessity, where a young Washington surrendered to the French before rising to lead our new nation. If you'd prefer to remain on-site, the campground has many planned activities like bingo, hayrides, and live music for your enjoyment.

Campsites, facilities: There are 130 sites for RVs up to 40 feet; 100 have full hookups; 30 have water and electricity. There are also 60 tent-only sites. Picnic tables and fire rings are provided. Drinking water, restrooms with flush toilets, a dump station, a laundry, a public phone, groceries, ice, wood, a rec hall, a pavilion, a swimming pool, a playground, two shuffleboard courts, badminton, volleyball, miniature golf, and LP gas are available. Some sites are wheelchair accessible. Leashed pets are permitted.

Reservations, fees: Reservations are accepted. The rate is $32 per night for up to two people. Each additional person is $8. Group and youth rates are available. Major credit cards are accepted. Open late April through September.

Directions: From the junction of Highway 381 and U.S. 40, travel one mile west on U.S. 40, then two miles north on Nelson Road to the campground entrance on the left.

Contact: Benner's Meadow Run Camping & Cabins, 315 Nelson Road, Farmington, PA 15437, 724/329-4097, bacamper@bell atlantic.net.

35 KENTUCK CAMPGROUND

🏕️ 🚴 🏊 🛶 🚤 ❄️ 🥾 ♿ 🚐 ⛺

Rating: 10

in Ohiopyle State Park

BEST (

Beautiful Ohiopyle State Park is an outdoor enthusiast's dream. Most visitors to Kentuck Campground spend their days rafting the Class III/IV Lower Youghiogheny River or floating down the calm Middle Yough in inflatable kayaks or canoes. Others use the numerous trails for horseback riding, biking, and hiking. There are an incredible 79 miles of hiking trails in the park. Meadow Run Trail is an easy three-mile trail that can be picked up near the park office, Cucumber Falls, or the natural waterslides. It follows beautiful Meadow Run, which has cascades, holes, and slides. As part of the Great Allegheny Passage that connects Pittsburgh to Cumberland, Maryland, the Youghiogheny River Bike Trail is 17 miles long and is also used for hiking. Ferncliff Peninsula boasts several trails along its fossil-strewn path; the easy, 1.7-mile Ferncliff Trail spins off into the other trails or loops back. Among the other trails in this area are Buffalo Nut, Fernwood, and Oakwoods Trails. Jonathan Run Trail crosses Jonathan Run several times, and its 1.7-mile trek takes you past Jonathan Run Falls before connecting to the Youghiogheny River Trail. During the winter, cross-country skiing, snowmobiling, sledding, and tobogganing are favorite activities. Be advised that hunting is allowed seasonally in Ohiopyle State Park.

Campsites, facilities: There are 226 sites for tents or RVs up to 50 feet: 28 are walk-ins; 32 have electricity; 166 have no hookups. Drinking water, restrooms with flush toilets, showers, and a playground are available.

Some sites are wheelchair accessible. No pets are permitted.

Reservations, fees: Reservations are accepted at 888/PA-PARKS (888/727-2757). The rate is $14–19 for up to five people; a fee may apply for additional guests. Senior and Pennsylvania resident discounts are available. Open March through December.

Directions: From Ohiopyle, travel 0.25 mile south on Highway 381, then follow signs to the campground entrance on the right.

Contact: Ohiopyle State Park, P.O. Box 105, Ohiopyle, PA 15470-0105, 724/329-8591, ohiopylesp@state.pa.us.

36 TALL OAKS CAMPGROUND, INC.

Rating: 6

near Ohiopyle State Park

This 150-acre campground is located only a few miles from Ohiopyle State Park. If it's privacy among the trees that you're looking for, then Tall Oaks is the place. You can choose from sites within the stream valley or further up on the ridge. At Ohiopyle you can spend your day rafting, kayaking, canoeing, fishing, hiking, biking, horseback riding, or just sightseeing. The Youghiogheny River has two sections for whitewater rafting, the Lower with Class III/IV rapids and the Middle with Class I/II rapids. You can join a guided trip if it's your first time or rent a raft and go it on your own. The 79 miles of hiking trails are rated easy, moderate, moderately difficult, and difficult. The easy trails include the Sproul Trail, Meadow Run Trail, McCune Trail, Jonathan Run Trail, and the Ferncliff Peninsula Trails. The moderate trails are Great Gorge Trail, Sugar Run Trail, and Old Mitchell Trail Loop. Kentuck Trail and Beech Trails are the only moderately difficult trails. Baughman Trail and Sugarloaf Trail are both rated difficult due to their steepness.

Sugarloaf Trail is also a multi-purpose trail for biking, horseback riding, and snowmobiling. Laurel Caverns Geologic Park and the Woodlands Zoo are nearby. Also in the area is the Christian Klay Winery, which has tastings and occasional festivals.

Campsites, facilities: There are 104 sites for tents or RVs up to 35 feet: 30 have electricity, 74 have no hookups. There are four pull-throughs. Drinking water, restrooms with flush toilets, a dump station, modern showers, a laundry, a pool, and a game room are available. Leashed pets are permitted.

Reservations, fees: Reservations are accepted. The rate is $12.50 per person per night. Open April through October.

Directions: From the junction of U.S. 40 and Highway 381, travel one mile south on Highway 381, then turn left onto Camp Riamo Road and travel one mile to the campground entrance on the left.

Contact: Tall Oaks Campground, 544 Camp Riamo Road, Farmington, PA 15437, 724/329-4777.

37 OUTFLOW RECREATION AREA

Rating: 8

near Ohiopyle State Park

One of the most unique campgrounds in Pennsylvania, Outflow Recreation Area is run by the Corps of Engineers like its sister site at Tub Run. All of its sites are open and offer a wonderful view of the outflow or spillway. Best known for its trout fishing most of the year, Outflow is also a through-way for the Youghiogheny River Hiking-Biking Trail. The cliffs that hang over the water between the area of the outflow and the spillway sport little cascades of their own during wetter seasons. If it's really wet, the water bursting from the outflow is like a mini–Niagara Falls. Obviously swimming is not allowed due to the danger, but being within a mile of Youghiogheny Lake makes up for this small inconvenience. A few miles down the road at Ohiopyle State Park, you can make use of 79 miles of hiking, biking, and horseback riding trails or take a trip down the Lower or Middle Youghiogheny River. You can go along on a guided tour or rent a raft yourself. If you're more into water watching, then you'll love the many benches back at the campground that face the outflow area. There are restaurants within walking distance in the tiny town of Confluence.

Campsites, facilities: There are 63 sites for tents or RVs up to 62 feet: four have full hookups; 32 have electricity; 27 have no hookups. Picnic tables and fire rings are provided. Drinking water, a dump station, restrooms with flush toilets, and showers are available. Some sites are wheelchair accessible. Leashed pets are permitted.

Reservations, fees: Reservations are accepted at 877/444-6777. The rates are $16–35 per night for up to eight people; a fee may apply for additional guests. Open mid-May through mid-September.

Directions: From Confluence, travel one mile south on Highway 281 to the campground entrance.

Contact: Outflow Recreation Area, Resource Manager, 497 Flanigan Road, Confluence, PA 15424, 814/395-3242.

38 TUB RUN RECREATION AREA

🏃🏊🚣🛶🐎🎣♿🚐⛺

Rating: 9

near Ohiopyle State Park

BEST (

Operated by the Corps of Engineers, Tub Run Recreation Area is a well-maintained camping facility nestled along the Youghiogheny Lake. As the lake is most likely the reason for choosing Tub Run or its sister site, Outflow Recreation Area, the campground provides a boat launch and swimming area exclusively for its campers. Though the little valley surrounding the campground is wooded, most sites are open. Even so, staying at Tub Run feels like stealing away to a private community built on a cove of the lake. Among the species in this fishery are largemouth and smallmouth bass, perch, catfish, crappie, trout, bluegill, sunfish, and muskie. Within a few miles is Ohiopyle State Park and its many trails. Among the most scenic and easiest to traverse are Meadow Run and Ferncliff. Meadow Run takes you past the natural rockslides and numerous swimming holes and falls, and ends at the scenic Cucumber Falls. Ferncliff has a series of small trails that split off of the main loop and take you through rhododendron forest, along the Youghiogheny River, and over large lepidodendron fossils that were left in the rocks underfoot over 300 million years ago. Tub Run also has planned activities like nature walks for your entertainment.

Campsites, facilities: There are 101 sites for tents or RVs up to 62 feet: 71 have no hookups; 30 have electricity. There are 14 lakeside sites. Picnic tables and fire rings are provided. Drinking water, restrooms with flush toilets, a dump station, showers, public phones and a playground are available. Some sites are wheelchair accessible. Leashed pets are permitted.

Reservations, fees: Reservations are accepted at 877/444-6777. The rate is $16–35 per night for up to eight people; a fee may apply for additional guests. Open Mid-May through early September.

Directions: From Confluence, travel eight miles south on Highway 281 to the campground entrance.

Contact: Tub Run Recreation Area, Resource Manager, 497 Flanigan Road, Confluence, PA 15424, 814/395-3242.

SOUTH CENTRAL

© JASON MILLER

BEST CAMPGROUNDS

Loosely bordered by mountains to the west, the Susquehanna River to the east and north, and the Mason-Dixon Line to the south, this region's treasures invite the traveler to go just a little further. Formed more than 300 million years ago when the African plate slammed into the North American plate, the mountains of central Pennsylvania stretch from northern New Jersey to Tennessee. Famous for their long, even ridges with continuous valleys in between, these remnants of ancient mountains formed when rock layers were pushed laterally from both sides. This corduroy of folds and the surrounding region hide a wealth of recreational activities.

Raystown Lake, the state's largest, draws anglers and boaters. Nestled in a mountain valley, this lake is surrounded by scenic Trough Creek State Park, with its wonderful gorge, and Warrior's Path, with its meandering streams. Campers are never far from trails that lead to scenic overlooks, quiet creeks, rushing waterfalls, and interesting geologic formations. Boats, powered either by gasoline or muscle, dominate here; canoeists can paddle in lazy bends without ever hearing the buzz of gas engines, and water-skiers can carve wakes in their very own cove. From swimming at a beach to hiking on the Keystone State's very own stretch of Appalachian Trail, visitors are never far from some type of recreational opportunity in these hills.

From President James Buchanan's birthplace, between McConnellsburg and Mercersburg, to Gettysburg National Battlefield, history comes alive in this part of the state. The site of the Civil War's largest battle is a sad, but significant stop for any visit to the region. A contemplative mind is needed to stroll along old defensive lines and infirmaries if one is to understand the growing pains our nation experienced at places like Little Round Top and Cemetery Hill, where bullets and other relics of war can still be found buried in the earth. The ghosts of the fallen are said to still walk at night, perhaps asking questions that will never be answered.

In the eastern half of the region lies the Susquehanna, the largest American river to find its way into the Atlantic. The Susquehanna River Trail is a wonderful way to experience a scenic land in the throes of revitalization. Where factories once stood, egrets and heron compete with anglers for a meal. Smallmouth bass, catfish, muskie, carp, and walleye all await the eminent return of the Atlantic shad, a migratory fish whose population decline mirrored the rise of industry in Pennsylvania. Osprey soar above once-polluted streams, witness to the recreational opportunities being reborn along the banks. Raccoons come to the river at night to take from its buffet of crayfish and insect larvae, and river otter play without a care. Many campgrounds in this region realize the importance of this waterway and provide campers with canoe and kayak rentals – some even go so far as to provide shuttles to convenient put-ins or take-outs.

The state's capital, Harrisburg, sits along the Susquehanna like a proud grandfather watching over his grandchildren. Even in this region, state parks are plentiful and activities are as varied as the lawmakers who arrive from Philly and the 'Burgh. Gifford Pinchot has a lake where visitors can sail on gentle breezes. South of the city, the Susquehanna makes a mad dash for the Atlantic, a trip that can be taken by pedal or paddle. Here wildlife is abundant, and a lucky few will spot black bear or coyote along the river's banks.

The south central region is where Pennsylvania confronts its visitors with experiences that can lead to a change of heart, a sense of history, a calmed spirit, a rush of adrenaline, a taste of wanderlust, or just peace of mind. After all, isn't that why a traveler fusses over maps and takes pictures? It isn't to remember the flavor of the cheeseburger at a roadside diner. It's to remember the laughs had by a family unified in their quest to see new sights, what's around the next bend or just a little further up the trail.

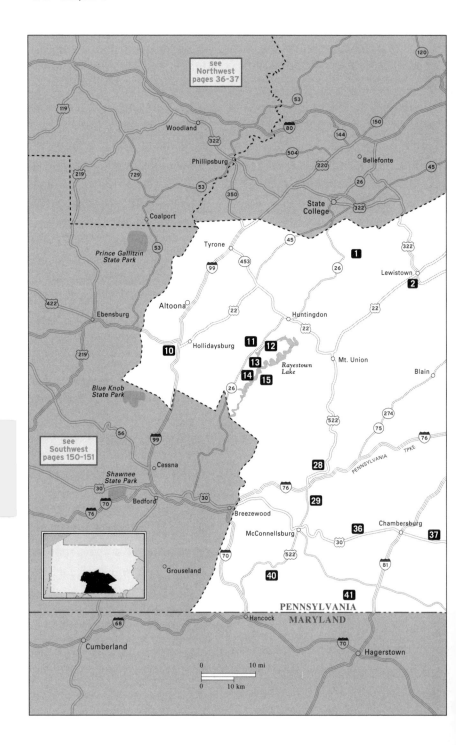

SOUTH CENTRAL

see North Central pages 80-81

see Southeast pages 212-213

220
80
80
Lewisburg
Danville
Bloomsburg
80
11
Susquehanna River
42
Aaronsburg
45
Sunbury
61
Selinsgrove
225
Shamokin
61
209
522
147
81
Pottsville
104
125
11
183
Mifflintown
322
17
209
78
3 4 6 Millersburg 7
Ickesburg 5 8
Licksdale
17 New Bloomfield 225 9
16 74 34 Dauphin 72 422
Landisburg 11 15 Annville Lebanon 19
20 17 18 Hershey 322
21 81 Harrisburg
22 23 24 PENNSYLVANIA TPKE
Carlisle 76 27 76
25 74 Manheim
81 15 Elizabethtown 222
Mount Holly 26 72
32 Dillsburg
30 34 Rossville Lancaster 30
Bendersville 74
31 33 272
35 30
94 York
30 15 38
Gettysburg Abbottstown 74 39
43 47 83 272
42 44 Hanover
116 45 48
46 Gettysburg Natl Mil Park
16 Emmitsburg
15 140 30
Westminster Hereford Gibson

© AVALON TRAVEL PUBLISHING, INC.

❶ GREENWOOD FURNACE STATE PARK

🚶 🏊 ⛴ 🎣 ❄️ 🐎 🚴 🚐 ⛰️

Rating: 9

near Huntingdon

In Pennsylvania's Seven Mountains region lies Greenwood Furnace State Park. This area is known for its rugged landscape, plentiful wildlife, and breathtaking beauty. Greenwood Furnace is a 423-acre park surrounded by 80,000 acres of Rothrock State Forest. Fishing and ice fishing are permitted on six-acre Greenwood Lake. From Memorial Day to Labor Day, visitors can swim from a 300-foot sand beach, though there is no lifeguard stationed. The area's abundant wildlife can be experienced along numerous hiking trails in the park and in the state forest. Hikers might spot white-tailed deer, black bear, turkey, grouse, and other small game, but are encouraged not to feed animals. Duck, great blue heron, and osprey can sometimes be seen near the lake. The park has planned activities such as guided walks and interpretive programs on weekends. During the winter, ice skating, snowmobiling, and cross-country skiing are favorite activities. Be advised that hunting is allowed seasonally in Greenwood Furnace State Park.

Campsites, facilities: There are 51 sites for tents or RVs up to 26 feet: 46 have electricity; five have no hookups. No sites have full hookups. Picnic tables and fire rings are available. Drinking water, restrooms with flush toilets, a dump station, showers, a laundry, a public phone, groceries, ice, wood, a camp store, a pavilion, a playground, horseshoes, and volleyball are available. Leashed pets are permitted.

Reservations, fees: Reservations are accepted at 888/PA-PARKS (888/727-2757). The rate is $14–19 per night for up to five people. Pets are $2 for up to two pets per night. Senior and Pennsylvania resident discounts are available. Open April through December.

hemlocks in Greenwood Furnace State Park

© JASON MILLER

Directions: From Huntingdon, travel west five miles on Highway 305 to the entrance on the left.

Contact: Greenwood Furnace State Park, RR 2, Box 118, Huntingdon, PA 16652-9006, 814/667-1800, greenwoodfurnacesp@ state.pa.us.

❷ LOCUST CAMPGROUND

🚶 🚴 ⛴ 🎣 ❄️ 🐎 🚴 ♿ 🚐 ⛰️

Rating: 6

near Reeds Gap State Park

So near the Juniata River, you can expect to do lots of fishing and boating while staying at Locust Campground. The campground has pedal boats and bikes for rent. Hiking trails run on the property and you can also take a boat ride on the Historic Pennsylvania Canal. On weekends there are planned activities like bingo. Hiking trails run throughout nearby Reeds Gap State Park. There are two loops:

1.8-mile Honey Creek Trail and 1.3-mile Blue Jay Trail. The Self-Guided Interpretive Trail follows portions of both of these trails. Flicker Path is a 0.5-mile offshoot of Blue Jay. The longest trail, at 18 miles, is Reeds Gap Spur Trail. Its rugged terrain makes it a more challenging hike. During the winter, most of these trails are open to cross-country skiing. Be advised that hunting is allowed in Reeds Gap State Park seasonally.

Campsites, facilities: There are 220 sites for tents or RVs up to 29 feet: 170 have full hookups; 30 have water and electricity; 20 have no hookups. Picnic tables and fire rings are provided. Drinking water, restrooms with flush toilets, a dump station, showers, a laundry, a phone hookup, cable TV hookup, ice, wood, a playground, a rec hall, a basketball court, badminton, horseshoes, and a volleyball court are available. Some sites are wheelchair accessible. Leashed pets are permitted.

Reservations, fees: Reservations are accepted. The rate is $18–22 per night for up to two people. Each additional person is $4. Weekly and seasonal rates and group discounts are available. Open year-round.

Directions: From the junction of U.S. 322 and U.S. 22/522, travel 3.5 miles southwest on U.S. 22/522, then one mile south on Industrial Road, then one mile southeast on Locust Road to the campground entrance at the end.

Contact: Locust Campground, 475 Locust Road, Lewistown, PA 17044, 717/248-3974, www.locustcampground.com.

3 SHOOP'S COUNTRY CAMPGROUND

Rating: 2

near Little Buffalo State Park

This new campground is nestled in the Tuscarora Mountains by the Juniata River. You can choose from shaded and open sites. Shoop's specialty is horse-drawn rides. Whether in a wagon, a carriage, or, during the winter, a sleigh, just sit back and enjoy the beautiful scenery while someone else takes the reins. Other planned activities include battle reenactments. For additional outdoor recreational opportunities, visit nearby Little Buffalo State Park. You can go fishing and boating on 88-acre Holman Lake. This warm-water fishery is known for its native bass population, but you can also cast for stocked rainbow, brook, and brown trout, muskie, walleye, catfish, bluegill, crappie, sunfish, and carp. Only motorboats with electric motors and non-powered boats are permitted on the lake. The park also has a swimming pool with a water slide, two picnic areas, and a playground. There are seven hiking trails in Little Buffalo State Park; two are difficult, but the rest are labeled easy. The one-mile Fishermen's Trail is a nice walk through a hemlock forest to an overlook of the dam and lake. During the winter, ice skating, ice fishing, and cross-country skiing are favorite activities.

Campsites, facilities: There are 30 sites for tents or RVs up to 30 feet. No sites have hookups. Picnic tables and fire rings are provided. Drinking water, restrooms with flush toilets, a dump station, showers, a pavilion, a playground, and a sports field are available. Leashed pets are permitted.

Reservations, fees: Reservations are accepted. The rate is $16–20 per night for up to two people. Each additional person is $3. Weekly and seasonal rates are available. Open year-round.

Directions: From the junction of Route 322 Port Royal Exit and Route 75, travel nine miles south on Route 75 to the campground entrance.

Contact: Shoop's Country Campground, RD 1 Box 758, Port Royal, PA 17082, 717/527-4885, www.shoopfarm.20m.com.

▲ BUTTONWOOD CAMPGROUND

👥 🏊 🛶 🎣 🚶 🚐 ⛺

Rating: 8

near Juniata River

Located right next to the scenic Juniata River, Buttonwood Campground is an ideal site from which to explore the Juniata River Water Trail, which was still under development at press time. When completed, this trail will provide flat-water paddling experiences and opportunities to cast a line in Pennsylvania's scenic center. Try it alone, or contact one of the many local outfitters. Also nearby is Little Buffalo State Park, a place with natural and historical significance. Besides a lake for boating and fishing, plentiful picnic areas, and hiking trails, Little Buffalo has its share of history. Visitors can see a restored, operating gristmill, covered bridges, an old farmhouse, and an old railcar on a narrow gauge railroad trace. Back at the campground, visitors can participate in one of the planned activities on weekends like hayrides and bingo. There are both wooded and shaded sites on this level property, which is located less than 0.5 mile from the banks of the Juniata.

Campsites, facilities: There are 79 sites for tents or RVs up to 28 feet: 74 have full hookups; five have water and electricity. There are 11 pull-throughs. Picnic tables and fire rings are provided. Drinking water, restrooms with flush toilets, a dump station, a portable dump, showers, a laundry, modem access, phone hookup, cable TV hookup, a public phone, groceries, ice, LP gas, wood, fishing supplies, a camp store, a pavilion, a rec room, a game room, ping-pong, a playground, a sandbox, a swimming pool, basketball, horseshoes, badminton, volleyball, bocce, and a sports field are available. Leashed pets are permitted.

Reservations, fees: Reservations are accepted.

The rate is $18–26 for up to two people per night. Each additional person is $3. Weekly, monthly, and group rates are available. Open year-round.

Directions: From the junction of U.S. 22/322 and Highway 75, travel 0.5 mile south on Highway 75, then one mile southeast on Old U.S. 322, then 0.25 mile on River Road. Follow signs to the campground entrance on the right.

Contact: Buttonwood Campground, P.O. Box 223, Mexico, PA 17056, 717/436-8334, www.buttonwoodcamp.com.

⑤ LITTLE BUFFALO FAMILY CAMPING

👥 🚴 🛶 🎣 🚐 ❄ 🐕 🚶 ♿ 🚐 ⛺

Rating: 8

near Little Buffalo State Park

This campground has mostly wooded sites around a lake and a pond. There is catch-and release-fishing in the pond, and lake and stream fishing for stocked trout. You can rent canoes, paddleboats, and rowboats at the campground. If you'd prefer to stay on land, check out the hiking and biking trails. At nearby Little Buffalo State Park, you have your choice of more trails, including six easy trails and two difficult trails. Blue Ball Trail is paved and wheelchair accessible. It begins in the East Picnic Area and travels 0.25 mile to the Blue Ball Tavern. The park has a large swimming pool complete with water slide. During the winter, ice skating and cross-country skiing are favorite activities. Be advised that hunting is allowed seasonally in Little Buffalo State Park.

Campsites, facilities: There are 40 sites for tents or RVs up to 40 feet: 12 have full hookups; 19 have water and electricity; nine have no hookups. There are five pull-throughs. Picnic tables and fire rings are provided. Drinking water, restrooms with flush toilets, a dump station, showers, ice, wood, a pavil-ion, a rec hall, a playground, badminton, horseshoes, volleyball, and an archery range are available. Some sites are wheelchair accessible. Leashed pets are permitted.

Reservations, fees: Reservations are accepted. The rate is $20–26 per night for up to two people. Each additional person is $5. Major credit cards are accepted. Open year-round.

Directions: From the junction of U.S. 22/322 and Highway 34, travel south three miles on Highway 34, three miles on a paved road, then 0.5 mile on a gravel road. Follow signs to the campground entrance on the left.

Contact: Little Buffalo Family Camping, RR2 Box 257A, Newport, PA 17074, 717/567-7370, www.littlebuffalofamilycamping.com.

6 FERRYBOAT CAMPSITES

Rating: 7

near the Susquehanna River

Located north of Harrisburg along the Susquehanna, Ferryboat Campsites is a great place to begin a trip along the Susquehanna River Trail. Paddlers can view wildlife, including otter, beaver, turtles, raccoons, foxes, mink, muskrat, skunks, squirrels, coyote, and bats. Anglers can wet a line for smallmouth bass, muskie, walleye, catfish, and carp. Waterfowl and other birds that can be observed include green-wing teal, gadwall, mallards and other puddle ducks, and diving ducks. Herons can appear in eddies, and egrets show up as far north as Wade Island. During the peak of spring migration, flycatchers, thrushes, vireos, warblers, orioles, and tanagers all pass through. During the summer Canada geese, tree swallows, cormorants, ring-billed gulls, and birds of prey can appear at any time. Many of these species can be viewed from Ferryboat without the aid of a canoe since the property

has waterfront campsites, both shaded and open, along the river. Here campers can fish, swim, launch boats, or rent kayaks. There are plenty of hiking trails here, as well as planned activities on weekends.

Campsites, facilities: There are 305 sites for tents or RVs up to 28 feet: 287 have full hookups; 3 have water and electricity; 15 have no hookups. There are 20 pull-throughs. Picnic tables and fire rings are provided. Drinking water, restrooms with flush toilets, a dump station, showers, modem access, a phone hookup, cable TV hookup, a public phone, groceries, ice, LP gas, wood, fishing supplies, miniature golf, two shuffleboard courts, basketball, badminton, volleyball, a sports field, a general store, a pavilion, a rec hall, an arcade, a playground, and RV storage are available. Some sites are wheelchair accessible. Leashed pets are permitted.

Reservations, fees: Reservations are accepted. The rate is $19–35 per night for up to four people. Each additional person is $5. Weekly and monthly rates are available. Major credit cards are accepted. Open mid-April through beginning of November.

Directions: From the junction of Highway 17 and U.S. 11/15, travel two miles south on U.S. 11/15, then turn right onto a paved road and travel 0.25 mile to the campground entrance on the right.

Contact: Ferryboat Campsites, 32 Ferry Lane, Liverpool, PA 17045, 717/444-3200 or 800/759-8707, www.ferryboatcampsites.com.

7 PINE GROVE KOA AT TWIN GROVE PARK

Rating: 9

near Swatara State Park

BEST (

You can rent a bike and enjoy the trails on this campground's property or just take a leisurely walk. At nearby Swatara State Park, you have your choice of three fishing spots: Trout Run's cold water has stocked trout; Swatara Creek is a warm-water fishery with smallmouth bass and panfish; Irving's Pond also has panfish and largemouth bass. Non-powered boats are allowed on Swatara Creek. You can bike or hike the Swatara Multi-Use Trail. During the winter you can trade in the bike for cross-country skis. Horseback riding is permitted on the state park roadways. Back at the campground, you can enjoy planned activities on weekends such as live music and hayrides.

Campsites, facilities: There are 143 sites for tents or RVs up to 38 feet: 134 have full hookups; 9 have no hookups. There are 10 pull-throughs. Picnic tables and fire rings are provided. Drinking water, restrooms with flush toilets, a dump station, showers, a laundry, modem access, phone hookup, cable TV hookup, a public phone, groceries, ice, LP gas, wood, a camp store, a pavilion, a rec hall, an arcade, a playground, a swimming pool, a water slide, miniature golf, basketball, volleyball, a sports field, a mini carnival, a restaurant, and RV supplies are available. Leashed pets are permitted. The campground has a traffic control gate for security.

Reservations, fees: Reservations are accepted at 800/562-5471. The rate is $22–45 per night for up to two people. Each additional person is $4. Major credit cards are accepted. Open year-round.

Directions: From the junction of I-81 and Highway 443 Exit 100, travel five miles west on Highway 443 to the campground entrance on the right.

Contact: Pine Grove KOA, 1445 Suedburg Road, Pine Grove, PA 17963, 717/865-4602, www.koa.com/where/pa/38180.

8 LICKDALE CAMPGROUND & GENERAL STORE

Rating: 7

near Swatara State Park

This wooded property has its own hiking and biking trails, and you can rent canoes, tubes, kayaks, and bikes from the campground. At nearby Swatara State Park, anglers have their choice of fisheries. Irving's Pond has largemouth bass, sunfish, catfish, crappie, suckers, and bluegill. Trout Run is stocked with brown and brook trout. Swatara Creek has panfish and smallmouth bass. Canoes and non-powered boats are welcome on the creek. Trails and roadways are open to hiking, biking, and horseback riding. A small portion of the Appalachian National Scenic Trail runs through Swatara State Park. Fossil collecting is also permitted at the park. You can then return to the campground to enjoy planned activities like bingo and hayrides.

Campsites, facilities: There are 99 sites for tents or RVs up to 35 feet: 55 have full hookups; 28 have water and electricity; 16 have no hookups. There are 35 pull-throughs. Picnic tables and fire rings are provided. Drinking water, restrooms with flush toilets, a dump station, a portable dump, showers, a laundry, modem access, a phone hookup, a public phone, groceries, ice, LP gas, wood, fishing supplies, a general store, a rec hall, an arcade, a playground, basketball, horseshoes, volleyball, and RV storage and supplies are available. Some sites are wheelchair accessible. Leashed pets are permitted.

Reservations, fees: Reservations are accepted at 877/865-6411. The rate is $21–26 per night for up to two people. Each additional person is $4. Weekly rates are available. Major credit cards are accepted. Open year-round.

Directions: From the junction of I-81 Exit 90/30 and Highway 72, travel 200 yards on a paved road. Follow signs to the campground entrance on the left.

Contact: Lickdale Campground, 11 Lickdale Road, Jonestown, PA 17038, 717/865-6411, www.lickdalecampground.com.

9 KOA JONESTOWN

Rating: 7

near Swatara State Park

Nearby 3,515-acre Swatara State Park provides many outdoor recreational opportunities. Trout Run is a cold-water stream stocked with brown and brook trout. Swatara Creek is a warm-water fishery with species like bluegill, sunfish, crappie, and smallmouth bass, and is open to canoes and other non-powered boats. Irving's Pond has other panfish and largemouth bass. Be advised that hunting is allowed seasonally in Swatara State Park. Horseback riding and biking are permitted on state park roads, and Swatara Multi-Use Trail is open to hikers and bikers. The Appalachian National Scenic Trail runs for two miles through the southern section of the park on its way from Georgia to Maine. The campground offers planned activities like bingo and hayrides on weekends.

Campsites, facilities: There are 129 sites for tents or RVs up to 25 feet: 67 have full hookups; 36 have water and electricity; 26 have no hookups. There are 50 pull-throughs. Picnic tables and fire rings are available. Drinking water, restrooms with flush toilets, a dump station, showers, a laundry, a public phone, groceries, ice, LP gas, wood, a camp store, a rec room, a playground, a swimming pool, miniature golf, badminton, and volleyball are available. Some sites are wheelchair accessible. Leashed pets are permitted.

Reservations, fees: Reservations are accepted at 800/562-1501. The rate is $25–41 per night for up to two people. Each additional person is $5. Open mid-March through October.

Directions: From the junction of Highway 72 and U.S. 22, travel east two miles on U.S. 22, then turn right onto a paved road and travel 0.5 mile to the campground entrance on the right.

Contact: KOA Jonestown, 500 Old Route 22, Jonestown, PA 17038, 717/865-2526.

10 WRIGHT'S ORCHARD STATION CAMPGROUND

Rating: 8

near Canoe Creek State Park

Wright's Orchard Station Campground is located near Canoe Creek State Park, a scenic place enjoyed by locals from nearby Altoona. The scenic highlight of the 958-acre park is the panorama that greets visitors when they climb Canoe Creek Road. The park has a 155-acre where guests can fish for walleye, muskie, bass, trout, chain pickerel, catfish, crappie, and other panfish. Boats with electric motors are permitted on the lake, and a concession rents rowboats, kayaks, canoes, and paddleboats. From Memorial Day to Labor Day, visitors can swim at a 350-feet sand beach that has grass and sand areas for sunbathing. There are trails for biking and riding horses, and eight miles of hiking trails that meander through fields, forests, and along the lakeshore. Be advised that hunting is allowed seasonally in Canoe Creek State Park. Winter activities include cross-country skiing, ice skating, ice boating, and ice fishing when the ice is at least four inches thick.

Campsites, facilities: There are 42 sites for tents or RVs up to 30 feet: 17 have full hookups; 20 have water and electricity; five have no hookups. There are nine pull-throughs. Picnic tables and fire rings are provided. Drinking water, restrooms with flush toilets, a dump station, a portable dump, showers, a laundry, a public phone, groceries, ice, wood, a camp store, and a pavilion are available. Some sites are wheelchair accessible. Leashed pets are permitted.

Reservations, fees: Reservations are accepted. The rate is $18–28 per night for up to two people. Each additional person is $5. Major credit cards are accepted. Open May through October.

Directions: From the junction of I-99 and U.S. 220 Exit 31/Plank Road, travel south one mile on Business U.S. 220 to the campground entrance on the right.

Contact: Wright's Orchard Station Campground, 2381 Old Route 220 North Business, Duncansville, PA 16635, 814/695-2628, wrightcamp@aol.com.

11 PIONEER FAMILY CAMPGROUND

Rating: 8

near Raystown Lake

Located where Pennsylvania's folded mountains begin their swing to the northeast, Pioneer Family Campground's wooded and open sites provide a quintessential outdoor experience. With on-site features like hiking trails, a fishing pond, boat rentals, and even a racetrack for radio-controlled vehicles, there are few reasons to leave. But with its location near 29,000-acre Raystown Lake and numerous state parks, Pioneer Family is a good base camp for those wishing to explore Pennsylvania's scenic beauty. Raystown Lake has beaches, trails, picnicking, fishing, and hunting. There is no limit to engine strength, and you're just as likely to see personal watercraft as a 70-foot houseboat. Raystown Lake is one of the best places in the area to fish for catfish, carp, striped, largemouth, smallmouth, or rock bass, walleye, muskie, lake, brown, or rainbow trout, perch, and other species of fish. Many marinas nearby rent boats. Since the campground adjoins 20,000 acres of state game lands you can begin your exploration just outside of your tent.

Campsites, facilities: There are 135 sites for RVs up to 40 feet; all sites have water and electricity. No tents can be accommodated. Picnic tables and fire rings are provided. Drinking water, restrooms with flush toilets, a dump station, showers, a laundry, ice, wood, a pavilion, a rec room, an arcade, a playground, a swimming pool, miniature golf, horseshoes, basketball, volleyball, an archery range, and a sports field are available. Leashed pets are permitted.

Reservations, fees: Reservations are recommended at 814/658-2267. The rate is $25–35 per night for up to four people. Each additional person is $5. Weekly, monthly, and yearly rates are available. Open year-round.

Directions: From Huntington, travel south on Highway 26 to its junction with Highway 994, then travel 100 yards south on Highway 26 to the campground entrance on the right.

Contact: Pioneer Family Campground, RR 1, James Creek, PA 16657, 814/627-5943, www.pioneerfamilycampground.com.

12 PLEASANT HILLS RESORT

Rating: 8

near Raystown Lake

Pleasant Hills provides easy access to Pennsylvania's largest lake and all that it has to offer. Raystown Lake is large enough for water-skiers and tubers to find coves of their own, and houseboaters won't feel at all crowded. If you plan on bringing a boat, there are plenty of mooring possibilities close to the campground. Raystown has many species of fish and was where the state's record-holding largemouth bass was caught. On the other side of Raystown Lake is Trough Creek State Park, a scenic gorge with hiking trails leading to hidden coves and scenic overlooks. Pleasant Hills is conveniently located close to Penn State and attractions like water slides, amusement parks, and farmer's markets. The campground has planned activities like bingo and ceramics on weekends.

Campsites, facilities: There are 130 sites for tents or RVs up to 28 feet: 90 have full hookups; 24 have water and electricity; 16 have no hookups. There are 28 pull-throughs. Picnic tables and fire rings are provided. Drinking water, restrooms with flush toilets, a dump station, a portable dump, showers, a laundry, a public phone, groceries, ice, wood, a camp store, a pavilion, a rec room, a playground, a swimming pool, miniature golf, badminton, horseshoes, volleyball, and a sports field are available. Leashed pets are permitted.

Reservations, fees: Reservations are accepted. The rate is $23–28 per night for up to two people. Each additional person is $3. Weekly rates and seasonal discounts are available. Open mid-April through mid-October.

Directions: From East Hesston, travel 1.5 miles east on Seven Points Road, then turn left onto a paved road and travel one mile to the campground entrance at the end.

Contact: Pleasant Hills Resort, P.O. Box 86, Hesston, PA 16647, 814/658-3986, www.pleasanthills.net.

13 LAKE RAYSTOWN RESORT AND LODGE

Rating: 10

near Raystown Lake

BEST (

Raystown Lake is Pennsylvania's largest, with just over 118 miles of shoreline. Pennyslvania's record-holding striped bass, weighing in at just over 53 pounds, was caught at the lake. It's also a great spot to cast for largemouth and smallmouth bass, lake, rainbow, and brook trout, muskie, walleye, catfish, carp, and perch. Raystown Resort and Lodge's very own pleasure cruiser, the *Proud Mary,* has weekly cruises departing from the lodge. The resort has one of Pennsylvania's largest full-service

marinas, has slip rentals at a variety of service levels, and rents pontoons, rowboats, canoes, motorboats, and fishing boats. The resort owns over 400 acres of shoreline with swimming beaches and woods with hiking trails, and offers fireworks nights and live music to entice campers to linger on the property.

Campsites, facilities: There are 232 sites for tents or RVs up to 32 feet; all have water and electricity. There are eight pull-throughs. Picnic tables and fire rings are provided. Drinking water, restrooms with flush toilets, a dump station, showers, a laundry, modem access, cable TV hookup, a public phone, groceries, ice, marine gas, wood, two general stores, grills, a pavilion, a rec room, an arcade, a playground, miniature golf, basketball, badminton, volleyball, a sports field, a marina, and RV supplies are available. Some sites are wheelchair accessible. Leashed pets are permitted.

Reservations, fees: Reservations are accepted at 814/658-3500. The rate is $30–42 per night for up to two people. Each additional person is $6. Weekly rates are available. Major credit cards are accepted. Open mid-April through October.

Directions: From the junction of Highway 26 and Highway 994, travel four miles east on Highway 994 to the entrance on the right.

Contact: Lake Raystown Resort and Lodge, 100 Chipmunk Crossing, Entriken, PA 16638, 814/658-2717, www.raystownresort.com.

14 HEMLOCK HIDEAWAY CAMPGROUND

Rating: 7

near Raystown Lake

This pleasantly wooded site is located near gigantic Raystown Lake and scenic Trough Creek State Park. The highlight of the 554-acre state park is a pretty gorge that was created when the creek cut through Terrace Mountain. Rainbow Falls, Balanced Rock, and other natural features can be reached via rugged hiking trails.

The tiny park is located between Raystown Lake and Rothrock State Forest, making one large contiguous area for public use. The fully accessible Trough Creek Lodge is a renovated stone mansion available for rent; it has large porches that look out onto great views. Anglers can wet a line in Trough Creek for trout and smallmouth bass, and can fish in a sheltered cove of Raystown Lake via Terrace Mountain Trail. Please note that 100 acres of the park are open to seasonal hunting. Hemlock Hideaway has a small pond for fishing and hiking trails on the property, and offers planned activities such as fishing derbies, bingo, and movies.

Campsites, facilities: There are 116 sites for tents or RVs up to 30 feet: 108 have water and electricity; eight have no hookups. Picnic tables and fire rings are available. Drinking water, restrooms with flush toilets, a dump station, showers, a laundry, cable hookup, a public phone, groceries, ice, LP gas, wood, a camp store, a pavilion, a playground, a game room, badminton, horseshoes, and volleyball are available. Leashed pets are permitted.

Reservations, fees: Reservations are accepted. The rate is $20–30 for up to four people per night. Each additional person is $3. Weekly and monthly rates are available. Open year-round.

Directions: From the junction of Highway 26 and Highway 994, travel east six miles on Highway 994 to the campground entrance on the right.

Contact: Hemlock Hideaway Campground, Box 189B1, James Creek, PA 16657, 814/658-3663, www.hemlockhidecamp.com.

15 TROUGH CREEK STATE PARK

🚶‍♂️ 🛶 ❄️ 🐕 🏠 ♿ 🚐 ⛺

Rating: 10

near James Creek

BEST (

Great Trough Creek flows into Trough Creek State Park, a 554-acre scenic gorge in the

Terrace Mountains. Because the creek empties into Raystown Lake, it is a common spawning ground for sucker, brook and brown trout, bluegill, smallmouth and rock bass, catfish, and sunfish. Ten hiking trails offer 12 miles of scenery and wildlife; all but one are moderate hikes. The 2.4-mile Brumbaugh Trail is classified as difficult because it has many climbs up and down ridges and cliffs with drop-offs. Gentler Abbot Run Trail has two stream crossings, and may be the most scenic trail in the park. Snowmobiling is a favorite winter activity. Be advised that hunting is allowed seasonally in Trough Creek State Park.

Campsites, facilities: There are 32 sites for tents or RVs up to 26 feet; all have electricity. Picnic tables and fire rings are provided. Drinking water, non-flush toilets, a dump station, a public phone, and a pavilion are available. Some sites are wheelchair accessible. Leashed pets are permitted.

Reservations, fees: Reservations are accepted at 888/PA-PARKS (888/727-2757). The rate is $14–19 per night for up to five people; a fee may apply for additional guests. Pets are $2 for up to two pets per night. Senior and Pennsylvania resident discounts are available. Open mid-April through mid-December.

Directions: From the junction of Highway 26 and Highway 994, travel south three miles on Highway 994, then east two miles at the park sign to the campground entrance.

Contact: Trough Creek State Park, RR 1 Box 211, James Creek, PA 16657-9302, 814/658-3847, troughcreeksp@state.pa.us.

16 PARADISE STREAM FAMILY CAMPGROUND

🚶‍♂️ 🛶 🏊 🎣 🏠 🚿 🚐 ⛺

Rating: 7

near Little Buffalo State Park

You can take advantage of the campground's location along Paradise Stream through boating and fishing. They offer canoe and pedal boat rentals. On weekends, you can join in on planned activities like bingo and potluck dinners. Nearby Little Buffalo State Park offers several miles of hiking trails. For leisurely walks, try 0.5-mile Mill Race Trail, 1.2-mile Exercise Trail, one-mile Fishermen's Trail, or one-mile Little Buffalos Creek Trail. Blue Ball Trail is paved and wheelchair accessible. It runs 0.25 mile from the East Picnic Area to Blue Ball Tavern. There are also two difficult trails. You can catch the 2.5-mile Middle Ridge Trail from Exercise Trail and follow it to the west end of the park. Buffalo Ridge Trail begins at the East Picnic Area and travels 1.5 miles to the Main Picnic Area. The state park also has a swimming pool with slide.

Campsites, facilities: There are 105 sites for tents or RVs up to 40 feet: 52 have full hookups; 53 have water and electricity. There are 12 pull-throughs. Picnic tables and fire rings are provided. Drinking water, restrooms with flush toilets, a dump station, a portable dump, showers, groceries, ice, LP gas, wood, a camp store, a pavilion, a rec hall, a playground, badminton, horseshoes, and volleyball are available. Leashed pets are permitted.

Reservations, fees: Reservations are accepted. The rate is $22–30 per night for up to two people. Each additional person is $5. Weekly rates are available. Major credit cards are accepted. Open mid-April through October.

Directions: From the junction of East Highway 850 and Highway 274, travel west five miles on Highway 274, then south 0.25 mile on Highway 308, then 0.5 mile on a gravel road. Follow the signs to the campground entrance on the right.

Contact: Paradise Stream Family Campground, P.O. Box 124, Loysville, PA 17047, 717/789-2117, www.campparadise stream.com.

17 RIVERFRONT CAMPGROUND

Rating: 5

near the Susquehanna River

Located at the confluence of the Susquehanna and Juniata Rivers, Riverfront Campground is all about angling. The campground has angler-friendly amenities, rather than family comforts. Waterfront acreage is the biggest draw, and the campground offers a choice of wooded and riverside sites. The campground rents boats and canoes, and provides a shuttle service that takes anglers and their boats upstream; a number of access points that allow anglers to vary trip length due to time considerations, water level, or other factors. The take-out is right at the campground, so going from the river to your tent is as easy as crossing a street. Smallmouth bass are the main draw, but catfish, carp, suckers, muskie, and walleye can be caught as well. The area's wildlife include mink, otter, beaver, muskrat, raccoons, heron, egrets, osprey, eagles, ducks, Canada geese, and other migratory or seasonal birds.

Campsites, facilities: There are 40 sites for tents or RVs up to 30 feet. No sites have hookups. Non-flush toilets, ice, a camp store, fishing supplies, and wood are available. Leashed pets are permitted.

Reservations, fees: Reservations are accepted. The rate is $10–20 per night for up to two people. Each additional person is $2. Open year-round.

Directions: From the junction of Route 22 and Highway 11, travel three miles south on Highway 11, then turn left onto Newport Road to the campground entrance on the right.

Contact: Riverfront Campground, Box 64, Duncannon, PA 17020, 717/834-5252, www.riverfrontcampground.com.

18 HERSHEY HIGHMEADOW CAMPGROUND

Rating: 8

in Hershey

Located almost close enough to smell chocolate, Hershey Highmeadow Campground is a great starting point for a wide variety of recreational activities in Hershey. The amusement park is the big attraction, and local tours to HersheyPark, ZooAmerica, North American Wildlife Park, Florida's Grassy Waters, Chocolate World, Hershey Museum, and Hershey Gardens help you see that there is more to Hershey than roller coasters. HersheyPark is home to outdoor concerts and sporting events, including playoffs for Pennsylvania's high school athletes. The campground provides a free shuttle to these attractions so you don't have to drive after you've arrived. But with planned activities like bingo, hayrides, and theme weekends on the site's 55 acres of wooded and open property, there's also plenty to do back at the campground.

Campsites, facilities: There are 300 sites for tents or RVs up to 29 feet: 87 have full hookups; 151 have water and electricity; 62 have no hookups. There are 87 pull-throughs. Picnic tables and fire rings are provided. Drinking water, restrooms with flush toilets, a dump station, a laundry, modem access, phone hookup, cable TV hookup, a public phone, groceries, ice, LP gas, wood, a general store, a gift shop, grills, a pavilion, a rec room, an arcade, a playground, two swimming pools, a wading pool, a basketball court, two shuffleboard courts, a volleyball court, a sports field, and RV storage and supplies are available. Some sites are wheelchair accessible. Leashed pets are permitted.

Reservations, fees: Reservations are accepted at 800/437-7439. The rate is $28.50–40.50 per night for up to two people. Each additional person is $6. Major credit cards are accepted. Open year-round.

Directions: From the junction of U.S. 422 and U.S. 322 and Highway 39, travel 0.5 mile northwest on Highway 39 to the campground entrance on the left.

Contact: Hershey Highmeadow Campground, P.O. Box 866, Hershey, PA 17033, 717/534-8999, www.hersheys.com/discover/campground.asp.

19 SHADY OAKS CAMPGROUND

Rating: 5

near Swatara State Park

Nearby Swatara State Park has three fisheries: Trout Run is a cold-water stream with stocked brown and brook trout; Irving's Pond has species such as largemouth bass, sunfish, crappie, bluegill, catfish, and carp; Swatara Creek is a warm-water fishery for smallmouth bass, sunfish, crappie, bluegill, suckers, catfish, and carp. The creek allows canoeing and boating with non-powered boats. You can hike, bike, or horseback ride along the state park roadways, or take nine-mile Swatara Multi-Use Trail from Lickdale to Pine Grove. During the winter you can cross-country ski here. Across the Waterville Bridge, two miles of the Appalachian National Scenic Trail pass through the southern section of the park. Back at the campground, there are planned activities like bingo and theme weekends.

Campsites, facilities: There are 87 sites for tents or RVs up to 25 feet: 61 have full hookups; 20 have water and electricity; six have no hookups. Picnic tables and fire rings are provided. Drinking water, restrooms with flush toilets, a dump station, showers, a laundry, groceries, ice, LP gas, wood, a camp store, a playground, a rec hall, a swimming pool, a shuffleboard court, volleyball, and a sports field are available. Leashed pets are permitted.

Reservations, fees: Reservations are accepted

at 800/807-3177. The rate is $25 per night for up to five people. Each additional person is $5. Open year-round.

Directions: From West Newmanstown, travel one mile southwest on Highway 419, then two miles on a paved road. Follow signs to the campground entrance on the left.

Contact: Shady Oaks Campground, 40 Round Barn Road, Newmanstown, PA 17073, 717/949-3177, www.shadyoakscamp.com.

20 COLONEL DENNING STATE PARK
🏃 🏊 ⛵ ❄️ 🐕 🚶 🚐 ⛺

Rating: 8

near Newville

BEST (

This park is named after William Denning, a Revolutionary War veteran who was not actually a colonel. Doubling Gap Lake stands in the middle of the park's 273 wooded acres. The 3.5-acre lake has some of the best brook, brown, and rainbow trout fishing around, and offers swimming from the sand beach along its shoreline. Eighteen miles of hiking trails run through the park, including one-mile Doubling Gap Trail, a self-guided moderate hike and 2.5-mile Flat Rock Trail, which leads to its namesake for a view of the Cumberland Valley. The park is also the starting point for the 105-mile Tuscarora Trail. During the winter, you can cross-country ski on some of these same trails and ice skate on the lake. In the summer, the park offers environmental and interpretive programs such as guided walks and campfires. There is also a visitor center with exhibits of local flora, fauna, and minerals. Be advised that hunting is allowed seasonally in Colonel Denning State Park.

Campsites, facilities: There are 52 sites for tents or RVs up to 30 feet: 18 have electricity; 34 have no hookups. Picnic tables and fire rings are provided. Drinking water, non-flush toilets, a dump station, a public phone, wood, grills, a snack bar,

a pavilion, a playground, and a sports field are available. Leashed pets are permitted.

Reservations, fees: Reservations are accepted at 888/PA-PARKS (888/727-2757). The rate is $14–19 for up to five people per night; a fee may apply for additional guests. Pets are $2 for up to two pets per night. Senior and Pennsylvania resident discounts are available. Open April through December.

Directions: From Newville, travel nine miles north on Highway 233 to the campground entrance.

Contact: Colonel Denning State Park, 1599 Doubling Gap Road, Newville, PA 17241-9756, 717/776-5272, coloneldenningsp@state.pa.us.

21 FREE SPIRIT RECREATION CENTER
🏃 🏊 ⛵ 🚐 ❄️ 🏠 🚐 ⛺

Rating: 6

near Colonel Denning State Park

Anglers can cast for trout and bass in the stream that runs through the property and in the campground's two stocked ponds. You can also take out a paddleboat or just watch Canada geese, mallards, and wood ducks from shore. The campground has hiking trails near its spacious, wooded sites and offers planned activities such as live music and dances. At nearby Colonel Denning State Park, there's swimming and more trout fishing in 3.5-acre Doubling Gap Lake, and the sandy shoreline beach has a snack bar. The state park has 18 miles of hiking trails and is also the trailhead for the 105-mile Tuscarora Trail, which travels into nearby Tuscarora State Forest. During the winter, cross-country skiing and ice skating are favorite activities.

Campsites, facilities: There are 69 sites for tents or RVs up to 40 feet. All sites have full hookups. Picnic tables and fire rings are provided. Drinking water, restrooms with flush toilets, a dump station, showers, ice, LP gas, wood, a pavilion, a rec hall, an arcade, a swimming pool, miniature golf, volleyball, and RV rentals are available. Leashed pets are permitted.

Reservations, fees: Reservations are accepted. The rate is $16–24 per night for up to two people. Each additional person is $4. Weekly, monthly, and seasonal rates are available. Open year-round.

Directions: From the junction of Route 11/15 and Highway 850, travel west on Highway 850 to Route 74, then 1.5 miles south on Route 74, then turn right onto McCabe Road and travel 3.75 miles to a gravel campground entrance on the right.

Contact: Free Spirit Recreation Center, RR 1, Kennedys Valley Road, Landisburg, PA 17043, 717/582-4443, www.freespiritreccenter.com.

22 DOGWOOD ACRES CAMPGROUND

Rating: 8

near Colonel Denning State Park

All sites at this campground are spacious and shaded. You can take advantage of the property's pond for swimming, fishing, canoeing, and non-motorized boating. Dogwood rents pedal boats and has planned activities on weekends such as boat races and fishing contests. For fun on dry land, try the hiking trails. Nearby Colonel Denning State Park offers 18 more miles of trails, and 3.5-acre Doubling Gap Lake, where trout fishing and swimming are available from a sandy shoreline beach. Check the visitor center for exhibits of local flora and fauna, as well as a list of environmental and interpretive programs that are offered in the summer. You can participate in campfires, hands-on activities, and guided walks. Other nearby attractions include Tuscarora State Forest and Hemlocks Natural Area.

Campsites, facilities: There are 90 sites for tents or RVs up to 30 feet: 80 have full hookups; 10 have no hookups. There are two pull-throughs. Picnic tables and fire rings are provided. Drinking water, restrooms with flush toilets, a dump station, a portable dump, showers, a public phone, groceries, ice, wood, a camp store, a pavilion, a rec hall, a playground, a game room, ping-pong, a swimming pool, a shuffleboard court, a Frisbee golf course, and volleyball are available. Some sites are wheelchair accessible. Leashed pets are permitted.

Reservations, fees: Reservations are accepted. The rate is $18–34 per night for up to two people. Each additional person is $3. Group and senior discounts are available. Major credit cards are accepted. Open end of April through mid-October.

Directions: From the junction of Highway 641 and Highway 233, travel five miles north on Highway 233, then 2.5 miles east on Highway 944 to the campground entrance on the left.

Contact: Dogwood Acres Campground, 4500 Enola Road, Newville, PA 17241, 717/776-5203, www.dogwoodcamping.com.

23 CARLISLE CAMPGROUND

Rating: 5

near Colonel Denning State Park

Anglers can cast for crappie, trout, sunfish, catfish, and bluegill in this property's stream or fish for rainbow, brook, and brown trout on 3.5-acre Doubling Gap Lake at nearby Colonel Denning State Park. A sand beach is available for swimming along the lakeshore and a picnic area and pavilions are available. There are 18 miles of hiking trails in the state park, as well as the trailhead for the 105-mile Tuscarora Trail. Flat Rock Trail travels 2.5 miles to Flat Rock, where you have a wonderful view of the expansive Cumberland Valley. Doubling Gap Trail is a one-mile moderate hike through the woodlands. Keep an eye out for the local wildlife like red and gray squirrels, raccoons, opossums, skunks, chipmunks, cottontail rabbits, and woodchucks. Other nearby attractions include Tuscarora State Forest, Hemlocks Natural Area, and State Game Land 169. Be advised that hunting is allowed seasonally in Colonel Denning State Park.

Campsites, facilities: There are 140 sites for tents or RVs up to 27 feet: 60 have full hookups; 40 have water and electricity; 40 have no hookups. There are 70 pull-throughs. Picnic tables and fire rings are available. Drinking water, restrooms with flush toilets, a dumping station, showers, a laundry, a public phone, groceries, ice, LP gas, wood, a camp store, grills, a pavilion, a rec room, a swimming pool, a playground, badminton, horseshoes, and volleyball are available. Leashed pets are permitted.

Reservations, fees: Reservations are accepted. The rate is $27–29 per night for up to two people. Each additional person is $5. Open year-round.

Directions: From the junction of Pennsylvania Turnpike Exit 226/16 and U.S. 11, travel one mile south on U.S. 11 to the campground entrance on the left.

Contact: Carlisle Campground, 1075 Harrisburg Pike, Carlisle, PA 17013, 717/249-4563.

24 HARRISBURG EAST CAMPGROUND

Rating: 6

near the Susquehanna River

The Susquehanna is the sixteenth-largest river in the United States, and the largest American river that empties into the Atlantic. Excellent wildlife opportunities abound here. Visitors can spot river otters, beaver, muskrat, various turtles, mink, bats, cottontail rabbits, striped skunks, wood-chucks, raccoons, foxes, and maybe even an eastern coyote. This campground's proximity to the Susquehanna makes it an excellent base for activities on the river. Canoeists and kayakers can see diverse natural and man-made habitats on the 65-mile Lower Section of the Susquehanna Water Trail. From Steelton to Conejohela Flats paddlers will experience a transition from industrial-use areas to serene bird habitat, a contrast that increases as one approaches the Chesapeake. There are 21 access points between Harrisburg and the Mason-Dixon Line, and soon the water trail will continue all of the way to Havre de Grace, Maryland, where the river meets the bay. Take care during times of high and potentially dangerous water levels. A hiking trail, the Mason-Dixon, parallels the river for much of the water trail's length. The Mason-Dixon is a great way for hikers to explore and experience riparian wildlife, and provides many access points for anglers. Muskie, walleye, smallmouth bass, panfish, catfish, and carp can all be caught here.

Campsites, facilities: There are 74 sites for tents or RVs up to 40 feet: 44 have full hookups; 15 have water and electricity; 15 have no hookups. There are 54 pull-throughs. Picnic tables and fire rings are provided. Drinking water, restrooms with flush toilets, a dump station, showers, a laundry, modem access, a phone hookup, a public phone, ice, LP gas, wood, grills, a playground, a swimming pool, and volleyball are available. Leashed pets are permitted.

Reservations, fees: Reservations are accepted. The rate is $26 per night for up to four people. Each additional person is $6. Open year-round.

Directions: From I-283 Exit 2, travel west 200 feet to Eisenhower Boulevard, then turn left onto Eisenhower Boulevard, then 0.75 mile to Campground Road. The campground entrance is on the left.

Contact: Harrisburg East Campground, 1134 Highspire Road, Harrisburg, PA 17111, 717/939-4331, hbgeastcamp@comcast.net.

25 WESTERN VILLAGE RV PARK

🚶 🚲 🏊 🎣 🛶 ♿ 🚐 ⛺

Rating: 6

near Kings Gap State Park

The spacious sites here are open or shaded. You can take advantage of hiking and biking trails in the northern edge of the campground and participate in bingo and campfires on weekends. Nearby Kings Gap State Park has 16 more miles of trails. Whispering Pines and White Oak Trails are both paved for wheelchair accessibility and run 0.3 mile each. The easiest trails are 0.6-mile Woodland Ecology Trail, 1.7-mile Kings Gap Hollow Trail, and 0.6-mile Pine Plantation Trail. Orienteering is also a popular sport within the state park. Be advised that hunting is allowed seasonally in Kings Gap State Park.

Campsites, facilities: There are 250 sites for RVs tents or up to 27 feet: 140 have full hookups; 110 have water and electricity. There are 20 pull-throughs. Picnic tables and fire rings are provided. Drinking water, restrooms with flush toilets, a dump station, showers, a laundry, modem access, a public phone, groceries, ice, LP gas, wood, a camp store, a pavilion, a rec hall, an arcade, a swimming pool, a playground, miniature golf, basketball, horseshoes, volleyball, a sports field, and RV storage and supplies are available. Some sites are wheelchair accessible. Leashed pets are permitted.

Reservations, fees: Reservations are accepted. The rate is $27–28 per night for up to two people. Each additional person is $3. Weekly, monthly, and seasonal rates are available. Major credit cards are accepted. Open year-round.

Directions: From I-81 Exit 45/13, travel southwest 1.5 miles on Walnut Bottom Road, then turn left on Greenview Drive and travel 0.25 mile. Follow the signs to the campground entrance at the end.

Contact: Western Village RV Park, 200 Greenview Drive, Carlisle, PA 17013, 717/243-1179, www.westernvillagervpark.com.

26 PARK AWAY PARK FAMILY CAMPGROUND

🚶 🏊 🚣 🚐 ❄ 🎣 🛶 🚐 ⛺

Rating: 8

near the Susquehanna River

Located near the state capital and the Susquehanna River, Park Away Park Family Campground is ideally located for visits to the region's attractions. Trips to Hershey, Gettysburg, and Lancaster County's Amish Country are all just short jaunts away, and entertainment of the natural sort can be found at nearby Gifford Pinchot State Park. The 2,338-acre park is mainly composed of old farm fields reverting back to forest and wooded hills. Pinchot Lake is suitable for boats with electric motors, and is increasingly popular for those with small sailboats and catamarans. Mooring is available. The 340-acre lake contains largemouth bass, striped bass, muskie, catfish, carp, and crappie, and is classified as a big bass lake. Visitors can swim at a large beach in the Quaker Race Day Use Area, which is open from Memorial Day to Labor Day. In the northeast section of the park, there are trails through old fields, pine plantations and wooded areas for horseback riding. There is a Frisbee golf course in the Conewago Day Use Area, as well as trails for biking and hiking. Winter activities include ice-skating, iceboating, ice fishing, and cross-country skiing. At the campground there are hiking trails and planned activities like bingo and theme weekends.

Campsites, facilities: There are 142 sites for tents or RVs up to 28 feet: 49 have full hookups; 93 have water and electricity. There are 90 pull-throughs. Picnic tables and fire rings are provided. Drinking water, restrooms with flush toilets, a dump station, a portable dump, showers, a laundry, a public phone, ice, LP gas, wood, a pavilion, a rec hall, a playground, a swimming pool, a shuffleboard court, tennis, badminton, volleyball, and a sports field are available. Leashed pets are permitted.

Reservations, fees: Reservations are accepted. The rate is $23.50–26 per night for up to two people. Each additional person is $5. Open April through beginning of November.

Directions: From the junction of I-83 Exit 33/14 and Highway 392, travel 0.1 mile east on Highway 392 to the campground entrance on the right.

Contact: Park Away Park, 1300 Old Trail Road, Etters, PA 17319, 717/938-1686, parkawaypark@webtv.net.

27 HERSHEY CONEWAGO CAMPGROUND

Rating: 9

near Hershey

Located south of Hershey's attractions and factories, Hershey Conewago is a 26-acre campground with planned activities on weekends, nightly movies for children, and plenty of hiking trails. Some of the open and shaded sites overlook a one-acre pond. In Hershey, attractions range from the sedate Hershey Museum, which tells the story of the man behind the bean, to HersheyPark, a sprawling complex with roller coasters and a zoological park. If you have kids, this is most likely where you are headed. With 10 coasters, six water rides, and over 20 kiddie rides the park has 60 different ways to make your head spin, knees wobble, and belly drop. Next door, ZooAmerica is a wildlife park specializing in North American animals. Here you can see black bear, river otter, great horned owls, Canada lynx, porcupine, gray wolves, mountain lions, American bison, American alligators, and crocodiles. No trip to Hershey would be complete without

a trip to Chocolate World, which explains the process of making the sweet treat and hands out free samples.

Campsites, facilities: There are 160 sites for tents or RVs up to 30 feet: 55 have full hookups; 85 have water and electricity; 20 have no hookups. There are 18 pull-throughs. Picnic tables and fire rings are provided. Drinking water, restrooms with flush toilets, a dump station, showers, a laundry, modem access, a phone hookup, a public phone, groceries, ice, LP gas, wood, a country store, grills, a pavilion, a gazebo, a rec room, an arcade, a playground, a swimming pool, miniature golf, a basketball court, a tennis court, badminton, horseshoes, a sand volleyball court, a sports field, and RV supplies are available. Leashed pets are permitted.

Reservations, fees: Reservations are accepted. The rate is $25–35 per night for up to two people. Each additional person is $6. Weekly and monthly rates are available. Major credit cards are accepted. Open April through October.

Directions: From the junction of U.S. 322 and Highway 743, travel six miles south on Highway 743 to the campground entrance on the left.

Contact: Hershey Conewago Campground, P.O. Box 449, Hershey, PA 17033, 717/367-1179 or 866/246-1809, www.hersheyconewago.com.

28 YE OLDE MILL CAMPGROUND

Rating: 7

near Cowans Gap State Park

Located between Tuscarora Mountain to the east and Shade Mountain to the west, Ye Olde Mill is situated in the heart of Pennsylvania's forested ridges. You can hike these folded mountains, which formed over 300 million years ago when the African plate slammed into the North American plate and compressed the earth's crust like a rug pushed into a wall. Along the highways near Ye Olde Mill, you can see places where the rock is folded into a vertical layer rather than a horizontal layer. At nearby Cowan's Gap State Park, you can fish from a pier or from your own electric motorboat, rent rowboats and pedal boats, or swim at a 500-foot sand beach that is guarded from Memorial Day to Labor Day. On the Ye Olde Mill property, there is stream fishing for those more inclined to stay put.

Campsites, facilities: There are 30 sites for tents or RVs up to 25 feet; all sites have water and electricity. There are 12 pull-throughs. Picnic tables and fire rings are provided. Drinking water, restrooms with flush toilets, a dump station, showers, a laundry, groceries, ice, LP gas, wood, a camp store, a pavilion, a playground, horseshoes, and a sports field are available. Leashed pets are permitted.

Reservations, fees: Reservations are accepted. The rate is $20–25 per night for up to five people. Each additional person is $5. Open April through beginning of November.

Directions: From the junction of Pennsylvania Turnpike Exit 180/13 and U.S. 522, travel 4.5 miles northeast on U.S. 522, then 0.5 mile east on a paved road to the campground entrance on the right.

Contact: Ye Olde Mill Campground, 599 Grist Mill Road, Burnt Cabins, PA 17215, 717/987-3244, gristmill@cun.net.

29 COWANS GAP STATE PARK

🏃 🏊 🚣 🚐 ❄ 🐎 ♿ 🚍 ⛺

Rating: 9

near Fort Loudon

Cowans Gap State Park is 1,085 acres of scenic beauty in Fulton County's Allens Valley. The scenic highlight is Cowans Gap Lake where visitors can swim at a 500-foot sand beach, which is guarded from Memorial Day to Labor Day. Picnic areas, some with fireplaces, are available nearby. The lake provides 42 acres of fishable surface area. Anglers may wet a line for trout, smallmouth bass, perch, and panfish. An accessible fishing pier makes casting easy, and electric motors are permitted on the lake. A concession at the beach area rents rowboats and paddleboats, and sells camp supplies and snacks. Good trout fishing can also be found at Little Aughwick Creek. There are several miles of hiking trails in the park. Please note that hunting is permitted in season. Winter activities include cross-country skiing, ice fishing, and ice skating on the lake. The park is adjacent to Buchanan State Forest and the birthplace of President James Buchanan.

Campsites, facilities: There are 224 sites for tents or RVs up to 30 feet: 64 have electricity; 160 have no hookups. Picnic tables and fire rings are provided. Drinking water, restrooms with flush toilets, a dump station, showers, a public phone, groceries, a camp store, a pavilion, and volleyball are available. Some sites are wheelchair accessible. Leashed pets are permitted.

Reservations, fees: Reservations are accepted at 888/PA-PARKS (888/727-2757). The rate is $14–19 per night for up to five people; a fee may apply for additional guests. Pets are $2 for up to two pets per night. Senior and Pennsylvania resident discounts are available. Open April through December.

Directions: From the junction of U.S. 30 and Highway 75, travel north four miles on Highway 75, then turn left onto Richmond Furnace Road and travel 8.5 miles to the campground entrance.

Contact: Cowans Gap State Park, 6235 Aughwick Road, Fort Loudon, PA 17224-9801, 717/485-3948, cowansgapsp@state.pa.us.

30 PINE GROVE FURNACE STATE PARK

Rating: 9

near Gardners

BEST (

You'll find plenty of water activities on this 696-acre park's two lakes. Laurel Lake covers 25 acres and Fuller Lake covers only 1.7 acres; both offer good fishing opportunities for perch, pickerel, sunfish, catfish, crappie, bluegill, and stocked trout. You can also fish for rainbow, brown, and brook trout in Mountain Creek. Only Laurel Lake permits boating, but both lakes have sandy beaches for swimming. For pursuits on land, try the three miles of park hiking trails or jump onto the small section of the Appalachian National Scenic Trail that runs through state park property. Pine Grove is where AT thru-hikers take the infamous half-gallon ice cream challenge, an attempt to down 3,200 calories before hitting the trail again. Biking is permitted on the state park roadways. The campground has planned activities. During the winter, you can go ice skating and ice fishing on Laurel Lake and snowmobiling and cross-country skiing. Be advised that hunting is allowed seasonally in Pine Grove Furnace State Park.

Campsites, facilities: There are 74 sites for tents or RVs up to 30 feet: 27 have electricity; 47 have no hookups. There are four pull-throughs. Picnic tables and fire rings are provided. Drinking water, non-flush toilets, a dump station, a public phone, groceries, ice, wood, a camp store, grills, a pavilion, and a sports field are available. Some sites are wheelchair accessible. Leashed pets are permitted.

Reservations, fees: Reservations are accepted at 888/PA-PARKS (888/727-2757). The rate is $14–19 per night for up to five people; a fee may apply for additional guests. Pets are $2 for up to two pets per night. Senior and Pennsylvania resident discounts are available. Open year-round.

Directions: From the junction of I-81 Exit 37 and Highway 233, travel eight miles south on Highway 233 to the campground entrance.

Contact: Pine Grove Furnace State Park, 1100 Pine Grove Road, Gardners, PA 17324, 717/486-7174, pinegrovesp@state.pa.us.

31 MOUNTAIN CREEK CAMPGROUND

Rating: 8

near Pine Grove Furnace State Park

There are both wooded and open sites here. You can cast for trout in the property's stocked stream or take advantage of access to a section of the Appalachian Trail and the Cumberland County Hiker-Biker Trail. Mountain Creek offers weekend activities such as hayrides. At 25-acre Laurel Lake in nearby Pine Grove Furnace State Park, you can continue fishing or just rent a boat and explore. Boats with electric motors and non-powered boats are welcome on the lake.

Campsites, facilities: There are 200 sites for tents or RVs up to 40 feet: 186 have water and electricity; 14 have no hookups. There are 10 pull-throughs. Picnic tables and fire rings are provided. Drinking water, restrooms with flush toilets, a dump station, a portable dump, showers, a laundry, modem access, a phone hookup, a public phone, groceries, ice, LP gas, wood, fishing supplies, a general store, a snack bar, a pavilion, a rec hall, an arcade, a playground, a swimming pool, a wading pool, a whirlpool, horseshoes, basketball, volleyball, and RV rentals, storage, and supplies are available. Some sites are wheelchair accessible. Leashed pets are permitted. The campground has a traffic control gate for security.

Reservations, fees: Reservations are required. The rate is $28–36 per night for up to two people. Each additional person is $5. Monthly, seasonal, and group rates are available. Major credit cards are accepted. Open year-round.

Directions: From the junction of I-81 and Highway 34 Exit 47A, travel seven miles south on Highway 34, then turn right onto Green Mountain Road and travel 0.5 mile, then bear right onto Pine Grove Road and travel one mile to the campground entrance on the right.

Contact: Mountain Creek Campground, 349 Pine Grove Road, Gardners, PA 17324, 717/486-7681, www.mtncreekcg.com.

32 DEER RUN APPALACHIAN CAMPGROUND

🚶🏊🎣🏕🛶🚐⛺

Rating: 10

near Kings Gap State Park

BEST (

This campground lies just 75 yards off the Appalachian Trail; live music from the campground often brings in travel-weary hikers during the summer. The campground is located in a mountain valley, and all of its sites are wooded and shaded. In addition to the bands, you can enjoy other planned activities such as car shows and hayrides. Deer Run also has a pond for fishing. Nearby Kings Gap State Park has a permanent orienteering course, so bring your compass and grab a course map from the park office. Also at Kings Gap are 16 miles of hiking trails. Whispering Pines Trail and White Oak Trail are both paved and wheelchair accessible. Each loop is only 0.3 mile and has interpretive signs in script and Braille.

Campsites, facilities: There are 225 sites for tents or RVs up to 30 feet: 105 sites have full hookups; 10 have electricity; 110 have no hookups. There are 21 pull-throughs. Picnic tables and fire rings are provided. Drinking water, restrooms with flush toilets, a dump station, showers, a laundry, cable TV hookup, groceries,

ice, wood, a camp store, a snack bar, an arcade, two playgrounds, two swimming pools, a hut tub, horseshoes, volleyball, and a sports field are available. Leashed pets are permitted.

Reservations, fees: Reservations are accepted at 800/955-0208. The rate is $18–31.50 for up to four people per night. Each additional person is $4. Weekly, monthly, and seasonal rates are available. Senior, law enforcement, and military personnel discounts are available. Open year-round.

Directions: From the junction of I-81 Exit 48E/14E and Route 34, travel south on Route 34 to Route 94 then turn left and travel 1.5 miles to the campground entrance.

Contact: Deer Run Campground, 111 Sheet Iron Roof Road, Gardners, PA 17324, 717/486-8168, www.deerruncampground.fcpages.com.

33 HERSHEY'S FUR CENTER CAMPING AREA

🚶🚴🏊🎣🚐🏕🛶♿🚐⛺

Rating: 6

near Gifford Pinchot State Park

This small campground has mostly shaded sites in a cozy setting. There are many recreational opportunities at nearby 2,338-acre Gifford Pinchot State Park, including water sports on 340-acre Pinchot Lake. Motorboats with electric motors and non-motorized boats are welcome at three launch areas and 286 mooring spaces. Anglers can fish for largemouth, smallmouth, and hybrid striped bass, muskie, carp, crappie, sunfish, bluegill, walleye, and catfish. There is also a guarded sand beach for swimming along part of the shoreline. The park offers miles of trails for hiking, biking, and horseback riding. The 11 hiking trails cover 18 miles; 3.5 of them are designated as the Multipurpose Trail Network and can accommodate bikes. The park also offers educational and interpretive programs such as guided walks and pontoon-boat tours. Check the park office for a schedule of these changing events.

Campsites, facilities: There are 25 sites for tents or RVs up to 22 feet: six have full hookups; 15 have water and electricity; four have no hookups. Picnic tables and fire rings are provided. Drinking water, a dump station, restrooms with flush toilets, a pavilion, ice, wood, a tennis court, badminton, a playground, volleyball, and RV storage are available. Some sites are wheelchair accessible. Leashed pets are permitted.

Reservations, fees: Reservations are accepted. The rate is $24–28 per night for up to four people. Each additional person is $5. Open May through October.

Directions: From the junction of U.S. 15 and Highway 94, travel 0.25 mile south on Highway 94 to the campground entrance on the right.

Contact: Hershey's Fur Center, 8164 Carlisle Pike, York Springs, PA 17372.

34 GIFFORD PINCHOT STATE PARK

🚶 🚵 🏊 🛶 � 🎿 🤾 ♿ 🚐 ⛺

Rating: 10

near Lewisberry

BEST (

The centerpiece of Gifford Pinchot State Park is 340-acre Pinchot Lake. The lake has three launch areas and 286 mooring spaces for motorboats with electric motors and canoes. You can cast for muskie, crappie, hybrid striped, largemouth, and smallmouth bass, carp, walleye, catfish, sunfish, and bluegill. The Quaker Race Day Use Area has a large sand beach for guarded swimming. You can also rent a boat here. You can choose from 11 trails for foot travel and the Multipurpose Trail Network in the Conewago Day Use Area has trails that are open to bikers. You can find the horseback riding trails in the northeastern corner of the park. The campground offers planned activities like

guided walks and nature programs. During the winter, ice skating, ice fishing, iceboating, and cross-country skiing are popular activities. Be advised that Gifford Pinchot State Park allows hunting seasonally.

Campsites, facilities: There are 339 sites for tents or RVs up to 30 feet: 75 have electricity; 264 have no hookups. Picnic tables and fire rings are provided. Drinking water, restrooms with flush toilets, a dump station, showers, a snack bar, a pavilion, a playground, horseshoes, volleyball, a sports field, a Frisbee golf course, and an amphitheater are available. Some sites are wheelchair accessible. No pets are permitted.

Reservations, fees: Reservations are accepted at 888/PA-PARKS (888/727-2757). The rate is $14–19 per night for up to five people; a fee may apply for additional guests. Senior and Pennsylvania resident discounts are available. Open April through October.

Directions: From the junction of Highway 177 and Highway 74, travel south one mile on Highway 74, then east on the camping area road to the campground entrance.

Contact: Gifford Pinchot State Park, 2200 Rosstown Road, Lewisberry, PA 17339-9787, 717/292-4112, giffordpinchotsp@state.pa.us.

35 CONEWAGO ISLE CAMPGROUND

🚶 🚵 🏊 🛶 🚐 🎿 🤾 🐎 🛶 🚐 ⛺

Rating: 7

near Gifford Pinchot State Park

Conewago Creek borders the northern part of the campground and offers views of the property's two waterfalls. Take out a canoe or paddleboat or cast your line for trout, bass, sunfish, bluegill, and catfish. You can also rent a bike to travel the trails around the campground or just take your time with a leisurely walk. At nearby 2,338-acre Gifford Pinchot State Park, you can hike, bike, go horseback riding, fish and boat at Pinchot Lake, or swim at a guarded sand beach. In the Conewago Day Use Area, you can try your hand at completing the park's 18-hole Frisbee golf course. During the winter, you can ice fish, ice skate, iceboat, and cross-country ski. The campground has a choice of grassy and water's edge sites. On weekends, you can participate in planned activities such as bingo and hayrides.

Campsites, facilities: There are 98 sites for tents or RVs up to 30 feet: 47 have full hookups; 51 have water and electricity. Picnic tables and fire rings are provided. Drinking water, restrooms with flush toilets, a dump station, showers, groceries, ice, wood, a camp store, a pavilion, a playground, basketball, horseshoes, and volleyball are available. Leashed pets are permitted.

Reservations, fees: Reservations are accepted. The rate is $24 per night for up to two people. Each additional person is $5. Weekly rates are available. Open year-round.

Directions: From the junction of Highway 194 and Highway 234, travel east four miles on Highway 234, then turn left onto Big Mount Road and travel three miles to the campground entrance on the left. There is a bridge with a seven-ton limit on Big Mount Road.

Contact: Conewago Isle Campground, 6220 Big Mount Road, York, PA 17315, 717/292-1461, www.conewagoisle.com.

36 TWIN BRIDGE MEADOW FAMILY CAMPGROUND

Rating: 8

near Cowans Gap State Park

Twin Bridge Meadow Family Campground is located amidst a variety of state parks and historical sites. At nearby Cowans Gap State Park, there's a lake for fishing, beaches for swimming, and plenty of hiking. Tuscarora Trail, a spur of the Appalachian Trail, winds up at Big Mountain Overlook, which has views of the surrounding area. Also along the trail are interesting rock fields and outcroppings. Buchanan State Forest is adjacent to the park and offers additional opportunities for hiking, fishing, and hunting. Buchanan's birthplace is a little further south, nestled in a crook of Tuscarora Mountain. This small but scenic park is home to a fine trout stream, Buck Run. The campground has planned activities like bingo and hayrides on weekends.

Campsites, facilities: There are 132 sites for tents or RVs up to 30 feet: hookupsall have water and electricity. There are 28 pull-throughs. Picnic tables and fire rings are provided. Drinking water, restrooms with flush toilets, a dump station, a portable dump, showers, modem access, a public phone, groceries, ice, wood, a camp store, a pavilion, a rec hall, a playground, miniature golf, basketball, horseshoes, volleyball, a sports field, and RV storage are available. Leashed pets are permitted.

Reservations, fees: Reservations are accepted. The rate is $18 per night for up to two people per night. Each additional person is $4. Open April through October.

Directions: From the junction of I-81 Exit 16/6 and U.S. 30, travel west six miles on U.S. 30, then turn right onto Twin Bridge Road and travel 1.25 miles to the campground entrance on the left.

Contact: Twin Bridge Meadow Family Campground, 1345 Twin Bridge Road, Chambersburg, PA 17201, 717/369-2216.

37 CALEDONIA STATE PARK

Rating: 9

near Fayetteville

Located in the Blue Ridge Mountains, 1,125-acre Caledonia State Park is named after a charcoal iron furnace that operated here in the late 1800s. The campground is divided into a main section and the smaller Hosack Run area, which gets its name from the nearby stream. You can enjoy the beautiful valley scenery by hiking the park's 10 miles of trails. The Appalachian National Scenic Trail also runs through the center of Caledonia State Park on its 2,000-mile run from Maine to Georgia. You can cool off in the swimming pool or play 18 holes at the oldest golf course in south-central Pennsylvania. The park is also home to Totem Pole Playhouse, a summer theater, and the Thaddeus Steven's Blacksmith Shop. You can participate in environmental and interpretive programs such as guided walks and campfires. Check the park office for a schedule of these changing events. Be advised that hunting is allowed seasonally in Caledonia State Park.

Campsites, facilities: There are 184 sites for tents or RVs up to 30 feet; 35 have electricity; 149 have no hookups. There are 10 pull-throughs. No sites have full hookups. Picnic tables and fire rings are available. Drinking water, restrooms with flush toilets, a dump station, showers, a public phone, a snack bar, a pavilion, a swimming pool, a playground, a golf course, and a sports field are available. Some sites are wheelchair accessible. Leashed pets are permitted.

Reservations, fees: Reservations are accepted at 888/PA-PARKS (888/727-2757). The rate is $14–19 per night for up to five people; a fee may apply for additional guests. Pets are $2 for up to two pets per night. Senior and Pennsylvania resident discounts are available. Open April through December.

Directions: From the junction of U.S. 30 and Highway 233, travel north 0.25 mile on Highway 233 to the campground entrance.

Contact: Caledonia State Park, 40 Rocky Mountain Road, Fayetteville, PA 17222-9610, 717/352-2161, caledoniasp@state.pa.us.

38 INDIAN ROCK CAMPGROUND

🏃 🚲 🏕 🛶 ♿ 🚐 ⛰

Rating: 5

near Samuel S. Lewis State Park

BEST (

You have your choice of shaded and open sites at Indian Rock. The property's hiking trail connects to York Heritage Bike and Rail Trail. For more hiking options, you can visit nearby Samuel S. Lewis State Park. The 85-acre park has interesting rock formations and pine forests to explore, as well as views from its centerpiece, 885-foot Mount Pisgah. Kite flying is a favorite activity from the mountain's peak. During the day you can see vistas of farmlands and the Susquehanna River from this vantage point, and at night a sky full of stars. The state park is also home to the George E. Stein Arboretum. Created before the area became a state park, the arboretum protects several tree species such as English yew, persimmon, concolor fir, and European beech. You can also pack a picnic lunch and enjoy it at the park. The picnic area has a sports field and a playground.

Campsites, facilities: There are 40 sites for tents or RVs up to 32 feet: all sites have full hookups. There are three pull-throughs. Picnic tables and fire rings are provided. Drinking water, a dump station, restrooms with flush toilets, showers, public phones, groceries, ice, wood, a camp store, a pavilion, a playground, volleyball, and RV storage and supplies are available. Some sites are wheelchair accessible. Leashed pets are permitted.

Reservations, fees: Reservations are accepted. The rate is $24 per night for up to two people. Each additional person is $5. Open year-round.

Directions: From the junction of I-83 Exit 14/4 and Highway 182, travel 2.5 miles west on Highway 182 to the campground entrance on the left.

Contact: Indian Rock Campground, 436

Indian Rock Dam Road, York, PA 17403, 717/741-1764, www.indianrockcampground.com.

39 OTTER CREEK CAMPGROUND

Rating: 3

on the Susquehanna River

This campground on the calm western bank of the Susquehanna River has scenic, wooded, and spacious sites. The campground has a ramp and a dock, as well as hiking trails. A public boat launch is 0.25 mile away for boating, canoeing, kayaking, waterskiing, and fishing. Among the species you can cast for are largemouth and smallmouth bass, carp, muskie, white suckers, and channel catfish. Some wildlife you may spot are white-tailed deer, raccoons, red and gray squirrels, opossums, chipmunks, woodchucks, and cottontail rabbits. Birders can watch for great blue herons, white herons, mallard ducks, cormorants, mergansers, osprey, bald eagles, terns, Canada geese, and kingfishers. Otter Creek has planned activities on weekends, such as hayrides, live music, and dances.

Campsites, facilities: There are 92 sites for tents or RVs up to 35 feet: all have water and electricity. There are 12 pull-throughs. Picnic tables and fire rings are available. Drinking water, restrooms with flush toilets, a dump station, a portable dump, showers, a laundry, a public phone, groceries, ice, wood, a camp store, a pavilion, a rec area, an arcade, a playground, basketball, a shuffleboard court, horseshoes, ping-pong, and volleyball are available. Some sites are wheelchair accessible. Leashed pets are permitted. The campground has a traffic control gate for security.

Reservations, fees: Reservations are accepted at 877/336-8837. The rate is $24 per night for up to two people. Each additional person

is $6. Weekly and group rates are available. Major credit cards are accepted. Open April through October.

Directions: From the junction of Highway 74 and Highway 425, travel north four miles on Highway 425 to the campground entrance on the left.

Contact: Otter Creek Campground, 1101 Furnace Road, Airville, PA 17302, 717/862-3628, www.ottercreekcamp.com.

40 LONGVIEW CAMPGROUND

Rating: 6

near Cowans Gap State Park

At nearby 1,085-acre Cowans Gap State Park, you can choose from a variety of outdoor recreational opportunities. Cowans Gap Lake covers 42 acres. You can launch your electric-motored boat or canoe from two launch areas or rent a rowboat or paddleboat from the boating concession in the day use area. While you're on the lake, cast your line for smallmouth and largemouth bass, perch, sunfish, brook, brown, and rainbow trout, bluegill, catfish, muskie, black crappie, and suckers. There is a 500-foot sand beach for swimming along the shoreline in the day-use area. You can also picnic by the lake at tables and pavilions, or just grab something from the snack bar. For drier pursuits, hop onto a hiking trail and explore the park. Among the wildlife you may encounter are white-tailed deer, raccoons, red and gray squirrels, opossums, chipmunks, and cottontail rabbits. During the winter, ice skating, ice fishing, and cross-country skiing are favorite activities.

Campsites, facilities: There are 106 sites for tents or RVs up to 40 feet: all sites have water and electricity. Picnic tables and fire rings are provided. Drinking water, restrooms with flush toilets, a dump station, a portable dump, showers, ice, and wood are available. Leashed pets are permitted.

Reservations, fees: Reservations are accepted. The rate is $16–30 per night for up to two people. Each additional person is $4. Open year-round.

Directions: From the junction of I-81 Exit 5 and Route 16, travel 10 miles west on Route 16 to Mercersburg, then turn left at the traffic light onto Park Avenue and travel one mile on Park Avenue, then turn right onto Mt. Pleasant Road and stay left as it turns into Charlestown Road. After three miles, turn right onto Robinson Road. The campground entrance is on the left.

Contact: Longview Campground, 7570 Robinson Road, Mercersburg, PA 17236, 717/328-3593, www.longviewcampground.net.

41 KEYSTONE RV CAMPGROUND

Rating: 3

near Mont Alto State Park

The rustic setting for this small campground includes cozy woodlands. At nearby Mont Alto State Park, anglers can spend the day casting for brook and brown trout in the West Branch of Antietam Creek. Hikers can follow the roadways for short hikes to glimpse wildlife such as white-tailed deer, woodchucks, raccoons, red and gray squirrels, opossums, skunks, chipmunks, and cottontail rabbits. Birders can follow these same roads to spy warblers, red-tailed hawks, eagles, cardinals, chickadees, and wrens. During the winter, snowmobiling is a favorite activity. Also close by is Michaux State Forest. Almost 39 miles of the 2,100-mile Appalachian Trail runs through the forest on its way from Maine to Georgia. Michaux also has its own hiking trails, as well as trails for biking and horseback riding. The other two state parks located within the state forest are Caledonia and Pine Grove. Be advised that

hunting is allowed seasonally within Michaux State Forest.

Campsites, facilities: There are 25 sites for RVs up to 25 feet; all have water and electricity. No tents can be accommodated. Picnic tables and fire rings are provided. Drinking water, a dump station, and RV rentals and supplies are available. There are no restrooms. Leashed pets are permitted.

Reservations, fees: Reservations are accepted. The rate is $25 per night for up to four people. Each additional person is $5. A Pennsylvania resident discount is available. Open year-round.

Directions: From the junction of I-81 Exit 1 and the Maryland/Pennsylvania State Line, enter the campground on the left at the end of the exit.

Contact: Keystone RV Campground, 15799 Young Road, Greencastle, PA 17225, 800/232-3279.

42 GRANITE HILL CAMPGROUND & ADVENTURE GOLF

Rating: 10

near Gettysburg

BEST (

Granite Hill's 150 acres of woodlands and meadows have played host to the internationally acclaimed Gettysburg Bluegrass Festival since 1979. Held in early May and in late August, the festival presents top musicians on the main stage as well as workshops for pickers and meet-and-greets. History buffs should note that General Lee's retreat from Gettysburg took him past Granite Hill. His troops held the entire community while wounded soldiers were treated at Granite Hill barn. Campers still find Civil War bullets and other relics on the property. You can stay at open or wooded sites and enjoy kayaking, pedal boating, and fishing in Bass Lake. You can also escape into the woods on one of the site's hiking trails. There are daily planned activities such as hayrides, dances, and local tours to the battlefield.

Campsites, facilities: There are 300 sites for tents or RVs up to 90 feet: 100 have full hookups; 150 have water and electricity; 50 have no hookups. There are 109 pull-throughs. Picnic tables and fire rings are provided. Drinking water, restrooms with flush toilets, a dump station, a portable dump, showers, a laundry, modem access, phone hookup, cable TV hookup, groceries, ice, LP gas, wood, fishing supplies, a camp store, a pavilion, a rec hall, an arcade, a playground, a swimming pool, miniature golf, basketball, two shuffleboard courts, tennis, badminton, horseshoes, volleyball, a sports field, and RV storage and supplies are available. Some sites are wheelchair accessible. Leashed pets are permitted. The campground has a traffic control gate for security.

Reservations, fees: Reservations are accepted at 800/642-8368. The rate is $24–39 per night for up to two people. Each additional person is $8. Weekly and group rates are available. Major credit cards are accepted. Open year-round.

Directions: From the junction of U.S. 15 and Highway 116, travel west six miles on Highway 116 to the campground entrance on the left.

Contact: Granite Hill Campground, 3340 Fairfield Road, Gettysburg, PA 17325, 717/642-8749 or 800/642-8368, www.granitehillcampground.com.

43 GETTYSBURG KOA KAMPGROUND

Rating: 7

in Gettysburg

Gettysburg KOA has plenty of on-site activities to keep campers busy. Weekend activities include living history encampments, Civil War stories told by campfire, ghost walks, and wine tastings. The park's wooded sites all have easy access to hiking trails. Bus tours depart daily to Washington D.C. and Gettysburg National Battlefield, or you can explore Little Round Top or Pickett's Charge on your own. Nearby in Pennsylvania's Blue Ridge Mountains is the Strawberry Hill Nature Center, a 609-acre preserve that offers good birding opportunities. This stop along Pennsylvania Audubon's Susquehanna River Birding and Wildlife Trail is home to wet and dry woodlands, ponds, pristine mountain streams, and over 10 miles of blazed trails that lead to overlooks and rock formations.

Campsites, facilities: There are 93 sites for tents or RVs up to 26 feet: 48 have full hookups; 26 have water and electricity; 19 have no hookups. There are 13 pull-throughs. Picnic tables and fire rings are provided. Drinking water, restrooms with flush toilets, a dump station, showers, a laundry, a public phone, groceries, ice, LP gas, wood, a camp store, grills, a pavilion, a rec hall, a playground, a swimming pool, miniature golf, a shuffleboard court, and horseshoes are available. Some sites are wheelchair accessible. Leashed pets are permitted.

Reservations, fees: Reservations are accepted at 800/562-1869. The rate is $20–52 per night for up to two people per night. Each additional person is $6. Major credit cards are accepted. Open April through October.

Directions: From the junction of U.S. 15 and U.S. 30, travel three miles west on U.S. 30, then turn left onto Knoxlyn Road and travel 2.5 miles, then turn right onto Knox Road and travel 0.5 mile to the campground entrance on the left.

Contact: Gettysburg KOA Kampground, 20 Knox Road, Gettysburg, PA 17325, 717/642-5713, www.gettysburgkoa.com.

44 GETTYSBURG CAMPGROUND

Rating: 8

in Gettysburg

BEST (

Most visitors to this well-appointed campground will visit Gettysburg National

Battlefield, where the bloodiest battle of the Civil War was fought. Visitors wishing to pursue other activities can head to Codorus State Park, where mountain biking is possible on 6.5 miles of trails. If fishing is more your thing, the park has 1,275-acre Lake Marburg, a stocked warmwater fishery. Some guests will prefer to remain on the property, which offers both shaded and open sites, and take advantage of activities such as crafts, ceramics, and nightly movies. Anglers can fish for stocked trout in March Creek, which surrounds the campground on two sides.

Campsites, facilities: There are 250 sites for tents or RVs up to 30 feet: 90 have full hookups; 140 have water and electricity; 20 have no hookups. There are 40 pullthroughs. Picnic tables and fire rings are provided. Drinking water, restrooms with flush toilets, two dump stations, a portable dump, showers, a laundry, a public phone, groceries, ice, LP gas, wood, a camp store, a pavilion, a rec hall, a game room, a playground, a swimming pool, miniature golf, two shuffleboard courts, horseshoes, volleyball, a sporst field, and RV supplies are available. Some sites are wheelchair accessible. Leashed pets are permitted.

Reservations, fees: Reservations are accepted. The rate is $29.70–36.70 per night for up to two people. Each additional person is $3. Weekly rates are available. Major credit cards are accepted. Open April through mid-November.

Directions: From the junction of U.S. 15 and Highway 116, travel three miles west on Highway 116 to the campground entrance on the left.

Contact: Gettysburg Campground, 2030 Fairfield Road, Gettysburg, PA 17325, 717/334-3304, www.gettysburgcampground.com.

45 ROUND TOP CAMPGROUND

Rating: 9

near Gettysburg

BEST (

Just three miles from the battlefield, Round Top Campground is ideally located to be a great base camp for all Gettysburg-related activities. Outdoor enthusiasts can choose from a variety of nearby options. At Mont Alto State Park, anglers can wet a line for trout in Antietam Creek, an excellent stream. Diverse wildlife and interesting wildflowers can be spotted on short hikes along the park's wooded roads. Just east is Codorus State Park, home to 1,275-acre Lake Marburg. Visitors to the park can enjoy hiking, swimming, boating, fishing, and picnicking on the park's 3,329 acres.

Campsites, facilities: There are 278 sites for tents or RVs up to 30 feet: 202 have full hookups; 56 have water and electricity; 20 have no hookups. There are eight pull-throughs. Picnic tables and fire rings are provided. Drinking water, restrooms with flush toilets, a dump station, showers, a laundry, modem access, a phone hookup, cable TV hookup, a public phone, groceries, ice, LP gas, wood, a general store, a snack bar, a pavilion, a rec hall, an arcade, a playground, a swimming pool, a wading pool, miniature golf, basketball, two shuffleboard courts, tennis, badminton, horseshoes, volleyball, a sports field, and RV rentals, storage, and supplies are available. Some sites are wheelchair accessible. Leashed pets are permitted.

Reservations, fees: Reservations are accepted. The rate is $18–35.50 per night for up to two people. Each additional person is $4. Major credit cards are accepted. Open year-round.

Directions: From the junction of U.S. 15 and Highway 134, travel 0.2 mile north on Highway 134, then turn left onto Knight Road and travel 0.5 mile to the campground entrance on the left.

Contact: Round Top Campground, 180 Knight Road, Gettysburg, PA 17325, 717/334-9565, www.roundtopcamp.com.

46 ARTILLERY RIDGE CAMPING RESORT

Rating: 9

near Gettysburg

BEST (

One of the most noteworthy features of Artillery Ridge Camping Resort is the two-hour guided horseback tour of Gettysburg National Battlefield. The tour guide will describe the three-day battle and history and ramifications of the Civil War's bloodiest battle. The campground is located very close to Little Round Top, one of the park's most heavily visited sites. The rocky protrusion offered a natural position from which the Union could defend the end of their line. Reservations are required for guided tours. For those with less time, a one-hour trail ride is available as well. Horse lovers will appreciate that Artillery Ridge has facilities, box stalls, and corrals available for those traveling with their own horses. Visitors should note the 750-square foot diorama located on the property. The park campground boasts pedal boat rentals and pond fishing, and planned weekend activities that include country line dancing and pool parties.

Campsites, facilities: There are 155 sites for tents of RVs up to 27 feet: 52 have full hookups; 68 have water and electricity; 35 have no hookups. There are 44 pull-throughs. Picnic tables and fire rings are provided. Drinking water, restrooms with flush toilets, a dump station, a portable dump, showers, a laundry, a public phone, groceries, ice, wood, a camp store, a pavilion, an equipped pavilion, a playground, a swimming pool, horseshoes, and volleyball are available. Some sites are wheelchair accessible. Leashed pets are permitted.

Reservations, fees: Reservations are accepted. The rate is $30–33 per night for up to two people. Each additional person is $6. Open April through beginning of November.

Directions: From the junction of U.S. 30 and U.S. 15, travel 1.5 miles south on U.S. 15, then 1.25 miles southeast on Highway 134 to the campground entrance on the left.

Contact: Artillery Ridge Camping Resort, 610 Taneytown Road, Gettysburg, PA 17325, 717/334-1288, www.artilleryridge.com.

47 DRUMMER BOY CAMPING RESORT

Rating: 10

near Gettysburg

BEST (

Drummer Boy Campground is a well-appointed park just five minutes from the battlefield. The site's mostly shaded, wooded 90 acres contain a pond for fishing and hiking trails in the northern part of the property. There are nightly movies, as well as abundant activities that may include live music or theme weekends. On hot summer days, campers can enjoy the new pool complex with free-form pool and waterslide. At nearby Gettysburg, visitors have a variety of touring options to choose from, including battlefield bus tours or self-guided auto tour tape rentals.

Campsites, facilities: There are 348 sites for tents or RVs up to 32 feet: 275 have full hookups; 32 have water and electricity; 27 have no hookups. There are 51 pull-throughs. Picnic tables and fire rings are provided. Drinking water, restrooms with flush toilets, three dump stations, a portable dump, showers, two laundries, modem access, phone hookup, cable TV hookup, a public phone, groceries, ice, wood, a general store, a gift shop, a snack bar, a pavilion, a rec hall, a playground, an arcade, a mini movie theater, a swimming pool, a water slide, a whirlpool, miniature golf, basketball, badminton, horseshoes, volleyball, and RV supplies are available. Some sites are wheelchair accessible. Leashed pets are permitted.

Reservations, fees: Reservations are accepted at 800/293-2808. The rate is $27–48 per night for up to two people. Each additional person is $4. Weekly rates are available. Major credit cards are accepted. Open April through October.

Directions: From the junction of U.S. 15 and Highway 116, travel 100 yards east on Highway 116, then turn left onto Rocky Grove Road and travel 0.2 mile to the campground entrance on the left.

Contact: Drummer Boy Camping Resort, 1300 Hanover Road, Gettysburg, PA 17325, 717/334-3277, www.drummerboycamping.com.

48 CODORUS STATE PARK

Rating: 10

near Hanover

BEST (

This 3,329-acre state park is home to 1,275-acre Lake Marburg, which has 26 miles of shoreline and offers lots of water activities. If you have your own motorboat (up to 20 hp), you can choose from seven launch ramps in the park. There are also mooring spots for canoes and sailboats. Boat rental facilities are located near the marina and pool area. Choose from motorboats, canoes, pontoon boats, and rowboats. The park has trails for hiking, biking, and horseback riding. Mary Ann Furnace Trail consists of three interconnected loops that meander 3.5 miles through wetlands, hardwood forests, and pine groves. The 1.5-mile LaHo Trail follows the shoreline and winds through wetlands. During the winter, ice skating, ice fishing, iceboating, snowmobiling, cross-country skiing, and sledding are favorite activities. Be advised that hunting is allowed seasonally in Codorus State Park.

Campsites, facilities: There are 198 sites for tents or RVs up to 50 feet: 100 have electricity; 98 have no hookups. There are 13 walk-in sites. Picnic tables and fire rings are provided. Drinking water, restrooms with flush toilets, a dump station, showers, two pavilions, a swimming pool, a marina, and a Frisbee golf course are available. Some sites are wheelchair accessible. Leashed pets are permitted.

Reservations, fees: Reservations are accepted at 888/PA-PARKS (888/727-2757). The rate is $14–19 per night for up to five people; a fee may apply for additional guests. Pets are $2 for up to two pets per night. Senior and Pennsylvania resident discounts are available. Open April through October.

Directions: From the junction of Highway 116 and Highway 216, travel east two miles on Highway 216 to the park entrance, then turn right onto Dubb's Church Road and travel 0.5 mile to the campground entrance on the right.

Contact: Codorus State Park, 1066 Blooming Grove Road, Hanover, PA 17331-9545, 717/637-2816, codorussp@state.pa.us.

SOUTHEAST

© JASON MILLER

BEST CAMPGROUNDS

Pennsylvania's southeast corner represents a land set aside as a refuge for all people fleeing persecution and oppression. The first people to settle here helped William Penn establish a land where all were welcome. Yet immigration is the very thing that pushed Lenni Lenape people west, and eventually out of Pennsylvania. The Mennonites, Quakers, and Amish brought new traditions, many of which still flourish today just outside of William Penn's "City of Brotherly Love." In addition to Philadelphia's cultural events and cheesesteak, many visitors come for the Amish experience. Whether it's the novelty of antiquity, or the culture shock of seeing a foreign way of life within our borders, Amish Country is the main attraction here.

There are natural draws as well, and they're not difficult to find. At Evansburg State Park, Skippack Creek has shaped the land into scenic enclosed valleys and ridges. A mixture of northern and southern hardwoods provides habitats for many types of wildlife and wildflowers. This patchwork of meadows and mature woodlands attracts hikers, bikers, golfers, and others who are content to enjoy nature's handiwork amidst the urban confines of eastern Pennsylvania.

At Marsh Creek State Park, prevailing winds and good natural terrain provide excellent sailing conditions on the park's 535-acre lake on most days. Sailboat races are regularly held, and anglers can try for largemouth bass, channel catfish, black crappie, walleye, and other panfish. A lucky few will land a 40-inch tiger muskie.

Serving northern Bucks County, Lehigh, Northampton and Philadelphia Counties, 5,283-acre Nockamixon State Park is an oasis of green space in a desert of urbanization. There are four launch areas on the park's 1,450-acre lake: boaters with sailboats, catamarans, and sailboards head to the Marina and Tohickon launch ramps and those with motorboats, canoes, and inflatable watercraft use Three Mile Run and Haycock.

Philadelphia adrenaline junkies and rock jocks head to scenic Ralph Stover State Park, where Tohickon Creek cuts through the rolling landscape. Experienced climbers head for the High Rocks section, a 200-foot sheer rock face with over 200 routes for varying skill levels. Climbers coming south from Seneca Rocks or north from the Gunks may not think much of it, but Philly climbers love it. After hard rains, Tohickon Creek becomes a Class III run with play-spots for kayakers, and there are twice-yearly whitewater releases from Lake Nockamixon.

One of the main natural attractions in this corner of the state is French Creek State Park. Located amidst picturesque farmland, the park is home to 40 miles of hiking trails, riparian zones and wetlands, and extensive forests full of large oak, poplar, hickory, maple, and beech. The understory of mountain laurel and rhododendron is home to a wide variety of small animals and birds. French Creek has been called the orienteering capital of North America, and is internationally known for this sport.

The Susquehanna River lies at this region's western edge. Hawk Point, the main overlook in Susquehannock State Park, pro-vides outstanding views of the area's dams and reservoirs. From the overlook, visitors can see Mount Johnson Island, home to the world's first bald-eagle sanctuary. With binoculars, visitors should be able to see a nesting pair of eagles, as well as osprey, turkey vultures, and black vultures.

Campers looking to pedal away road fatigue can check out the region's bike trails. On its 19-mile route through the Perkiomen Creek Valley, Perkiomen Trail connects three county parks and two historic sites, and passes through 10 municipalities with connec-tions to numerous local parks and open spaces. Bikers can reach Valley Forge National Historic Park via the Schuylkill River Trail, which runs from downtown Philadelphia to Oaks in Montgomery County. Eventually the trail will extend the entire 100-mile length of the Schuylkill River.

Most recreational activities in this region take place well within the reach of human occupation. But not to worry, you can still sneak away from the bustle and get back to nature at one of the many camp-grounds in the area. In this part of the state, we sacrifice wilderness areas for the convenience of city life, but we don't have to sacrifice easy access to a plethora of outdoor activities as varied as those found in any other part of the state.

220

80

see
North Central
pages 80-81

11

80

Lewisburg

11

Danville

Bloomsburg

Hazleton

80

81

45

Susquehanna River

42

1

Sunbury

61

Tamaqua

3

Selinsgrove

Shamokin

2

209

Pottsville

4

522

147

225

125

5

61

81

8

104

11

6

183

7

78

322

17

209

Hamburg

78

22

Millersburg

78

12-14

Ickesburg

225

Licksdale

183

15

New
Bloomfield

81

72

422

Reading

74

34

Dauphin

Annville

Lebanon

176

11

15

Landisburg

Harrisburg

Hershey

322

28

29-31

Carlisle

81

76

76

PENNSYLVANIA TPKE

35-36

Elizabethtown

Manheim

37

38

39

Morgan-
town

74

15

34

40-41

222

Mount Holly

Dillsburg

33

283

72

New Holland

43

44-45

46

Rossville

74

47

48

Bendersville

30

Lancaster

53

54

57

10

see
South Central
pages 178-179

York

272

55

56

30

59

94

58

60

Gettysburg

Hanover

372

Cochranville

30

15

Abbottstown

74

61

Buck

63

Gettysburg
Natl Mil Park

83

62

1

PENNSYLVANIA

Emmitsburg

MARYLAND

Nottingham

140

30

Westminster

Hereford

Gibson

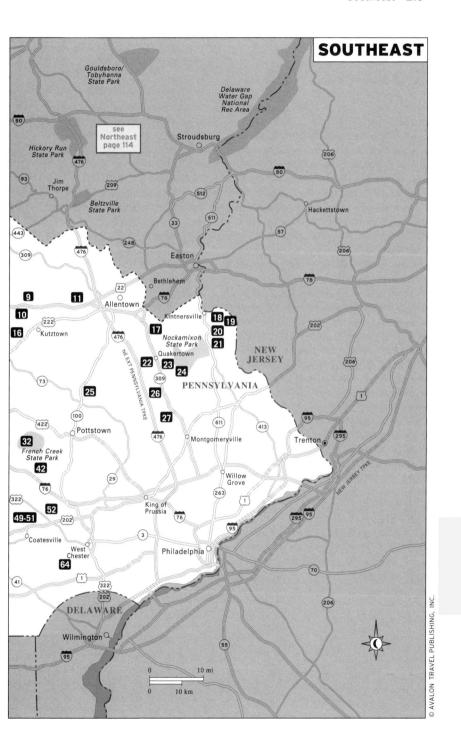

SOUTHEAST

Gouldsboro/
Tobyhanna
State Park

Delaware
Water Gap
National
Rec Area

see
Northeast
page 114

Stroudsburg

Hickory Run
State Park

Jim
Thorpe

Beltzville
State Park

Hackettstown

Easton

Bethlehem

Allentown

Kutztown

Kintnersville

Nockamixon
State Park

Quakertown

NEW
JERSEY

PENNSYLVANIA

Pottstown

Montgomeryville

Trenton

French Creek
State Park

Willow
Grove

King of
Prussia

NEW JERSEY TPKE

Coatesville

West
Chester

Philadelphia

DELAWARE

Wilmington

10 mi

10 km

© AVALON TRAVEL PUBLISHING, INC.

9 **11** **10** **16** **18** **19** **17** **20** **21** **22** **23** **24** **25** **26** **27** **32** **42** **52** **49-51** **64**

■ RED RIDGE LAKE CAMPGROUND

Rating: 8

near Locust Lake State Park

These spacious, wooded sites sit amongst pines and rhododendron in the foothills of the western Pocono Mountains. At nearby Locust Lake State Park, you can swim, boat, and fish in 52-acre Locust Lake. Swimming areas are marked by buoys. Motorboats with electric motors and non-powered boats are welcome on the lake. If you don't have your own, you can rent canoes, pedal boats, and rowboats at the park concessions. The lake is stocked with brown and brook trout several times a year, and also contains largemouth and smallmouth bass, pickerel, sunfish, and bluegill. For those of you who prefer dry land, check out the Oak, Hemlock, and Ridge Trails for hiking. The Oak Loop Trail is a difficult four-mile hike that encircles a ridge. Among the activities to enjoy back at the campground are fishing, bingo, ceramics, and live entertainment.

Campsites, facilities: There are 100 sites for tents or RVs up to 36 feet: 25 have full hookups; 68 have water and electricity; seven have electricity. Picnic tables and fire rings are provided. Drinking water, restrooms with flush toilets, a dump station, a portable dump, groceries, ice, wood, propane, a pavilion, a rec room, a fishing pond, badminton, a sports field, and a volleyball court are available. Some sites are wheelchair accessible. Leashed pets are permitted.

Reservations, fees: Reservations are accepted. The rate is $22–25 per night for up to five people. Each additional person is $5. Open May through September.

Directions: From South Zion Grove, travel one mile south on Millers Road. Follow signs to the campground entrance on the left.

Contact: Red Ridge Lake Campground, 61 Millers Road, Zion Grove, PA 17985, 570/384-4760.

■ LOCUST LAKE STATE PARK

Rating: 10

near Barnesville

BEST (

These wooded sites encircle 52-acre Locust Lake. You can tent on the north side or set up your RV on the south side. The lake provides opportunities for swimming, boating, and fishing. Swimming areas are marked by buoys and are open from Memorial Day to Labor Day. Motorboats with electric motors and non-powered boats are welcome on the lake. You can rent a canoe, pedal boat, or rowboat at the park concessions area. Anglers can cast for abundantly stocked brown and brook trout, pickerel, sunfish, largemouth and smallmouth bass, and bluegill. Hikers can choose from three trails with varying degrees of difficulty. The 0.75-mile Oak/Ridge Trail is an easy self-guided loop along a creek and through a mature forest. Oak/Hemlock Trail travels a moderate two miles and follows a wooded stream through a stand of hemlocks. The four-mile Oak Loop Trail is the most difficult because it encircles a forested ridge. During the winter, ice skating, ice fishing, and sledding are favorite activities. Be advised that hunting is allowed seasonally in Locust Lake State Park.

Campsites, facilities: There are 282 sites for tents or RVs up to 30 feet: 240 have water and electricity; three have electricity; 39 have no hookups. No sites have full hookups. There are six walk-in sites. Picnic tables and fire rings are provided. Drinking water, restrooms with flush toilets, a dump station, showers, groceries, ice, wood, fishing supplies, a camp store, and two playgrounds are available. Leashed pets are permitted.

Reservations, fees: Reservations are accepted at 888/PA-PARKS (888/727-2757). The rate is $14–19 per night for up to five people; a fee may apply for additional guests. Pets are $2 for up to two pets per night. Senior and Pennsylvania resident discounts are available.

Major credit cards are accepted. Open April through October.

Directions: From I-81 Exit 131A, travel southwest four miles on SR 106 to the campground entrance.

Contact: Locust Lake State Park, c/o Tuscarora, Barnesville, PA 18214-9715, 570/467-2404, tuscarorasp@state.pa.us.

❸ ROSEMOUNT CAMPING RESORT
🏃 ⛵ 🚣 🚐 🐕 🚵 ♿ 🚍 ⛺

Rating: 6

near Tuscarora State Park

This campground offers boating, canoeing, and lake fishing. If you don't have your own craft, you can rent pedal boats. You can also participate in planned activities like bingo and theme weekends. At nearby 1,618-acre Tuscarora State Park you can go boating, fishing, and swimming at Lake Tuscarora. Your electric motor or non-powered boats are welcome. Night fishing is permitted on the lake. Swimming areas are marked by buoys and guarded, and open from Memorial Day to Labor Day. You also have your choice of seven hiking trails. The two moderate trails are the 0.3-mile Hill Trail and the 0.4-mile Locust Mountain Trail. The others are labeled easy.

Campsites, facilities: There are 200 sites for tents or RVs up to 30 feet: 145 have full hookups; 50 have water and electricity; five have no hookups. Picnic tables and fire rings are provided. Drinking water, restrooms with flush toilets, a dump station, showers, a laundry, a public phone, cable TV hookup, groceries, ice, wood, a camp store, a rec hall, a pavilion, an arcade, a swimming pool, a wading pool, badminton, a sports field, volleyball, basketball, a playground, a shuffleboard court, and RV storage and supplies are available. Some sites are wheelchair accessible. Leashed pets are permitted.

Reservations, fees: Reservations are accepted. The rate is $24–25 per night for up to two people. Each additional person is $5. Major credit cards are accepted. Group rates are available. Open mid-April through mid-October.

Directions: From the junction of Highway 309 and U.S. 209, travel southwest four miles on U.S. 209, then turn left onto New Ringgold Road and travel 2.5 miles, then turn right onto Valley Road and travel 1.25 miles to the campground entrance on the right.

Contact: Rosemount Camping Resort, 285 Valley Road, Tamaqua, PA 18252, 570/668-2580.

❹ LAUREL LAKE CAMPSITES
🏃 ⛵ 🚣 🚐 🐕 🚵 🚍 ⛺

Rating: 8

near Leaser Lake

This campground offers its own fishing, plus it's close to 40-acre Leaser Lake. In this warmwater fishery, you can cast for yellow perch, largemouth bass, brown bullhead, bluegill, and sunfish. The lake is stocked several times a year with rainbow and brown trout. Motorboats with electric motors and non-powered boats are welcome on the lake. You have your choice of two launch ramps. A section of the Appalachian National Scenic Trail runs close by on its way from Georgia to Maine. For more outdoor recreational opportunities, try nearby Tuscarora State Park. Here you can continue your fishing, even at night, in Tuscarora Lake. If you don't have your own electric motor or non-powered boat, you can rent rowboats, pedal boats, and canoes at the park's concessions. Lake swimming areas are marked with buoys and are open from Memorial Day to Labor Day. Hikers can take advantage of the seven hiking trails that run throughout the park. All are easy to moderate in difficulty.

Campsites, facilities: There are 64 sites for

tents or RVs up to 27 feet: 60 have water and electricity; four have no hookups. Picnic tables and fire rings are provided. Drinking water, restrooms with flush toilets, a dump station, showers, ice, wood, a rec hall, a playground, badminton, horseshoes, and volleyball are available. Leashed pets are permitted.

Reservations, fees: Reservations are accepted. The rate is $17 per night for up to five people. Each additional person is $4. Open April through beginning of November.

Directions: From the junction of Highway 443 and Highway 895, travel 7.5 miles east on Highway 895 to the campground entrance on the right.

Contact: Laurel Lake Campsites, 3480 Summer Valley Road, New Ringgold, PA 17960, 570/386-5301, stival@ptd.net.

5 CAMP-A-WHILE, INC.
🏃 🚴 🏊 ⛵ 🚐 🏕 🐕 🎣 ⛺

Rating: 8

near Swatara State Park

On-site activities at Camp-A-While include pond fishing, hiking trails, and planned events on weekends. The nearby 3,515-acre Swatara State Park offers more outdoor recreational opportunities. The anglers in your group can cast at several fishing spots. Trout Run is a cold-water, stocked trout stream. Swatara Creek is a warm-water fishery for smallmouth bass, sunfish, and bluegill. Your non-powered boats are also welcome here. Irving's Pond has largemouth bass, bluegill, and sunfish. The Swatara Multi-Use Trail runs through nine miles of beautiful forest and is open to both hikers and bikers. Hikers and backpackers can also hop onto part of the Appalachian National Scenic Trail, which runs through the state park on its way from Georgia to Maine. Horseback riding is permitted on the berms of state park roadways. There are many bird boxes maintained throughout the park. You can look for red-tailed hawks, wrens, Eastern bluebirds, and

ducks. Other wildlife in the area include whitetailed deer, red and gray squirrels, raccoons, cottontail rabbits, skunks, woodchucks, and chipmunks. Be advised that hunting is permitted seasonally at Swatara State Park.

Campsites, facilities: There are 123 sites for tents or RVs up to 30 feet: 95 have full hookups; 28 have no hookups. There are four pull-throughs. Picnic tables and fire rings are provided. Drinking water, restrooms with flush toilets, a dump station, showers, a laundry, a public phone, groceries, ice, wood, a general store, a playground, a rec hall, an arcade, a swimming pool, basketball, horseshoes, volleyball, and RV supplies are available. Leashed pets are permitted.

Reservations, fees: Reservations are accepted. The rate is $25 per night for up to four people. Each additional person is $5. Major credit cards are accepted. Open mid-April through October.

Directions: From the junction of I-81 and Highway 25 Exit 112, travel 0.5 mile west on Highway 25 to the campground entrance on the left.

Contact: Camp-A-While, Inc., 1921 East Main Street, Hegins, PA 17938, 570/682-8696, camping@epix.com.

6 ECHO VALLEY CAMPGROUND
🏃 🚴 🏊 ⛵ 🚐 🎿 🏕 🐕 🎣 ⛺

Rating: 9

near Swatara State Park

At Echo Valley, some sites are located in the woods near the stream, but most are open. The campground offers stream fishing, but serious anglers should check out nearby Swatara State Park. The park's three major fisheries are Trout Run, Irving's Pond, and Swatara Creek. The cold waters of Trout Run are stocked with brook and brown trout. You can catch warm-water species such as largemouth bass, sunfish, and bluegill at Irving's Pond and smallmouth bass at Swatara Creek. Non-powered boats are welcome on the creek, and it is especially popular for canoeing. The park's nine-mile Swatara Multi-Use Trail is open to hikers, mountain bikers, and cross-country skiers. A two-mile section of the Appalachian National Scenic Trail also runs through part of the park. Horseback riding is allowed on the berm of state park roads. Be advised that hunting is allowed seasonally in Swatara State Park.

Campsites, facilities: There are 114 sites for tents or RVs up to 25 feet: 96 have full hookups; 11 have water and electricity; seven have no hookups. There are 10 pull-throughs. Picnic tables and fire rings are provided. Drinking water, restrooms with flush toilets, a dump station, showers, a laundry, modem access, a phone hookup, cable TV hookup, a public phone, groceries, ice, wood, a general store, a restaurant, a pavilion, a playground, a rec room, an arcade, a swimming pool, miniature golf, basketball, volleyball, and RV rentals are available. Leashed pets are permitted.

Reservations, fees: Reservations are accepted. The rate is $23–24 per night for up to four people. Each additional person is $5. Open year-round.

Directions: From the junction of I-81 Exit 104/32 and Highway 125, travel one mile north on Highway 125 to the campground entrance on the right.

Contact: Echo Valley Campground, 52 Camp Road, Tremont, PA 17981, 570/695-3659, echovly@f-tech.net.

◼ CHRISTMAS PINES CAMPGROUND

🚶 🏊 🎣 🚐 🐕 🚴 ♿ 🚙 ⛺

Rating: 8

near the Schuylkill River

You have your choice of shaded and open sites here. Take advantage of the catch-and-release fishing pond and the campground's hiking trails. You can also participate in planned activities on the weekends such as bingo and hayrides. Christmas Pines is the closest campground to Hawk Mountain Sanctuary and with its proximity to the Schuylkill River, you can spend your days on and around the water. Cast a line for muskie, northern pike, sucker, pickerel, smallmouth bass, rainbow and brown trout, sunfish, bluegill, and catfish. If you have your own boat, you can use one of the river's launches. There are also rental outfitters nearby. Hikers can explore the shore and surrounding woodlands in search of wildlife.

Campsites, facilities: There are 101 sites for tents or RVs up to 27 feet: 92 have water and electricity; 9 have no hookups. There are nine pull-throughs. No sites have full hookups. Picnic tables and fire rings are provided. Drinking water, restrooms with flush toilets, a dump station, a portable dump, showers, a laundry, a public phone, groceries, ice, LP gas, wood, a camp store, a gift shop, a pavilion, a playground, a rec room, an arcade, a swimming pool, badminton, a basketball court, and volleyball are available. Some sites are wheelchair accessible. Leashed pets are permitted.

Reservations, fees: Reservations are accepted. The rate is $19–22 per night for up to two people. Each additional person is $4. Weekly and monthly rates are available. Open April through October.

Directions: From the northern junction of Highway 61 and Highway 895, travel west 1.95 miles on Highway 895, then turn right onto a steeply graded, paved road and travel 1.25 miles to the campground entrance on the left.

Contact: Christmas Pines Campground, P.O. Box 375, Auburn, PA 17922, 570/366-8866, www.christmaspines.com.

◼ BLUE ROCKS FAMILY CAMPGROUND

🚶 🏊 🎣 🏕 🚴 ♿ 🚙 ⛺

Rating: 10

near Lenhartsville

Hikers will love this campground, located just off the Appalachian Trail. From Blue

Rocks you can access several trails of varying difficulty, including Pulpit and Pinnacle Trails. When you reach the top of Pulpit Rock or the Pinnacle, your view includes 100 acres of wooded state game lands. Anglers in your group won't feel left out thanks to a one-acre stocked pond on the property that contains trout, sunfish, catfish, and bluegill. There are also planned activities like bingo on weekends.

Campsites, facilities: There are 200 sites for tents or RVs up to 26 feet: 45 have full hookups; 60 have water and electricity; 95 have no hookups. There are 24 pull-throughs. Picnic tables and fire rings are provided. Drinking water, restrooms with flush toilets, a dump station, a portable dump, showers, a laundry, modem access, a phone hookup, a public phone, groceries, ice, LP gas, wood, a camp store, a gift shop, a rec room, a pavilion, an arcade, a swimming pool, a wading pool, basketball, a playground, a badminton court, two shuffleboard courts, horseshoes, volleyball, and RV storage and supplies are available. Some sites are wheelchair accessible. Leashed pets are permitted.

Reservations, fees: Reservations are accepted at 800/525-5605. The rate is $22–32 per night for up to two people. Each additional person is $5. Weekly rates are available. Major credit cards are accepted. Open through beginning of November.

Directions: From the junction of I-78/U.S. 22 and Highway 143, travel north 0.75 mile on Highway 143, then west 100 yards on Mountain Road, then 0.75 mile on a paved road. Follow signs to the campground entrance on the left.

Contact: Blue Rocks Family Campground, 341 Sousley Road, Lenhartsville, PA 19534, 610/756-6366, www.bluerockscampground.com.

9 PINE HILL RV PARK

Rating: 8

near Leaser Lake Recreation Area

Anglers will appreciate a stay at Pine Hill RV Park due its proximity to 40-acre Leaser Lake, a warm-water fishery. Among the species you can cast for are largemouth bass, brown bullhead, bluegill, yellow perch, and stocked rainbow trout. Motorboats with electric motors and non-powered boats are welcome on the lake, and two launch ramps are available for water access. Among the wildlife and bird life that hikers can spot are white-tailed deer, red and gray squirrels, raccoons, woodchucks, chipmunks, cottontail rabbits, orioles, warblers, vireos, osprey, heron, red-tailed hawks, and bluebirds. The campground is also near Crystal Cave, Hawk Mountain Bird Sanctuary, and Lehigh Valley Wine Trail.

Campsites, facilities: There are 125 sites for RVs up to 30 feet; all sites have full hookups. There are 90 pull-throughs. No tents can be accommodated. Picnic tables and fire rings are provided. Drinking water, restrooms with flush toilets, a dump station, showers, a laundry, modem access, a phone hookup, cable TV hookup, a public phone, groceries, ice, wood, a camp store, an ice cream parlor, a gift shop, a playground, a rec hall, an arcade, miniature golf, horseshoes, a kite-flying field, and a sports field are available. Leashed pets are permitted.

Reservations, fees: Reservations are accepted at 800/217-6776. The rate is $28–32 per night for up to two people. Each additional person is $3. Major credit cards are accepted. Open April through November.

Directions: From the junction of I-78/U.S. 22 and Highway 737, travel 0.2 mile north on Highway 737, then 1.5 miles east on Old U.S. 22 to the campground entrance on the right.

Contact: Pine Hill RV Park, 268 Old Route 22, Kutztown, PA 19530, 610/285-6776, www.pinehillrvpark.com.

10 ROBIN HILL CAMPING RESORT

Rating: 7

near Lake Ontelaunee

While visiting the campground you can enjoy boating and fishing on Lake Ontelaunee. Motor boats, canoes, kayaks, and other non-powered boats are welcome on the lake. If you don't have your own watercraft, you can rent a pedal boat. The anglers in your group will be pleased with the variety of fish in the lake. Among the species are white and channel catfish, pumpkinseed, black and white crappie, golden shiner, carp, yellow and white perch, quillback, brown and yellow bullhead, largemouth bass, and white sucker. The campground also offers planned weekend activities like bingo.

Campsites, facilities: There are 268 sites for tents or RVs up to 40 feet: 221 have full hookups; 47 have water and electricity. There are 40 pull-throughs. Picnic tables and fire rings are provided. Drinking water, restrooms with flush toilets, a dump station, showers, a laundry, modem access, a phone hookup, cable TV hookup, a public phone, groceries, ice, LP gas, wood, a camp store, a rec room, an arcade, a swimming pool, basketball, a playground, badminton, horseshoes, a sports field, volleyball, and RV storage and supplies are available. Some sites are wheelchair accessible. Leashed pets are permitted.

Reservations, fees: Reservations are accepted at 800/732-5267. The rate is $25–35 per night for up to two people. Each additional person is $4. Weekly, monthly, and group rates are available. Major credit cards are accepted. Open April through October.

Directions: From the junction of I-78/U.S. 22 and Highway 143, travel south 0.5 mile on Highway 143, then east 1.5 miles on Old U.S. 22, then one mile on a paved road. Follow signs to the campground entrance on the right.

Contact: Robin Hill Camping Resort, 149 Robin Hill Road, Lenhartsville, PA 19534, 610/756-6117, robinhillcamp@aol.com.

11 ALLENTOWN KOA CAMPGROUND

Rating: 7

near Allentown

You can spend your day fishing in the property's stream or hiking the campground trails. There are also planned activities like bingo and hayrides on the weekends. Nearby Allentown has many recreational opportunities. Little Lehigh Creek, Cedar Creek, Jordan Creek, and Trout Creek are all stocked with brown and brook trout. In the Cedar Beach area, you can rent a pedal boat for Lake Muhlenberg or hike the fitness trail. There are also pool and picnic facilities located here. Lehigh Canal Park offers hiking, canoeing, and fishing facilities, as well as a boat launch for the Lehigh River. You can also visit East Side Reservoir and Kimmets Lock Park.

Campsites, facilities: There are 110 sites for tents or RVs up to 28 feet: 39 have full hookups; 68 have water and electricity; 3 have no hookups. There are 23 pull-throughs. Picnic tables and fire rings are provided. Drinking water, restrooms with flush toilets, a dump station, a portable dump, showers, a laundry, modem access, phone hookup, cable TV hookup, groceries, ice, LP gas, wood, a general store, a pavilion, a playground, a rec hall, an arcade, a swimming pool, a wading pool, basketball, horseshoes, volleyball, and RV supplies are available. Some sites are wheelchair accessible. Leashed pets are permitted.

Reservations, fees: Reservations are accepted at 800/KOA-2138 (800/562-2138). The rate is $26–35 per night for up to two people. Each additional person is $6. Major credit cards are accepted. Open April through November.

Directions: From the junction of PA Turnpike Exit 56/33 and U.S. 22, travel three miles west on U.S. 22, then 6.5 miles north on Highway 100, then turn left onto Narris Road and travel 0.5 mile to the campground entrance on the right.

Contact: Allentown KOA Campground, 6750 KOA Drive, New Tripoli, PA 18066, 610/298-2160, allentownkoa@entermail.net.

⓬ APPALACHIAN CAMPSITES

🚶 🚴 🏊 🛶 🚐 🐴 🤸 ♿ 🚍 ⛺

Rating: 9

near the Schuylkill River

This campground offers pond fishing for sunfish, bluegill, and bass, as well as bike rentals for the hiking and biking trails. At the nearby Schuylkill River, you can boat or fish for bass, trout, perch, bluegill, catfish, sunfish, and pickerel. Motorboats and non-powered boats are welcome on the river. If you prefer to stay dry, you can hike or bike the Schuylkill River Trail. You may see are muskrats, white-tailed deer, opossums, raccoons, red and gray squirrels, chipmunks, woodchucks, turtles, cottontail rabbits, herons, terns, osprey, teal, wood and mallard ducks, Canada geese, or bluebirds. Back at the campground, you can participate in planned activities like bingo and ceramics on the weekends.

Campsites, facilities: There are 374 sites for tents or RVs up to 30 feet: 350 have full hookups; seven have water and electricity; 17 have no hookups. There are 50 pull-throughs. Picnic tables and fire rings are provided. Drinking water, restrooms with flush toilets, a dump station, showers, a laundry, modem access, a phone hookup, cable TV hookup, a public phone, groceries, ice, LP gas, wood, a camp store, a rec hall, a pavilion, an arcade, a swimming pool, a wading pool, basketball, a playground, a sports field, miniature golf, volleyball, and RV storage and supplies are available. Some sites are wheelchair accessible. Leashed pets are permitted.

Reservations, fees: Reservations are accepted at 800/424-5746. The rate is $27–43 per night for up to two people. Each additional person is $7. Major credit cards are accepted. Open year-round.

Directions: From the junction of I-78/U.S. 22 and Shartlesville Road, travel 0.25 mile west on North Service Road to the campground entrance on the right.

Contact: Appalachian Campsites, 60 Motel Drive, Shartlesville, PA 19554, 610/488-6319, www.appalachianrvresort.com.

⓭ PENNSYLVANIA DUTCH CAMPSITE

🚶 🚴 🏊 🛶 🚐 🐴 🤸 🚍 ⛺

Rating: 9

near the Schuylkill River

This campground has hiking trails and planned activities like bingo and hayrides on weekends. Nearby is the Schuylkill River. The Multi-Use Schuylkill River Trail runs from Valley Forge National Historic Park to Philadelphia for 11.5 miles and is recognized by the U.S. Department of Interior as a National Recreation Trail. Bikers and hikers alike can enjoy this paved trail built on the Pennsylvania Railroad right-of-way as it follows the river. If you prefer to be on the river itself, you can launch your boat from several designated areas or cast a line from shore. Among the species you can catch are smallmouth and largemouth bass, carp, northern pike, muskie, crappie, catfish, pickerel, sunfish, and bluegill. There is also abundant wildlife and bird life along the shore and in the surrounding woodlands.

Campsites, facilities: There are 230 sites for tents or RVs up to 27 feet; five have full hookups; 225 have water and electricity. Picnic tables and fire rings are provided. Drinking water, restrooms with flush toilets, a dump station, showers, groceries, ice, LP gas, wood, a general store, a rec hall, a swimming pool, a playground, two shuffleboard courts, badminton, horseshoes, a sports field, volleyball, and RV storage and supplies are available. Leashed pets are permitted.

Reservations, fees: Reservations are accepted at 800/228-0206. The rate is $28–30 per night for up to four people. Each additional person is $6. Open mid-April through mid-October.

Directions: From the junction of I-78/U.S. 22 and Shartlesville Road, travel 0.2 mile south on Shartlesville Road, then one mile west on Old U.S. 22, then turn right onto Northkill Road and travel 0.25 mile, then turn left onto Campsite Road and travel 0.75 mile to the campground entrance on the left.

Contact: Pennsylvania Dutch Campsite, P.O. Box 337, Campsite Road, Shartlesville, PA 19554, 610/488-6268.

14 MOUNTAIN SPRINGS CAMPING RESORT

🏃 ⛵ 🚣 🛶 🐕 🎣 ♿ 🚐 ⛺

Rating: 8

near the Schuylkill River

Mountain Springs has many activities and amenities onsite to encourage campers to kick back and relax on the property. The campground has a pond for fishing and canoeing, hiking trails, and planned weekend activities. For a little isolation, check out Swatara State Park. This 3,515-acre park is made up mostly of woodlands and rolling hills situated between Second Mountain and Blue Mountain. Many canoeists are already well aware of the fine, eight-mile stretch of Swatara Creek that runs through the park. Some of the facilities are still under development, but your opportunities include canoeing, fishing, hiking, picnicking, bicycling, swimming, and environmental programs. Check the park office for a schedule of these changing events.

Campsites, facilities: There are 300 sites for tents or RVs up to 30 feet: 87 have full hookups; 208 have water and electricity; five have no hookups. There are 18 pull-throughs. Picnic tables and fire rings are provided. Drinking water, restrooms with flush toilets, a dump station, showers, a laundry, a public phone, groceries, ice, LP gas, wood, a camp store, a rec hall, a pavilion, an arcade, a swimming pool, a wading pool, basketball, a playground, a shuffleboard court, badminton, a sports field, volleyball, and RV storage and supplies are available. Some sites are wheelchair accessible. Leashed pets are permitted.

Reservations, fees: Reservations are accepted. The rate is $25–29 per night for up to five people. Each additional person is $5. Major credit cards are accepted. Open April through October.

Directions: From the junction of I-78/U.S. 22 and Shartlesville Road, travel one mile east on Mountain Road to the campground entrance on the left.

Contact: Mountain Springs Camping Resort, P.O. Box 365, Shartlesville, PA 19554, 610/488-6859, mtsprings@fast.net.

15 BLUE FALLS GROVE CAMPGROUND

🏃 ⛵ 🚣 🚐 🐕 🎣 🚐 ⛺

Rating: 7

near Lake Ontelaunee

You can expect lots of fun in the water at Blue Falls Grove Campground, which borders Lake Ontelaunee and has its own water park on the property. You have your choice of open and shaded sites, some of which are along the water. If you don't have your own motorboat or non-powered boat, you can rent a pedal boat from the campground. Anglers will appreciate the variety of catch in the 1,000-acre lake. You can cast for white and black crappie, largemouth bass, white and yellow perch, quillback, white sucker, brown and yellow bullhead, bluegill, carp, channel and white catfish, and golden shiner. Those who prefer to stay dry can hike along the lakeshore or any of the trails in search of birds and wildlife. Among the animals you may spot are gulls, herons, osprey, mallard and wood ducks, teal, Canada geese, red-tailed hawks, vireos, muskrats, raccoons, red and gray squirrels, white-tailed deer, opossums, cottontail rabbits, woodchucks, chipmunks, and turtles. You can also participate in the campground's planned activities such as hayrides, live music, bingo, and pony rides.

Campsites, facilities: There are 100 sites for tents or RVs up to 50 feet: 60 have water and electricity; 40 have no hookups; 24 are pullthroughs. Picnic tables and fire rings are provided. Drinking water, restrooms with flush toilets, a dump station, showers, a pavilion, a playground, a swimming pool, water slides, basketball, horseshoes, and volleyball are available. Leashed pets are permitted.

Reservations, fees: Reservations are accepted. The rate is $25–34 per night for up to two people. Each additional person is $5. Open April through October.

Directions: From the junction of Route 61 and Route 73, turn right onto Ontelaunee Drive, then turn left onto Wiley's Road and travel to the campground entrance at the end.

Contact: Blue Falls Grove Campground, 91A Bower & Wiley's Road, Reading, PA 19605, 610/926-4017, www.bluefallsgrove.com.

16 SACONY PARK CAMPSITES & CABINS

🚶‍♂️🏊‍♀️🛶🚐❄️🐴🚵♿🚙⛺

Rating: 7

near Lake Ontelaunee

Anglers will appreciate Sacony Park's location near 1,082-acre Lake Ontelaunee. Among the species you can cast for are muskie, white and black crappie, channel and white catfish, brown and yellow bullhead, bluegill, largemouth bass, yellow perch, carp, northern pike, pickerel, and

sucker. Ice fishing is a favorite winter activity on the lake. You can also boat and canoe on these waters. A hike around the shore provides wildlife- and bird-viewing opportunities. You can see white-tailed deer, red fox, woodchucks, minks, warblers, vireos, osprey, herons, and red-tailed hawks. The campground also has its own stocked stream for fishing. Other nearby attractions are Dorney Park and Wildwater Kingdom, Crystal Cave, and Hawk Mountain Sanctuary.

Campsites, facilities: There are 113 sites for tents or RVs up to 26 feet: 100 have water and electricity; 13 have no hookups. Picnic tables and fire rings are available. Drinking water, restrooms with flush toilets, a dump station, a portable dump, showers, a public phone, groceries, ice, LP gas, wood, a camp store, a pavilion, a playground, a swimming pool, basketball, horseshoes, and ping-pong are available. Some sites are wheelchair accessible. Leashed pets are permitted.

Reservations, fees: Reservations are accepted. The rate is $20–24 per night for up to two people. Each additional person is $5. Weekly, monthly, and seasonal rates are available. Open April through beginning of November.

Directions: From the junction of Highway 737 and U.S. 222, travel southwest two miles on U.S. 222 to the Virginville Exit, then north three miles on Crystal Cave Road, then turn right onto Saucony Road and travel 0.5 mile to the campground entrance on the left.

Contact: Sacony Park Campsites & Cabins, 1583 Saucony Road, Katztown, PA 19530, 610/683-3939, drbrown_1@yahoo.com.

17 COLONIAL WOODS FAMILY CAMPING RESORT

🚶‍♂️🚴🏊‍♀️🛶🐴🚵🚙⛺

Rating: 8

near Nockamixon State Park

Among the activities that you can enjoy at Colonial Woods are boating, canoeing, kayaking, and pond fishing. At nearby Nockamixon State Park, you have more outdoor recreational options. The 1,450-acre Lake Nockamixon has four launch areas. Three Mile Run and Haycock are best for motorboats, canoes, and inflatable craft. Marina and Tohickon are for sailboats, catamarans, and windsurfers. The lake is also a warm-water fishery. There are hiking, biking, and equestrian trials that run throughout the park.

Campsites, facilities: There are 208 sites for tents or RVs up to 30 feet: 204 have water and electricity; four have no hookups. There are 10 pull-throughs. No sites have full hookups. Picnic tables and fire rings are provided. Drinking water, restrooms with flush toilets, a dump station, showers, a laundry, modem access, phone hookup, cable TV hookup, a public phone, groceries, ice, LP gas, wood, a camp store, a rec hall, a pavilion, an arcade, a swimming pool, a wading pool, a whirlpool, a basketball court, a playground, two shuffleboard courts, a tennis court, badminton, horseshoes, miniature golf, a sports field, a volleyball court, and RV storage and supplies are available. Leashed pets are permitted.

Reservations, fees: Reservations are accepted at 800/877-2267. The rate is $29–34 per night for up to two people. Each additional person is $6. Weekly, monthly, and seasonal rates are available. Major credit cards are accepted. Open mid-April through November.

Directions: From the junction of South Highway 412 and Highway 611, travel 1.5 miles north on Highway 611, then turn right onto Marienstein Road and travel 1.5 miles, then turn left onto Lonely Cottage Drive and travel 0.75 miles to the campground entrance on the right.

Contact: Colonial Woods Family Campground, 545 Lonely College Drive, Upper Black Eddy, PA 18972, 610/847-5808, www.colonialwoods.com.

18 RINGING ROCKS FAMILY CAMPGROUND

Rating: 8

near the Delaware River

All of the sites here are wooded. Located near the Delaware River and Delaware Canal State Park, you can expect lots of water activities to help you while away the hours. Motorboats and non-powered boats are welcome on the river. Anglers can cast a line for shad, largemouth, smallmouth, and rock bass, carp, black and white crappie, bluegill, northern pike, yellow and brown bullhead, sunfish, and white and channel catfish. There are also many paths and trails for hiking and biking in the area. Among the wildlife you may see are osprey, gulls, ducks, cormorants, pheasants, red-tailed hawks, white-tailed deer, red fox, raccoons, muskrats, otters, turtles, and bobcats. Back at the campground you can participate in planned weekend activities such as dances and bonfires.

Campsites, facilities: There are 129 sites for tents or RVs up to 30 feet: 110 have water and electricity; 19 have no hookups. No sites have full hookups. Picnic tables and fire rings are provided. Drinking water, restrooms with flush toilets, a dump station, a laundry, a public phone, groceries, ice, LP gas, wood, a camp store, a rec hall, a pavilion, a swimming pool, a playground, a shuffleboard court, a tennis court, horseshoes, volleyball, and RV storage and supplies are available. Leashed pets are permitted.

Reservations, fees: Reservations are accepted. The rate is $22–25 per night for up to two people. Each additional person is $5. Major credit cards are accepted. Open April through beginning of November.

Directions: From North Upper Black Eddy, travel 0.5 mile north on Highway 32, then turn left onto Bridgeton Hill Road and travel 2.5 miles, then turn right onto Woodland Drive and travel 0.25 mile. Follow signs to the campground entrance on the right.

Contact: Ringing Rocks Family Campground, 75 Woodland Drive, Upper Black Eddy, PA 18972, 610/982-5552, www.ringingrocks.qpg.com.

19 DOGWOOD HAVEN FAMILY CAMP GROUNDS

🚶 🚴 🛶 🚤 ❄️ 🐕 🚙 ⛺

Rating: 6

near the Delaware River

The anglers in your group will appreciate the proximity to the Delaware River. Among the species you can cast for are herring, stripers, fallfish, shad, walleye, carp, smallmouth, largemouth, and rock bass, sunfish, brown, brook, and rainbow trout, and suckers. Motor boats and non-powered boats are welcome on the river. There are several boat launches, ramps, and access points along the shoreline. Canoeing and kayaking are especially popular pastimes on the Delaware. The campground is also near Delaware Canal State Park, where you can continue your water pursuits or settle on dry land. Part of the 60-mile Delaware Canal Towpath runs through the park. Hikers, bikers, and cross-country skiers are all welcome on this National Historic Trail that was once trod by mules carrying cargo back and forth to the river. You can also take advantage of the campground's hiking trails.

Campsites, facilities: There are 50 sites for tents or RVs up to 26 feet: 35 have water and electricity; 15 have no hookups. There are pull-throughs. No sites have full hookups. Picnic tables and fire rings are provided Drinking water, restrooms with flush toilets, a dump station, showers, ice, wood, horseshoes, and RV storage and supplies are available. Leashed pets are permitted.

Reservations, fees: Reservations are accepted. The rate is $17–19 per night for up to two people. Each additional person is $4. Seasonal rates are available. Open April through beginning of November.

Directions: From South Upper Black Eddy, travel one mile south on Highway 32, then turn right onto Lodi Hill Road and travel 0.2 mile, then another 0.2 mile on a gravel road. Follow signs to the campground entrance on the left.

Contact: Dogwood Haven Family Camp Grounds, 16 Lodi Hill Road, Upper Black Eddy, PA 18972, 610/982-5402.

20 MELODY LAKES COUNTRY ESTATES

🚶 🛶 🚤 🚌 🐕 🚙 ⛺

Rating: 8

near Nockamixon State Park

The wooded sites of this small campground are big on beauty. Located near two state parks, Melody Lakes Country Estates is well suited for a variety of day trips to either. With just over 5,280 acres, Nockamixon State Park is the obvious choice. Its large lake is suited for pleasure boats of nearly any size, and anglers will enjoy wetting a line in such a scenic setting. A boat rental concession has rowboats, canoes, motorboats, sailboats, paddleboats and pontoon boats during the summer season. Nearly 20 miles of equestrian trails beckon riders to bring their animals, or rent one at an outfitter just off of state park property. A large pool has a lifeguard and is open from May to September. Ralph Stover State Park, Nockamixon's smaller cousin, is home to a particularly scenic stretch of Tohickon Creek. Hikers will enjoy the short trail to the overlook, and even casual visitors can watch climbers put routes up the 200-foot cliffs that line the creek. Regular releases from Lake Nockamixon turn Tohickon into a popular Class III whitewater run. There are also many hiking trails.

Campsites, facilities: There are 10 sites for tents or RVs up 25 feet; all have full hookups. Picnic tables and fire rings are provided. Drinking water, restrooms with flush toilets, a dump station, showers, a public phone, a swimming pool, miniature golf, and RV storage and supplies are available. Leashed pets are permitted.

Reservations, fees: Reservations are accepted. The rate is $15 per night for up to two people. Each additional person is $4. Open year-round.

Directions: From the junction of Highway 663 and Highway 309, travel north two miles on Highway 309, then turn right onto North West End Boulevard and travel 100 yards to the campground entrance at the end.

Contact: Melody Lakes Country Estates, 1045 North West End Boulevard #600, Quakertown, PA 18951, 215/536-6640.

21 BEAVER VALLEY FAMILY CAMPGROUND

Rating: 6

near Nockamixon State Park

At nearby 5,283-acre Nockamixon State Park, you can go hiking, biking, and horseback riding on the various trails that run throughout the park. There are designated trails for each activity. If you have your own motorboat (up to 20 hp) or non-powered boat, you can choose from four launch areas around the 1,450-acre Lake Nockamixon. There are also boat rental facilities available. Anglers can cast for muskie, pickerel, channel catfish, carp, smallmouth, largemouth, and hybrid striped bass, and walleye. There are also picnic areas, a swimming facility, and a hostel available. You can also participate in environmental and interpretive programs. Check the office for a schedule of these changing events. Back at the campground, you can enjoy the hiking trails and planned activities like bingo and theme weekends.

Campsites, facilities: There are 85 sites for tents or RVs up to 30 feet; all sites have water and electricity. Picnic tables and fire rings

are provided. Drinking water, restrooms with flush toilets, a dump station, showers, a laundry, modem access, phone hookup, cable TV hookup, a public phone, groceries, ice, LP gas, wood, a camp store, a rec hall, a pavilion, a swimming pool, a playground, two shuffleboard courts, horseshoes, a sports field, volleyball and RV storage and supplies are available. Leashed pets are permitted.

Reservations, fees: Reservations are accepted. The rate is $24.50 per night for up to two people. Each additional person is $5. Open April through October.

Directions: From Ottsville, travel 2.5 miles east on Geigel Hill Road, then turn left onto Beaver Run Road and travel 0.25 mile, then turn left onto Clay Ridge Road and travel 100 yards to the campground entrance on the right.

Contact: Beaver Valley Family Campground, 80 Clayridge Road, Ottsville, PA 18942, 610/847-5643.

22 QUAKERWOODS CAMPGROUND

Rating: 6

near Nockamixon State Park

At nearby Nockamixon State Park you can choose from a variety of outdoor activities on and off the water. The 1,450-acre Lake Nockamixon, which gets its name from the Lenni Lenape words for "at the place of soft soil," allows boating and fishing. Four launch areas cater to motorboats, canoes, sailboats, inflatables, and other non-powered craft. The lake is also a favorite spot for windsurfers. Trails for biking, hiking, and horseback riding run throughout the area. Nockamixon State Park also offers environmental and interpretive programs. Check the park office for a schedule of these changing events. Back at the campground, you can go pond fishing or participate in planned activities like bingo and theme weekends.

Campsites, facilities: There are 213 sites for tents or RVs up to 28 feet: 110 have full hookups; 83 have water and electricity; 20 have no hookups. There are three pull-throughs. Picnic tables and fire rings are provided. Drinking water, restrooms with flush toilets, a dump station, a laundry, a public phone, groceries, ice, LP gas, wood, a camp store, a rec hall, a pavilion, a swimming pool, a playground, two shuffleboard courts, miniature golf, badminton, horseshoes, a sports field, volleyball, and RV storage and supplies are available. Leashed pets are permitted.

Reservations, fees: Reservations are accepted at 800/235-2350. The rate is $21–32 per night for up to two people. Each additional person is $4. Weekly, monthly, and seasonal rates are available. Open April through October.

Directions: From the junction of Highway 309 and Highways 313 and 663, travel 0.25 mile southwest on Highway 663, then turn rigbt onto Old Bethlehem Road and travel 2.5 miles, then turn left onto Rosedale Road and travel 0.25 mile to the campground entrance on the left.

Contact: Quakerwoods Campground, 2225 Rosedale Road, Quakertown, PA 18951, 215/536-1984.

23 TOHICKON FAMILY CAMPGROUND
🚶 🚴 🛶 🎣 🏊 🐕 🏕 🚐 ⛺
Rating: 6

near Nockamixon State Park

You have your choice of creekside and shaded sites at this campground situated on 64 wooded acres. You can take out your canoe or other non-powered boat or try a little fishing on Tohickon Creek. There are also hiking trails that run on the property. The campground has planned activities on the weekends such as clambakes, pig roasts, hayrides, and bingo. At nearby Nockamixon State Park, you can find more outdoor recreational opportunities. The

1,450-acre Lake Nockamixon allows boating and fishing, and there are hiking, biking, and equestrian trails throughout the park. During the winter, sledding, cross-country skiing, ice skating, and ice fishing are favorite pursuits. Be advised that hunting is allowed seasonally in Nockamixon State Park.

Campsites, facilities: There are 200 sites for tents or RVs up to 50 feet; 104 have full hookups; 71 have water and electricity; 25 have no hookups. Picnic tables and fire rings are provided. Drinking water, restrooms with flush toilets, a dump station, showers, a laundry, a public phone, groceries, ice, LP gas, wood, a general store, a rec hall, a swimming pool, a wading pool, a playground, badminton, a sports field, volleyball, and RV storage and supplies are available. Leashed pets are permitted.

Reservations, fees: Reservations are accepted at 866/536-2267. The rate is $30–36 per night for up to four people. Each additional person is $6. Weekly, monthly, and seasonal rates and group discounts are available. Major credit cards are accepted. Open year-round.

Directions: From the junction of Highway 309 and Highway 313, travel 2.5 miles east on Highway 313, then turn left onto Thatcher Road and travel 2.75 miles, then turn right onto Covered Bridge Road and travel 0.25 mile to the campground entrance on the left.

Contact: Tohickon Family Campground, 8308 Covered Bridge Road, Quakertown, PA 18951, 215/536-7951, www.tohickoncampground.com.

24 BOULDER WOODS CAMPGROUND
🚶 🚴 🛶 🎣 🚐 🐕 🏕 ♿ 🚐 ⛺
Rating: 9

near Nockamixon State Park

At nearby 5,283-acre Nockamixon State Park, you can boat or fish on Lake Nockamixon. This 1,450-acre body of water has trout, bass, perch, pickerel, catfish, carp, sunfish, and bluegill. Motorboats (up to 20 hp) and nonpowered boats are welcome on the lake. You can choose from four different launch areas. Marina and Tohickon are for sailboats, catamarans, and windsurfers. Three Mile Run and Haycock are better for canoes, inflatable watercraft, and motorboats. There are also trails for hiking, biking, and horseback riding available. Back at the campground you can fish in the catch-and-release lake or participate in planned activities on the weekend including clam bakes and chili cook-offs.

Campsites, facilities: There are 188 sites for tents or RVs up to 30 feet: 165 have water and electricity; 23 have no hookups. Picnic tables and fire rings are provided. Drinking water, restrooms with flush toilets, a dump station, showers, a laundry, a public phone, groceries, ice, LP gas, wood, a camp store, rec hall, a pavilion, an arcade, two swimming pools, a wading pool, basketball, playground, two shuffleboard courts, miniature golf, horseshoes, a sports field, volleyball and RV storage and supplies are available. Some sites are wheelchair accessible. Leashed pets are permitted. The campground has a traffic control gate for security.

Reservations, fees: Reservations are accepted. The rate is $24–28.50 per night for up to two people. Each additional person is $6. Weekly, monthly, and seasonal rates are available. Major credit cards are accepted. Open April through October.

Directions: From the junction of Highway 309 and Highway 313, travel six miles south on Highway 309, then 0.25 mile south on Highway 563, then turn right onto Ridge Valley Road and travel 2.5 miles, then turn right onto Allentown Road and travel 100 yards, then turn left onto Finland Road and travel for two miles, and finally turn left onto Camp Skymont Road and travel 0.25 mile to the campground entrance on the right.

Contact: Boulder Woods Campground, 1050 Camp Skymount Road, Green Lane, PA 18054, 215/257-7178, www.boulderwoods.com.

25 LAZY-K CAMPGROUND

Rating: 5

near the Schuylkill River

This 46-acre campground has a fishable stream and two fishing ponds, one of which is limited to catch-and-release fishing. You have your choice of open and wooded sites. You can continue fishing at the Schuylkill River nearby. Among the species you can cast for are channel catfish, muskie, northern pike, black and white crappie, sunfish, rainbow and brook trout, sucker, bluegill, and pickerel. Boating is also a favorite sport on the river. The Multi-Use Trail that runs along the Schuylkill from Valley Forge to Philadelphia is recognized by the U.S. Department of Interior's National Trails System as a National Recreation Trail. You are welcome to bike, hike, jog, or rollerblade on its 11.5 miles. French Creek State Park is also nearby.

Campsites, facilities: There are 146 sites for tents or RVs up to 25 feet: 46 have full hookups; 100 have water and electricity. Picnic tables and fire rings are provided. Drinking water, restrooms with flush toilets, a dump station, a portable dump, showers, a laundry, cable TV hookup, a public phone, groceries, ice, wood, a camp store, a pavilion, a playground, a rec hall, a shuffleboard court, badminton, volleyball, and RV storage are available. Some sites are wheelchair accessible. Leashed pets are permitted.

Reservations, fees: Reservations are accepted at 888/367-8576. The rate is $23–27 per night for up to two people. Each additional person is $2. Weekly, monthly, and seasonal rates and group discounts are available. Open year-round.

Directions: From the junction of Highway 73 and Highway 100, travel north 2.5 miles on Highway 100, then turn right onto Township Line Road and travel 0.2 mile to the campground entrance on the right.

Contact: Lazy-K Campground, 102 Township Line Road, Bechtelsville, PA 19505, 610/367-8576, www.lazykcamping.com.

26 LITTLE RED BARN CAMPGROUND

Rating: 6

near Nockamixon State Park

Little Red Barn is located in Quakertown, near Nockamixon State Park and Lake Nockamixon. At 1,450 acres, the lake is large enough to give almost all boaters their own space. There are four public launching areas, Haycock and Three Mile Run are popular for motorboats, and Tohickon and the Marina are popular for sailboats, catamarans, and windsurfs. Lake Nockamixon empties into Tohickon Creek, which passes through Ralph Stover State Park. This scenic park is home to a 200-foot rock face popular with rock climbers. Over 200 routes of varying difficulty have been put up here. Scheduled releases from Lake Nockamixon provide reliable flows for whitewater paddlers looking for a different sort of thrill. Ralph Stover's Class III rapids can get pushy at higher levels, so keep an eye on the weather. Hiking trails lead to overlooks and some of the more scenic sections of the park.

Campsites, facilities: There are 150 sites for tents or RVs up to 27 feet: 100 have water and electricity; 50 have no hookups. Picnic tables and fire rings are provided. Drinking water, restrooms with flush toilets, a dump station, showers, a laundry, groceries, ice, LP gas, wood, a camp store, a rec hall, a pavilion, a playground, a swimming pool, horseshoes, a sports field, volleyball, and RV storage and supplies are available. Leashed pets are permitted.

Reservations, fees: Reservations are accepted. The rate is $26–29.50 per night for up to two people. Each additional person is $5. Open year-round.

Directions: From the junction of Highway 309 and Highway 313, travel four miles east on Highway 313, then 2.25 miles north on Highway 563, then turn left onto Old Beth-lehem Road and travel 0.75 mile to the campground entrance on the left.

Contact: Little Red Barn Campground, 367 Old Bethlehem Road, Quakertown, PA 18951, 215/536-3357, lrbcampground@msn.com.

27 VILLAGE SCENE PARK

Rating: 5

near Evansburg State Park

At nearby Evansburg State Park, you can golf 18 holes at the Skippack Golf Course along scenic Skippack Creek or enjoy numerous other activities. The creek is also a warm-water fishery. You can cast for eel, brook and brown trout, smallmouth bass, channel catfish, sucker, carp, sunfish, and bluegill. A wheelchair-accessible fishing dock is available at the Lewis Road picnic area. A larger picnic area is on May Hall Road. If you like to hike, the park has six miles of easy and moderate trails. Bikers can enjoy the five-mile mountain bike trail at the southern end of the property or on the state park roadways. A 15-mile equestrian trail is also available. While out and about, be on the look-out for white-tailed deer, red and gray squirrels, woodchucks, chipmunks, and cottontail rabbits. Birders can get out the binoculars to watch vireos, wrens, Eastern bluebirds, orioles, red-tailed hawks, and tanagers. You can participate in environmental and interpretive programs while visiting the park. Check the state park office for a schedule of these changing events. Be advised that hunting is allowed seasonally in Evansburg State Park.

Campsites, facilities: There are 35 sites for RVs up to 25 feet. All sites have full hookups. No tents can be accommodated. Picnic tables and fire rings are provided. Drinking water, restrooms with flush toilets, a dump station, a laundry, and a playground are available.

Some sites are wheelchair accessible. Leashed pets are permitted.

Reservations, fees: Reservations are accepted. The rate is $23 per vehicle per night. Open April through November.

Directions: From the junction of Highway 63 and Highway 463, travel northeast one mile on Highway 463, then turn right onto Koffel Road and travel 0.25 mile to the campground entrance on the left.

Contact: Village Scene Park, 2151 Koffel Road, Hatfield, PA 19440, 215/362-6030.

28 COCALICO CREEK CAMPGROUND
🏍 🏊 🛶 🚣 🎣 🐕 🚶 🚐 ⛺

Rating: 7

near Blue Marsh Lake

BEST (

The one-acre lake on this property has a wonderful sand swimming beach. You can also launch canoes, kayaks, rowboats, and other non-powered boats. If you don't have your own, you can rent a pedal boat from the campground. Anglers can cast for trout, catfish, sunfish, and bluegill in the lake or pond. On weekends, you can participate in planned activities including bingo and hayrides. At nearby Blue Marsh Lake you can cast your line or launch your watercraft. Other outdoor recreational opportunities include swimming, waterskiing, sailing, picnicking, hiking, and birding. Among the species of birds you may view are ospreys, great blue herons, egrets, mallard and wood ducks, Canada geese, teal, cormorants, gulls, pheasants, woodcocks, and ruffed grouse. This is also a good spot for viewing wildlife like white-tailed deer, raccoons, muskrats, red and gray squirrels, opossums, chipmunks, and beavers.

Campsites, facilities: There are 136 sites for tents or RVs up to 27 feet: 126 have full hookups; four have water and electricity; six have no hookups. Picnic tables and fire rings are provided. Drinking water, restrooms with flush toilets, a dump station, a portable dump, showers, a laundry, a public phone, groceries, ice, wood, a camp store, a pavilion, a playground, a rec hall, an arcade, basketball, a sports field, and RV storage are available. Leashed pets are permitted.

Reservations, fees: Reservations are accepted. The rate is $22–26 per night for up to four people. Each additional person is $3. Weekly, monthly, and seasonal rates are available. Open April through October.

Directions: From northern Cocalico, travel 0.25 mile north on Cocalico Road, then 0.25 mile west on Gluft Road to the campground entrance on the left.

Contact: Cocalico Creek Campground, 560 North Cocalico Road, Denver, PA 17517, 717/336-2014, www.holiday-guide.com/camp_usa/pennsylvania/cocalico.

29 SHADY GROVE CAMPGROUND
🏍 🏊 🛶 🚣 🚐 🐕 🚶 🚐 ⛺

Rating: 9

near Blue Marsh Lake

So close to Blue Marsh Lake, you can expect lots of fun on the water. You can choose from three boat launches. Motorboats, sailboats, canoes, kayaks, rowboats, and other non-powered boats are welcome, and waterskiing is a favorite activity. You can also swim from the large sand beach. For pursuits on land, try the 16 miles of hiking and nature trails. You can explore the surrounding forests of red and white oaks. Be on the lookout for wildlife such as white-tailed deer, red and gray squirrels, chipmunks, raccoons, opossums, woodchucks, cottontail rabbits, ruffed grouse, pheasants, and woodcocks. Nearer to the lake, you may see minks, muskrats, heron, osprey, gulls, teal and mallard ducks, and Canada geese. The campground also has planned activities on the weekends.

Campsites, facilities: There are 96 sites for

tents or RVs up to 25 feet: all sites have full hookups. There are three pull-throughs. Picnic tables and fire rings are provided. Drinking water, restrooms with flush toilets, a dump station, showers, a laundry, a public phone, groceries, ice, LP gas, wood, a camp store, an equipped pavilion, a rec room, a playground, a swimming pool, volleyball, and a sports field are available. Leashed pets are permitted.

Reservations, fees: Reservations are accepted at 800/742-3947. The rate is $32 per night for up to two adults and two children aged 14 and under. Each additional adult is $5 and each additional child is $3. Group, weekly, monthly, and seasonal rates are available. Open year-round.

Directions: At the junction of PA Turnpike Exit 286/21 and Highway 272, travel 1.25 miles north on Highway 272, then 0.5 mile northwest on Highway 897, and another 0.2 mile south on a paved road to the campground entrance on the right.

Contact: Shady Grove Campground, Route 897, P.O. Box 812, Adamstown, PA 19501, 717/484-4225 or 800/742-3947, www.shadygrovecampground.com.

30 SILL'S FAMILY CAMPGROUND

🥾 🏊 🛶 🎣 🐕 🚴 🚐 ⛺

Rating: 6

near Blue Marsh Lake

This mostly wooded property offers shaded sites. At nearby Blue Marsh Lake, you can take out your sailboat or motorboat. Other non-powered boats are also welcome. Anglers can cast for muskie, trout, smallmouth and largemouth bass, pickerel, catfish, northern pike, sunfish, carp, and bluegill. Birders can find waterfowl around the lake area such as osprey, cormorants, blue and white heron, egrets, Canada geese, teal, wood, and mallard ducks, and gulls.

Other birds and animal life may be spotted along the 16 miles of hiking and nature trails. You can walk the oak forests and look for ruffed grouse, red-tailed hawks, woodcocks, pheasants, white-tailed deer, cottontail rabbits, opossums, raccoons, red and gray squirrels, skunks, woodchucks, and chipmunks.

Campsites, facilities: There are 140 sites for tents or RVs up to 30 feet: 100 have full hookups; 30 have water and electricity; 10 have no hookups. There are 22 pull-throughs. Picnic tables and fire rings are provided. Drinking water, restrooms with flush toilets, a dump station, showers, a laundry, modem access, phone hookup, cable TV hookup, a public phone, groceries, ice, LP gas, wood, a camp store, a pavilion, a playground, a rec room, an arcade, a swimming pool, badminton, and a sports field are available. Leashed pets are permitted. The campground has a traffic control gate for security.

Reservations, fees: Reservations are required at 800/325-3002. The rate is $26 per night for up to two people. Each additional person is $6. Major credit cards are accepted. Open April through October.

Directions: From the junction of Pennsylvania Turnpike Exit 286/21 and Highway 272, travel north 3.5 miles on Highway 272, then turn right onto Bowmansville Road and travel 0.25 mile to the campground entrance on the left.

Contact: Sill's Family Campground, 1906 Bowmansville Road, Adamstown, PA 19501, 717/484-4806, campsills@aol.com.

31 DUTCH COUSINS CAMPGROUND

🥾 🚴 🏊 🛶 🎣 🐕 🚴 🚐 ⛺

Rating: 6

near Blue Marsh Lake

You have your choice of shaded or sunny sites on this mid-sized property. Located near Blue Marsh Lake and French Creek State

Park, Dutch Cousins makes a convenient home base for many outdoor activities. Blue Marsh Lake has three boat launches and a swimming beach. Motorboats, sailboats, canoes, rowboats, and kayaks are all welcome on the lake. Anglers can fish for muskie, smallmouth and largemouth bass, northern pike, perch, black crappie, channel catfish, sucker, pickerel, sunfish, carp, and bluegill. Around the lake are three interpretive trails and a 30-mile multi-use trail for hiking and biking. French Creek State Park has two lakes for boating or fishing. There are nine hiking trails totaling 30 miles. All are labeled moderate except for the difficult Mill Creek Trail. This six-mile loop begins and ends at Shed Road and connects to Raccoon and Lenape Trails. Raccoon Trail continues 1.7 miles to Hopewell Furnace.

Campsites, facilities: There are 81 sites for tents or RVs up to 25 feet: 18 have full hookups; 58 have water and electricity; five have no hookups. Picnic tables and fire rings are provided. Drinking water, restrooms with flush toilets, a dump station, a portable dump, showers, a laundry, cable TV, a public phone, groceries, ice, LP gas, wood, a camp store, a rec room, a playground, and RV rentals are available. Leashed pets are permitted.

Reservations, fees: Reservations are accepted at 800/992-0261. The rate is $26–28 per night for up to two people. Each additional person is $6. Major credit cards are accepted. Open year-round.

Directions: From the junction of Pennsylvania Turnpike Exit 286/21 and Highway 272, travel north 0.25 mile on Highway 272, then turn left onto Hill Road and travel one mile. The campground entrance is on the left.

Contact: Dutch Cousins Campground, 446 Hill Road Denver, PA 17517, 717/336-6911, www.dutchcampsite.com.

32 FRENCH CREEK STATE PARK

🏃 🏊 🚣 🚐 🐕 ♿ 🚗 ⛺

Rating: 10

near Elverson

BEST (

All of the sites here are wooded. Fishing and boating rule at French Creek State Park thanks to its two lakes. The largest is 68-acre Hopewell Lake, a warm-water fishery where you can cast for muskie, chain pickerel, smallmouth and largemouth bass, walleye, northern pike, sunfish, and bluegill. Scotts Run is a 22-acre cold-water lake that is stocked with brown, brook, and rainbow trout. Motorboats with electric motors and non-powered boats are welcome on both lakes. Hopewell has a boat rental facility. French Creek also offers 30 miles of hiking trails and orienteering for the adventurous among you. All trails, except the difficult Mill Creek, are labeled moderate. Check the park office for a schedule of weekend activities. Be advised that hunting is allowed seasonally in French Creek State Park.

Campsites, facilities: There are 210 sites for tents or RVs up to 30 feet: 60 have electricity; 151 have no hookups. No sites have full hookups. Picnic tables and fire rings are provided. Drinking water, restrooms with flush toilets, a dump station, showers, a public phone, a pavilion, a swimming pool, two Frisbee golf courses, and a sports field are available. Some sites are wheelchair accessible. Leashed pets are permitted.

Reservations, fees: Reservations are accepted at 888/PA-PARKS (888/727-2757). The rate is $14–19 for up to five people per night; a fee may apply for additional guests. Pets are $2 for up to two pets per night. Senior and Pennsylvania resident discounts are available. Open April through December.

Directions: From the junction of Highway 23 and Highway 345, travel north on Highway 345 to the campground entrance on the right.

Contact: French Creek State Park, 843 Park Road, Elverson, PA 19520-9523, 610/582-9680, frenchcreeksp@state.pa.us.

33 ELIZABETHTOWN/ HERSHEY KOA

🚶 🏊 ⛵ 🚐 🏠 ⛺ 🚍 ⛰️

Rating: 8

near the Susquehanna River

You have your choice of shaded and open sites here. With the Susquehanna River so close, you have a variety of water sports at your disposal. Motor and non-powered boats are welcome on the river. If you don't have your own, you can visit any of several outfitters to rent one. Fishermen can cast for muskie, smallmouth bass, channel catfish, carp, bluegill, and sunfish. You may be able to spot white-tailed deer, minks, otters, muskrats, raccoons, osprey, egrets, cormorants, teal, gadwall, and mallard ducks, and heron along the shoreline. Back at the campground, you can enjoy hiking trails and planned activities on weekends.

Campsites, facilities: There are 134 sites for tents or RVs up to 27 feet: 92 have full hookups; 32 have water and electricity; 10 have no hookups. There are 17 pull-throughs. Picnic tables and fire rings are provided. Drinking water, restrooms with flush toilets, a dump station, showers, a laundry, modem access, a phone hookup, a public phone, groceries, ice, LP gas, wood, a general store, a pavilion, a playground, a rec room, an arcade, a swimming pool, miniature golf, basketball, badminton, horseshoes, volleyball, a sports field, and RV rentals and supplies are available. Leashed pets are permitted.

Reservations, fees: Reservations are accepted at 800/562-4774. The rate is $25–44.50 per night for up to two people. Each additional person is $6. Major credit cards are accepted. Weekly specials and group rates are available. Open late March through mid-November.

Directions: From the junction of Highway 283 and Highway 743, travel 1.5 miles south on Highway 743, then 0.5 mile southwest on Highway 241/High Street, then 2.5 miles northwest on Turnpike Road to the campground entrance on the left.

Contact: Elizabethtown/Hershey KOA, 1980 Turnpike Road, Elizabethtown, PA 17022, 717/367-7718, www.campwithrusty.com.

34 RED RUN CAMPGROUND

🏊 🚣 🚐 🏠 ♿ 🚍 ⛰️

Rating: 6

near Lancaster

Red Run Campground is located in the heart of Amish Country. Visitors can take advantage of this prime spot for trips to the scenic countryside for sightseeing and farm tours. The campground itself provides plenty for campers to do. Weekend activities are varied and creative. Steak fry weekends, hayrides, chili cook-offs, murder mystery weekends, and luaus keep campers entertained. Anglers can wet a line in the pond or overflow, or just explore the lake in a rented canoe or pedal boat. Muddy Creek has some fine fishing spots along its banks; be sure to ask campground staff where fishing is permitted, and never cross private property to access a stream.

Campsites, facilities: There are 110 sites for tents or RVs up to 26 feet: all sites have water and electricity. There are 24 pull-throughs. Picnic tables and fire rings are provided. Drinking water, restrooms with flush toilets, a dump station, showers, a laundry, modem access, phone hookup, cable TV hookup, a public phone, groceries, ice, LP gas, wood a camp store, a rec hall, a swimming pool, badminton, a sports field, volleyball, and RV storage and supplies are available. Some sites are wheelchair accessible. Leashed pets are permitted.

Reservations, fees: Reservations are accepted. The rate is $25–30 per night for up to two people. Each additional person is $5. Weekly rates are available. Major credit cards are accepted. Open April through beginning of November.

Directions: From the junction of Highway 23 and U.S. 322, travel three miles west on U.S.

322, then turn right onto Grist Mill Road and travel three miles, then turn right onto Martin Church Road and travel 0.2 mile to the campground entrance on the right.
Contact: Red Run Campground, 877 Martin Church Road, New Holland, PA 17557, 717/445-4526, www.redruncampground.com.

35 GRETNA OAKS CAMPING

Rating: 6

near Lancaster

The wooded sites here get their shade from the surrounding white oaks on the property. Because the campground is in the middle of Pennsylvania Dutch Country, you can explore the Amish countryside on several different types of tours. For the more traditional route you can go for a buggy or van ride. There are more thrilling options as well, such as train, helicopter, and hot air balloon tours. Among the attractions you can visit are the Hans Herr House and Museum, the Fulton Opera House, Kettle Kitchen Village, Dutch Wonderland Family Amusement Park, Eagle Falls Thrills & Spills, the Amish Experience Theater, Indian Echo Caverns, the Landis Valley Museum, Longwood Gardens, the National Civil War Museum, and Mill Bridge Village. For hiking, try Muhlenberg Native Plant and Wildflower Meadow and Lancaster County Central Park.

Campsites, facilities: There are 40 sites for tents or RVs up to 27 feet: 14 have full hookups; six have water and electricity; 20 have no hookups. Picnic tables, fire rings and wood, drinking water, restrooms with flush toilets, a dump station, a laundry, a pavilion, a shuffleboard court, and RV storage and supplies are available. Leashed pets are permitted.

Reservations, fees: Reservations are accepted. The rate is $24–29 per night for up to two people. Each additional person is $3. Weekly,

monthly, and seasonal rates are available. Major credit cards are accepted. Open mid-April through October.

Directions: From the junction of Pennsylvania Turnpike Exit 266/20 and Highway 72, travel one mile south on Highway 72, then turn right onto Cider Press Road and travel 0.5 mile, then turn right onto Pinch Road and travel 0.75 mile, and finally turn left onto Camp Road and travel 0.5 mile to the campground entrance on the left.
Contact: Gretna Oaks Camping, 2649 Camp Road, Manheim, PA 17545, 717/665-7120, www.gretnaoaks.com.

36 PINCH POND FAMILY CAMPGROUND AND RV PARK

Rating: 8

near Lancaster

Pinch Pond Family Campground and RV Park is a large property with plenty of amenities to keep campers busy. You can participate in planned weekend activities such as Christmas in July, a haunted house, tie-dyeing, and powwows. There is a pond for fishing, and a traffic control gate to help campers rest easy. If you need to experience the great outdoors, camp staff will most likely direct you to Governor Dick. This 66-foot high tower stands at the end of a relatively short trail, and provides views of Lancaster, Lebanon, York, Dauphin, and Berks Counties. Please note that the trail may be rocky and steep at times, but the climb to the top of the tower makes it well worth it.

Campsites, facilities: There are 225 sites for tents or RVs up to 35 feet: 165 have full hookups; 35 have water and electricity; 25 have no hookups. There are 20 pull-throughs. Picnic tables and fire rings are provided. Drinking water, restrooms with flush toilets, a dump station, a laundry, phone hookup, cable TV hookup, a public phone, groceries, ice, LP gas, wood, a camp store, a rec hall, an equipped pavilion, an arcade, a swimming pool, fishing supplies, basketball, a playground, two shuffleboard courts, badminton, a sports field, volleyball, and RV storage and supplies are available. Some sites are wheelchair accessible. Leashed pets are permitted.

Reservations, fees: Reservations are accepted at 800/659-7640. The rate is $27–37 per night for up to two people. Each additional person is $7. Weekly rates and senior discounts are available. Major credit cards are accepted. Open year-round.

Directions: From the junction of Pennsylvania Turnpike Exit 266/20 and Highway 72, travel one mile south on Highway 72, then turn right onto Cider Press Road and travel 0.5 mile, then turn right onto Pinch Road and travel one mile to the campground entrance on the right.

Contact: Pinch Pond Family Campground, 3075 Pinch Road, Manheim, PA 17545, 717/665-7640, www.pinchpond.com.

37 STARLITE CAMPING RESORT

Rating: 7

near Lancaster

While staying at Starlite Camping Resort, you have a home base that is close to many attractions in Pennsylvania Dutch country. The area has seven theaters, including several that offer dinner with your show. For more active pursuits, try the Dutch Wonderland Family Amusement Park or Eagle Falls Thrills & Spills. Hikers and birders can walk along trails at Lancaster County Central Park and Muhlenberg National Native Plant and Wildflower Meadow. Among the species you can spot are warblers, vireos, wrens, bluebirds, red-tailed hawks, flycatchers, and tanagers. You can explore the area via buggy, train, helicopter, or balloon. Back at the campground

you can enjoy planned activities or take a walk on the hiking trails.

Campsites, facilities: There are 220 sites for tents or RVs up to 28 feet: 143 have full hookups; 77 have water and electricity. Picnic tables and fire rings are provided. Drinking water, restrooms with flush toilets, a dump station, showers, a laundry, a public phone, groceries, ice, LP gas, wood, a general store, a pavilion, a playground, a rec hall, an arcade, a swimming pool, a wading pool, miniature golf, basketball, tennis, badminton, volleyball, a sports field, and RV storage and supplies are available. Leashed pets are permitted. The campground has a traffic control gate for security.

Reservations, fees: Reservations are accepted. The rate is $34 per night for up to two people. Each additional person is $5. Weekly rates and senior and group discounts are available. Major credit cards are accepted. Open end of April through October.

Directions: From the junction of Highway 272 and U.S. 322, travel four miles west on U.S. 322, then one mile north on Clay Road, then two miles on a paved road. Follow signs to the campground entrance on the left.

Contact: Starlite Camping Resort, 1500 Furnace Hill Road, Stevens, PA 17578, 717/733-9655, www.starlitecampingresort.com.

38 HICKORY RUN FAMILY CAMPING RESORT

Rating: 8

near French Creek State Park

You have your choice of wooded, shaded, and open sites at this campground. Water enthusiasts will appreciate the three-acre lake on the property. You can launch your own non-powered boat, or rent a rowboat, a canoe, or a pedal boat. You can also cast a line for catfish, bluegill, crappie, and sunfish. If you prefer drier pursuits, you can hop on one of the hiking trials. The campground also offers live music, movies, and hayrides. At nearby French Creek State Park you can enjoy even more outdoor recreation.

Campsites, facilities: There are 209 sites for tents or RVs up to 32 feet: 85 have full hookups; 118 have water and electricity; two have electricity; four have no hookups. There are 24 pull-throughs. Picnic tables and fire rings are provided. Drinking water, restrooms with flush toilets, a dump station, a portable dump, showers, a laundry, modem access, a phone hookup, a public phone, groceries, ice, LP gas, wood, a general store, a pavilion, a playground, a rec hall, an arcade, a swimming pool, a wading pool, miniature golf, basketball, tennis, horseshoes, volleyball, a sports field, and RV rentals, storage, and supplies are available. Some sites are wheelchair accessible. Leashed pets are permitted.

Reservations, fees: Reservations are accepted at 800/458-0612. The rate is $29–34.50 per night for up to two people. Each additional person is $6. Seasonal rates are available. Major credit cards are accepted. Open April through October.

Directions: From the junction of Pennsylvania Turnpike Exit 286/21 and Highway 272, travel 1.75 miles south on Highway 272, then turn right onto Church/Main Street and travel two miles, then another two miles on a paved road. Follow signs to the campground entrance on the left.

Contact: Hickory Run Family Camping Resort, 285 Greenville Road, Denver, PA 17517, 717/336-5564, stanst@ptdprolog.net.

39 OAK CREEK CAMPGROUND

Rating: 9

near French Creek State Park

You can choose from wooded and open sites here, and anglers can take advantage of the stocked pond and creek fishing. More fishing awaits at French Creek State Park on Scotts Run Lake and Hopewell Lake. You can also take out a boat here. The park has 30 miles of mostly moderate trails. Back at the campground, you can hike or participate in planned activities like bingo and hayrides.

Campsites, facilities: There are 307 sites for tents or RVs up to 26 feet: 157 have full hookups; 150 have water and electricity. There are eight pull-throughs. Picnic tables and fire rings are provided. Drinking water, restrooms with flush toilets, a dump station, a portable dump, showers, a laundry, modem access, phone hookup, cable TV hookup, a public phone, groceries, ice, LP gas, wood, a camp store, a snack bar, a gift shop, a pavilion, a playground, a rec hall, an arcade, a swimming pool, basketball, two shuffleboards, badminton, horseshoes, a sports field, and RV storage and supplies are available. Leashed pets are permitted. The campground has a traffic control gate for security.

Reservations, fees: Reservations are accepted at 800/446-8365. The rate is $33–38 per night for up to two adults. Each additional person is $6. Seasonal discounts and weekly rates are available. Major credit cards are accepted. Open year-round.

Directions: From the junction of Pennsylvania Turnpike Exit 286/21 and Highway 272, travel north on Highway 272 to Route 897, then south 2.1 miles on Route 897, turn left onto Lauschtown Road, then right onto Route 625 South to the intersection and turn left onto Maple Grove Road, and finally travel 1.5 miles to the campground entrance on the right.

Contact: Oak Creek Campground, P.O. Box 128, Bowmansville, PA 17507, 717/445-6161, www.oakcreekcamp.com.

40 LAKE-IN-WOOD RESORT

Rating: 8

near French Creek State Park

Lake-In-Wood Resort is a large property with many activities for campers. Golf cart and bike rentals make getting around a little easier, and a traffic control gate for security helps campers to rest easy at night. At the heart of the property is a lake where campers can paddle or pedal a variety of watercraft. A concession rents rowboats and pedal boats, and if boating isn't your thing you can wet a line in the lake instead. Lake-In-Wood plans a large variety of activities for its campers such as ceramics, bingo, hayrides, fire engine rides, movie nights, and live music. Hikers and fitness buffs should check out the Total Fitness World Trail. French Creek State Park is nearby if campers want to get back to nature. This large park has a variety of hiking trails that allow visitors to experience flora and fauna in a natural setting.

Campsites, facilities: There are 350 sites for RVs up to 32 feet and tents; 338 have full hookups; 11 have water and electricity; one has no hookups; There are 36 pull-throughs. Picnic tables and fire rings are provided. Drinking water, restrooms with flush toilets, a dump station, a portable dump, showers, a laundry, modem access, a phone hookup, cable TV hookup, a public phone, groceries, ice, wood, a general store, a café, a pavilion, a playground, a rec hall, an arcade, a swimming pool, a wading pool, a whirlpool, miniature golf, basketball, four shuffleboard courts, badminton, horseshoes, volleyball, a sports field, and RV rentals, storage, and supplies are available. Leashed pets are permitted.

Reservations, fees: Reservations are accepted. The rate is $25–50 per night for up to two people. Each additional person is $6. Seasonal rates are available. Major credit cards are accepted. Open April through November.

Directions: From the junction of the Pennsylvania Turnpike and Highway 897 South, travel on Highway 897 to Lauschtown Road for 2.5 miles to Route 625. Follow signs to the campground entrance.

Contact: Lake-In-Wood Resort, 576 Yellow Hill Road, Narvon, PA 17555, 717/445-5525, www.lakeinwoodcampground.com.

41 SUN VALLEY CAMPGROUND

Rating: 7

near French Creek State Park

You can fish in this property's pond or check out Sun Valley's hiking trails. There are also planned activities such as Wild West and medieval weekends. At nearby French Creek State Park, you can fish and boat in Scotts Run and Hopewell Lakes. For the hikers in your group there are 30 miles of trails running throughout the park.

Campsites, facilities: There are 265 sites for tents or RVs up to 32 feet: 200 have full hookups; 55 have water and electricity; 10 have no hookups. There are 10 pull-throughs. Picnic tables and fire rings are provided. Drinking water, restrooms with flush toilets, a dump station, a portable dump, showers, a laundry, modem access, a phone hookup, cable TV hookup, a public phone, groceries, ice, LP gas, wood, a general store, a snack bar, a library, a playground, a rec hall, an arcade, a swimming pool, a putting green, a basketball court, badminton, a volleyball court, and a sports field are available. Some sites are wheelchair accessible. Leashed pets are permitted. The campground has a traffic control gate for security.

Reservations, fees: Reservations are accepted at 800/700-3370. The rate is $28–39 per night for up to two people. Each additional person is $6. Weekly, monthly, and seasonal rates and group discounts are available. Major credit cards are accepted. Open year-round.

Directions: From the junction of Pennsylvania Turnpike Exit 286/21 and Highway 272, travel north 1.2 miles on Highway 272, then turn right onto Route 897 South and travel two miles, then turn left onto Lauschtown Road and travel 2.2 miles to Route 625 South, then 0.25 miles on Route 625, turn left onto Maple Grove Road and travel two miles to the campground entrance on the left.

Contact: Sun Valley Campground, 451 East

Maple Grove Road, Bowmansville, PA 17507, 717/445-6262, www.sunvalleycamping.com.

42 WARWICK WOODS FAMILY CAMPING RESORT

Rating: 8

near French Creek State Park

BEST (

There are many activities you can enjoy while staying at 100-acre Warwick Woods Family Camping Resort. You can hike and bike on the property's trails, fish in the pond, or participate in hayrides, live music, bingo, or ceramics. For more fun, you can check out French Creek State Park. There are 30 miles of hiking trails that run throughout the 7,339-acre park. All but the difficult Mill Creek Trail are moderate hikes. The park also boasts two lakes for boating and fishing. Scotts Run Lake is a 22-acre cold-water fishery that is stocked with trout. Hopewell Lake covers 68 acres and offers bass, walleye, chain pickerel, northern pike, and muskie. You can also go orienteering or try your hand at the Frisbee golf course.

Campsites, facilities: There are 183 sites for tents or RVs up to 30 feet: 18 have full hookups; 132 have water and electricity; 33 have no hookups. Picnic tables and fire rings are provided. Drinking water, restrooms with flush toilets, a dump station, showers, a laundry, a public phone, groceries, ice, wood, a camp store, two playgrounds, a rec room, an arcade, horseshoes, a swimming pool, a wading pool, a basketball court, badminton, shuffleboard, a volleyball court, and RV supplies are available. Leashed pets are permitted.

Reservations, fees: Reservations are accepted at 610/286-9655. The rate is $30–42 per night for up to two people. Each additional person is $6. Open year-round.

Directions: From Pennsylvania Turnpike Exit 298, travel one mile south on Route 10, then 7.5 miles east on Route 23, then 0.5 mile on Trythall Road. Follow signs to the campground entrance.

Contact: Warwick Woods Family Camping Resort, 401 Trythall Road, Elverson, PA 19520, 610/286-9655, www.warwickwoods.com.

43 BRANDYWINE MEADOWS FAMILY CAMPGROUND

Rating: 8

near Marsh Creek State Park

This campground offers pond fishing, motorboating (for craft with electric motors), canoeing, and planned weekend activities. At nearby Marsh Creek State Park, you can take advantage of the many hiking and horseback riding trails or go birding for waterfowl along Marsh Lake. The 535-acre lake also allows boating and fishing. There are two boat launches and 220 mooring slips for sailboats, motorboats, and canoes. If you don't have your own watercraft, you can rent rowboats, canoes, and sailboats at the East Launch. Among the fish you can cast for are tiger muskie (a hybrid of northern pike and native muskie), largemouth bass, channel catfish, black crappie, and walleye. Be advised that hunting is allowed seasonally in Marsh Creek State Park.

Campsites, facilities: There are 160 sites for tents or RVs up to 29 feet: 36 have full hookups; 124 have water and electricity. There are 27 pull-throughs. Picnic tables and fire rings are provided. Drinking water, restrooms with flush toilets, a dump station, a portable dump, showers, a laundry, groceries, ice, wood, a camp store, a pavilion, a playground, a rec hall, a swimming pool, miniature golf, two shuffleboard courts, badminton, horseshoes, volleyball, and a sports field are available. Some sites are wheelchair accessible. Leashed pets are permitted.

Reservations, fees: Reservations are accepted. The rate is $26–40 per night for up to two people. Each additional person is $5. Open April through October.

Directions: From the junction of Highway 10 and U.S. 322, travel three miles east on U.S. 322, then turn right onto Birdell Road and travel 0.5 mile, then turn left onto Icedale Road and travel 0.5 mile to the campground entrance on the left.

Contact: Brandywine Meadows Family Campground, 429 Icedale Road, Honey Brook, PA 19344, 610/273-9753.

44 SPRING GULCH RESORT CAMPGROUND

Rating: 9

near Lancaster

BEST (

Spring Gulch is located on 115 acres of farmland and forest. The property has hiking trails, and a trout-stocked lake for fishing, and a white sand beach for swimming. You can also participate in planned activities such as movies, square dancing, and the annual Folk Festival in May. The campground offers its own local tours or you can see Amish Country via train, buggy, helicopter, or hot air balloon. If you have a bike, you'll enjoy riding the scenic country roads.

Campsites, facilities: There are 450 sites for tents or RVs up 32 feet: 290 have full hookups; 110 have water and electricity; 50 have no hookups. There are 40 pull-throughs. Picnic tables and fire rings are provided. Drinking water, restrooms with flush toilets, a dump station, showers, a laundry, modem access, a phone hookup, cable TV hookup, a pubic phone, groceries, ice, LP gas, wood, a camp store, a rec hall, a pavilion, an arcade, two swimming pools, a whirlpool, basketball, a playground, two shuffleboard courts, tennis, miniature golf, badminton, horseshoes, a sports field, volleyball, a day spa, a fitness center, and RV storage and supplies are available. Some sites are wheelchair accessible. Leashed pets are permitted. Spring Gulch has a traffic control gate for security.

Reservations, fees: Reservations are accepted at 866/864-8524. The rate is $26.50–49.50 for up to four people per night. Weekly rates and senior and group discounts are available. Major credit cards are accepted. Open April through mid-November.

Directions: From the junction of Highway 23 and Highway 897, travel four miles south on Highway 897, then turn left onto Lynch Road and travel 45 yards to the campground entrance on the left.

Contact: Spring Gulch Resort Campground, 475 Lynch Road, New Holland, PA 17557, 717/354-3100, www.springgulch.com.

45 TWO LOG CAMPGROUND

Rating: 8

near Marsh Creek State Park

This campground offers lots of water activities. You can swim in the lake from a sand beach, go boating (electric motors only), canoe, or fish. If you don't have your own boat, you can rent canoes and pedal boats. At nearby Marsh Creek State Park, you can go horseback riding or hiking on various trails. There is also Marsh Lake for your fishing and boating enjoyment. The 535-acre has two boat launches and 220 mooring slips and rentals for canoes, rowboats, and sailboats. You can cast a line for tiger muskie (a hybrid of northern pike and native muskie), black crappie, walleye, sunfish, bluegill, channel catfish, and largemouth bass. For swimming, the state park has a pool complex open from Memorial Day to Labor Day. Be advised that hunting is allowed seasonally in Marsh Creek State Park. Back at the campground, you can enjoy planned activities on weekends and on-site hiking trails.

Campsites, facilities: There are 75 sites for tents or RVs up to 28 feet: 60 have water and electricity; 15 have no hookups. Picnic tables and fire rings are provided. Drinking water, restrooms with flush toilets, a dump station, a portable dump, showers, groceries, ice, LP gas, wood, a camp store, a pavilion, a playground, badminton, horseshoes, volleyball, and RV storage are available. Leashed pets are permitted.

Reservations, fees: Reservations are accepted. The rate is $25–28 per night for up to two people. Each additional person is $5. Open mid-April through mid-October.

Directions: From the junction of U.S. 322 and Highway 10, travel south 2.75 miles on Highway 10, then turn left onto Beaver Dam Road and travel 1.75 miles to the campground entrance on the right.

Contact: Two Log Campground, 960 Beaver Dam Road, Honey Brook, PA 19344, 610/273-3068, twologcampground@ccis.net.

46 RIDGE RUN FAMILY CAMPGROUND

Rating: 7

near the Susquehanna River

The large pond on this property is great for fishing or taking out a pedal boat. You can rent a boat right from the campground. There are also planned activities on weekends. The nearby Susquehanna River offers even more fishing and boating opportunities. Motorboats and non-powered boats are welcome on the river. Several outfitters in the area have boat and canoe rentals. Anglers can cast for smallmouth bass, crappie, walleye, muskie, catfish, bluegill, sucker, carp, and sunfish. Hiking near the shoreline not only provides wonderful views, but also a chance to spot the area's wildlife. You may see otters, white-tailed deer, minks, muskrats, cottontail rabbits, woodchucks, red and gray squirrels, and chipmunks. Birders can get out the binoculars for cormorants, osprey, heron, orioles, vireos, tanagers, teal and mallard ducks, gulls, Canada geese, and flycatchers.

Campsites, facilities: There are 135 sites for tents or RVs up to 28 feet: 86 have full hookups; 28 have water and electricity; 21 have no hookups. There are six pull-throughs. Picnic tables and fire rings are provided. Drinking water, restrooms with flush toilets, a dump station, showers, a laundry, a public phone, groceries, ice, LP gas, wood, a camp store, a pavilion, an equipped pavilion, a playground, a rec room, a swimming pool, a shuffleboard court, badminton, horseshoes, volleyball, and a sports field are available. Some sites are wheelchair accessible. Leashed pets are permitted.

Reservations, fees: Reservations accepted at 800/827-3464. The rate is $24–28 per night for up to two people. Each additional person is $4. Seasonal rates are available. Open year-round.

Directions: From Highway 283, take the Rheems-Elizabethtown Exit, then travel one mile on Schwanger Road. Follow signs to the campground entrance on the right.

Contact: Ridge Run Family Campground, 867 Schwanger Road, Elizabethtown, PA 17022, 717/367-3454.

47 BRANDYWINE CREEK CAMPGROUND

Rating: 7

near Marsh Creek State Park

You have your choice of wooded and creekside sites at this campground. The Brandywine Creek is stocked with trout. There is also a fishing pond where you can cast for catfish, bluegill, and sunfish. Because Brandywine Creek Campground borders 1,705-acre Marsh Creek State Park, you have even more opportunities for outdoor recreational activities. The 535-acre Marsh Lake has two boat launches for motorboats and non-powered boats. If you don't have your own craft, you can rent rowboats, canoes, and sailboats through the park's concessions area. Anglers can cast for tiger muskie (a hybrid of muskie and northern pike), black crappie, channel catfish, walleye, largemouth bass, sunfish, and bluegill. Those who prefer to stay on land can take advantage of the many hiking and horseback riding trails that run throughout the park. You may spot osprey, gulls, terns, herons, red-tailed hawks, warblers, bluebirds, vireos, and tanagers along the way. Be advised that hunting is allowed seasonally in Marsh Creek State Park.

Campsites, facilities: There are 57 sites for tents or RVs up to 40 feet: all have full hookups; eight are pull-throughs. Picnic tables and fire rings are provided. Drinking water, restrooms with flush toilets, a dump station, showers, a laundry, modem access, phone hookup, cable TV hookup, a playground, a rec hall, an arcade, ping-pong, and a swimming pool are available. Leashed pets are permitted.

Reservations, fees: Reservations are accepted. The rate is $25–49 per night for up to two people. Each additional person is $5. Weekly, monthly, and seasonal rates are available. Open April through October.

Directions: From the junction of I-76 and Highway 100 Exit 312, travel north on Highway 100, then turn left onto West Township Line Road, then turn right onto Creek Road to the campground entrance.

Contact: Brandywine Creek Campground, 1091 Creek Road, Lyndell, PA 19354, 610/942-9950, www.brandywinecreekcampground.com.

48 BERRY PATCH CAMPGROUND
🏃 🛶 🎣 🚐 🐎 🚣 ♿ 🚙 ⛺

Rating: 8

near Marsh Creek State Park

All of the sites here are wooded and spacious. Berry Patch Campground has lake fishing, hiking trails, and planned weekend activities such as live music, bingo, and hayrides. At nearby 1,705-acre Marsh Creek State Park, you can find lots of outdoor recreational opportunities. The

highlight of the park is 535-acre Marsh Lake. Boating enthusiasts can take out sailboats, motorboats with electric motors, and non-powered boats. The anglers in your group can cast a line for largemouth bass, channel catfish, muskie, black crappie, walleye, bluegill, and sunfish. If you prefer to stay on land, the state park has several hiking and horseback riding trails.

Campsites, facilities: There are 125 sites for tents or RVs up to 30 feet: 65 have full hookups; 40 have water and electricity; 20 have no hookups. There are 10 pull-throughs. Picnic tables and fire rings are provided. Drinking water, restrooms with flush toilets, a dump station, showers, a laundry, modem access, a phone hookup, a public phone, groceries, ice, wood, a general store, a playground, a rec room, an arcade, a swimming pool, a wading pool, basketball, horseshoes, volleyball, a sports field, a golf course, and RV supplies are available. Some sites are wheelchair accessible. Leashed pets are permitted.

Reservations, fees: Reservations are accepted. The rate is $20–38 per night for up to two people. Each additional person is $5. Weekly, monthly, and seasonal rates and senior discounts are available. Open May through October.

Directions: From the junction of U.S. 322 and Highway 10, travel 1.5 miles south on Highway 10, then turn right onto Mt. Pleasant Road and travel one mile, then turn left onto Ross Road and travel 0.25 mile to the campground entrance on the right.

Contact: Berry Patch Campground, 6225 Ross Road, Honey Brook, PA 19344, 610/273-3720, www.berrypatchcampground.com.

49 HIDDEN ACRES CAMPING GROUNDS
🏃 🛶 🎣 🚐 🐎 🚣 ♿ 🚙 ⛺

Rating: 9

near Marsh Creek State Park

BEST (

Hidden Acres Camping Grounds retains some of the character of nearby Marsh

Creek State Park. The rolling hills of Marsh Creek are home to 535-acre Marsh Creek Lake, a body of water well suited to sailing and fishing. Sailboat races are held regularly here, and the prevailing breezes and gentle terrain make Marsh Creek Lake a year-round favorite with skippers of small watercraft. A concession rents rowboats, canoes, and sailboats, weather permitting, from May to September. Anglers will find the warm waters of Marsh Creek Lake well suited for catching largemouth bass, channel catfish, black crappie, walleye and a variety of other panfish. Some anglers will even try for the tiger muskie that can occasionally grow to more than 40 inches here. This lake is a designated big bass lake. Other popular activities at Marsh Creek include horseback riding on the park's west side and hiking on a variety of trails that pass through wooded areas, wetlands, and marsh. Hikers and horseback riders should exercise caution during hunting season. Back at Hidden Acres, campers can wet a line in the property's pond or stretch their legs on some of the hiking trails.

Campsites, facilities: There are 255 sites for tents or RVs up to 25 feet: 65 have full hookups; 180 have water and electricity; 10 have no hookups. Picnic tables and fire rings are provided. Drinking water, restrooms with flush toilets, a dump station, showers, a laundry, modem access, phone hookup, a public phone, groceries, ice, wood, a camp store, a pavilion, a playground, a rec hall, an arcade, a swimming pool, basketball, badminton, volleyball, a sports field, and RV storage are available. Some sites are wheelchair accessible. Leashed pets are permitted.

Reservations, fees: Reservations are accepted. The rate is $22–28 per night for up to five people. Each additional person is $5. Seasonal and group rates are available. Open April through October.

Directions: From the junction of U.S. 30 and Highway 82, travel north 0.2 mile on Highway 82, then west five miles on Highway 340, then turn right onto Cambridge Road and travel 1.5 miles, and then turn right onto Baldwin Road and travel 0.25 mile to the campground entrance on the left.

Contact: Hidden Acres Camping Grounds, 103 Hidden Acres Road, Coatesville, PA 19320, 610/857-3990.

50 BIRCHVIEW FARM CAMPGROUND

🚶 ♒ 🛶 🚐 🎣 🐴 🚙 ⛺

Rating: 7

near Marsh Creek State Park

You can choose open or shaded sites at this spacious campground. Take advantage of the short hiking trails or fish in the mid-sized pond on property. At nearby Marsh Creek State Park, you can fish in 535-acre Marsh Creek Lake. Among the species you can cast for are tiger muskies (a hybrid of northern pike and native muskies), walleye, largemouth bass, channel catfish, black crappie, sunfish, and bluegill. Sailing can be quite enjoyable here; other non-powered boats and motorboats with electric motors are also welcome. If need to rent a boat, there is a concession at the East Launch. Horseback riding and hiking trails run throughout the park. Be advised that hunting is allowed seasonally in Marsh Creek State Park.

Campsites, facilities: There are 185 sites for tents or RVs up to 28 feet: 139 have full hookups; 46 have water and electricity. There are 10 pull-throughs. Picnic tables and fire rings are provided. Drinking water, restrooms with flush toilets, a dump station, a portable dump, showers, a laundry, modem access, a phone hookup, a public phone, groceries, ice, LP gas, wood, a general store, a pavilion, a playground, a rec hall, an arcade, a swimming pool, a wading pool, basketball, badminton, volleyball, a sports field, and RV rentals, storage, and supplies are available. Leashed pets are permitted.

Reservations, fees: Reservations are accepted at 610/384-0500. The rate is $20–25 per night for up to five people. Each additional person is $5. Major credit cards are accepted. Open May through October.

Directions: From the junction of U.S. 30 and Highway 82, travel 0.25 mile north on Highway 82, then three miles west on Highway 340, then turn right onto North Bonsall School Road and travel one mile, then turn right onto Martins Corner Road and travel 1.5 miles to the campground entrance on the left.

Contact: Birchview Farm Campground, 100 Birchview Drive, Coatesville, PA 19320, 610/384-1457.

51 BEECHWOOD CAMPGROUND

Rating: 8

near Marsh Creek State Park

If you prefer open sites, then set up camp along Fairview Lane or Sunshine Strips. For a site surrounded by trees, try Elm Drive, Dogwood Lane, Cherry Lane, Beechtree Lane, and Acorn Drive. You have many recreational opportunities available to you at nearby 1,705-acre Marsh Creek State Park. Sailing is very popular on 535-acre Marsh Lake, other non-powered boats and motorboats with electric motors are also welcome on the lake. If you don't have your own, you can rent one at the park. The anglers among you can cast for largemouth bass, channel catfish, walleye, black crappie, and tiger muskie. For land lovers, there are several scenic hiking and horseback riding trails. There is also a large picnicking area available. Be advised that hunting is allowed seasonally in Marsh Creek State Park. Back at the campground, you can participate in planned activities like bingo and hayrides.

Campsites, facilities: There are 315 sites for tents or RVs up to 30 feet: 135 have full hookups; 170 have water and electricity; 10 have no hookups. There are 50 pull-throughs. Picnic tables and fire rings are provided. Drinking water, restrooms with flush toilets, a dump station, a portable dump, showers, a laundry, a public phone, groceries, ice, LP gas, wood, a camp store, a pavilion, a playground, a rec hall, a swimming pool, badminton, volleyball, and a sports field are available. Leashed pets are permitted.

Reservations, fees: Reservations are accepted. The rate is $22–32 per night for up to two people. Each additional person is $5. Weekly, monthly, and seasonal rates are available. Major credit cards are accepted. Open April through October.

Directions: From the junction of Highway 82 and U.S. 30, travel east 1.74 miles on U.S. 30 to Veterans Hospital, then turn left onto Reeseville Road and travel for 1.5 miles, then another 0.25 mile on a paved road to the campground entrance on the right.

Contact: Beechwood Campground, 105 Beechwood Drive, Coatesville, PA 19320, 610/384-1457.

52 COUNTRY HAVEN CAMPSITE

Rating: 5

near Lancaster

You can explore all of Pennsylvania Dutch Country while using Country Haven as your base camp. There are many ways to tour this land of the Amish. If you have your own bikes, you can spend the days leisurely riding the country roads past farms and craft villages. For a more authentic experience, you can tour from a horse-drawn buggy or a train. But, if you're looking for something with a little more thrill, try either a hot air balloon or helicopter ride. There is even a ghost tour of Amish Country. Also in the area are Dutch Wonderland Family Amusement Park and Eagle Falls Thrills &

Spills. For those who prefer to get around by foot, you can try the hiking trails at Muhlenberg Native Plant and Wildflower Meadow and Lancaster County Central Park. These easy trails are also excellent spots for birding. Among the species you may see are warblers, vireos, tanagers, flycatchers, bluebirds, and wrens.

Campsites, facilities: There are 55 sites for RVs up to 26 feet and tents; 52 have full hookups; three have water and electricity. Picnic tables and fire rings are provided. Drinking water, restrooms with flush toilets, a dump station, showers, a laundry, modem access, a phone hookup, cable TV hookup, a public phone, groceries, ice, LP gas, wood, a camp store, a pavilion, a playground, and RV storage and supplies are available. Some sites are wheelchair accessible. Leashed pets are permitted.

Reservations, fees: Reservations are accepted. The rate is $27–32 per night for up to six people. Each additional person is $5. Major credit cards are accepted. Open year-round.

Directions: From the junction of Highway 23 and Highway 897, travel 5.5 miles south on Highway 897 to the campground entrance on the right.

Contact: Country Haven Campsite, 354 Springville Road, New Holland, PA 17557, 717/354-7926.

53 OLD MILL STREAM CAMPGROUND

Rating: 9

near Lancaster

BEST (

This campground adjoins Dutch Wonderland Family Amusement Park and Wonderland Mini-Golf. Its 15 acres offers shaded sites. Among the attractions at the amusement park are roller coasters, bumper cars, riverboat rides, gondola rides, a merry-go-round, a monorail, and a train. There are daily shows and live music. You can also cool off at Duke's Lagoon, a small family water park within Dutch Won-

derland. If you can pull yourself away from the amusement park fun, explore Amish Country and historic Lancaster with the campground's local auto tape tours. If you would like to stretch your legs in a more natural setting, check out the two Audubon Trails in Lancaster: Muhlenberg Native Plant and Wildlife Meadow and Lancaster County Central Park. Both provide excellent birding opportunities. You may spot vireos, tanagers, bluebirds, wrens, warblers, and red-tailed hawks.

Campsites, facilities: There are 168 sites for tents or RVs up to 30 feet: 108 have full hookups; 51 have water and electricity; nine have no hookups. Picnic tables and fire rings are provided. Drinking water, restrooms with flush toilets, two dump stations, a portable dump, showers, two laundries, modem access, phone hookup, cable TV hookup, a public phone, groceries, ice, wood, a camp store, grills, a pavilion, a playground, a rec room, an arcade, basketball, and volleyball are available. Some sites are wheelchair accessible. Leashed pets are permitted.

Reservations, fees: Reservations are accepted at 866/FUNATDW (866/386-2839). The rate is $27–36 per night for up to two people. Each additional person is $3. Major credit cards are accepted. Open year-round.

Directions: From the junction of East Highway 283 and U.S. 30, travel nine miles east on U.S. 30 to the campground entrance on the left.

Contact: Old Mill Stream Campground, 2249 Route 30 East, Lancaster, PA 17602, 717/299-2314, www.oldmillstreamcamping.com.

54 MILL BRIDGE VILLAGE & CAMP RESORT

Rating: 9

near Lancaster

BEST (

Home to two registered historic landmarks, Herr's Grist Mill and Covered Bridge, this campground is located next to a working Amish farm. Guests can take advantage of free tours of these historical sites as well as free admission to Mill Bridge Village. Take a buggy ride or visit the Farm Museum during your stay. The anglers in your group can cast a line on Pequea Creek, which borders the property. Among the species inhabiting these waters are sunfish, bluegill, and trout. You can join in planned activities such as pool volleyball, hayrides, candle dipping, and scavenger hunts. Choose from shaded and open sites and sites along the stream or adjacent to the Amish farm.

Campsites, facilities: There are 100 sites for tents or RVs up to 55 feet: 60 have full hookups; 40 have water and electricity. There are 15 pull-throughs. Picnic tables and fire rings are provided. Drinking water, restrooms with flush toilets, a dump station, showers, a laundry, modem access, phone hookup, cable TV hookup, a public phone, groceries, ice, wood, a camp store, a snack bar, a pavilion, a playground, a rec room, basketball, horseshoes, and shuffleboard are available. Some sites are wheelchair accessible. Leashed pets are permitted.

Reservations, fees: Reservations are accepted at 800/645-2744. The rate is $25–40 per night for up to two people. Each additional person is $6. Senior discounts are available. Major credit cards are accepted. Open March through November.

Directions: From the junction of East Highway 462 and U.S. 30, travel east 3.5 miles on U.S. 30, then turn right onto Ronks Road and travel 0.5 mile to the campground entrance at the left.

Contact: Mill Bridge Village, P.O. Box 7, Paradise, PA 17562, 717/687-8181, www.mill-bridgevillage.com.

55 FLORY'S COTTAGES & CAMPING

🏃 ⛱ 🐕 🚵 🚐 ⛺

Rating: 5

near Lancaster

The shaded sites here are level and grassy. Right in the heart of Amish Country, Flory's Cottages & Camping is centrally located to several local attractions. You can visit the Amish Village, the Freedom Chapel Dinner Theater, the Herr Family Homestead, Kitchen Kettle Village, the Sight and Sound's Millennium Theater, the Americana Museum, and the American Music Theater. Several companies offer guided tours of Amish farms, as well as buggy rides. There are also two public pools not affiliated with the campground, Lancaster and Leola Community Park & Pool. Day trips include HersheyPark and Gettysburg National Battlefield. Birders and hikers will enjoy the trails at 544-acre Lancaster County Central Park. Among the species you may spot are red-tailed hawks, herons, Eastern bluebirds, osprey, warblers, and orioles. If you prefer to partake in the on-site entertainment, the campground has weekend activities such as live music.

Campsites, facilities: There are 71 sites for tents or RVs up to 26 feet. All sites have full hookups. Picnic tables and fire rings are provided. Drinking water, restrooms with flush toilets, a dump station, showers, a laundry, modem access, a phone hookup, cable TV hookup, a public phone, groceries, ice, a pavilion, a playground, a rec hall, an arcade, basketball, and RV rentals and supplies are available. Leashed pets are permitted.

Reservations, fees: Reservations are accepted. The rate is $24–33 per night for up to two people. Each additional person is $5. Weekly rates are available. Major credit cards are accepted. Open year-round.

Directions: From the junction of East Highway 462 and U.S. 30, travel east 3.5 miles on U.S. 30, then turn left onto Ronks Road and travel 0.5 mile to the campground entrance on the right.

Contact: Flory's Cottages & Camping, P.O. Box 308, Ronks, PA 17572, 717/687-6670, www.floryscamping.com.

56 COUNTRY ACRES CAMPGROUND

Rating: 8

near Lancaster

As a guest at Country Acres Campground, you can take advantage of a complimentary two-hour tour of Pennsylvania Dutch Country. You may see authentic Amish farms and buggy transportation, handicraft centers, and even the occasional white-tailed deer or woodchuck. If you'd prefer to get around on foot, visit the hiking trails at nearby Muhlenberg Native Plant and Wildflower Meadow or Lancaster County Central Park. The 1.5-mile Mill Creek Trail passes through the Kiwanis Natural Area and connects to the 0.5-mile Wildflower Trail. Birders will also love these trails for opportunities to spy orioles, warblers, osprey, red-tailed hawks, herons, waxwings, bluebirds, and thrushes. Back at the campground, you have your choice of wooded and shaded sites.

Campsites, facilities: There are 83 sites for tents or RVs up to 32 feet: 59 have full hookups; 18 have water and electricity; six have no hookups. There are 22 pull-throughs. Picnic tables and fire rings are provided. Drinking water, restrooms with flush toilets, a dump station, showers, a laundry, modem access, a phone hookup, cable TV hookup, a laundry, a public phone, groceries, ice, wood, a camp store, a pavilion, a playground, a rec hall, an arcade, a swimming pool, a wading pool, two shuffleboard courts, badminton, horseshoes, croquet, volleyball, and a sports field are available. Some sites are wheelchair accessible. Leashed pets are permitted. There is a traffic control gate for security.

Reservations, fees: Reservations are accepted. The rate is $22–37 per night for up to two people. Each additional person is $3. Major credit cards are accepted. Open April through November.

Directions: From the junction of Highway 896 and U.S. 30, travel 2.75 miles east on U.S. 30 to the campground entrance on the left.

Contact: Country Acres Campground, 20 Leven Road, Gordonville, PA 17529, 717/687-8014 or 866/675-4745, www.countryacres-campground.com.

57 BEACON HILL CAMPING

Rating: 7

near Lancaster

You have your choice of shady and open sites at this campground. Devoted to the relaxing charm of its rural Amish setting, Beacon Hill Camping's recreation is limited to ice cream socials. But there is plenty to do in the surrounding Pennsylvania Dutch Country. Buggy rides and tours of Amish farms are just the beginning. You can also visit Dutch Wonderland Family Amusement Park, the Americana Museum, Kitchen Kettle Village, Longwood Gardens, Strasburg Rail Road, and Eagle Falls Thrills & Spills. For the outdoor lovers among you, check out the hiking and birding trails at Lancaster County Central Park and Muhlenberg Native Plant and Wildlife Meadow. There is also fishing and boating on the Conestoga River. Among the species you can cast for are crappie, trout, bass, carp, catfish, bluegill, sunfish, and perch.

Campsites, facilities: There are 45 sites for tents or RVs up to 25 feet: 40 have full hookups; five have water and electricity. There are 10 pull-throughs. Picnic tables and fire rings are provided. Drinking water, restrooms with flush toilets, a dump station, showers, a laundry, modem access, phone hookup, a public phone, ice, LP gas, wood, a pavilion, a playground, and RV supplies are available. Some sites are wheelchair accessible. Leashed pets are permitted.

Reservations, fees: Reservations are recommended. The rate is $24–29 per night for up to two people. Each additional person is $5. Weekly rates are available. Major credit cards are accepted. Open April through beginning of November.

Directions: From the junction of Highway 340 and Highway 722, travel northwest 0.5 mile on Highway 722, then east 0.25 mile on Beacon Hill Road to the campground entrance on the left.

Contact: Beacon Hill Camping, 128 Beacon Hill Road, Intercourse, PA 17534, 717/768-8775, www.beaconhillcamping.com.

58 WHITE OAK CAMPGROUND

🚶 🚲 🏕 🎣 🚐 ⛺

Rating: 7

near Lancaster

You have your choice of open meadow and shaded woodland sites at this 25-acre campground. Located in the middle of Amish Country, White Oak is a nice base camp for touring, hiking, biking, and birding. Pennsylvania Dutch Country can be seen by buggy, rain, van, bus, hot air balloon, and helicopter. The country roads offer bikers a scenic ride. Hikers and birders alike will find a wonderful morning or afternoon spent at Lancaster County Central Park or Muhlenberg Native Plant and Wildflower Meadow. Among the species you may spot are vireos, warblers, tanagers, red-tailed hawks, bluebirds, orioles, and wrens. Back at the campground, you can participate in planned activities like theme weekends.

Campsites, facilities: There are 200 sites for tents or RVs up to 30 feet: 140 have full hookups; 45 have water and electricity; 15 have no hookups; There are 20 pull-throughs. Picnic tables and fire rings are provided. Drinking water, restrooms with flush toilets, a dump station, modem access, phone hookup, a public phone, groceries, ice, wood, a general store, a rec room, a pavilion, an arcade, a playground, a sports field, and RV storage and supplies are available. Leashed pets are permitted.

Reservations, fees: Reservations are accepted. The rate is $22–28 per night for up to two people. Each additional person is $3. Weekly, monthly, and seasonal rates are available. Major credit cards are accepted. Open year-round.

Directions: From the junction of west Highway 741 and Highway 896 and Decatur Street, travel 3.5 miles south on Decatur Street and May Post Office Road, then turn left onto White Oak Road and travel 0.25 mile to the campground entrance on the left.

Contact: White Oak Campground, P.O. Box 90, Strasburg, PA 17579, 717/687-6207, www.whiteoakcampground.com.

59 ROAMERS' RETREAT CAMPGROUND

🚶 🏕 🎣 ♿ 🚐 ⛺

Rating: 4

near Lancaster

You have your choice of sunny or shaded sites at this campground in the heart of Pennsylvania Dutch Country. You can explore the scenic countryside in a horse-drawn buggy, in a helicopter, on a train, or in a hot air balloon. Among the attractions to see are the Herr Family Homestead, Strasburg Rail Road, Kitchen Kettle Village, the Americana Museum, the Brandywine River Museum, Dutch Wonderland Family Amusement Park, Eagle Falls Thrills & Spills, Twin Brook Winery, and the Fulton Opera House. Both Muhlenberg Native Plant and Wildflower Meadow and Lancaster County Central Park have hiking trails popular with birders. Back at the campground, you can participate in planned activities like bingo and hayrides on the weekends.

Campsites, facilities: There are 108 sites for tents or RVs up to 30 feet: 95 have full hookups; 13 have water and electricity. There are 41 pull-throughs. Picnic tables and fire rings are provided. Drinking water, restrooms with flush toilets, a dump station, showers, a laundry, modem access, phone hookup, cable TV hookup, a public phone, groceries, ice, LP gas, wood, a camp store, rec room, a pavilion, an arcade, a basketball court, a playground, badminton, horseshoes, a sports field, a volleyball court, and RV storage and supplies are available. Some sites are wheelchair accessible. Leashed pets are permitted.

Reservations, fees: Reservations are accepted at 800/525-5605. The rate is $30–43 per night for up to four people. Each additional person is $6. Major credit cards are accepted. Open April through beginning of November.

Directions: From the junction of Highway 896 and U.S. 30, travel 7.5 miles east on U.S. 30 to the campground entrance on the left.

Contact: Roamer's Retreat Campground, 5005 Lincoln Highway, Kinzers, PA 17535, 717/442-4287, www.roamerscampground.com.

60 PEQUEA CREEK CAMPGROUND

🏃 ⛵ 🚣 🐕 🚴 ♿ 🚐 ⛺

Rating: 9

near Susquehannock State Park

Pequea Creek Campground is just a short drive away from the Susquehanna River at Susquehannock State Park. This 224-acre park is located on a wooded plateau that provides spectacular views of the river from cliffs 380 feet above the river. From these overlooks, visitors can spot osprey, turkey vultures, black vultures, and even bald eagles. The island below is home to a bald eagle sanctuary, the world's first. Be sure to stay behind railings and supervise children at all times. Visitors can ride their horses at Susquehannock, but

horses are not permitted near the overlook. On the river itself you can boat and fish. Hikers will find five miles of trails with many interesting sites to behold. Rhododendron, native holly, wildflowers, deer, lizards, and other forms of wildlife await patient hikers. Back at Pequea Creek, you can hike, try your hand at stream fishing, or participate in planned weekend activities.

Campsites, facilities: There are 105 sites for tents or RVs up 27 feet: 102 have water and electricity; 3 have no hookups; 30 are pull-throughs. No sites have full hookups. Picnic tables and fire rings are provided. Drinking water, restrooms with flush toilets, a dump station, showers, a laundry, modem access, phone hookup, cable TV hookup, a public phone, groceries, ice, LP gas, wood, grills, a camp store, a rec room, a pavilion, a playground, volleyball, and RV storage and supplies are available. Some sites are wheelchair accessible. Leashed pets are permitted.

Reservations, fees: Reservations are accepted. The rate is $22–30 per night for up to two people. Each additional person is $6. Open March through November.

Directions: From the junction of Highway 372 and Highway 272, travel north five miles on Highway 272, then turn left onto Pennsy Road and travel five miles. Follow signs to the campground entrance on the right.

Contact: Pequea Creek Campground, 86 Fox Hollow Road, Pequea, PA 17565, 717/284-4587, pequeacamp@aol.com.

61 MUDDY RUN RECREATION PARK

🏃 ⛵ 🚣 🐕 🚴 🚐 ⛺

Rating: 9

near the Susquehanna River

So close to the Susquehanna River, you can expect lots of water activities during your stay at

Muddy Run Recreation Park. You can canoe, motorboat with electric motors, and kayak the river. The campground offers a ramp for access to Muddy Run and rents rowboats, pedal boats, and motorboats. Anglers can cast for muskie, walleye, smallmouth bass, carp, white and channel catfish, bluegill, sunfish, black crappie, and sucker. Birders can look for vireos, warblers, orioles, thrushes, tanagers, and other migratory birds, as well as heron, teal, wood, and mallard ducks, Canada geese, egrets, gulls, and cormorants. You might also glimpse white-tailed deer, muskrats, otters, cottontail rabbits, woodchucks, red and gray squirrels, raccoons, foxes, chipmunks, turtles, and skunks. Tucquan Nature Preserve and Pinnacle Overlook are nearby. Back at the campground you can participate in planned activities on weekends or hike along one of the trails.

Campsites, facilities: There are 163 sites for tents or RVs up to 28 feet: 136 have water and electricity; 27 have no hookups. Picnic tables and fire rings are provided. Drinking water, restrooms with flush toilets, a dump station, showers, a laundry, a public phone, groceries, ice, wood, a camp store, grills, a pavilion, a playground, a rec hall, volleyball, and a sports field are available. Leashed pets are permitted.

Reservations, fees: Reservations are accepted. The rate is $20 per night for up to six people; a fee may apply for additional guests. Open April through November.

Directions: From the junction of Highway 272 and Highway 372, travel 3.5 miles west on Highway 372, then turn left onto Bethesda Church Road and proceed 0.25 mile to the campground entrance on the left.

Contact: Muddy Run Recreation Park, 172 Bethesda Church Road, West Holtwood, PA 17532, 717/284-4325.

62 TUCQUAN PARK FAMILY CAMPGROUND

Rating: 9

near the Susquehanna River

The sites here are mostly wooded and shaded. You can take advantage of the stocked fishing pond, rent a pedal boat, hike a trail, or participate in bingo, ceramics, scavenger hunts, or other weekend activities. At the nearby Susquehanna River you can boat with electric motorboats or non-powered boats, or cast for muskie, bluegill, sunfish, catfish, perch, smallmouth bass, carp, walleye, and crappie. Birding opportunities abound at this migratory hot spot. You can spy flycatchers, thrushes, vireos, warblers, orioles, and tanagers. The campground is also near Tucquan Nature Preserve and Pinnacle Overlook.

Campsites, facilities: There are 198 sites for tents or RVs up to 31 feet: 128 have full hookups; 10 have water and electricity; 60 have no hookups. There are 20 pull-throughs. Picnic tables and fire rings are provided. Drinking water, restrooms with flush toilets, a dump station, showers, a laundry, modem access, phone hookup, a public phone, groceries, ice, LP gas, wood, a camp store, a snack bar, a pavilion, a playground, a rec hall, an arcade, a swimming pool, basketball, a shuffleboard court, badminton, horseshoes, volleyball, and a sports field are available. Some sites are wheelchair accessible. Leashed pets are permitted.

Reservations, fees: Reservations are accepted. The rate is $21–28 per night for up to two people. Each additional person is $6. Seasonal and group rates are available. Major credit cards are accepted. Open year-round.

Directions: From the junction of Highway 272 and Highway 372, travel five miles west on Highway 372, then two miles north on River Road to the campground entrance on the right.

Contact: Tucquan Park Family Campground, 917 River Road, Holtwood, PA 17532, 717/284-2156, www.800padutch.com/z/tucquanpark.htm.

63 YOGI BEAR'S JELLYSTONE PARK CAMP-RESORT

🚶🚴🏊🛶🚤🐕🎣♿🚐⛺

Rating: 7

near the Susquehanna River

At Yogi Bear's, you can fish on the lake or enjoy the hiking and biking trails. If you don't have your own bike, you can rent one from the campground. Motorboats and non-powered boats are welcome on the Susquehanna River, where you can cast for pickerel, perch, bass, trout, sunfish, catfish, bluegill, and sucker. Hiking along the shore or in the surrounding woodlands affords scenic views and opportunities to see herons, osprey, turtles, white-tailed deer, squirrels, and cottontail rabbits.

Campsites, facilities: There are 145 sites for tents or RVs up to 32 feet: 60 have full hookups; 70 have water and electricity; 15 have no hookups. There are 12 pull-throughs. Picnic tables and fire rings are provided. Drinking water, restrooms with flush toilets, a dump station, showers, a laundry, modem access, a phone hookup, a public phone, groceries, ice, LP gas, wood, a camp store, rec room, a pavilion, an arcade, a swimming pool, a basketball court, a playground, three shuffleboard courts, badminton, horseshoes, miniature golf, a sports field, volleyball, and RV storage and supplies are available. Some sites are wheelchair accessible. Leashed pets are permitted.

Reservations, fees: Reservations are accepted at 717/786-4514. The rate is $26–54 per night for up to two people. Each additional person is $10. Weekly rates and senior discounts are available. Major credit cards are accepted. Open April through October.

Directions: From the junction of East Highway 372 and U.S. 222, travel 2.5 miles south on U.S. 222, then turn left onto Blackburn Road and travel 1.5 miles to the campground entrance on the left.

Contact: Yogi Bear's Jellystone Park Camp-Resort, 340 Blackburn Road, Quarryville, PA 17566, 717/786-3458, www.jellystone-pa.com.

64 PHILADELPHIA/ WEST CHESTER KOA

🏊🛶🚐🐕🎣♿🚐⛺

Rating: 7

along the Brandywine River

You can rent a canoe or kayak from this campground, or use the campground's launch for your own craft. Anglers can cast for bass, brook and brown trout, pickerel, sunfish, channel catfish, carp, and bluegill. The Philadelphia/West Chester KOA offers two local van tours, one to Lancaster and Amish Country, the other to Philadelphia and Valley Forge. Kids will enjoy nearby Sesame Place Theme Park. There are special equestrian events at the campground, including fox hunts and steeplechase, as well as ice cream socials, live entertainment, and other activities. You have your choice of shaded, open, and riverside sites.

Campsites, facilities: There are 104 sites for tents or RVs up to 90 feet: 47 have full hookups; 27 have water and electricity; 3 have electricity; 27 have no hookups. There are 15 pull-throughs. Picnic tables and fire rings are provided. Drinking water, restrooms with flush toilets, a dump station, showers, a laundry, modem access, phone hookup, a public phone, groceries, ice, LP gas, wood, a general store, a snack bar, a pavilion, a playground, a rec room, an arcade, a swimming pool, a wading pool, miniature golf, badminton, volleyball, and RV supplies are available. Some sites are wheelchair accessible. Leashed pets are permitted.

Reservations, fees: Reservations are accepted at 800/KOA-1726 (800/562-1726). The rate is $25–50 per night for up to two people. Each additional person is $5. Group rates are available. Major credit cards are accepted. Open April through October.

Directions: From the junction of U.S. 202 and U.S. 1, travel nine miles south on U.S. 1, then three miles northwest on Highway 82, then three miles east on Highway 162 to the entrance on the left.

Contact: Philadelphia/West Chester KOA, P.O. Box 920, Coatesville, PA 19320, 610/486-0447 or 800/562-1726, www.philadelphiakoa.com.

RESOURCES

© JASON MILLER

Resources

Allegheny National Forest
www.fs.fed.us/r9/forests/allegheny

Go Camping America
www.gocampingamerica.com

Keystone Trails Association
www.kta-hike.org

National Park Service
www.nps.gov

Pennsylvania Campground Owners Association
www.pacamping.com

Pennsylvania Campgrounds
www.campgroundinfo.com

Pennsylvania Fish and Boat Commission
http://sites.state.pa.us/PA_Exec/Fish_Boat/mpag1.htm

Pennsylvania State Parks
www.dcnr.state.pa.us

Pennsylvania Visitors Network
www.pavisnet.com

Recreation Around the Water
www.lrp.usace.army.mil/rec

Rock Climbing.com
www.rockclimbing.com

Susquehanna River Birding and Wildlife
www.pabirdingtrails.org

Susquehanna River Trail
http://sites.state.pa.us/PA_Exec/Fish_Boat/watertrails/susqmid/trailguide.htm

Acknowledgments

We would like to thank the many people who have helped us throughout the completion of this project.

First and foremost our appreciation goes to our wonderful contacts at Avalon Travel Publishing: Rebecca Browning, Kathryn Ettinger, Kemi Oyesiku, Tabitha Lahr, Kevin Anglin, Jane Musser, and Leslie Walters. They were with us every step to make sure the process went smoothly.

Next, we are grateful for the additional pictures from our great photographers, our sister-in-law, Crystal Miller, Christopher Paul Carey, and Maria V. Snyder.

Finally, to our family and friends, we thank you for your patience and understanding when writing seemed to take precedence over everything else. And a special thanks goes to Heidi's mother, Sharon Ruby, who may be the fastest typist in southwest Pennsylvania.

Index

Notes

Notes

-email us a photo or story from your
  travels for our website
    webmaster@moonstonewritings.com
http://community.livejournal.com/penncamping

www.moon.com

For helpful advice on planning a trip, visit www.moon.com for the **TRAVEL PLANNER** and get access to useful travel strategies and valuable information about great places to visit. When you travel with Moon, expect an experience that is uncommon and truly unique.

HANDBOOKS • OUTDOORS • METRO • LIVING ABROAD

OUTDOORS

COLORADO CAMPING
The Complete Guide to Tent and RV Camping

NORTHERN CALIFORNIA CABINS & COTTAGES
Great Lodgings with Easy Access to Outdoor Recreation

OREGON CAMPING
The Complete Guide to Tent and RV Camping

PENNSYLVANIA CAMPING
The Complete Guide to Tent and RV Camping

TAKE A HIKE LOS ANGELES
Hikes Within Two Hours of the City

TAKE A HIKE NEW YORK CITY
Hikes Within Two Hours of Manhattan

TAKE A HIKE SEATTLE
Hikes Within Two Hours of the City

WASHINGTON CAMPING
The Complete Guide to Tent and RV Camping

"A smart new look provides just one more reason to travel with Moon Outdoors. Well written, thoroughly researched, and packed full of useful information and advice, these guides really do get you into the outdoors."

—GORP.COM

ALSO AVAILABLE AS FOGHORN OUTDOORS ACTIVITY GUIDES:

101 Great Hikes of the
San Francisco Bay Area
250 Great Hikes in
California's National Parks
Baja Camping
Bay Area Biking
California Beaches
California Camping
California Fishing
California Golf
California Hiking
California Recreational
Lakes & Rivers
California Waterfalls
California Wildlife
Camper's Companion
Easy Biking in Northern
California

Easy Hiking in Northern
California
Easy Hiking in Southern
California
Florida Beaches
Florida Camping
Georgia & Alabama Camping
Great Lakes Camping
Maine Hiking
Massachusetts Hiking
Montana, Wyoming & Idaho
Camping
New England Biking
New England Cabins
& Cottages
New England Camping
New England Hiking
New Hampshire Hiking

Northern California Biking
Oregon Hiking
Pacific Northwest Hiking
Southern California
Cabins & Cottages
Tom Stienstra's Bay Area
Recreation
Utah Camping
Utah Hiking
Vermont Hiking
Washington Boating
& Water Sports
Washington Fishing
Washington Hiking
West Coast RV Camping

MOON PENNSYLVANIA CAMPING

Avalon Travel Publishing
An Imprint of
Avalon Publishing Group, Inc.

AVALON
publishing group incorporated

1400 65th Street, Suite 250
Emeryville, CA 94608, USA
www.moon.com

Editor: Kathryn Ettinger
Series Manager: Sabrina Young
Acquisitions Manager: Rebecca K. Browning
Copy Editor: Ellie Behrstock
Graphics Coordinator: Elizabeth Jang
Production Coordinators: Elizabeth Jang,
   Tamara Gronet
Cover Designer: Gerilyn Attebery
Interior Designer: Darren Alessi
Map Editor: Kevin Anglin
Cartographer: Landis Bennett
Proofreader: Erika Howsare
Indexer: Greg Jewett

ISBN-10: 1-56691-986-X
ISBN-13: 978-1-56691-986-9
ISSN: 1930-1510

Printing History
1st Edition — May 2006
5 4 3 2 1

SOMERSET COUNTY LIBRARY
6022 GLADES PIKE, SUITE 120
SOMERSET, PA 15501
814-445-5907

Text © 2006 by Jason and Heidi Ruby Miller.
Maps © 2006 by Avalon Travel Publishing, Inc.
All rights reserved.

Front cover photo: Youghiogheny River in
   Ohiopyle State Park, © Michael D. McCumber
Back cover photo: © Digital Vision / Getty Images
Title page photo: South over Black Moshannon
   Lake, © Jason Miller

Printed in the United States by Worzalla

Some photos and illustrations are used by
permission and are the property of the original
copyright owners.

Moon Outdoors and the Moon logo are the
property of Avalon Travel Publishing, an imprint
of Avalon Publishing Group, Inc. All other marks
and logos depicted are the property of the
original owners. All rights reserved. No part of
this book may be translated or reproduced in any
form, except brief extracts by a reviewer for the
purpose of a review, without written permission
of the copyright owner.

Although every effort was made to ensure that
the information was correct at the time of going
to press, the author and publisher do not assume
and hereby disclaim any liability to any party for
any loss or damage caused by errors, omissions,
or any potential travel disruption due to labor
or financial difficulty, whether such errors or
omissions result from negligence, accident, or
any other cause.

KEEPING CURRENT

We are committed to making this book the most accurate and enjoyable camping
guide to the state. You can rest assured that every campground in this book has
been carefully reviewed in an effort to keep this book as up-to-date as possible.
However, by the time you read this book, some of the fees listed herein may have
changed and campgrounds may have closed unexpectedly.

   If you have a favorite gem you'd like to see included in the next edition, or
see anything that needs updating, clarification, or correction, please drop
us a line. Send your comments via email to feedback@moon.com, or use the
address above.